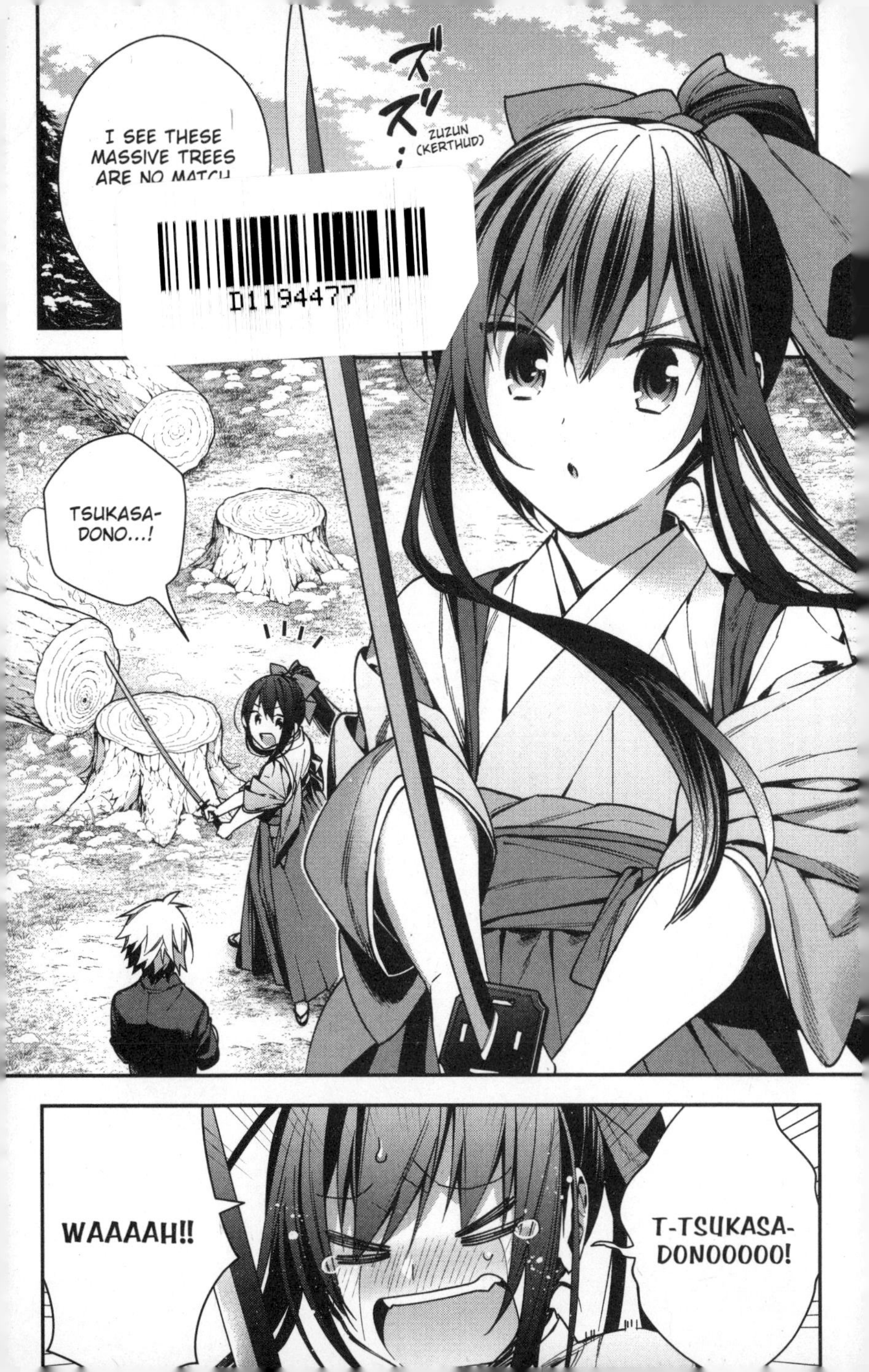
ZUZUN (KERTHUD)
I SEE THESE MASSIVE TREES ARE NO MATCH
TSUKASA-DONO...!
T-TSUKASA-DONOOOOO!
WAAAAH!!

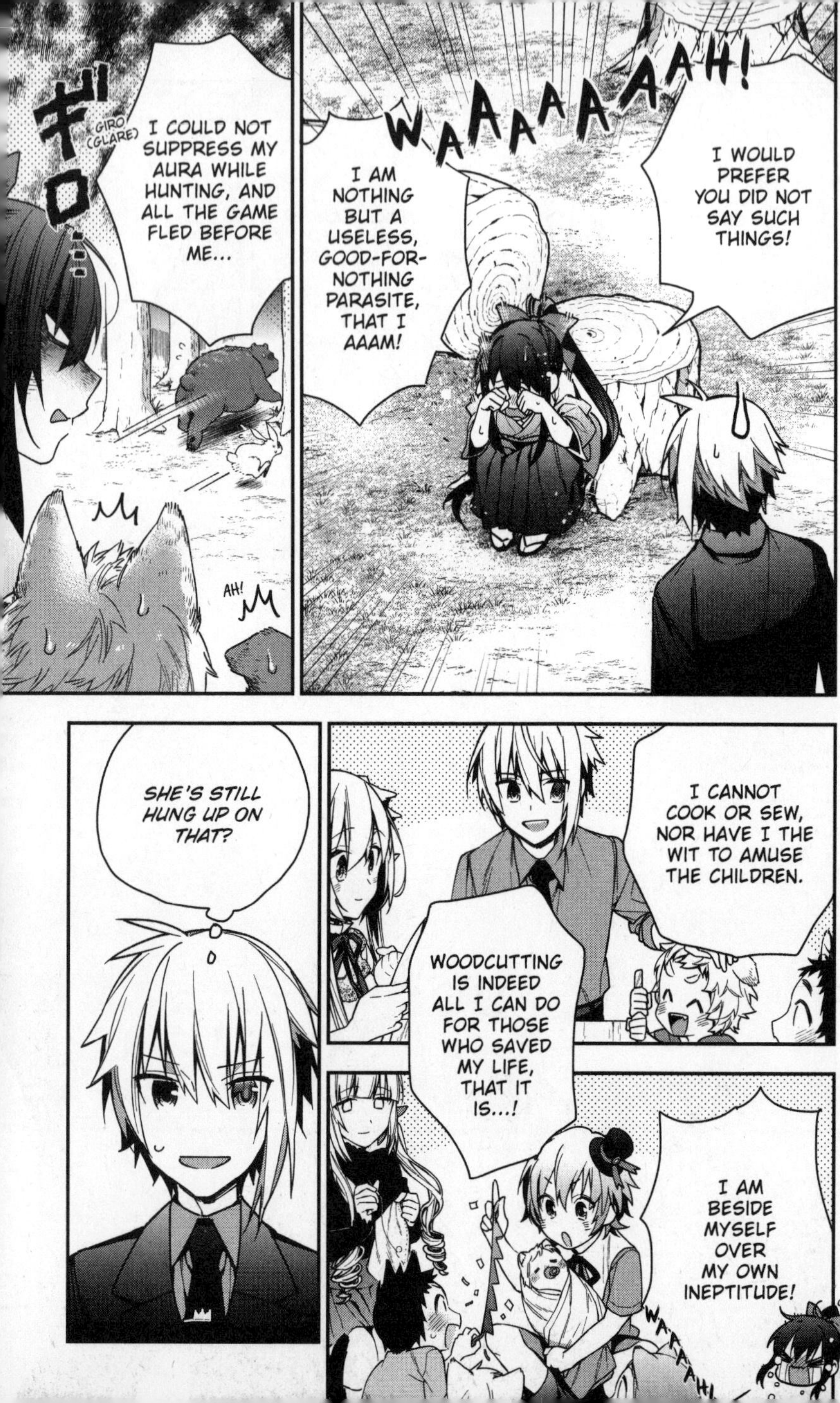
WAAAAAAAAH!
I AM NOTHING BUT A USELESS, GOOD-FOR-NOTHING PARASITE, THAT I AAAM!
I WOULD PREFER YOU DID NOT SAY SUCH THINGS!
ギロ
GIRO (GLARE)
I COULD NOT SUPPRESS MY AURA WHILE HUNTING, AND ALL THE GAME FLED BEFORE ME...
AH!
I CANNOT COOK OR SEW, NOR HAVE I THE WIT TO AMUSE THE CHILDREN.
WOODCUTTING IS INDEED ALL I CAN DO FOR THOSE WHO SAVED MY LIFE, THAT IT IS...!
I AM BESIDE MYSELF OVER MY OWN INEPTITUDE!
WAAAAAH!
SHE'S STILL HUNG UP ON THAT?

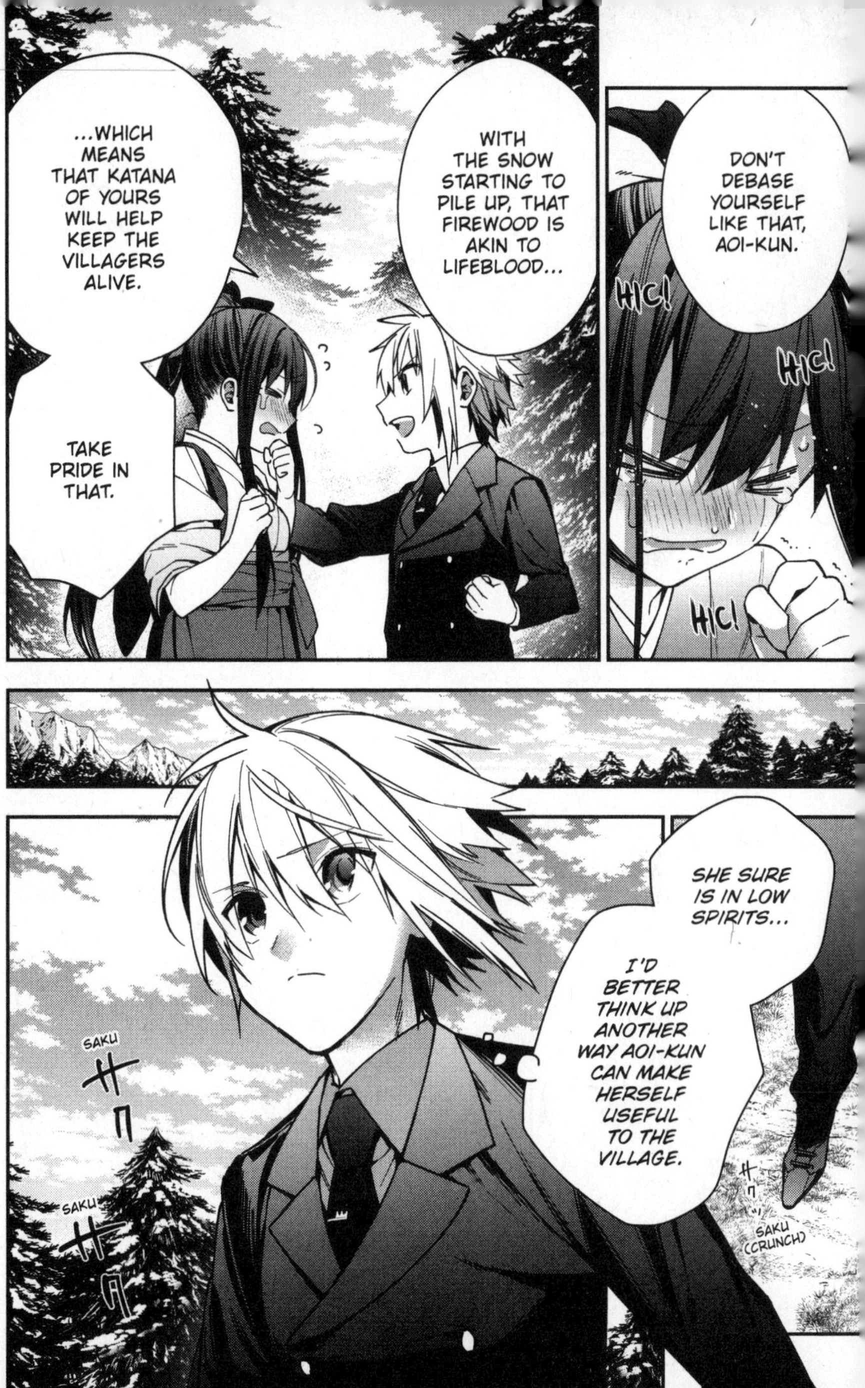
DON'T DEBASE YOURSELF LIKE THAT, AOI-KUN.
HIC!
HIC!
HIC!
WITH THE SNOW STARTING TO PILE UP, THAT FIREWOOD IS AKIN TO LIFEBLOOD...
...WHICH MEANS THAT KATANA OF YOURS WILL HELP KEEP THE VILLAGERS ALIVE.
TAKE PRIDE IN THAT.
SHE SURE IS IN LOW SPIRITS...
I'D BETTER THINK UP ANOTHER WAY AOI-KUN CAN MAKE HERSELF USEFUL TO THE VILLAGE.
SAKU (CRUNCH)
SAKU
SAKU

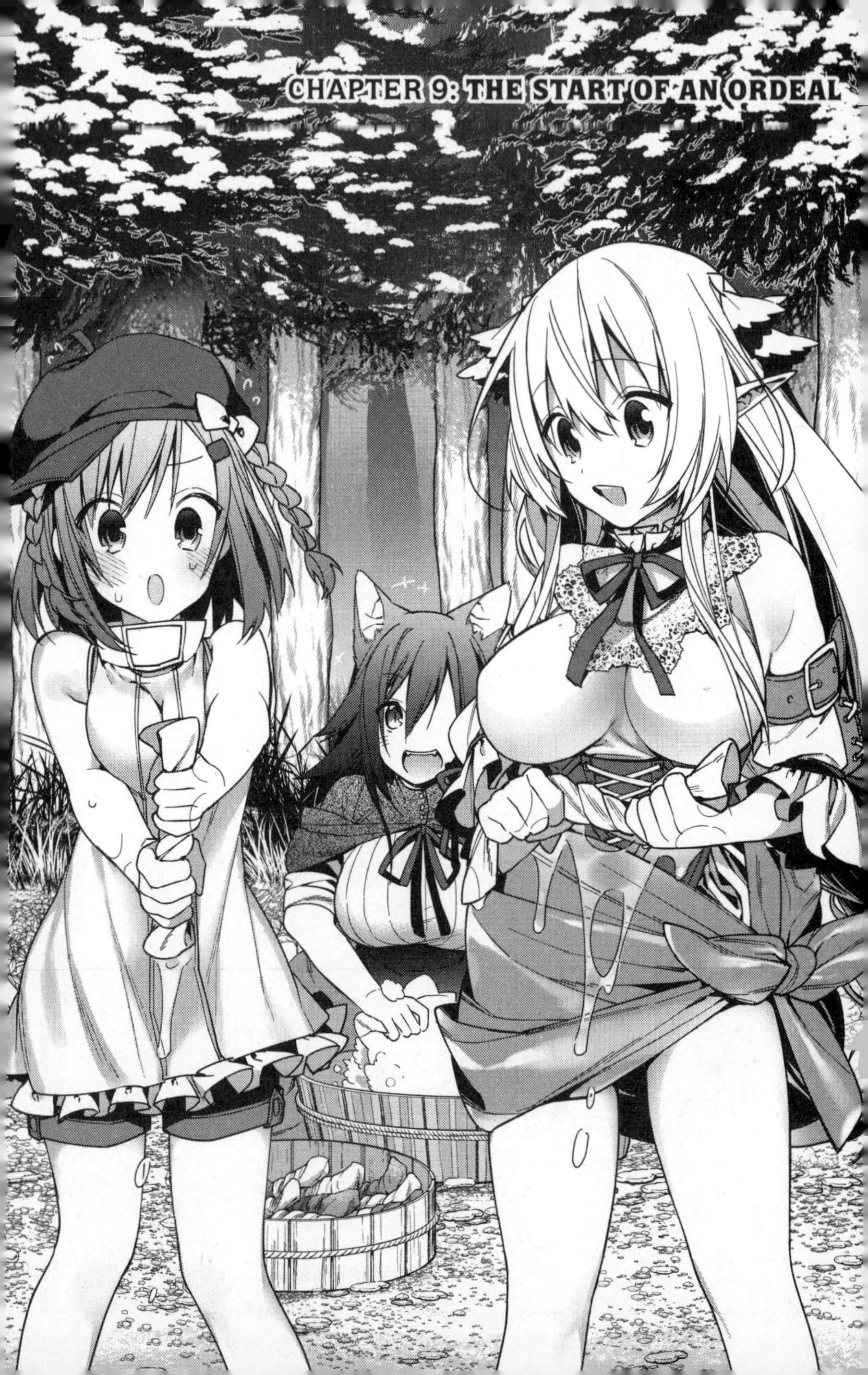
CHAPTER 9: THE START OF AN ORDEAL

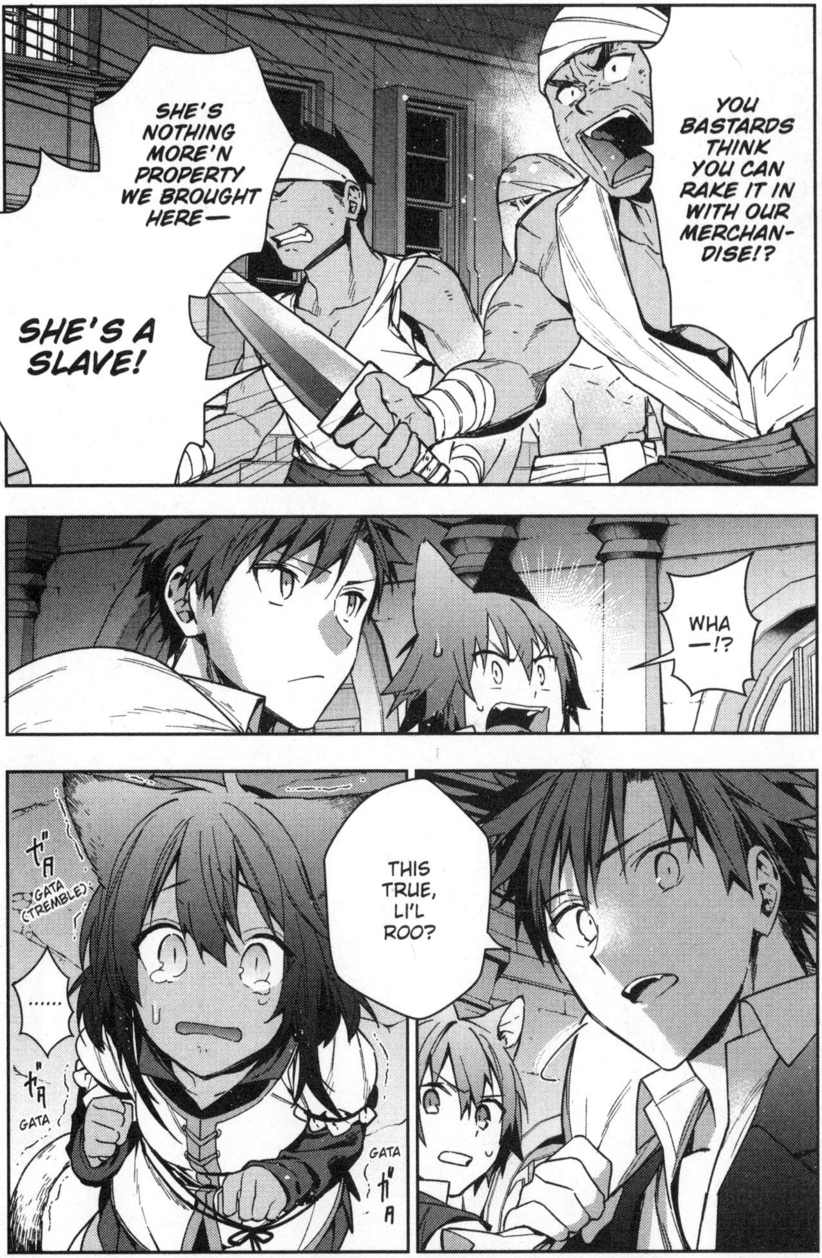
YOU BASTARDS THINK YOU CAN RAKE IT IN WITH OUR MERCHANDISE!?
SHE'S NOTHING MORE'N PROPERTY WE BROUGHT HERE—
SHE'S A SLAVE!
WHA—!?
THIS TRUE, LI'L ROO?
ガタ
GATA
ガタ
GATA (TREMBLE)
......
ガタ
GATA

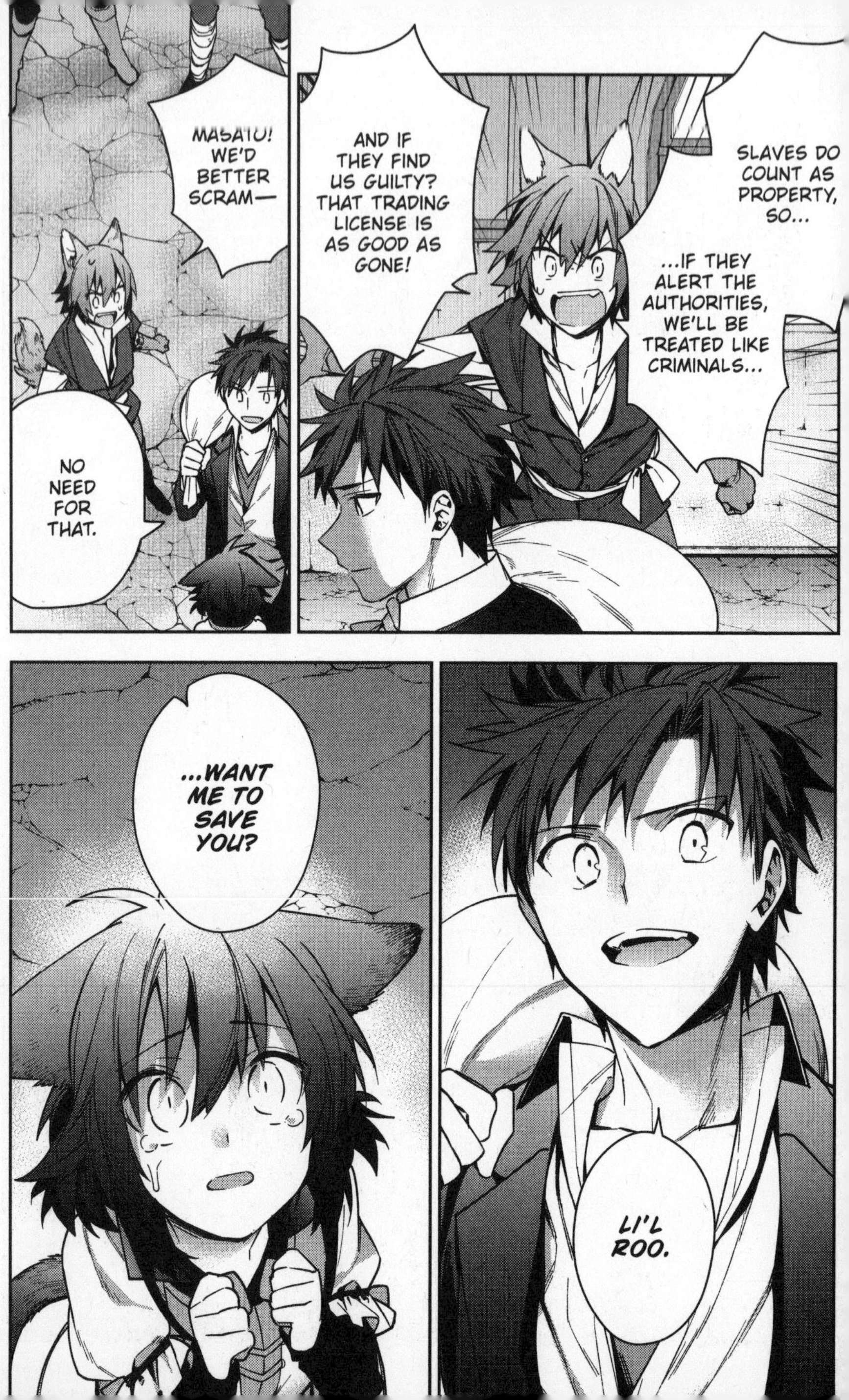
SLAVES DO COUNT AS PROPERTY, SO...
...IF THEY ALERT THE AUTHORITIES, WE'LL BE TREATED LIKE CRIMINALS...
AND IF THEY FIND US GUILTY? THAT TRADING LICENSE IS AS GOOD AS GONE!
MASATO! WE'D BETTER SCRAM—
NO NEED FOR THAT.
LI'L ROO.
...WANT ME TO SAVE YOU?

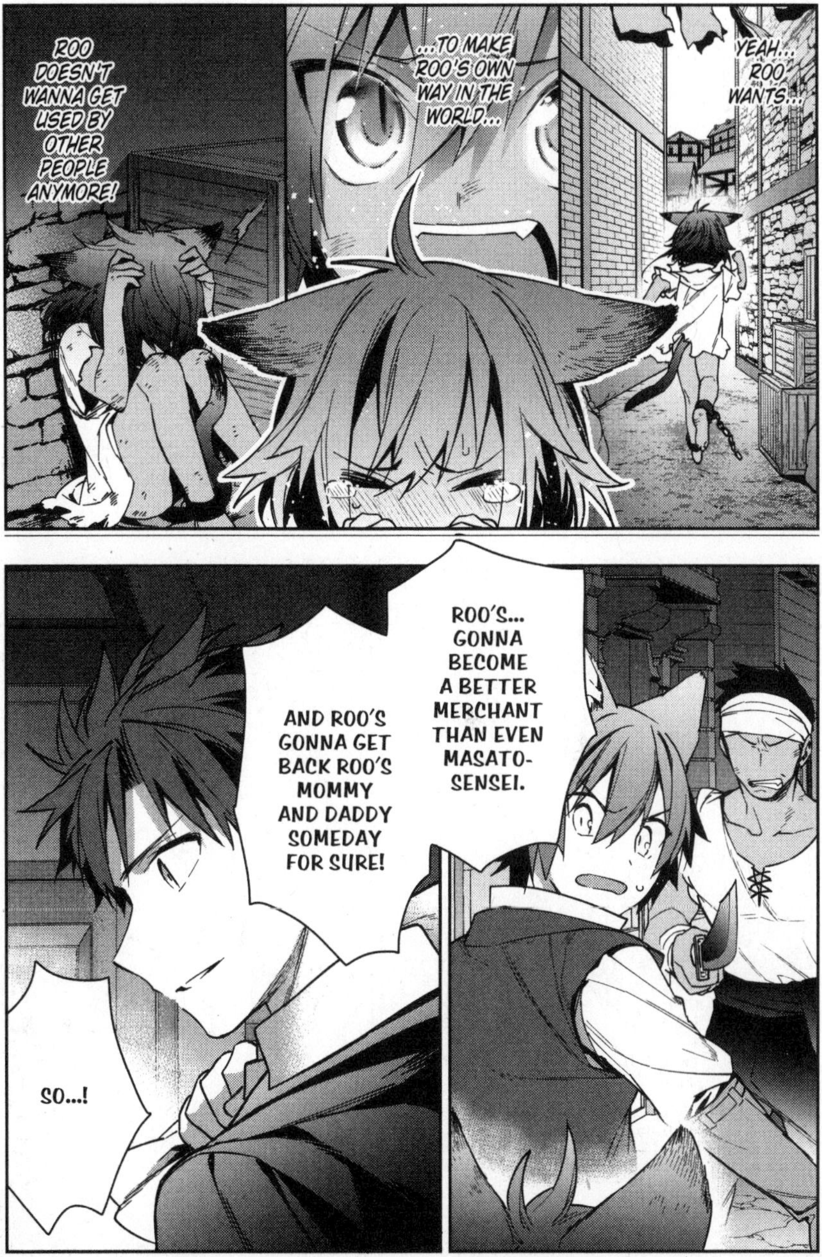
YEAH... ROO WANTS...
...TO MAKE ROO'S OWN WAY IN THE WORLD...
ROO DOESN'T WANNA GET USED BY OTHER PEOPLE ANYMORE!
ROO'S... GONNA BECOME A BETTER MERCHANT THAN EVEN MASATO-SENSEI.
AND ROO'S GONNA GET BACK ROO'S MOMMY AND DADDY SOMEDAY FOR SURE!
SO...!

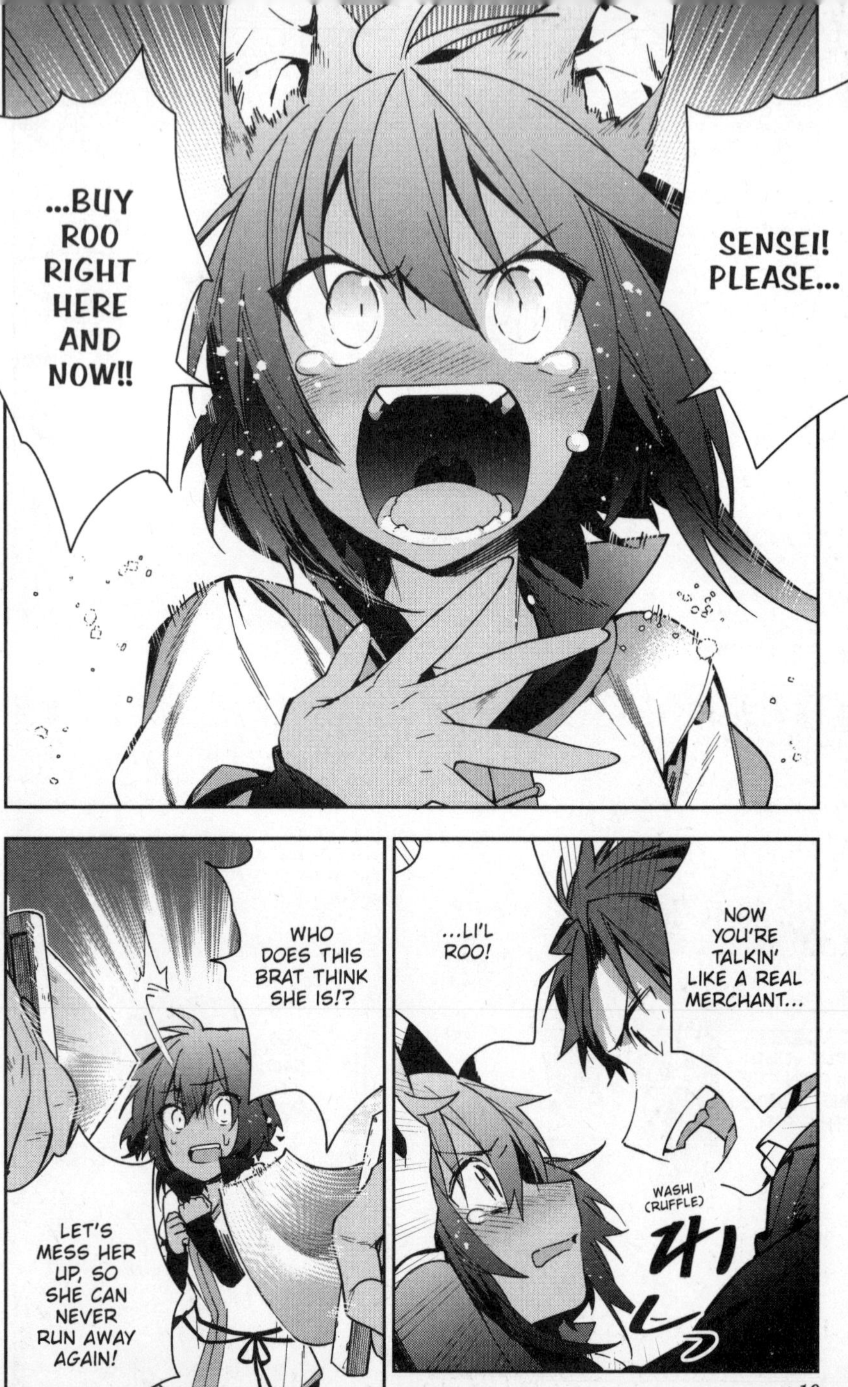
SENSEI! PLEASE...
...BUY ROO RIGHT HERE AND NOW!!
NOW YOU'RE TALKIN' LIKE A REAL MERCHANT...
...LI'L ROO!
WASHI (RUFFLE)
WHO DOES THIS BRAT THINK SHE IS!?
LET'S MESS HER UP, SO SHE CAN NEVER RUN AWAY AGAIN!

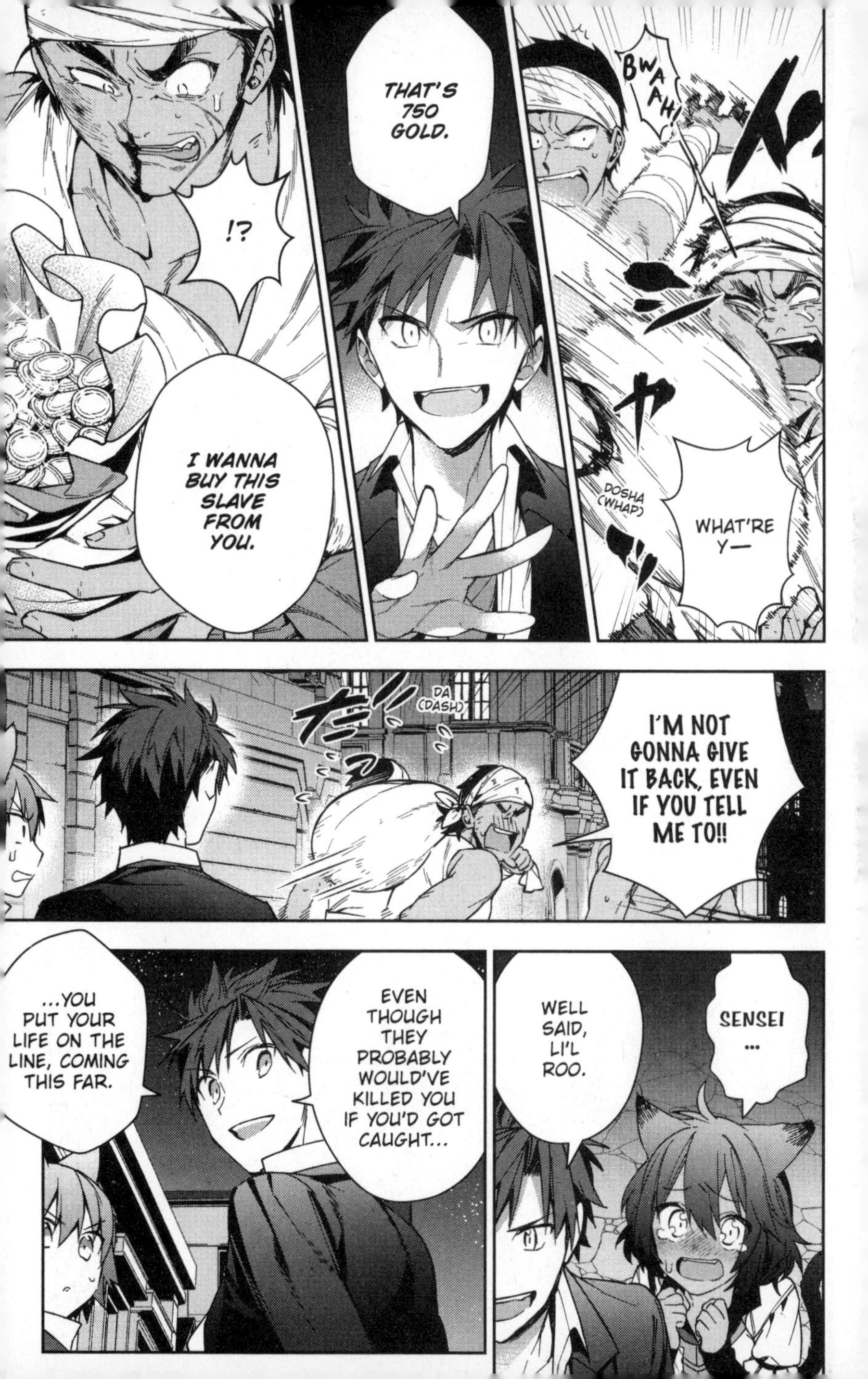
BWAAH!
DOSHA (WHAP)
WHAT'RE Y—
THAT'S 750 GOLD.
!?
I WANNA BUY THIS SLAVE FROM YOU.
DA (DASH)
I'M NOT GONNA GIVE IT BACK, EVEN IF YOU TELL ME TO!!
SENSEI...
WELL SAID, LI'L ROO.
EVEN THOUGH THEY PROBABLY WOULD'VE KILLED YOU IF YOU'D GOT CAUGHT...
...YOU PUT YOUR LIFE ON THE LINE, COMING THIS FAR.

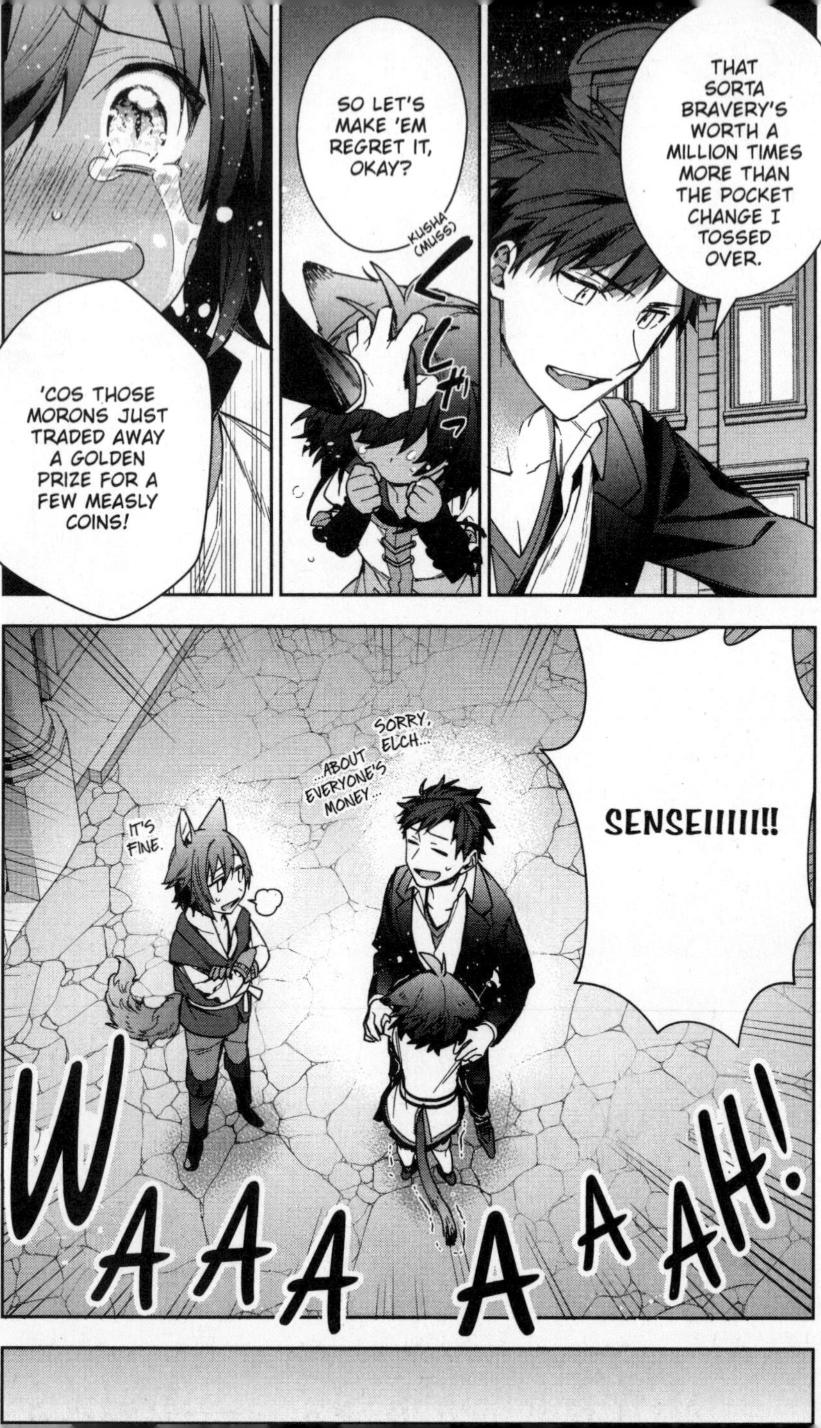

THAT SORTA BRAVERY'S WORTH A MILLION TIMES MORE THAN THE POCKET CHANGE I TOSSED OVER.
SO LET'S MAKE 'EM REGRET IT, OKAY?
KUSHA (MUSS)
'COS THOSE MORONS JUST TRADED AWAY A GOLDEN PRIZE FOR A FEW MEASLY COINS!
SENSEIIIIII!!
SORRY, ELCH...
...ABOUT EVERYONE'S MONEY...
IT'S FINE.
WAAAA AAAAH!

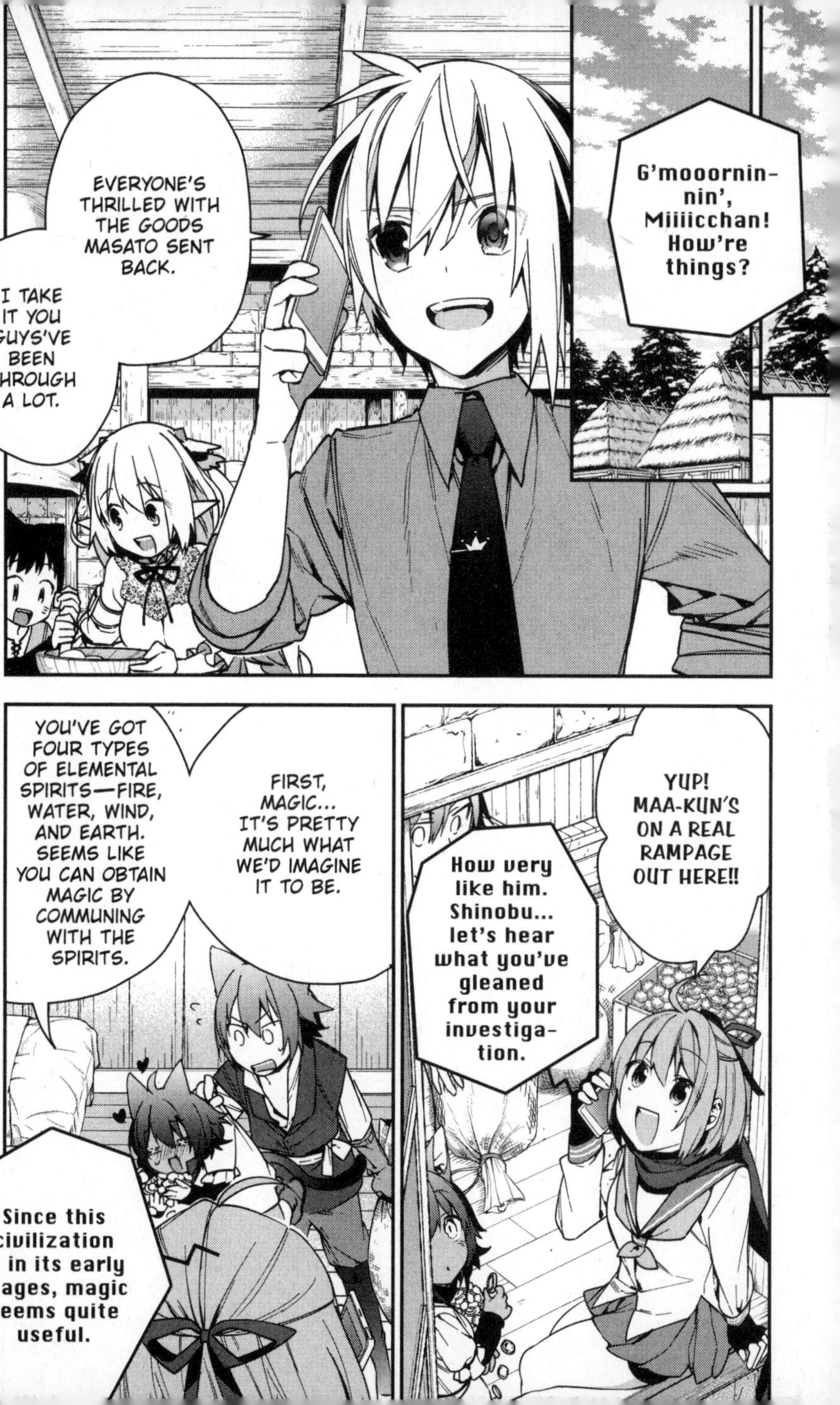
G'mooornin-nin', Miiiicchan! How're things?
EVERYONE'S THRILLED WITH THE GOODS MASATO SENT BACK.
I TAKE IT YOU GUYS'VE BEEN THROUGH A LOT.
YUP! MAA-KUN'S ON A REAL RAMPAGE OUT HERE!!
How very like him. Shinobu... let's hear what you've gleaned from your investiga-tion.
FIRST, MAGIC... IT'S PRETTY MUCH WHAT WE'D IMAGINE IT TO BE.
YOU'VE GOT FOUR TYPES OF ELEMENTAL SPIRITS—FIRE, WATER, WIND, AND EARTH. SEEMS LIKE YOU CAN OBTAIN MAGIC BY COMMUNING WITH THE SPIRITS.
Since this civilization is in its early stages, magic seems quite useful.

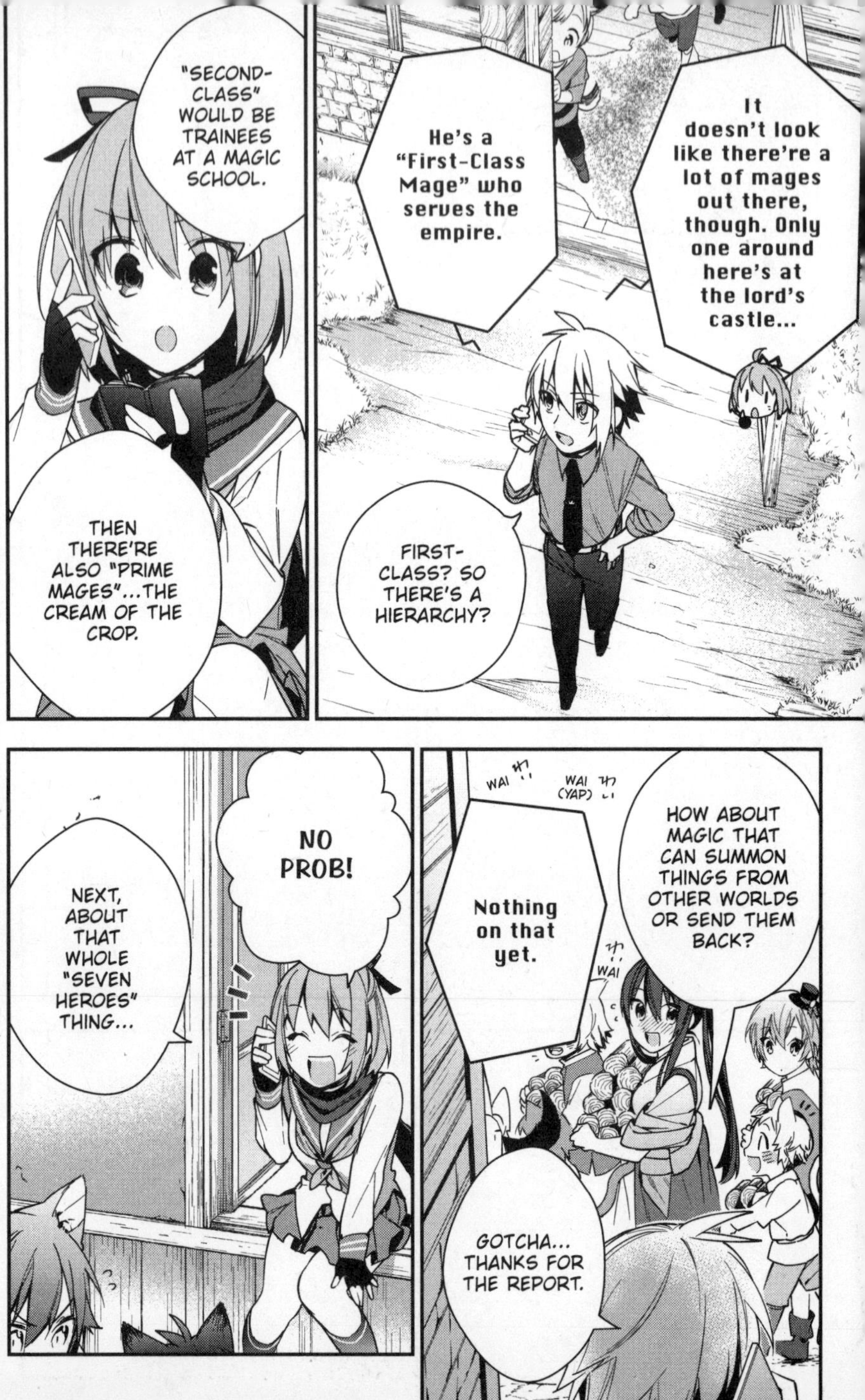
It doesn't look like there're a lot of mages out there, though. Only one around here's at the lord's castle...
He's a "First-Class Mage" who serves the empire.
FIRST-CLASS? SO THERE'S A HIERARCHY?
"SECOND-CLASS" WOULD BE TRAINEES AT A MAGIC SCHOOL.
THEN THERE'RE ALSO "PRIME MAGES"...THE CREAM OF THE CROP.
HOW ABOUT MAGIC THAT CAN SUMMON THINGS FROM OTHER WORLDS OR SEND THEM BACK?
WAI (YAP)
WAI
Nothing on that yet.
WAI
GOTCHA... THANKS FOR THE REPORT.
NO PROB!
NEXT, ABOUT THAT WHOLE "SEVEN HEROES" THING...

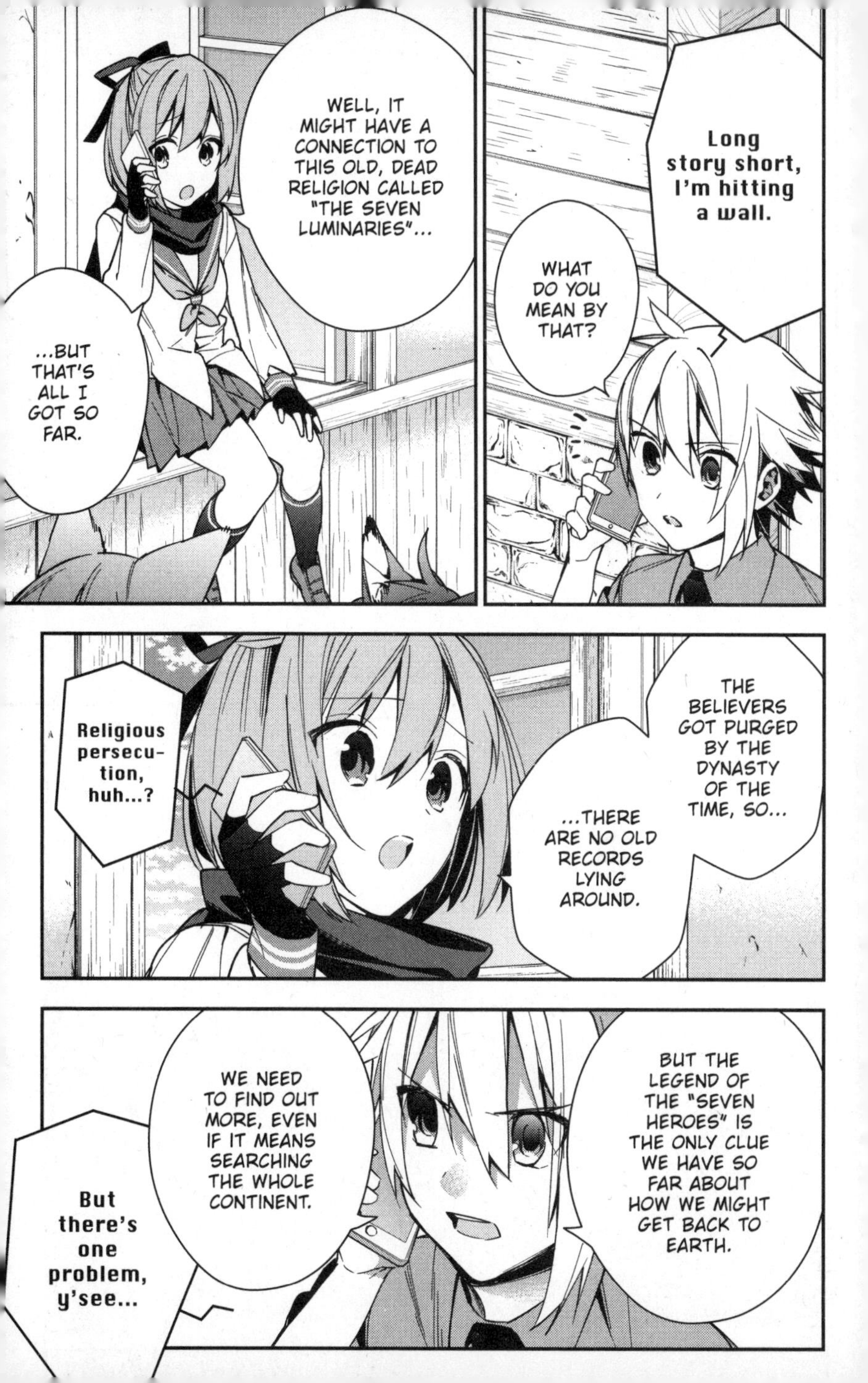
Long story short, I'm hitting a wall.
WHAT DO YOU MEAN BY THAT?
WELL, IT MIGHT HAVE A CONNECTION TO THIS OLD, DEAD RELIGION CALLED "THE SEVEN LUMINARIES"...
...BUT THAT'S ALL I GOT SO FAR.
THE BELIEVERS GOT PURGED BY THE DYNASTY OF THE TIME, SO...
...THERE ARE NO OLD RECORDS LYING AROUND.
Religious persecu-tion, huh...?
BUT THE LEGEND OF THE "SEVEN HEROES" IS THE ONLY CLUE WE HAVE SO FAR ABOUT HOW WE MIGHT GET BACK TO EARTH.
WE NEED TO FIND OUT MORE, EVEN IF IT MEANS SEARCHING THE WHOLE CONTINENT.
But there's one problem, y'see...

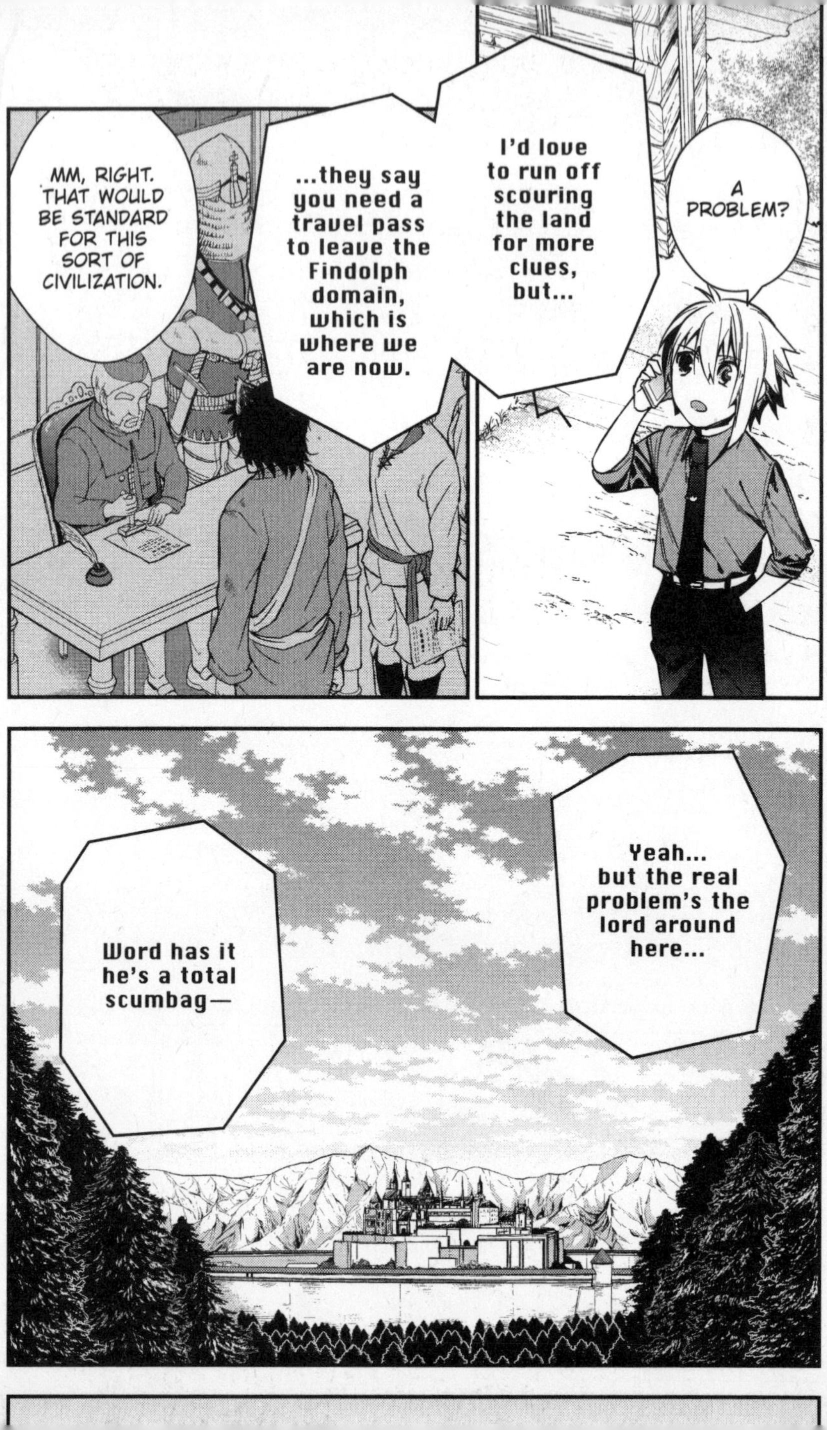
A PROBLEM?
I'd love to run off scouring the land for more clues, but...
...they say you need a travel pass to leave the Findolph domain, which is where we are now.
MM, RIGHT. THAT WOULD BE STANDARD FOR THIS SORT OF CIVILIZATION.
Yeah... but the real problem's the lord around here...
Word has it he's a total scumbag—

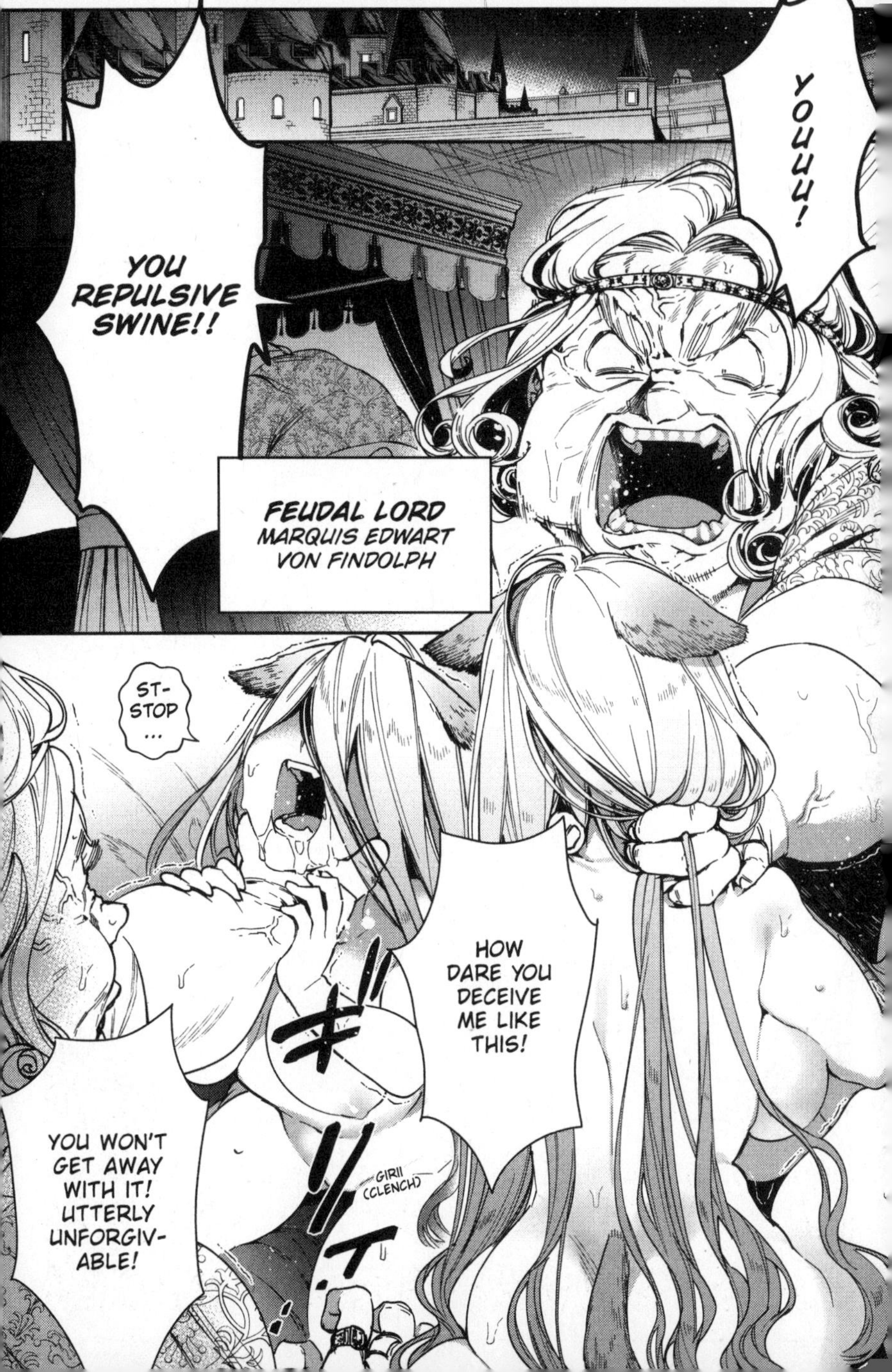
YOUUU!
YOU REPULSIVE SWINE!!
FEUDAL LORD MARQUIS EDWART VON FINDOLPH
ST-STOP ...
HOW DARE YOU DECEIVE ME LIKE THIS!
GIRII (CLENCH)
YOU WON'T GET AWAY WITH IT! UTTERLY UNFORGIV-ABLE!

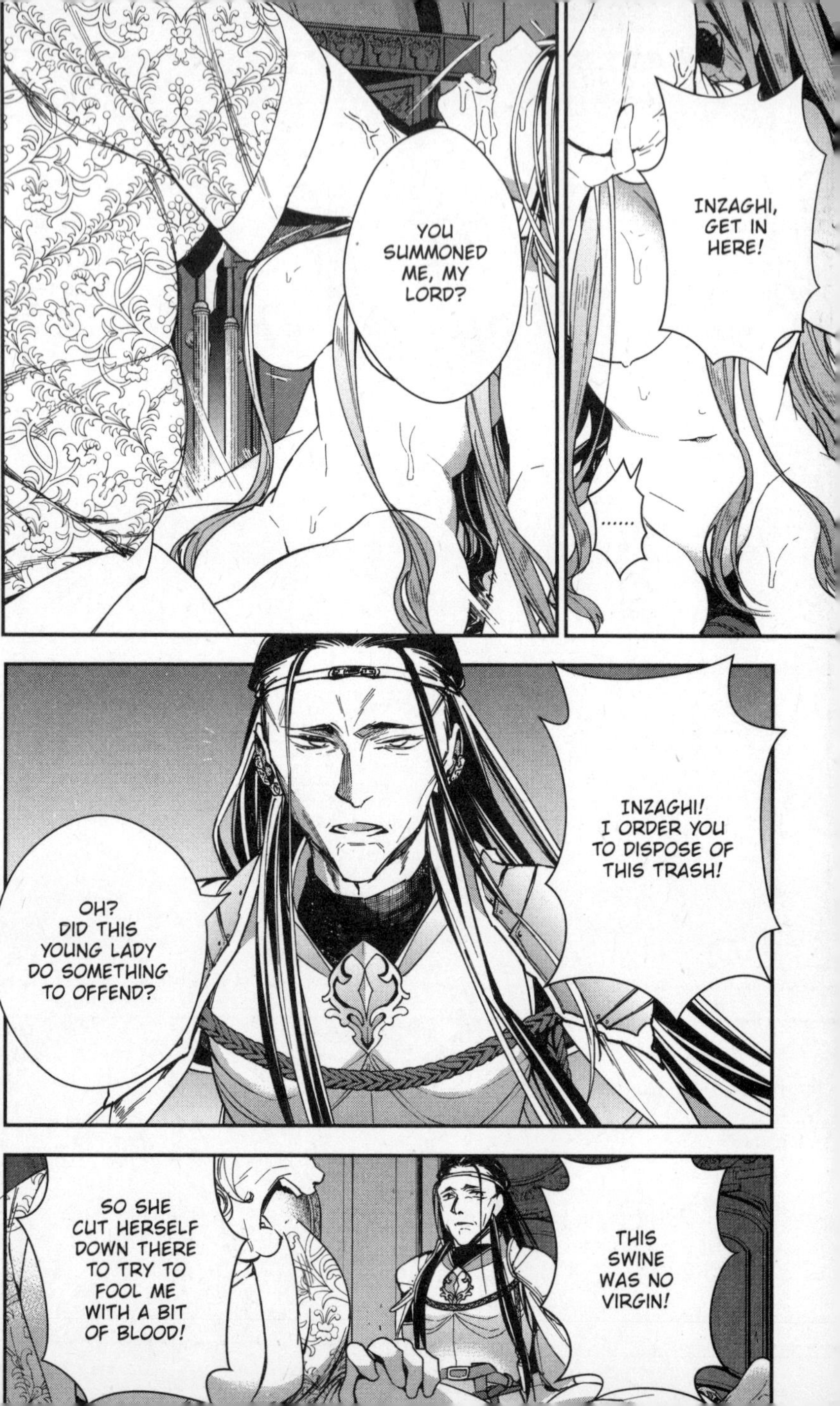
INZAGHI, GET IN HERE!
......
YOU SUMMONED ME, MY LORD?
INZAGHI! I ORDER YOU TO DISPOSE OF THIS TRASH!
OH? DID THIS YOUNG LADY DO SOMETHING TO OFFEND?
THIS SWINE WAS NO VIRGIN!
SO SHE CUT HERSELF DOWN THERE TO TRY TO FOOL ME WITH A BIT OF BLOOD!

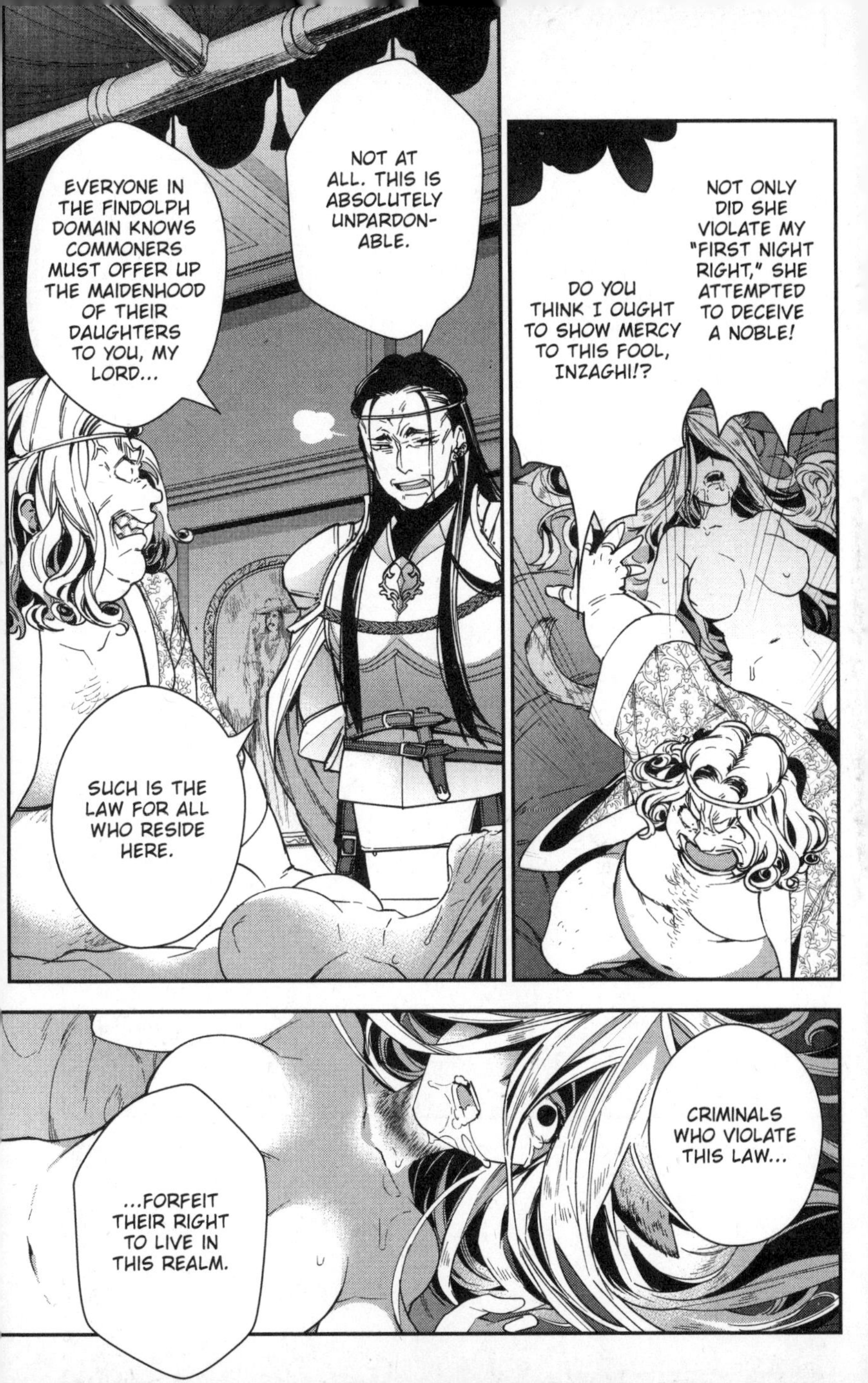
NOT ONLY DID SHE VIOLATE MY "FIRST NIGHT RIGHT," SHE ATTEMPTED TO DECEIVE A NOBLE!
DO YOU THINK I OUGHT TO SHOW MERCY TO THIS FOOL, INZAGHI!?
NOT AT ALL. THIS IS ABSOLUTELY UNPARDON-ABLE.
EVERYONE IN THE FINDOLPH DOMAIN KNOWS COMMONERS MUST OFFER UP THE MAIDENHOOD OF THEIR DAUGHTERS TO YOU, MY LORD...
SUCH IS THE LAW FOR ALL WHO RESIDE HERE.
CRIMINALS WHO VIOLATE THIS LAW...
...FORFEIT THEIR RIGHT TO LIVE IN THIS REALM.

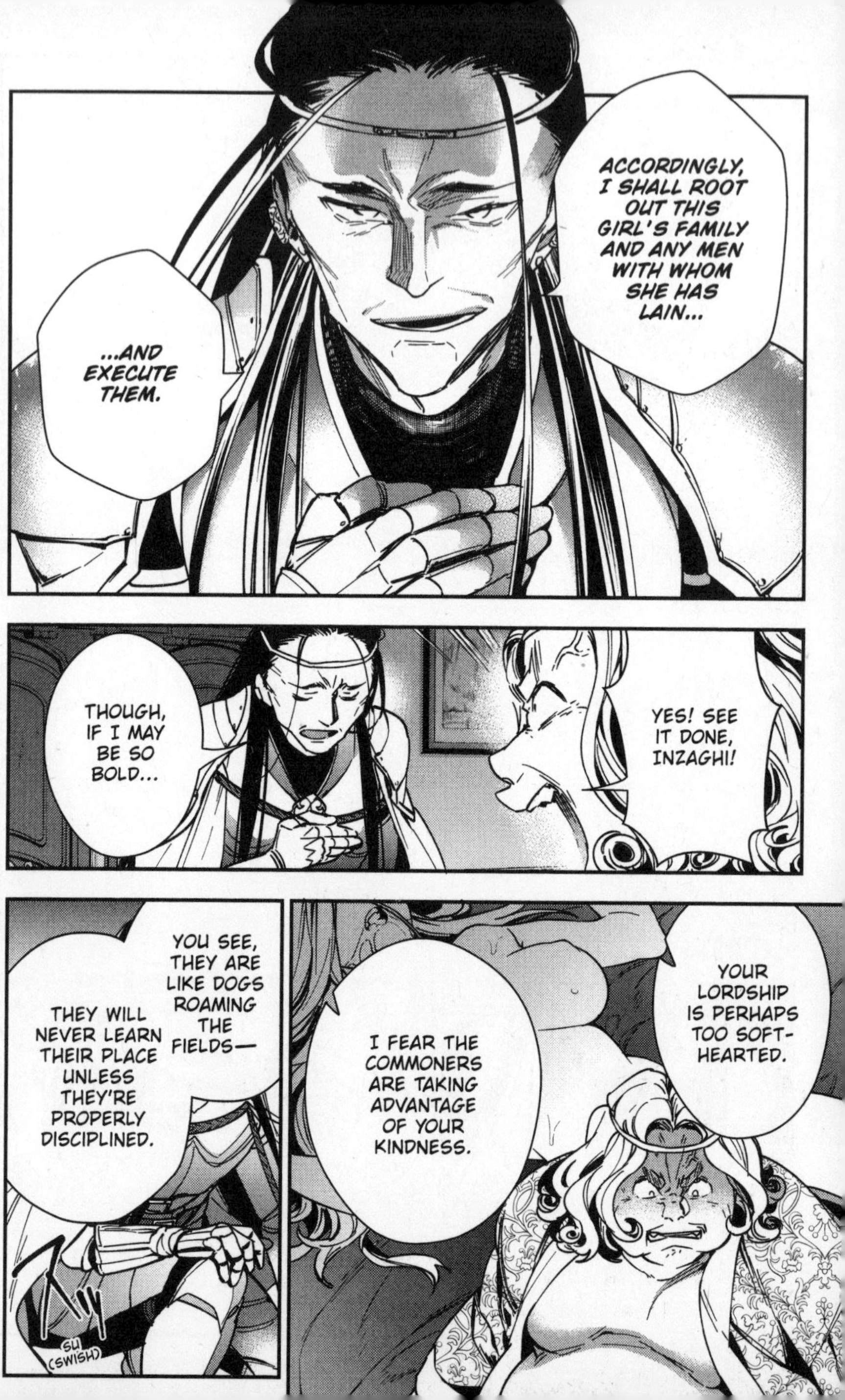
ACCORDINGLY, I SHALL ROOT OUT THIS GIRL'S FAMILY AND ANY MEN WITH WHOM SHE HAS LAIN...
...AND EXECUTE THEM.
YES! SEE IT DONE, INZAGHI!
THOUGH, IF I MAY BE SO BOLD...
YOUR LORDSHIP IS PERHAPS TOO SOFT-HEARTED.
I FEAR THE COMMONERS ARE TAKING ADVANTAGE OF YOUR KINDNESS.
YOU SEE, THEY ARE LIKE DOGS ROAMING THE FIELDS—
THEY WILL NEVER LEARN THEIR PLACE UNLESS THEY'RE PROPERLY DISCIPLINED.
SU (SWISH)

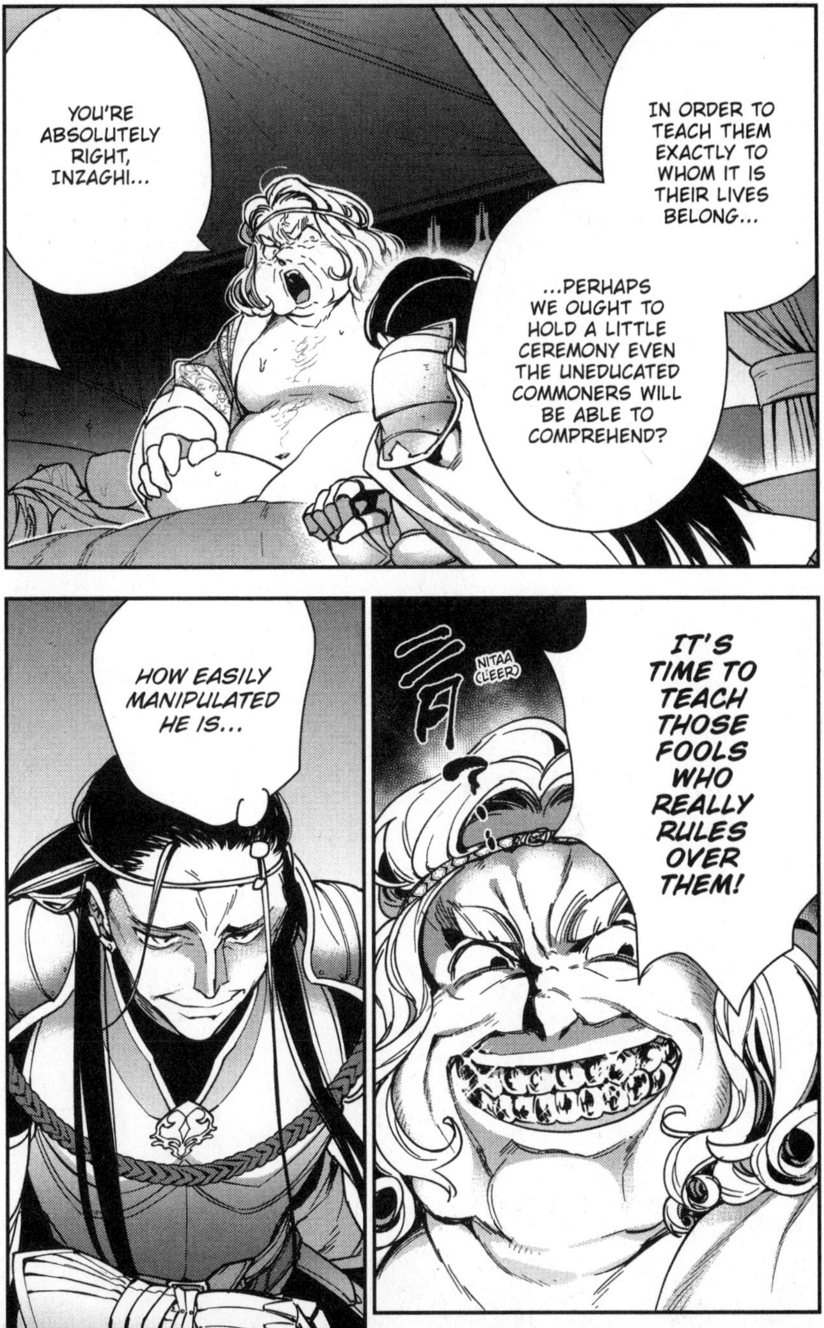
IN ORDER TO TEACH THEM EXACTLY TO WHOM IT IS THEIR LIVES BELONG...
...PERHAPS WE OUGHT TO HOLD A LITTLE CEREMONY EVEN THE UNEDUCATED COMMONERS WILL BE ABLE TO COMPREHEND?
YOU'RE ABSOLUTELY RIGHT, INZAGHI...
NITAA (LEER)
IT'S TIME TO TEACH THOSE FOOLS WHO REALLY RULES OVER THEM!
HOW EASILY MANIPULATED HE IS...

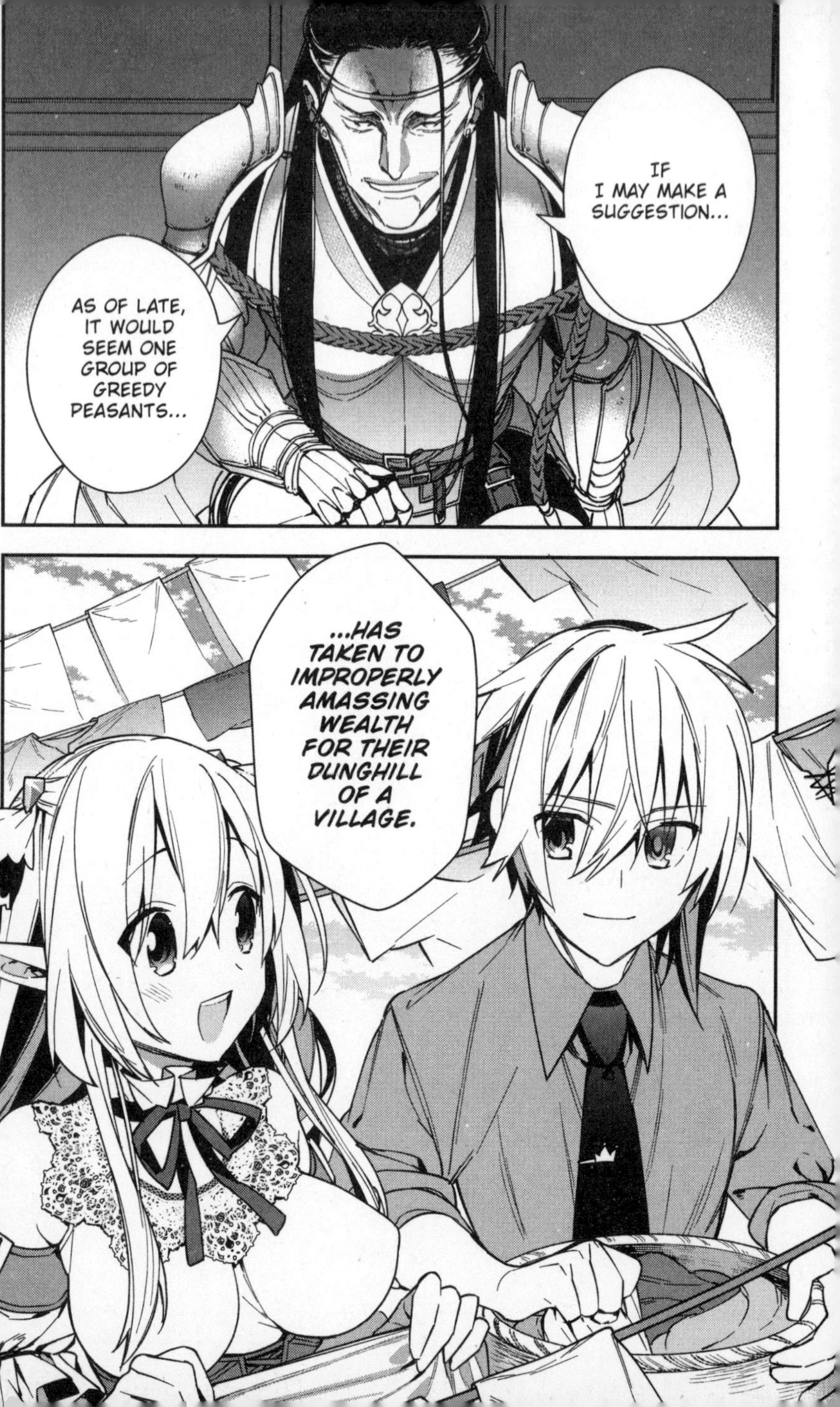
IF I MAY MAKE A SUGGESTION...
AS OF LATE, IT WOULD SEEM ONE GROUP OF GREEDY PEASANTS...
...HAS TAKEN TO IMPROPERLY AMASSING WEALTH FOR THEIR DUNGHILL OF A VILLAGE.

HIGH SCHOOL PRODIGIES HAVE IT EASY EVEN IN ANOTHER WORLD!

HAAH...

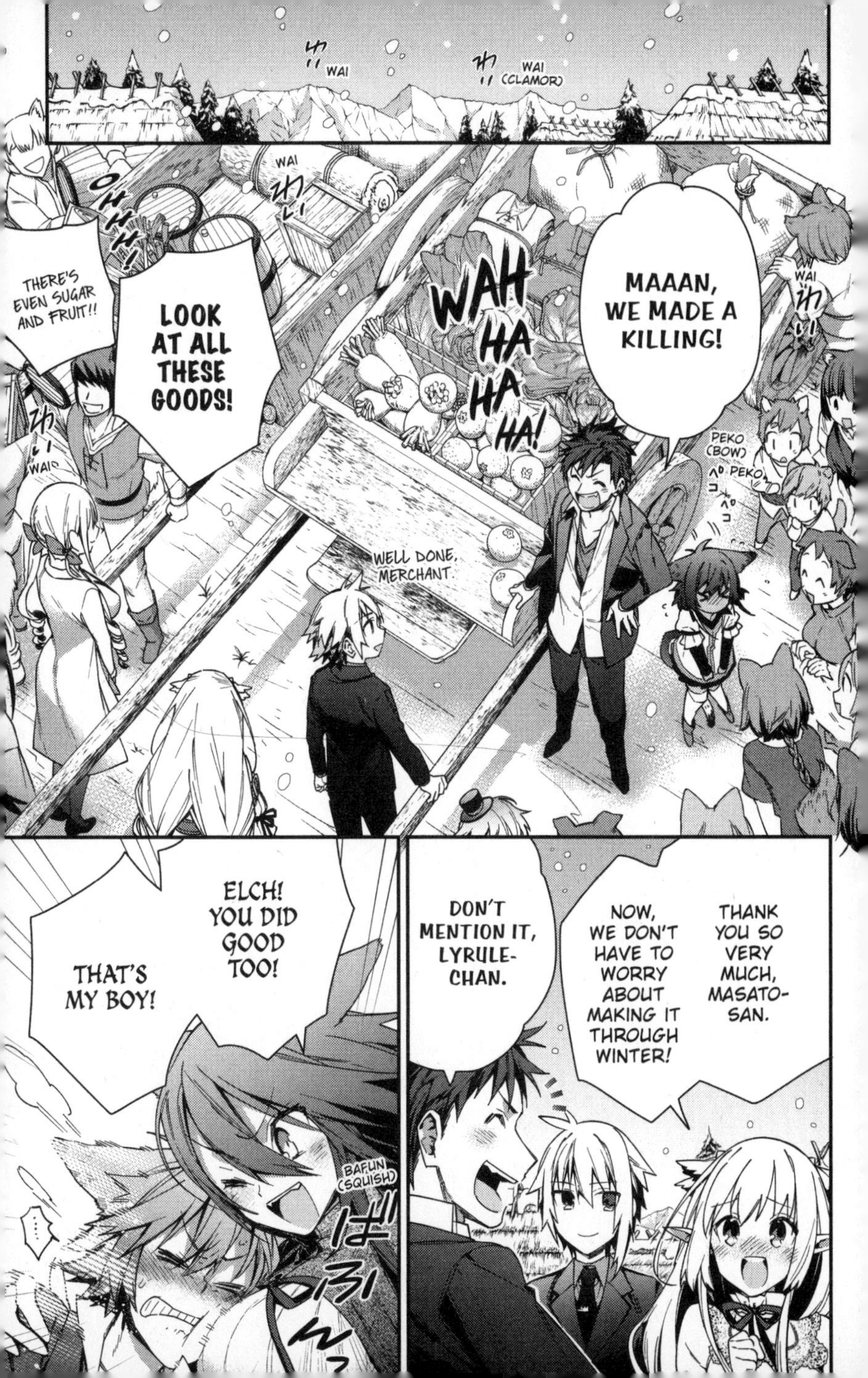
WAI (CLAMOR)
WAI
WAI
MAAAN, WE MADE A KILLING!
WAH HA HA HA!
PEKO (BOW) PEKO
WELL DONE, MERCHANT
WAI
LOOK AT ALL THESE GOODS!
THERE'S EVEN SUGAR AND FRUIT!!
OHHHH!
WAI
THANK YOU SO VERY MUCH, MASATO-SAN.
NOW, WE DON'T HAVE TO WORRY ABOUT MAKING IT THROUGH WINTER!
DON'T MENTION IT, LYRULE-CHAN.
ELCH! YOU DID GOOD TOO!
THAT'S MY BOY!
BAFUN (SQUISH)
......

CHAPTER 10: A NEW INITIATIVE

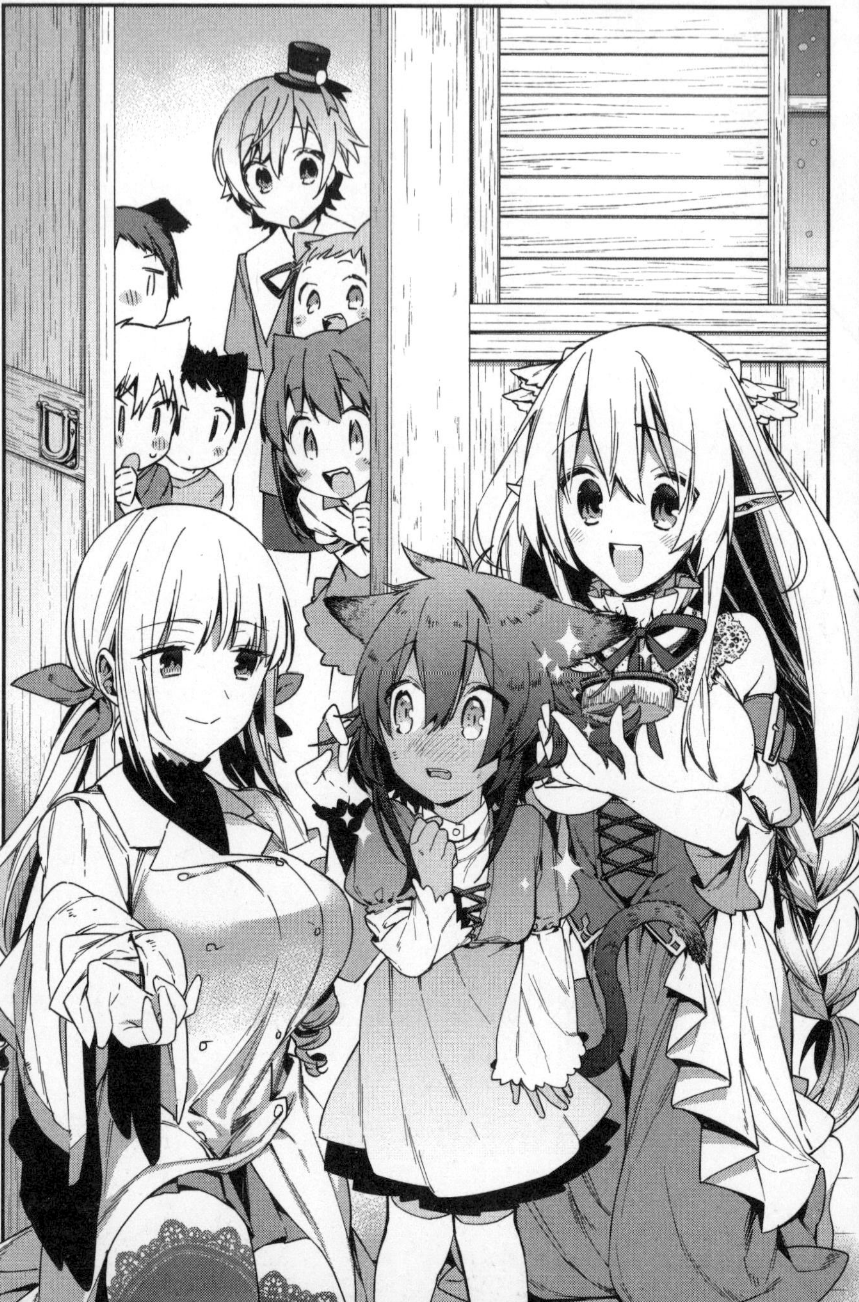

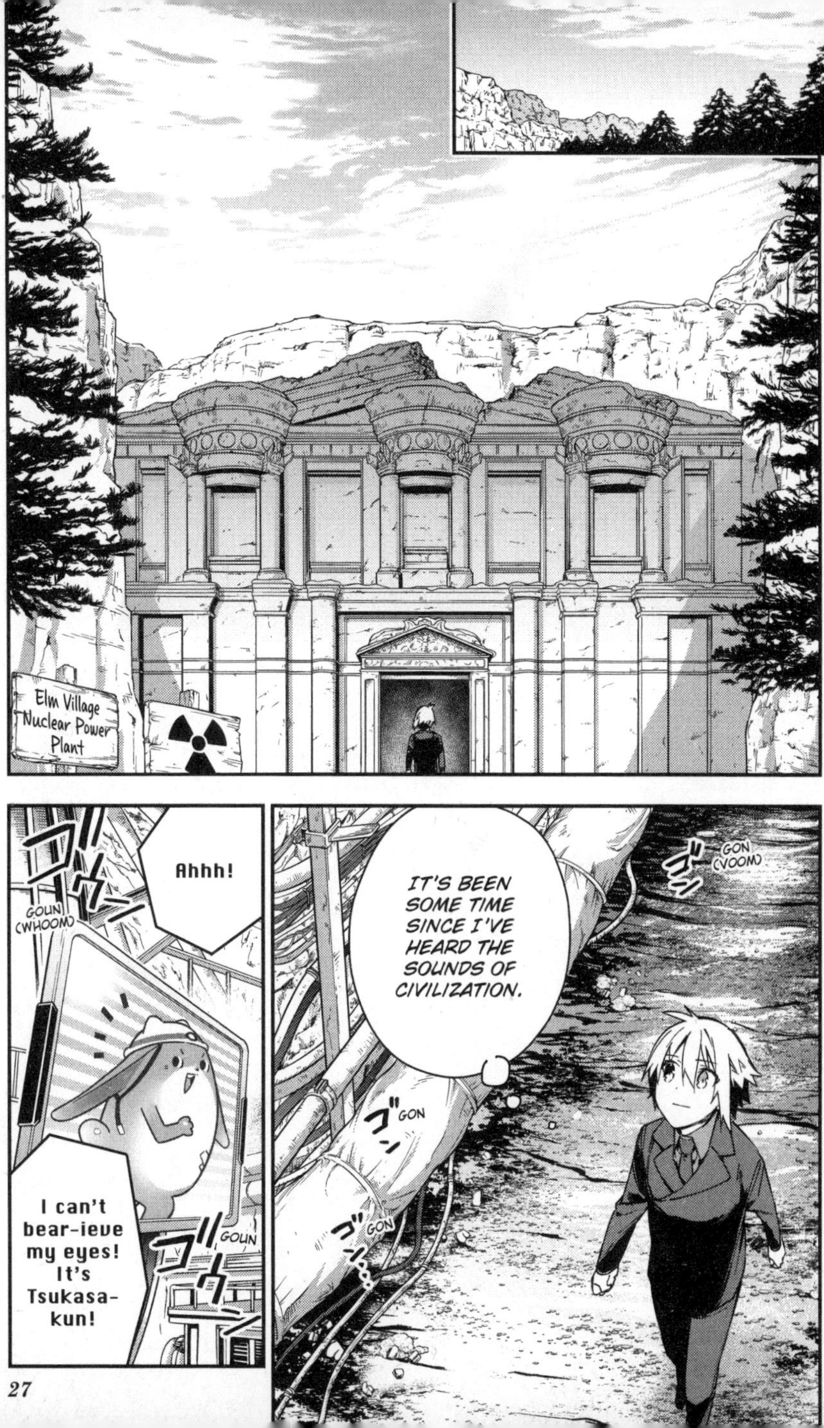
Elm Village Nuclear Power Plant
GON (VOOM)
IT'S BEEN SOME TIME SINCE I'VE HEARD THE SOUNDS OF CIVILIZATION.
GON
GON
Ahhh!
GOUN (WHOOM)
GOUN
I can't bear-ieve my eyes! It's Tsukasa-kun!

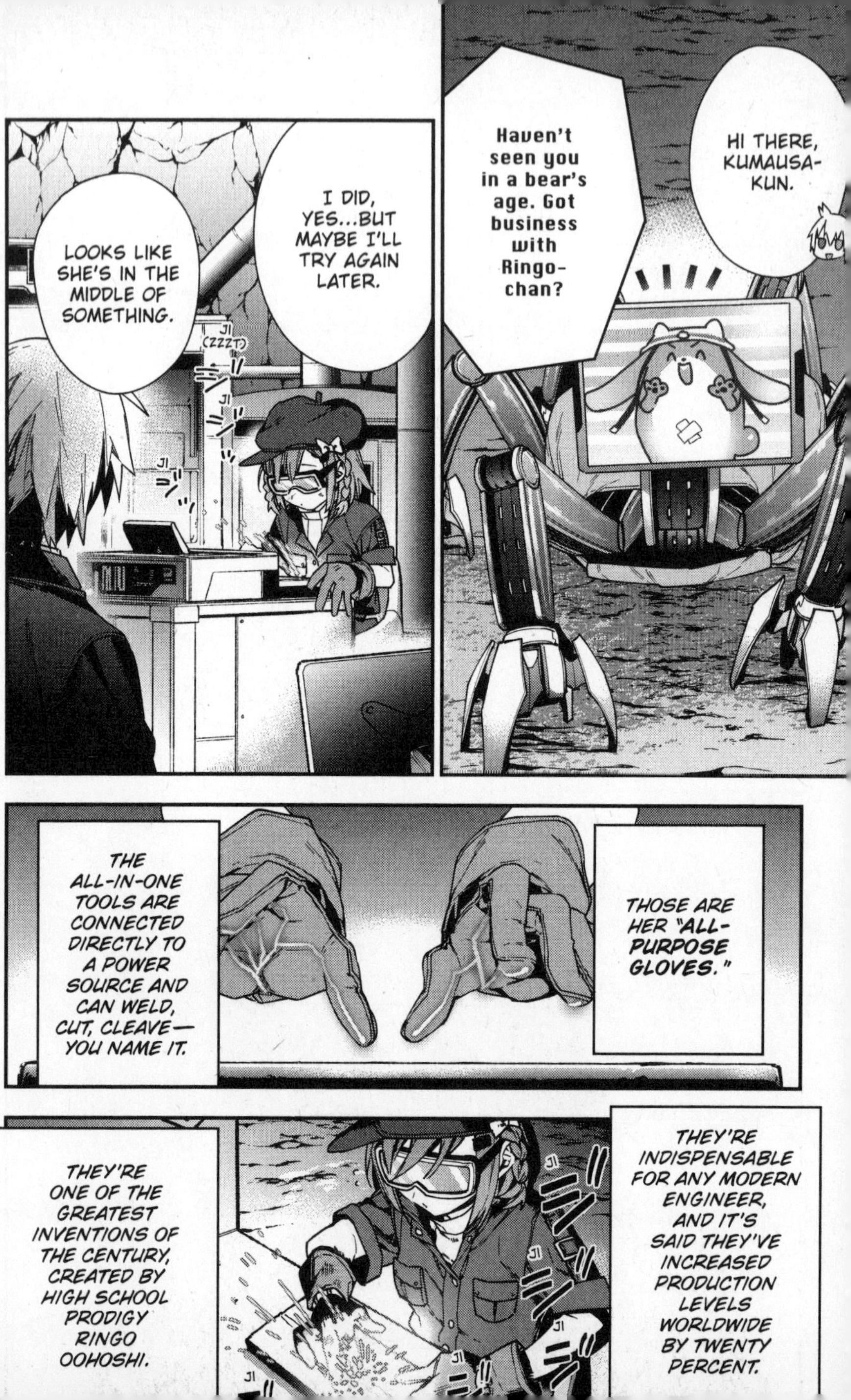
HI THERE, KUMAUSA-KUN.
Haven't seen you in a bear's age. Got business with Ringo-chan?
I DID, YES...BUT MAYBE I'LL TRY AGAIN LATER.
LOOKS LIKE SHE'S IN THE MIDDLE OF SOMETHING.
JI (ZZZT)
JI
JI
THOSE ARE HER "ALL-PURPOSE GLOVES."
THE ALL-IN-ONE TOOLS ARE CONNECTED DIRECTLY TO A POWER SOURCE AND CAN WELD, CUT, CLEAVE—YOU NAME IT.
THEY'RE INDISPENSABLE FOR ANY MODERN ENGINEER, AND IT'S SAID THEY'VE INCREASED PRODUCTION LEVELS WORLDWIDE BY TWENTY PERCENT.
JI
JI
JI
THEY'RE ONE OF THE GREATEST INVENTIONS OF THE CENTURY, CREATED BY HIGH SCHOOL PRODIGY RINGO OOHOSHI.
JI

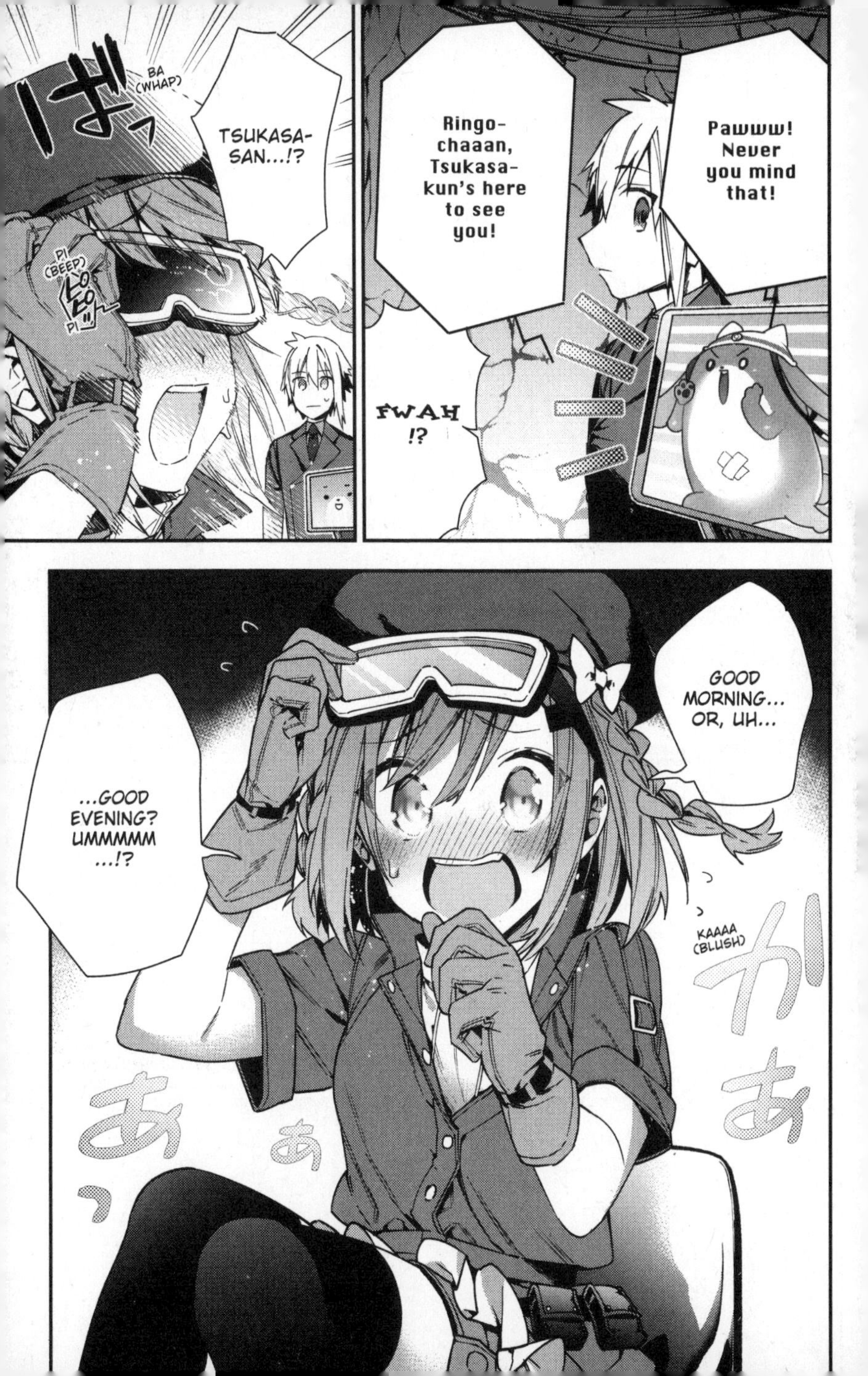
Pawww! Never you mind that!
Ringo-chaaan, Tsukasa-kun's here to see you!
FWAH !?
BA (WHAP)
TSUKASA-SAN...!?
PI (BEEP)
PI
GOOD MORNING... OR, UH...
KAAAA (BLUSH)
...GOOD EVENING? UMMMMM ...!?

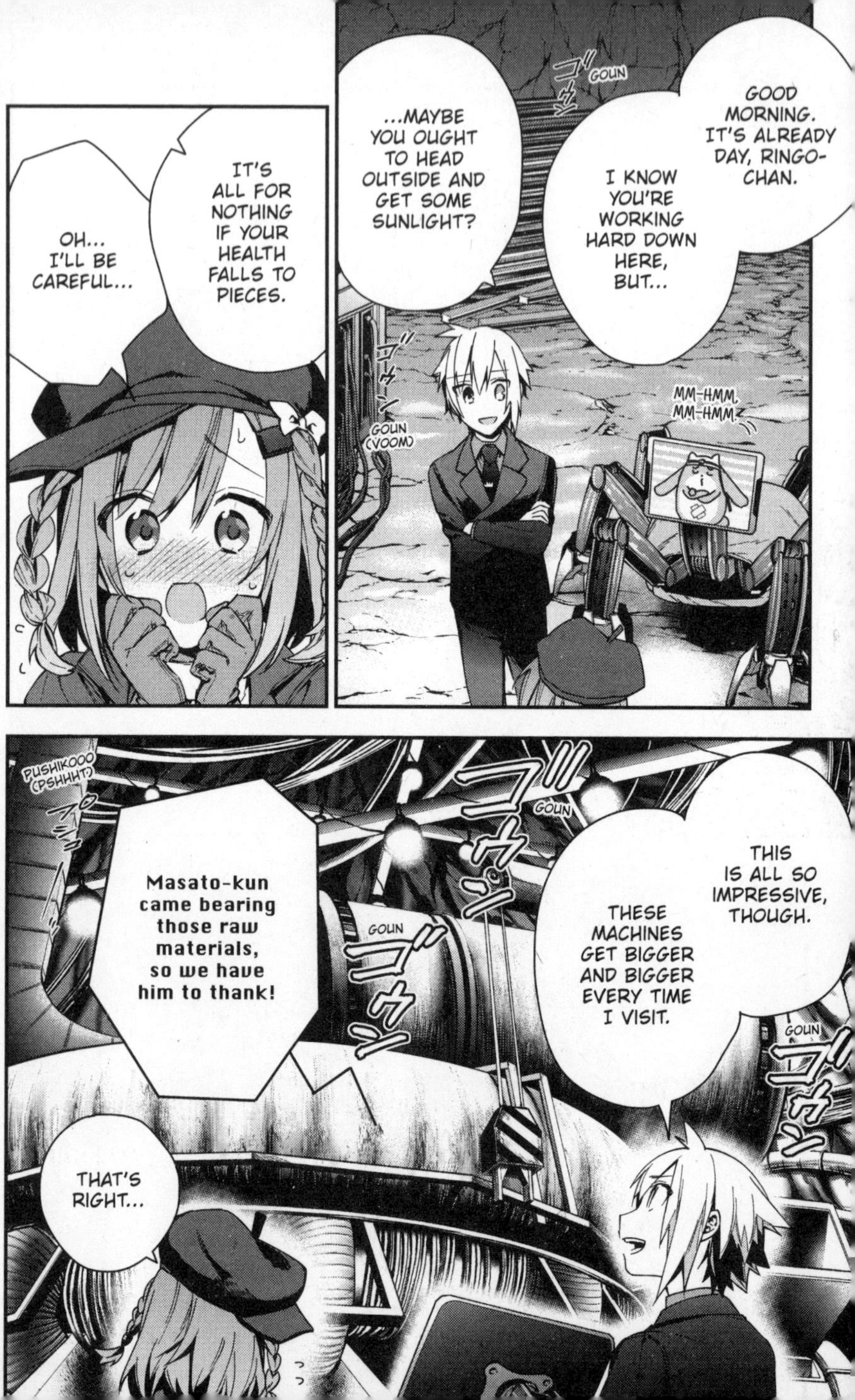
GOUN
GOOD MORNING. IT'S ALREADY DAY, RINGO-CHAN.
I KNOW YOU'RE WORKING HARD DOWN HERE, BUT...
...MAYBE YOU OUGHT TO HEAD OUTSIDE AND GET SOME SUNLIGHT?
MM-HMM, MM-HMM.
GOUN (VOOM)
IT'S ALL FOR NOTHING IF YOUR HEALTH FALLS TO PIECES.
OH... I'LL BE CAREFUL...
GOUN
THIS IS ALL SO IMPRESSIVE, THOUGH.
THESE MACHINES GET BIGGER AND BIGGER EVERY TIME I VISIT.
GOUN
GOUN
Masato-kun came bearing those raw materials, so we have him to thank!
PUSHIKOOO (PSHHHT)
THAT'S RIGHT...

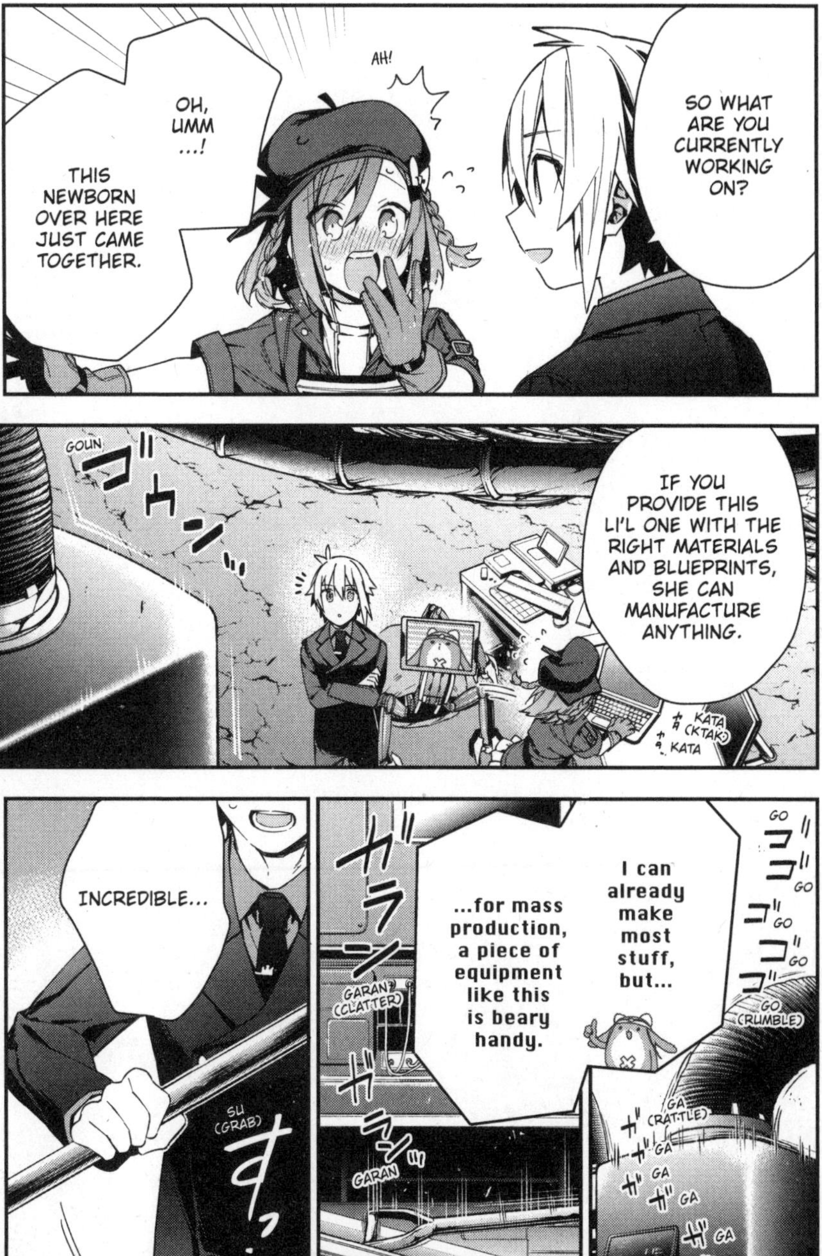
SO WHAT ARE YOU CURRENTLY WORKING ON?
AH!
OH, UMM ...!
THIS NEWBORN OVER HERE JUST CAME TOGETHER.
IF YOU PROVIDE THIS LI'L ONE WITH THE RIGHT MATERIALS AND BLUEPRINTS, SHE CAN MANUFACTURE ANYTHING.
GOUN
KATA (KTAK) KATA
GO GO GO GO GO (RUMBLE)
I can already make most stuff, but...
...for mass production, a piece of equipment like this is beary handy.
GARAN (CLATTER)
GARAN
GA (RATTLE) GA GA GA GA
INCREDIBLE...
SU (GRAB)

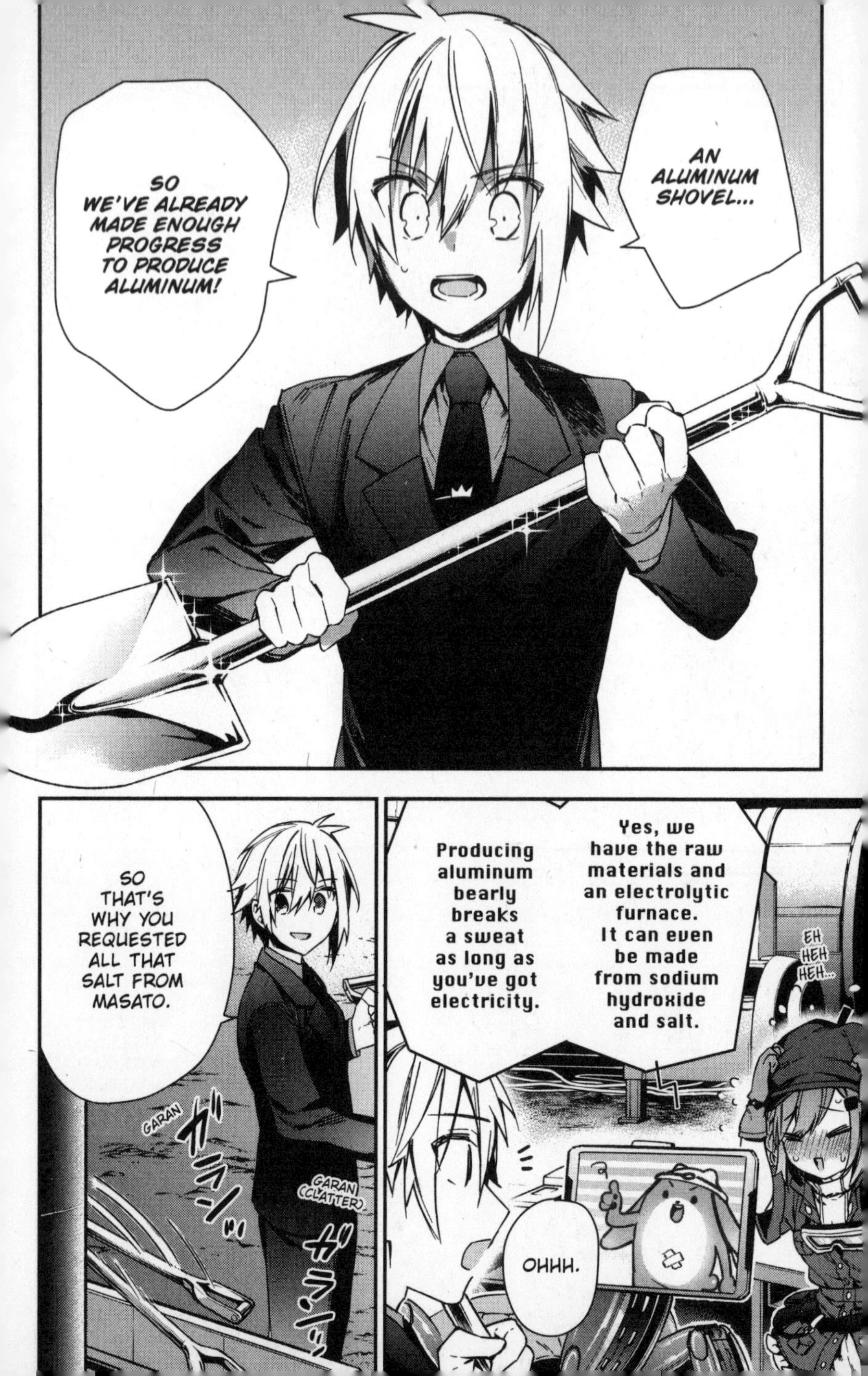
AN ALUMINUM SHOVEL...
SO WE'VE ALREADY MADE ENOUGH PROGRESS TO PRODUCE ALUMINUM!
Yes, we have the raw materials and an electrolytic furnace. It can even be made from sodium hydroxide and salt.
Producing aluminum bearly breaks a sweat as long as you've got electricity.
EH HEH HEH...
OHHH.
SO THAT'S WHY YOU REQUESTED ALL THAT SALT FROM MASATO.
GARAN
GARAN (CLATTER)

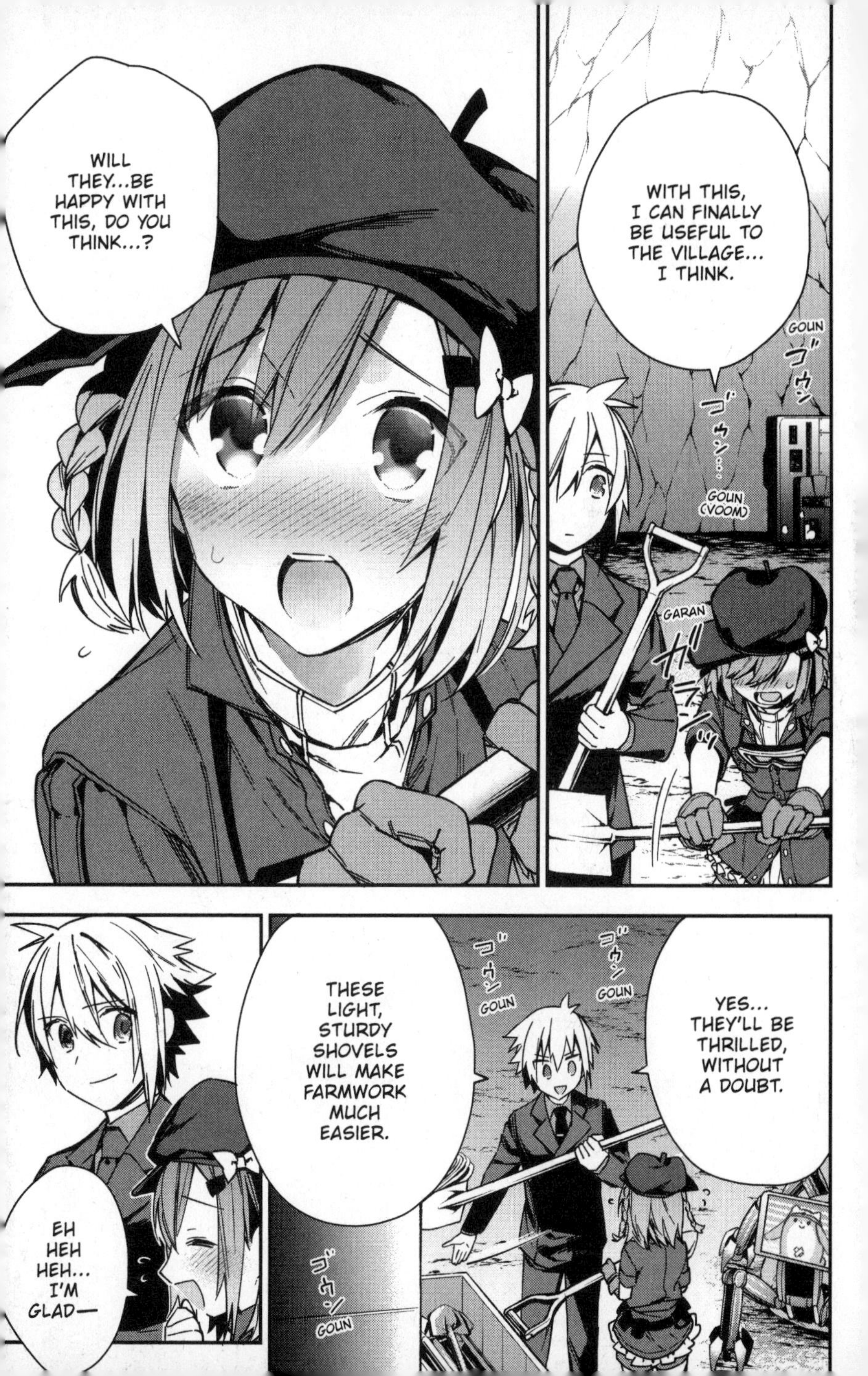

WITH THIS, I CAN FINALLY BE USEFUL TO THE VILLAGE... I THINK.
GOUN
ゴウン
ゴウン…
GOUN (VOOM)
GARAN
ガラン
WILL THEY...BE HAPPY WITH THIS, DO YOU THINK...?
YES... THEY'LL BE THRILLED, WITHOUT A DOUBT.
ゴウン
GOUN
ゴウン
GOUN
THESE LIGHT, STURDY SHOVELS WILL MAKE FARMWORK MUCH EASIER.
ゴウン
GOUN
EH HEH HEH... I'M GLAD—

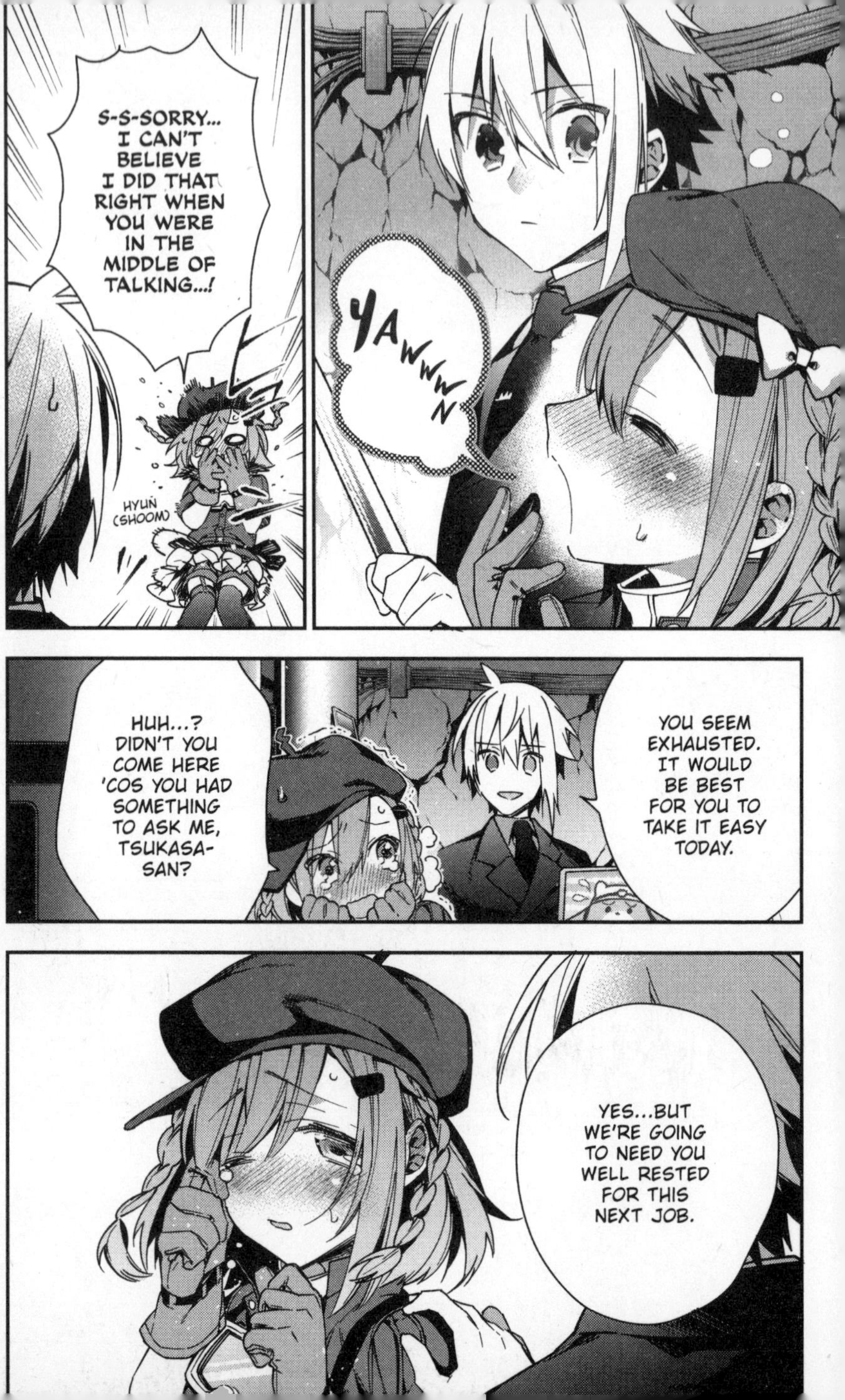
YAWWWN
S-S-SORRY... I CAN'T BELIEVE I DID THAT RIGHT WHEN YOU WERE IN THE MIDDLE OF TALKING...!
HYUN (SHOOM)
YOU SEEM EXHAUSTED. IT WOULD BE BEST FOR YOU TO TAKE IT EASY TODAY.
HUH...? DIDN'T YOU COME HERE 'COS YOU HAD SOMETHING TO ASK ME, TSUKASA-SAN?
YES...BUT WE'RE GOING TO NEED YOU WELL RESTED FOR THIS NEXT JOB.

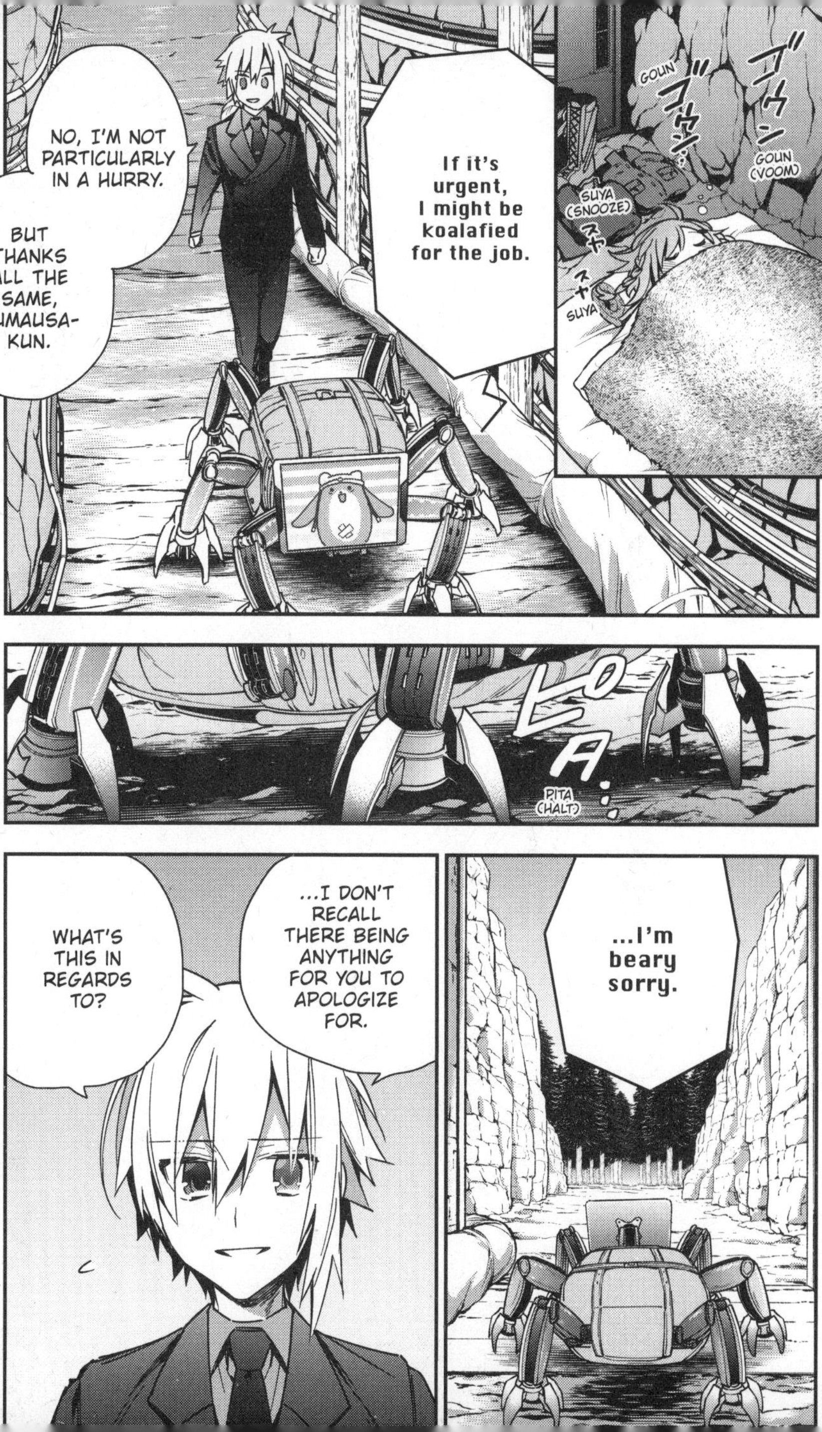
GOUN
GOUN (VOOM)
SUYA (SNOOZE)
SUYA
If it's urgent, I might be koalafied for the job.
NO, I'M NOT PARTICULARLY IN A HURRY.
BUT THANKS ALL THE SAME, KUMAUSA-KUN.
PITA (HALT)
...I'm beary sorry.
...I DON'T RECALL THERE BEING ANYTHING FOR YOU TO APOLOGIZE FOR.
WHAT'S THIS IN REGARDS TO?

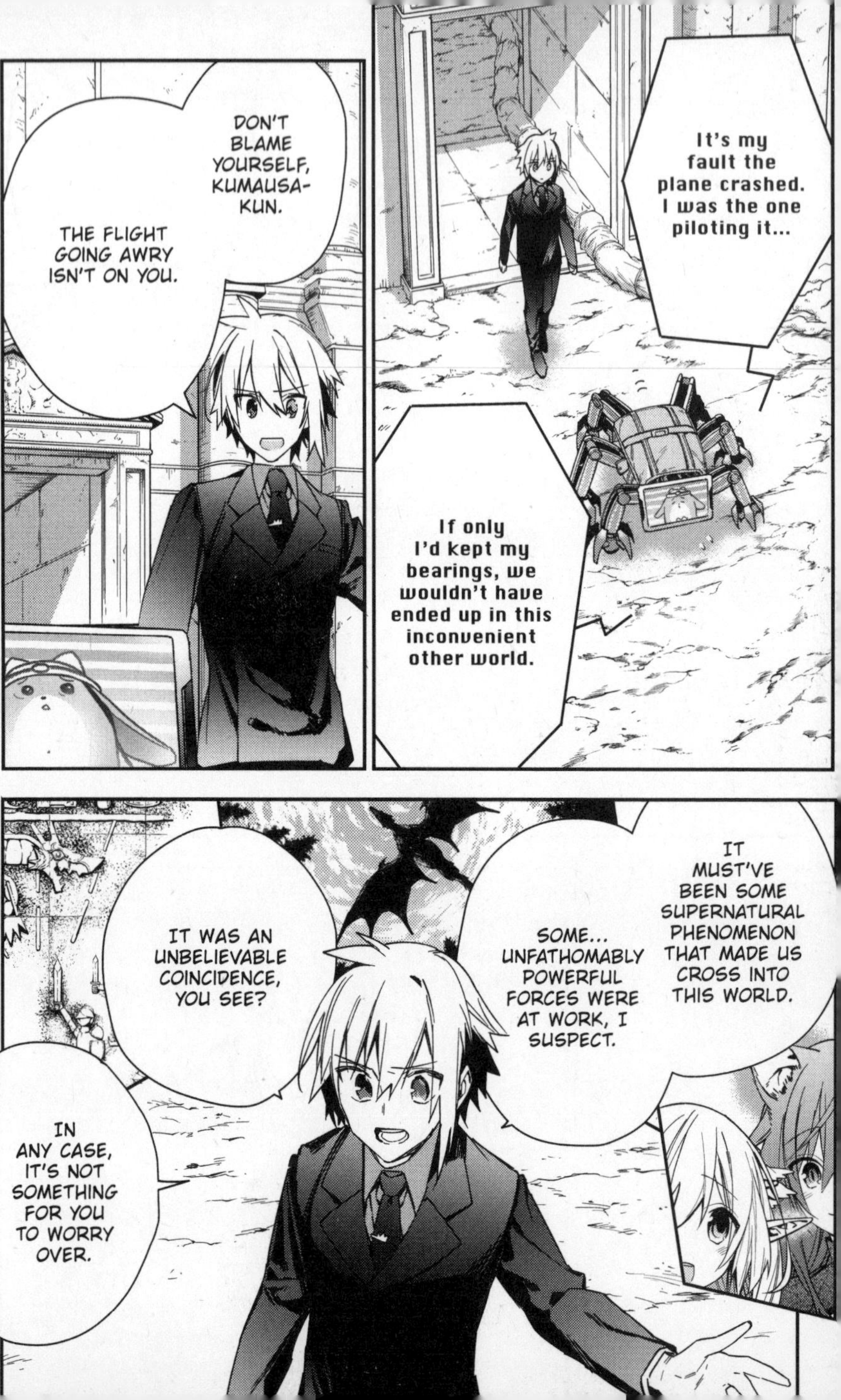
It's my fault the plane crashed. I was the one piloting it...
If only I'd kept my bearings, we wouldn't have ended up in this inconvenient other world.
DON'T BLAME YOURSELF, KUMAUSA-KUN.
THE FLIGHT GOING AWRY ISN'T ON YOU.
IT MUST'VE BEEN SOME SUPERNATURAL PHENOMENON THAT MADE US CROSS INTO THIS WORLD.
SOME... UNFATHOMABLY POWERFUL FORCES WERE AT WORK, I SUSPECT.
IT WAS AN UNBELIEVABLE COINCIDENCE, YOU SEE?
IN ANY CASE, IT'S NOT SOMETHING FOR YOU TO WORRY OVER.

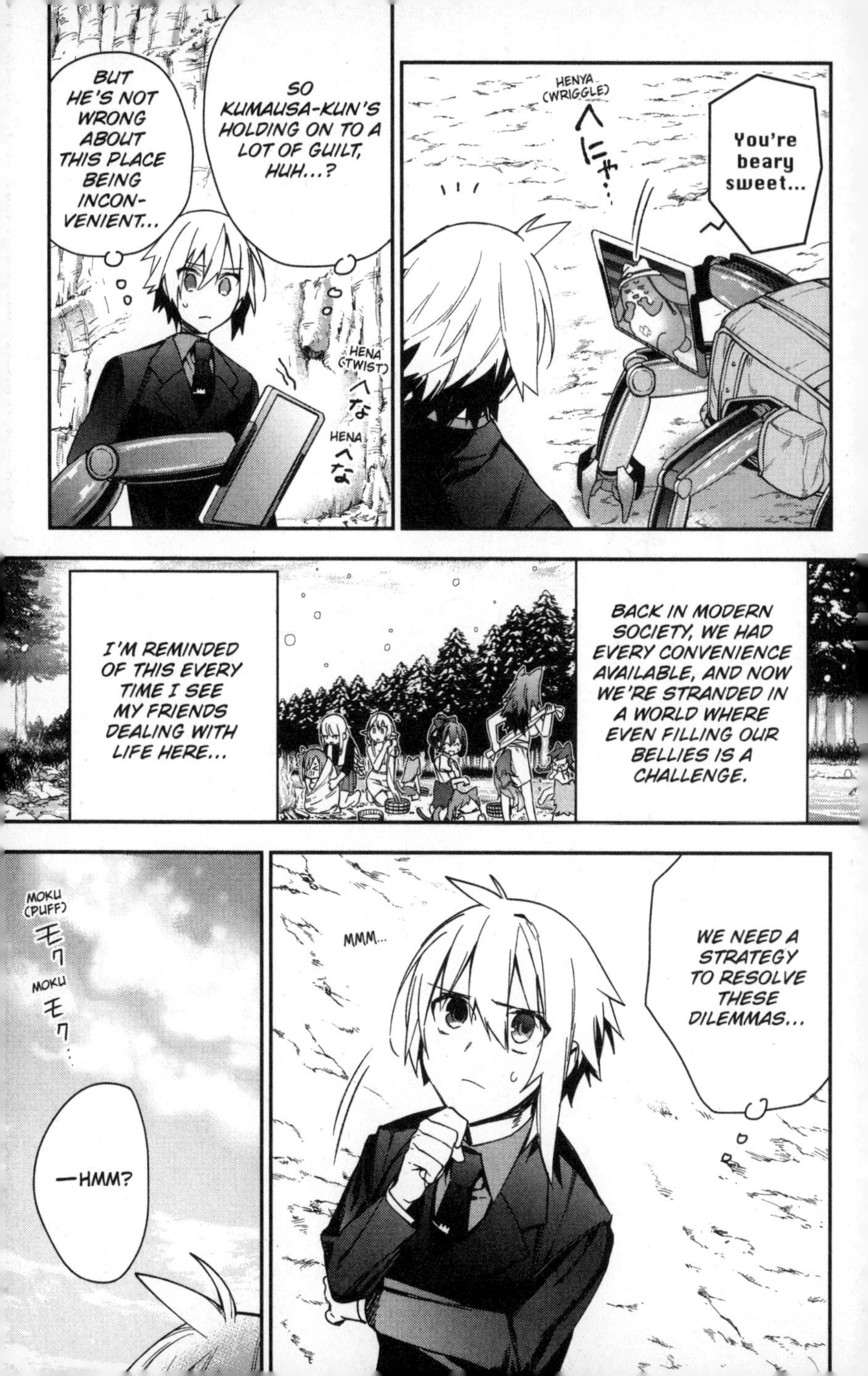
You're beary sweet...
HENYA (WRIGGLE)
へにゃ...
SO KUMAUSA-KUN'S HOLDING ON TO A LOT OF GUILT, HUH...?
BUT HE'S NOT WRONG ABOUT THIS PLACE BEING INCON-VENIENT...
HENA (TWIST)
へな
HENA
へな
BACK IN MODERN SOCIETY, WE HAD EVERY CONVENIENCE AVAILABLE, AND NOW WE'RE STRANDED IN A WORLD WHERE EVEN FILLING OUR BELLIES IS A CHALLENGE.
I'M REMINDED OF THIS EVERY TIME I SEE MY FRIENDS DEALING WITH LIFE HERE...
WE NEED A STRATEGY TO RESOLVE THESE DILEMMAS...
MMM...
MOKU (PUFF)
モク
MOKU
モク...
—HMM?

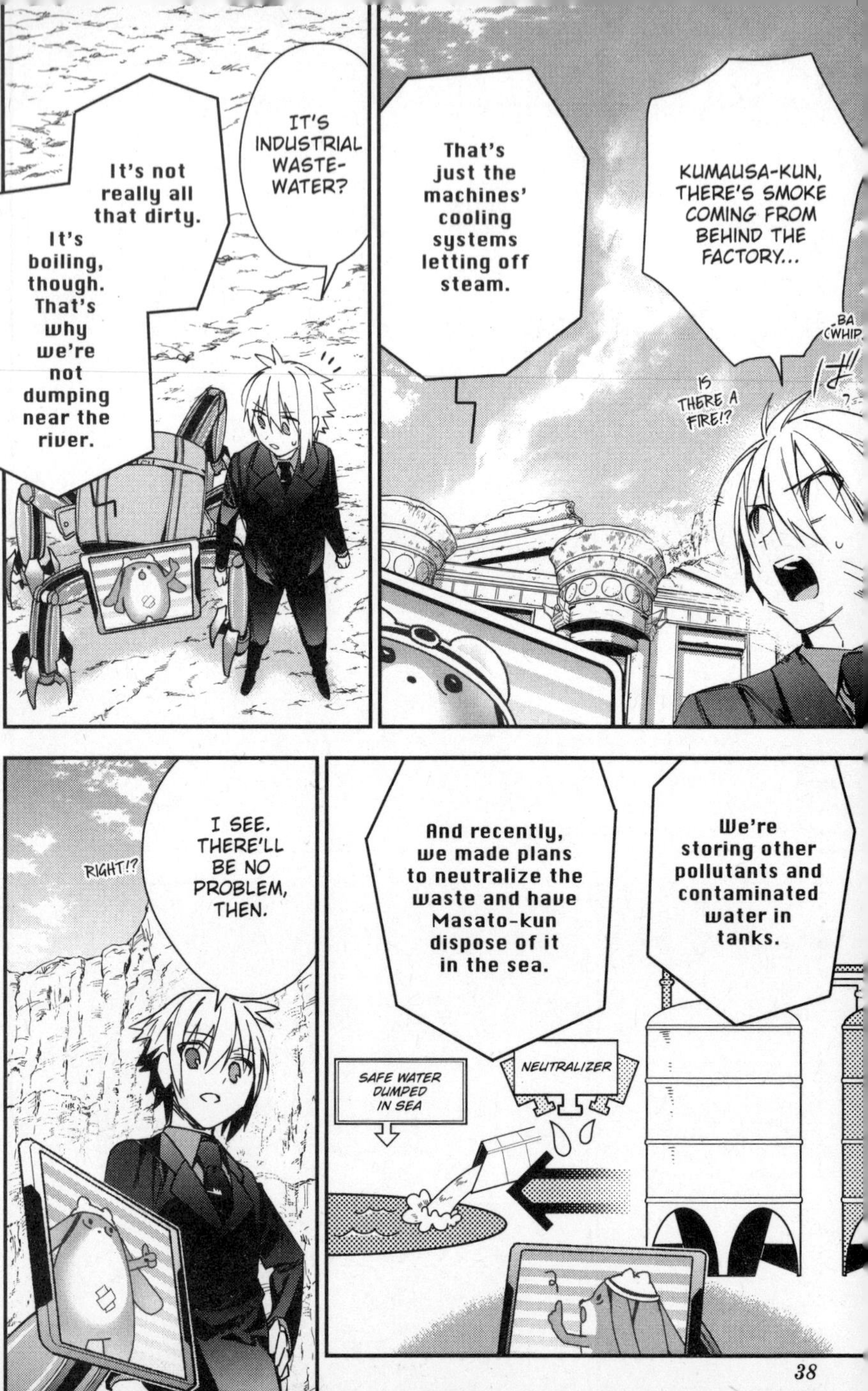
KUMAUSA-KUN, THERE'S SMOKE COMING FROM BEHIND THE FACTORY...
BA CWHIP
IS THERE A FIRE!?
That's just the machines' cooling systems letting off steam.
IT'S INDUSTRIAL WASTE-WATER?
It's not really all that dirty.
It's boiling, though. That's why we're not dumping near the river.
We're storing other pollutants and contaminated water in tanks.
And recently, we made plans to neutralize the waste and have Masato-kun dispose of it in the sea.
NEUTRALIZER
SAFE WATER DUMPED IN SEA
I SEE. THERE'LL BE NO PROBLEM, THEN.
RIGHT!?

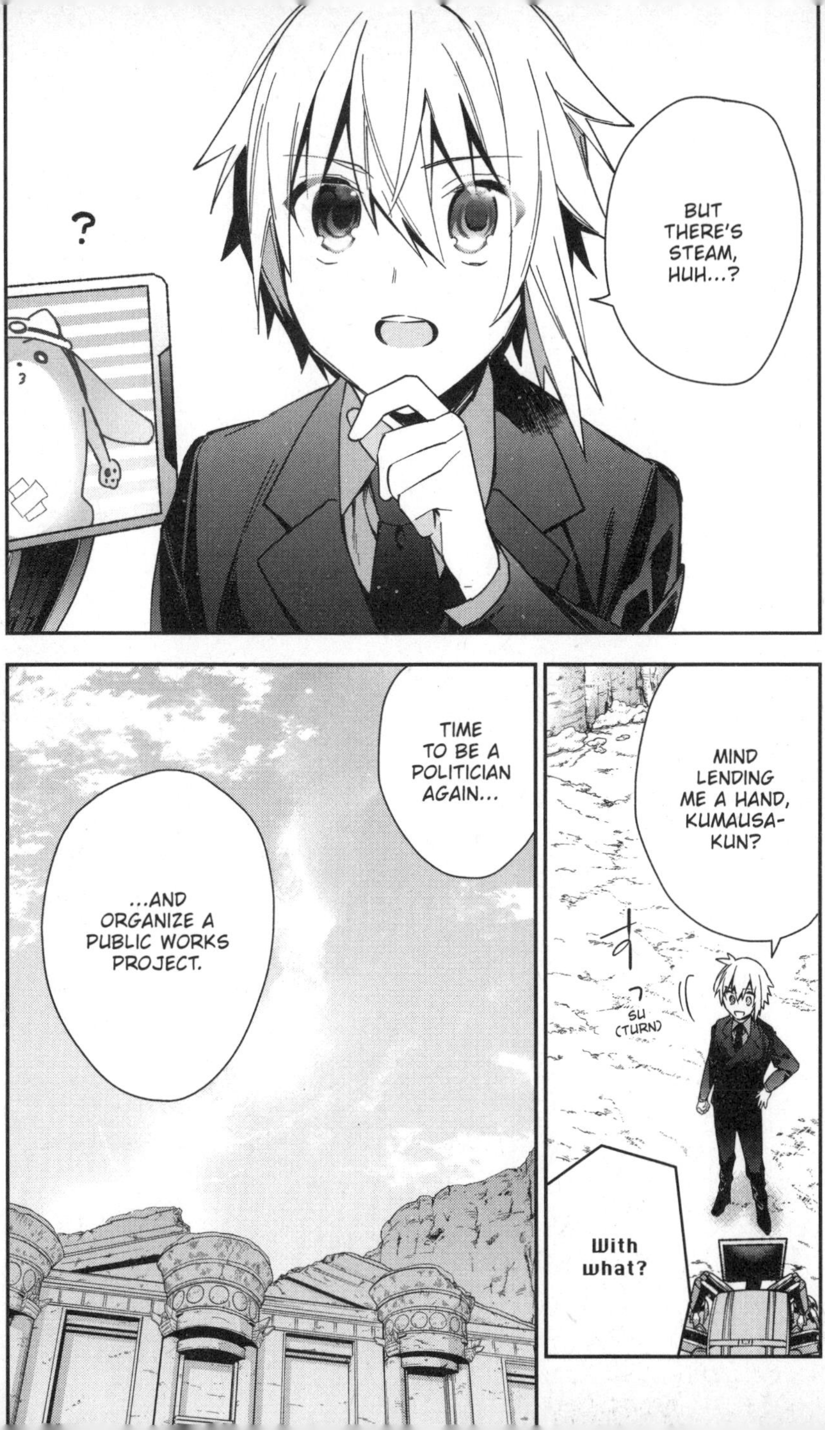
BUT THERE'S STEAM, HUH...?
?
MIND LENDING ME A HAND, KUMAUSA-KUN?
SU (TURN)
With what?
TIME TO BE A POLITICIAN AGAIN...
...AND ORGANIZE A PUBLIC WORKS PROJECT.

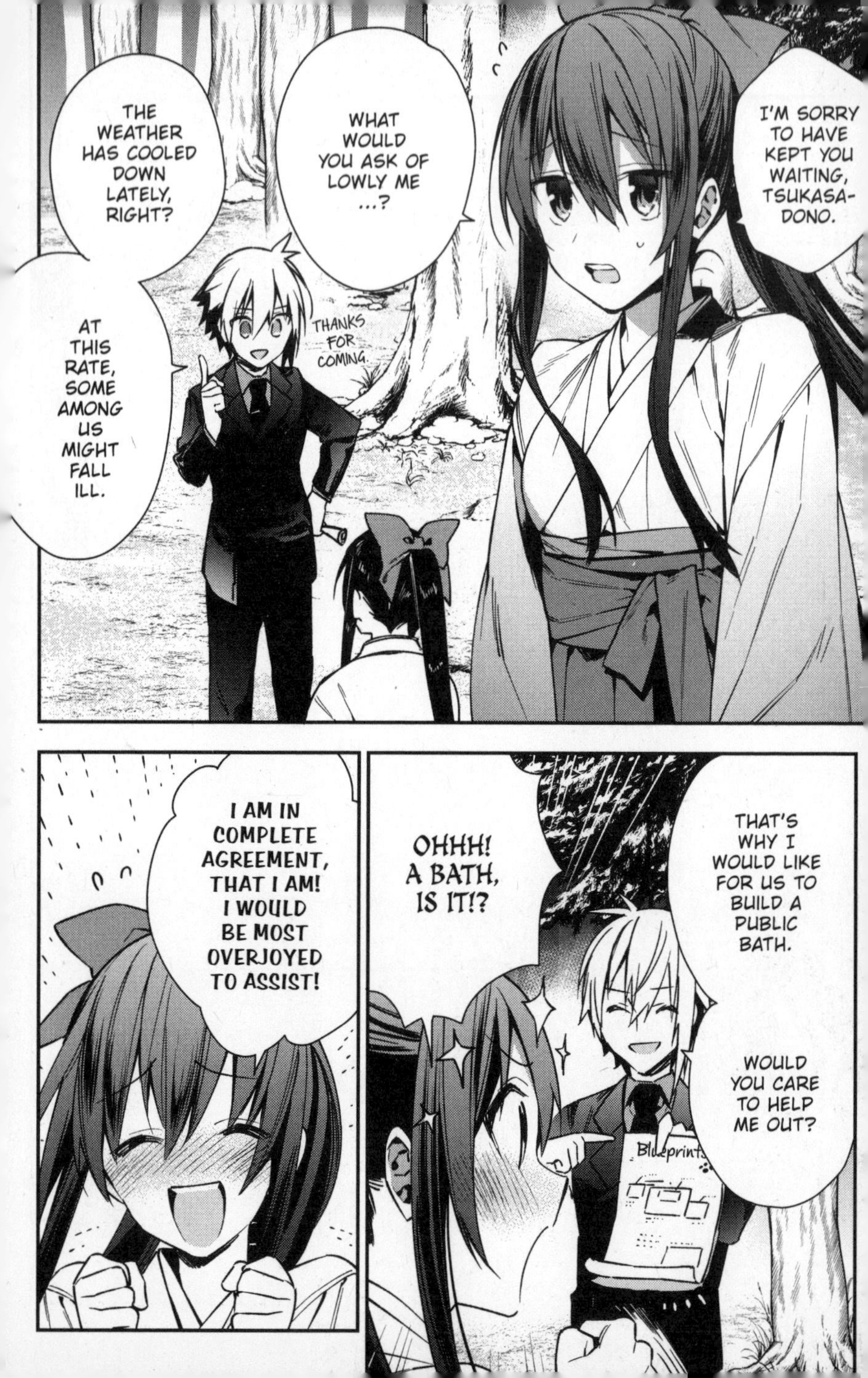
I'M SORRY TO HAVE KEPT YOU WAITING, TSUKASA-DONO.
WHAT WOULD YOU ASK OF LOWLY ME ...?
THE WEATHER HAS COOLED DOWN LATELY, RIGHT?
THANKS FOR COMING.
AT THIS RATE, SOME AMONG US MIGHT FALL ILL.
THAT'S WHY I WOULD LIKE FOR US TO BUILD A PUBLIC BATH.
OHHH! A BATH, IS IT!?
WOULD YOU CARE TO HELP ME OUT?
Blueprints
I AM IN COMPLETE AGREEMENT, THAT I AM! I WOULD BE MOST OVERJOYED TO ASSIST!

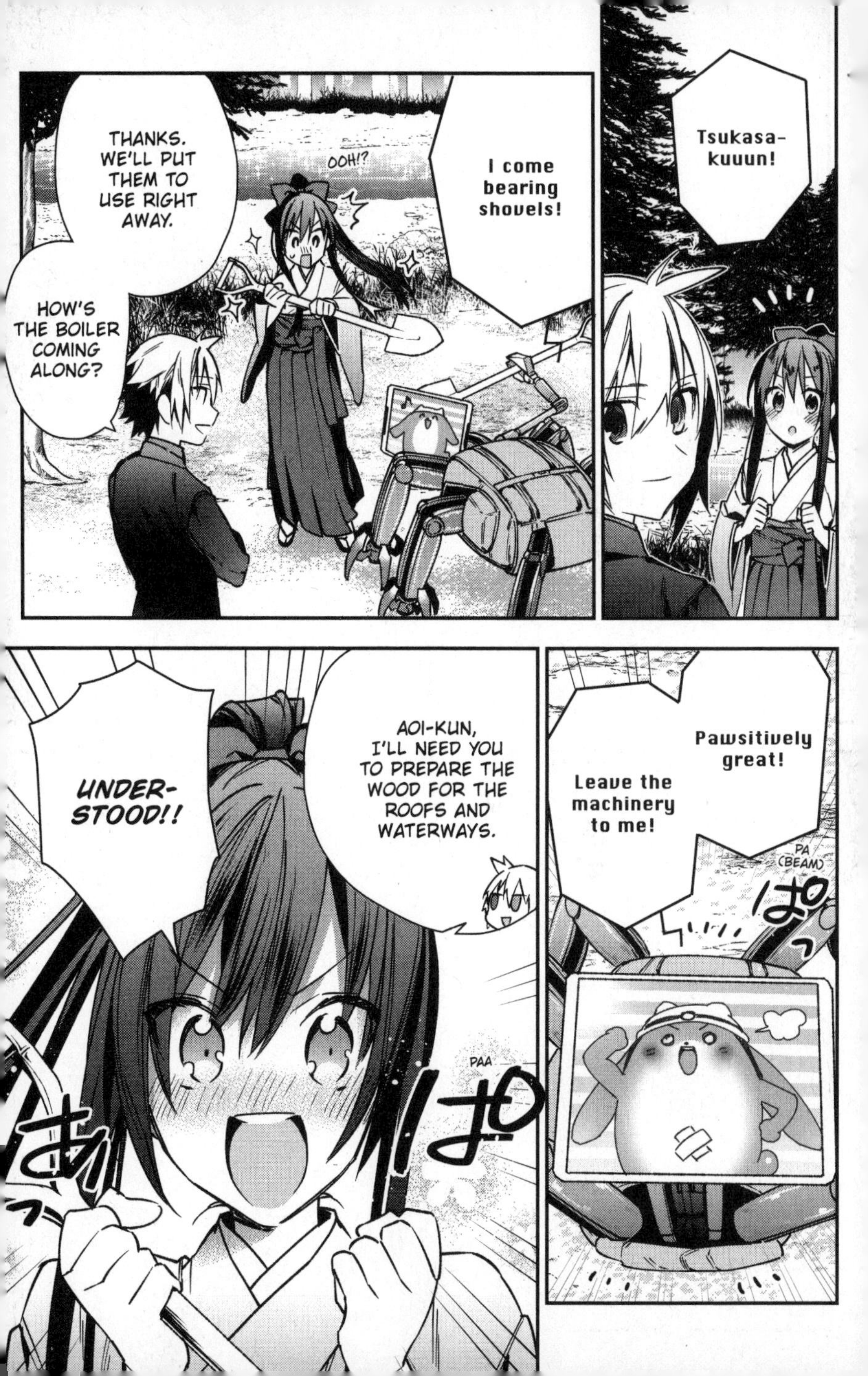
Tsukasa-kuuun!
I come bearing shovels!
OOH!?
THANKS. WE'LL PUT THEM TO USE RIGHT AWAY.
HOW'S THE BOILER COMING ALONG?
Pawsitively great!
Leave the machinery to me!
PA (BEAM)
ぱっ
AOI-KUN, I'LL NEED YOU TO PREPARE THE WOOD FOR THE ROOFS AND WATERWAYS.
UNDER-STOOD!!
PAA
ぱ
あ

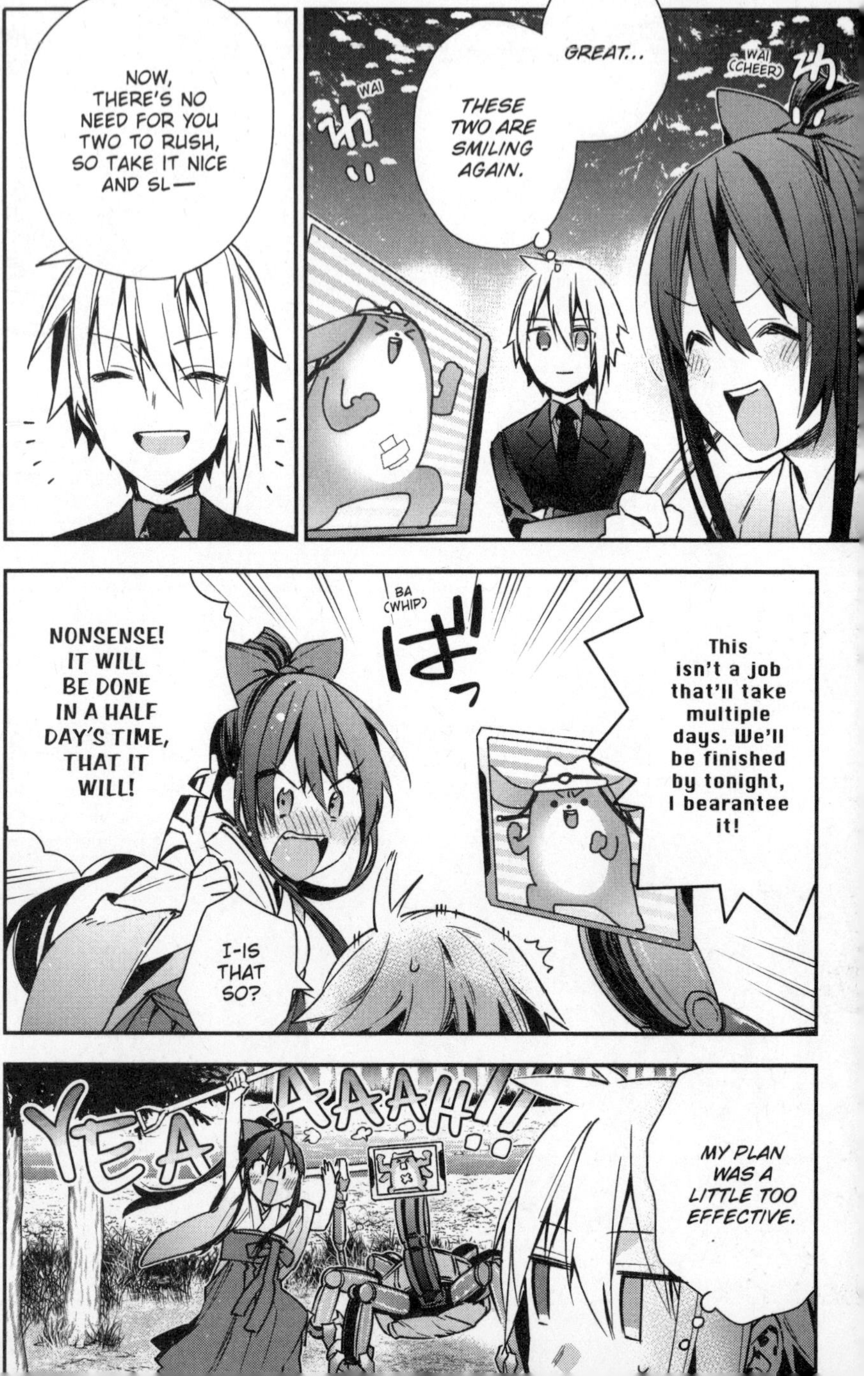
WAI (CHEER)
GREAT...
THESE TWO ARE SMILING AGAIN.
WAI
NOW, THERE'S NO NEED FOR YOU TWO TO RUSH, SO TAKE IT NICE AND SL—
BA (WHIP)
This isn't a job that'll take multiple days. We'll be finished by tonight, I bearantee it!
NONSENSE! IT WILL BE DONE IN A HALF DAY'S TIME, THAT IT WILL!
I-IS THAT SO?
MY PLAN WAS A LITTLE TOO EFFECTIVE.
YEAAAAH!!

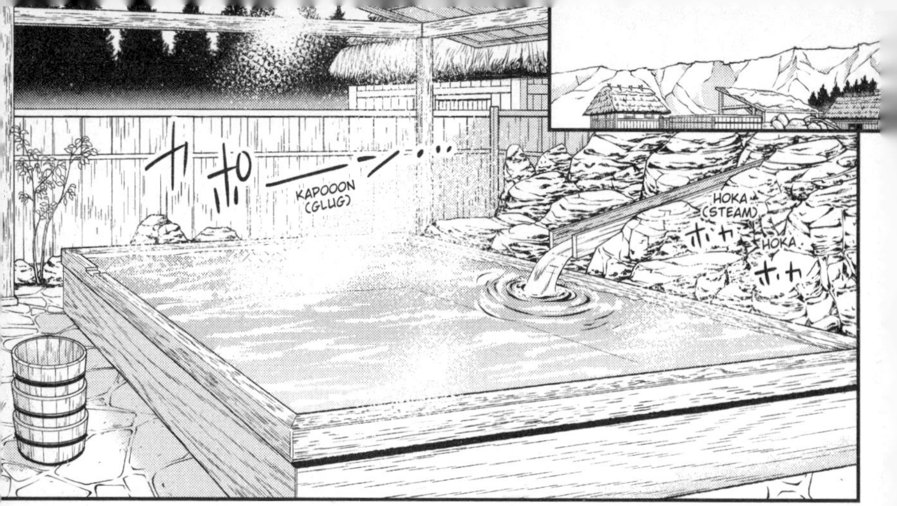
HOKA (STEAM)
HOKA
KAPOOON (GLUG)

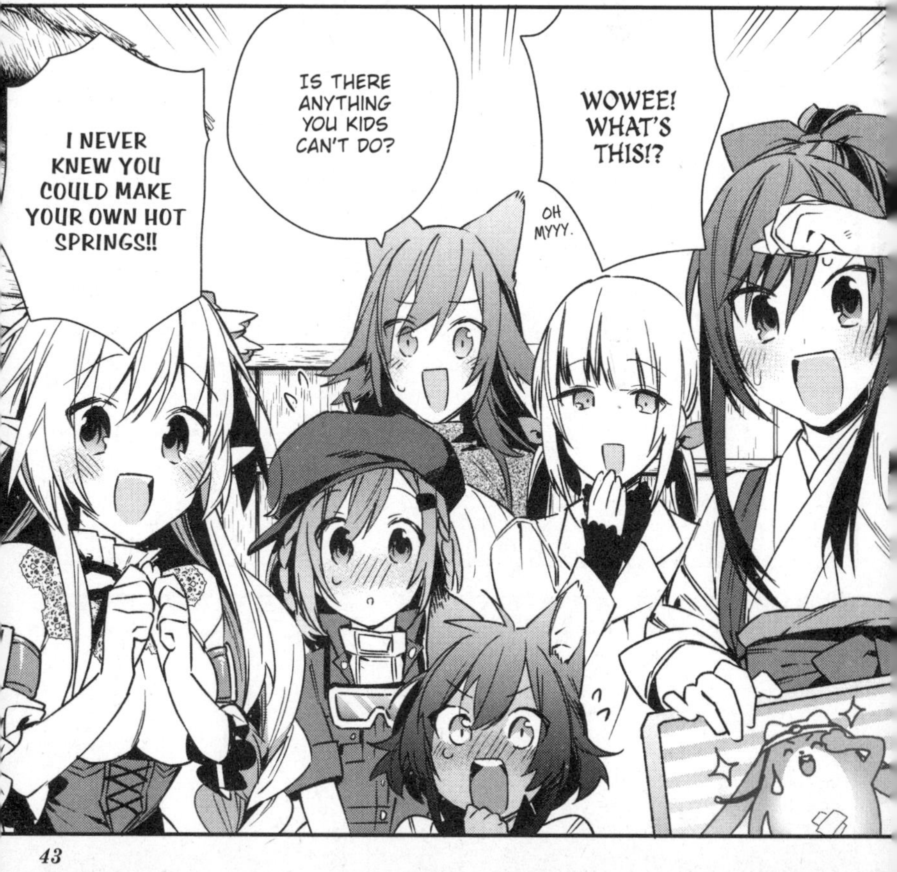
WOWEE! WHAT'S THIS!?
OH MYYY.
IS THERE ANYTHING YOU KIDS CAN'T DO?
I NEVER KNEW YOU COULD MAKE YOUR OWN HOT SPRINGS!!

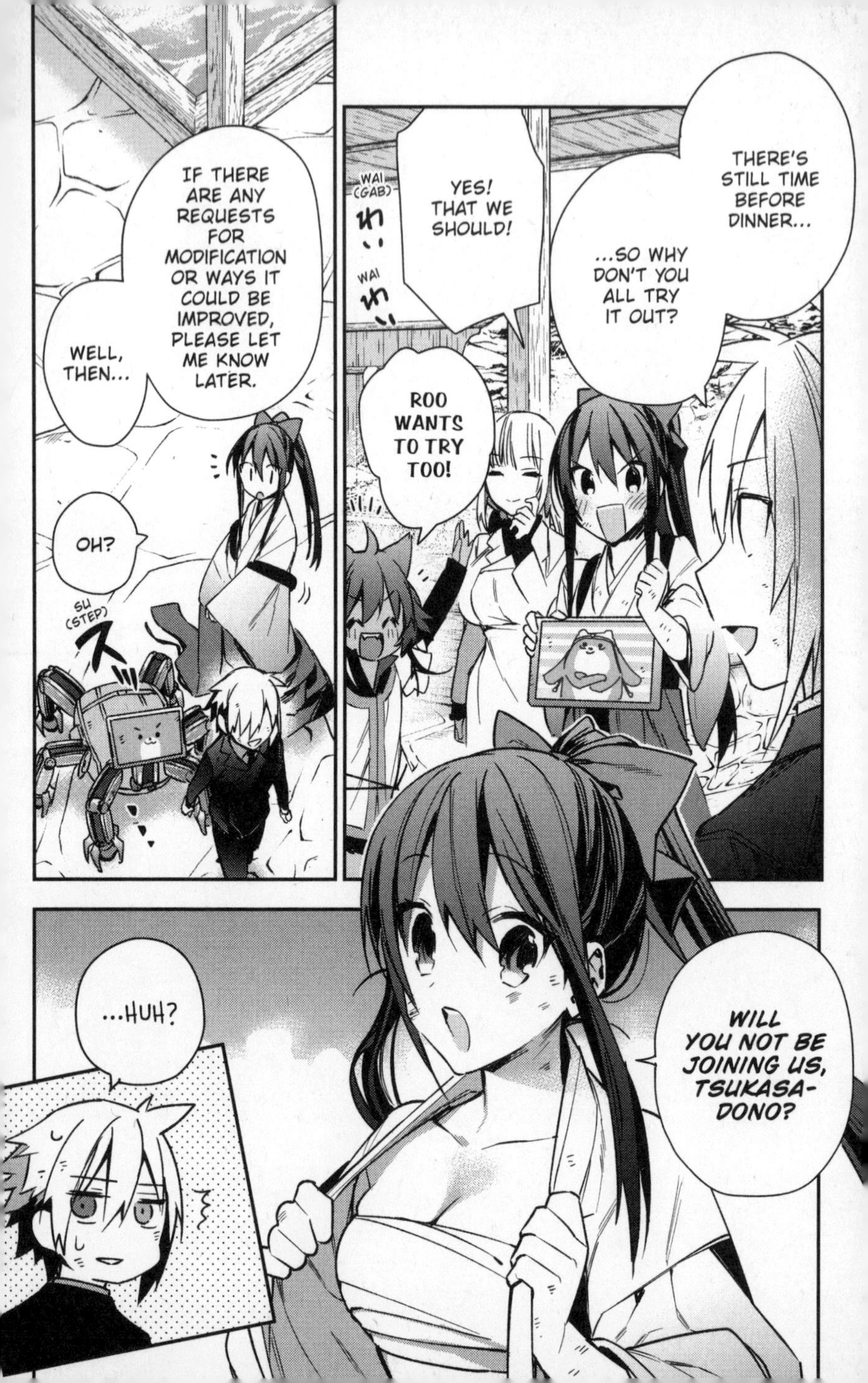
THERE'S STILL TIME BEFORE DINNER...
...SO WHY DON'T YOU ALL TRY IT OUT?
YES! THAT WE SHOULD!
WAI (GAB)
WAI
ROO WANTS TO TRY TOO!
IF THERE ARE ANY REQUESTS FOR MODIFICATION OR WAYS IT COULD BE IMPROVED, PLEASE LET ME KNOW LATER.
WELL, THEN...
OH?
SU (STEP)
WILL YOU NOT BE JOINING US, TSUKASA-DONO?
...HUH?

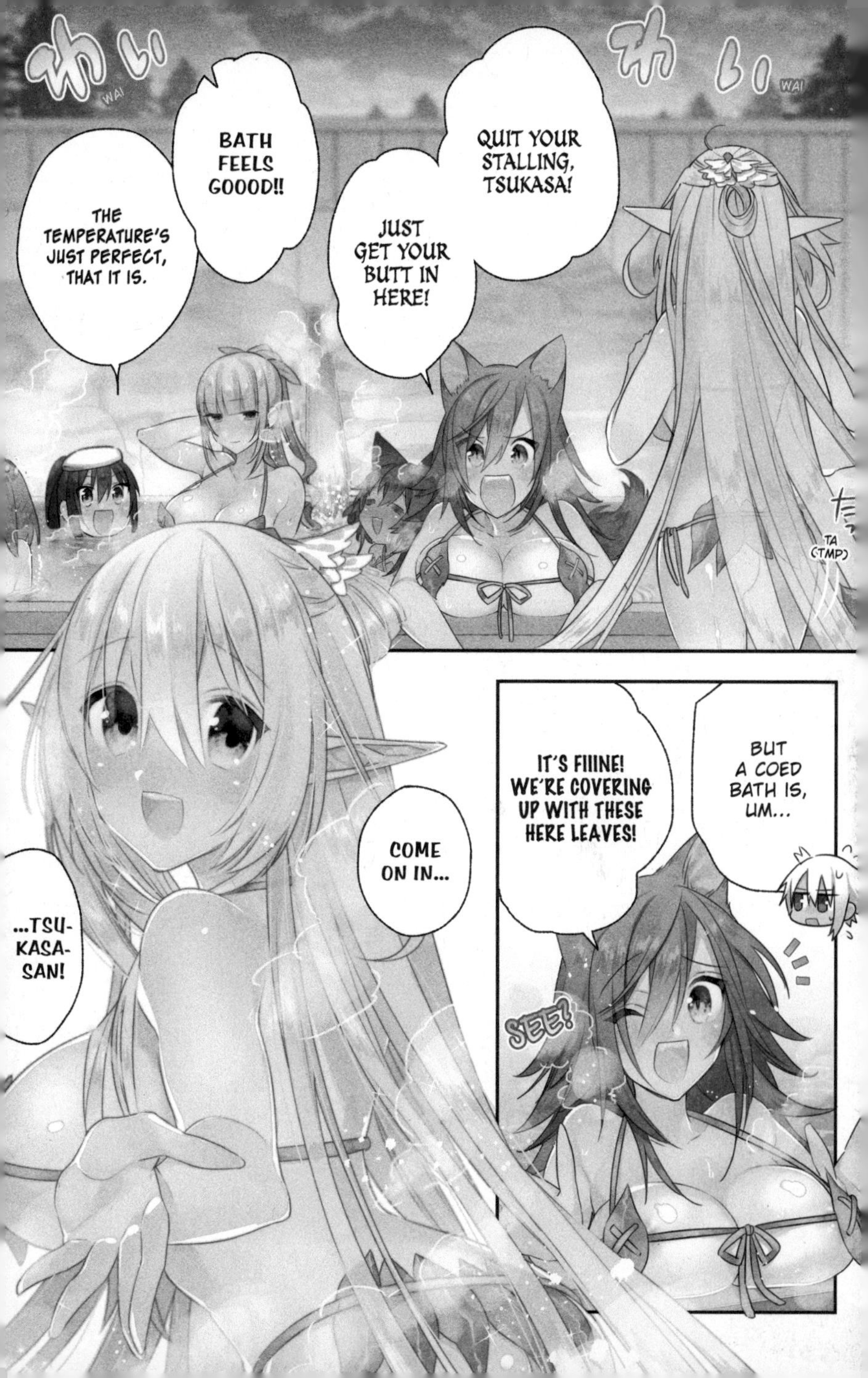
わい WAI
QUIT YOUR STALLING, TSUKASA!
JUST GET YOUR BUTT IN HERE!
BATH FEELS GOOOD!!
THE TEMPERATURE'S JUST PERFECT, THAT IT IS.
わい WAI
TA (TMP)
BUT A COED BATH IS, UM...
IT'S FIIINE! WE'RE COVERING UP WITH THESE HERE LEAVES!
SEE?
COME ON IN...
...TSU-KASA-SAN!

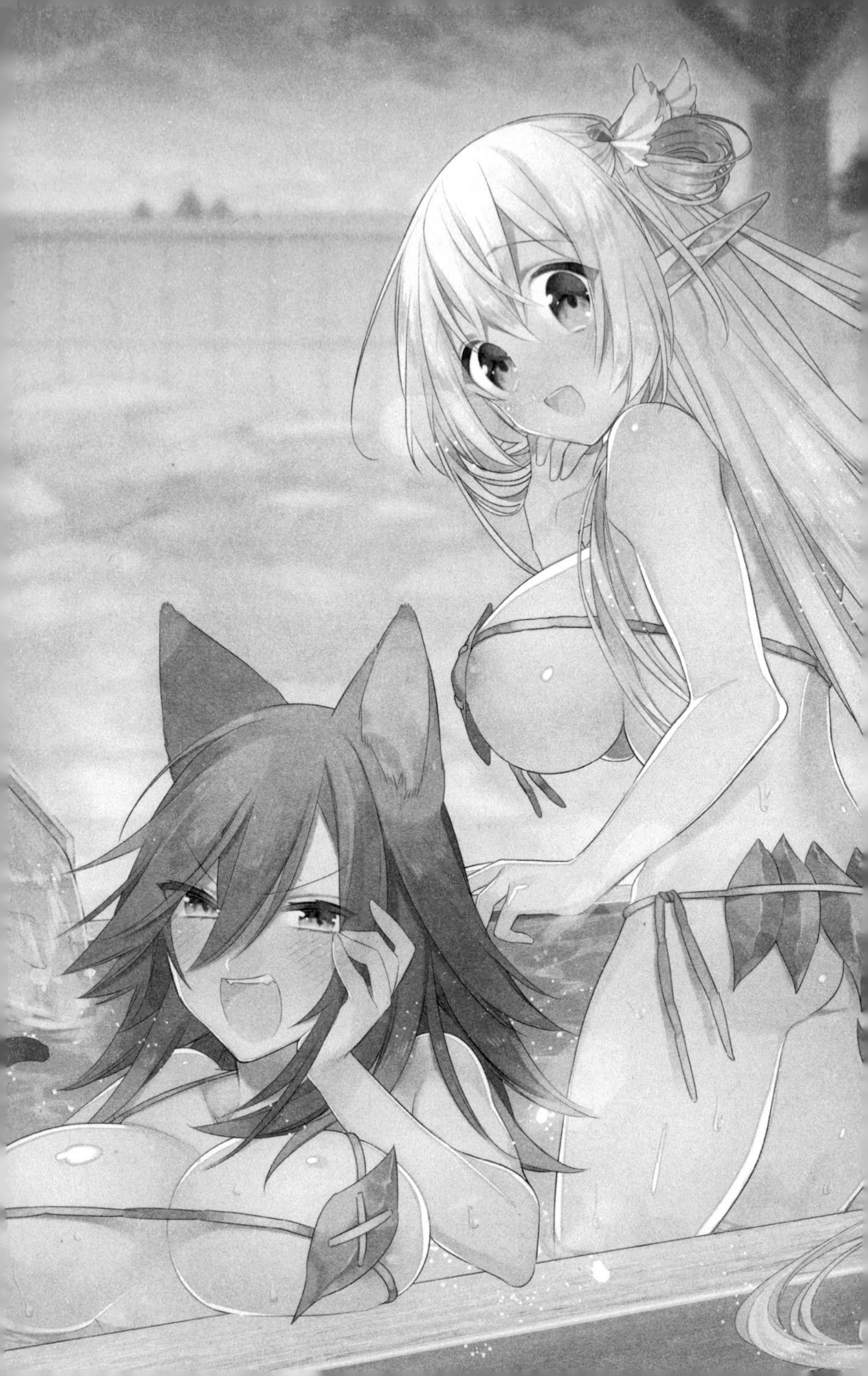

CHAPTER 11: PUBLIC BATH AND SUDDEN PANIC

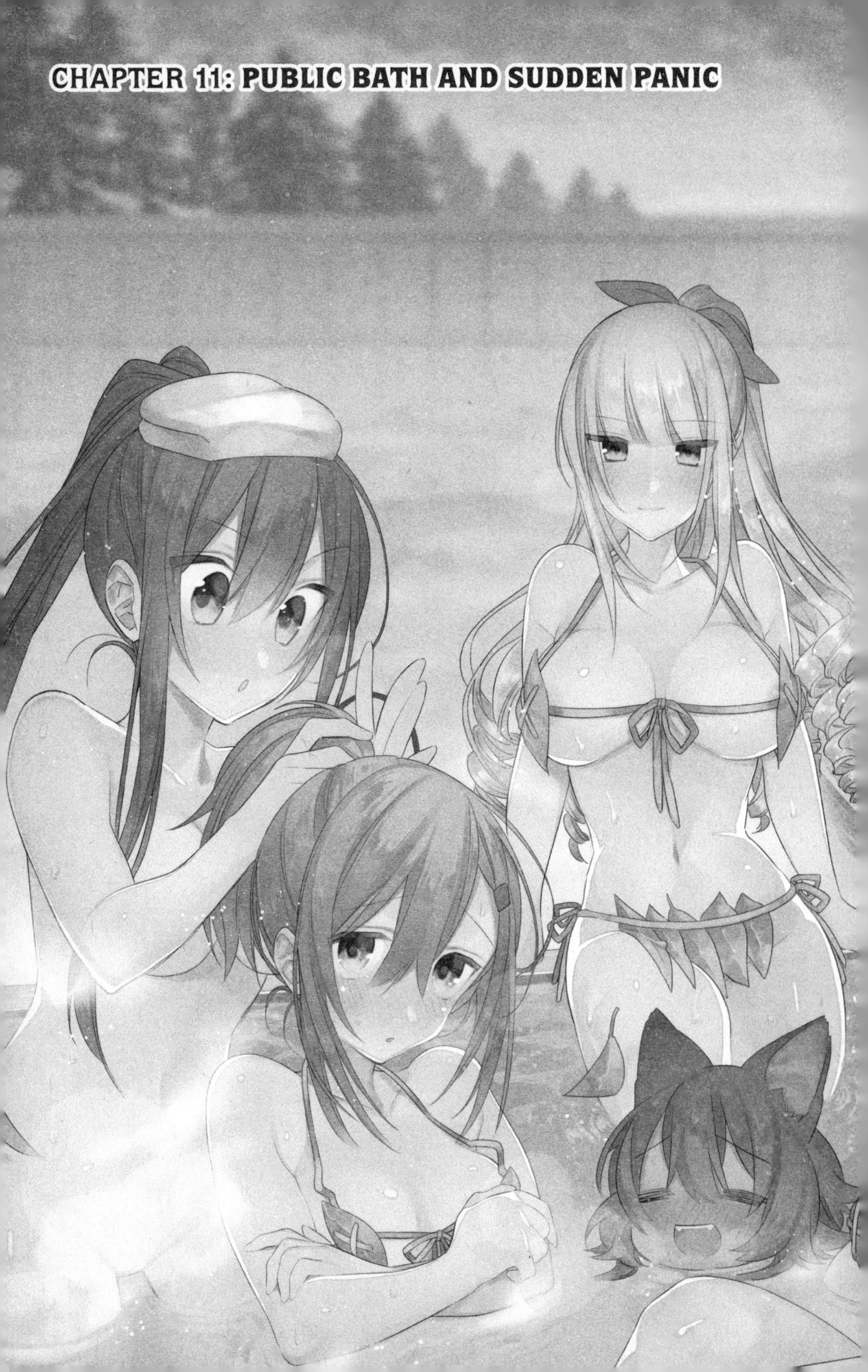

HIGH SCHOOL PRODIGIES HAVE IT EASY EVEN IN ANOTHER WORLD!

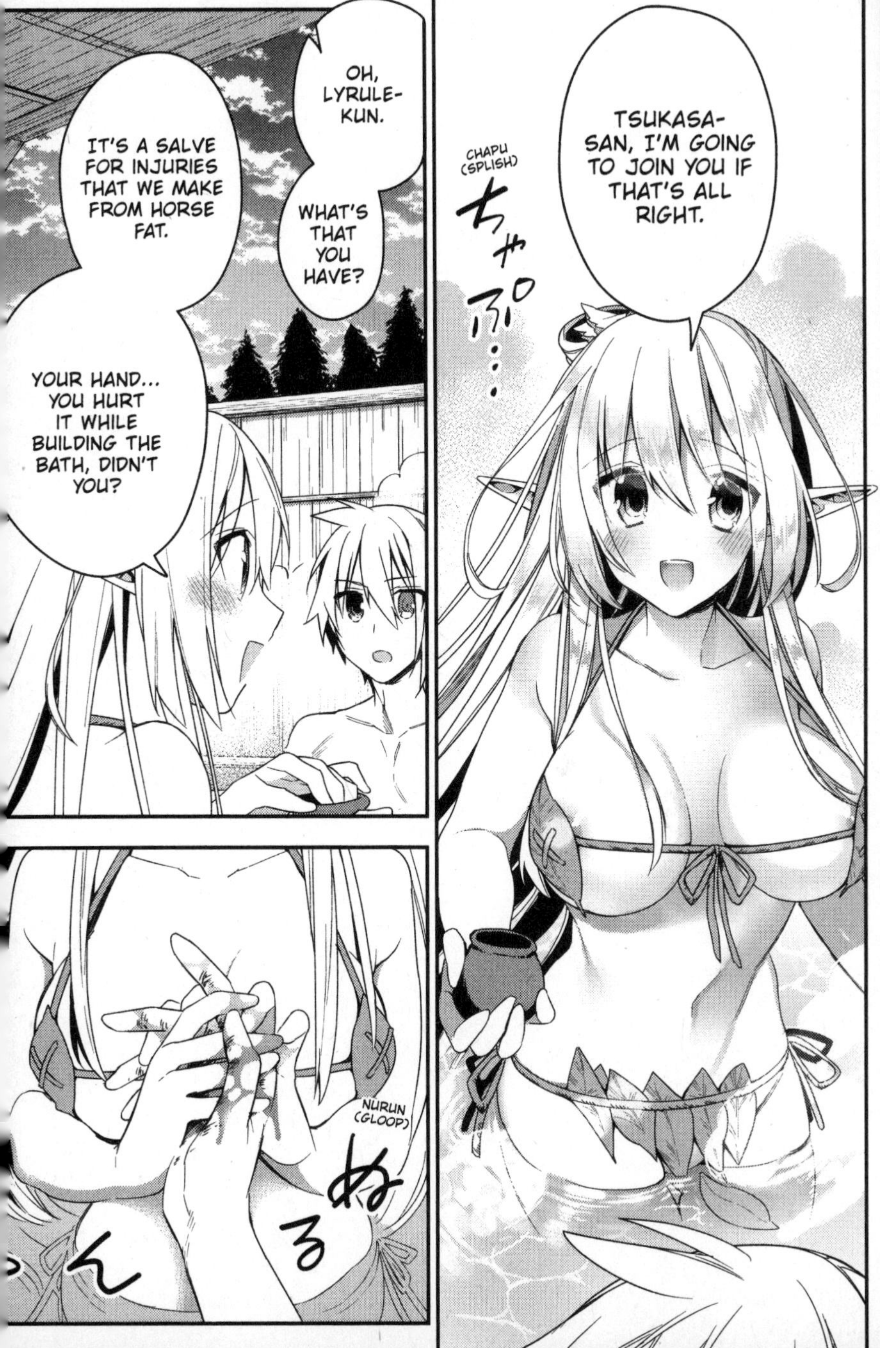
CHAPU (SPLISH)
ちゃぷ…
TSUKASA-SAN, I'M GOING TO JOIN YOU IF THAT'S ALL RIGHT.
OH, LYRULE-KUN.
WHAT'S THAT YOU HAVE?
IT'S A SALVE FOR INJURIES THAT WE MAKE FROM HORSE FAT.
YOUR HAND... YOU HURT IT WHILE BUILDING THE BATH, DIDN'T YOU?
NURUN (GLOOP)
ぬるん

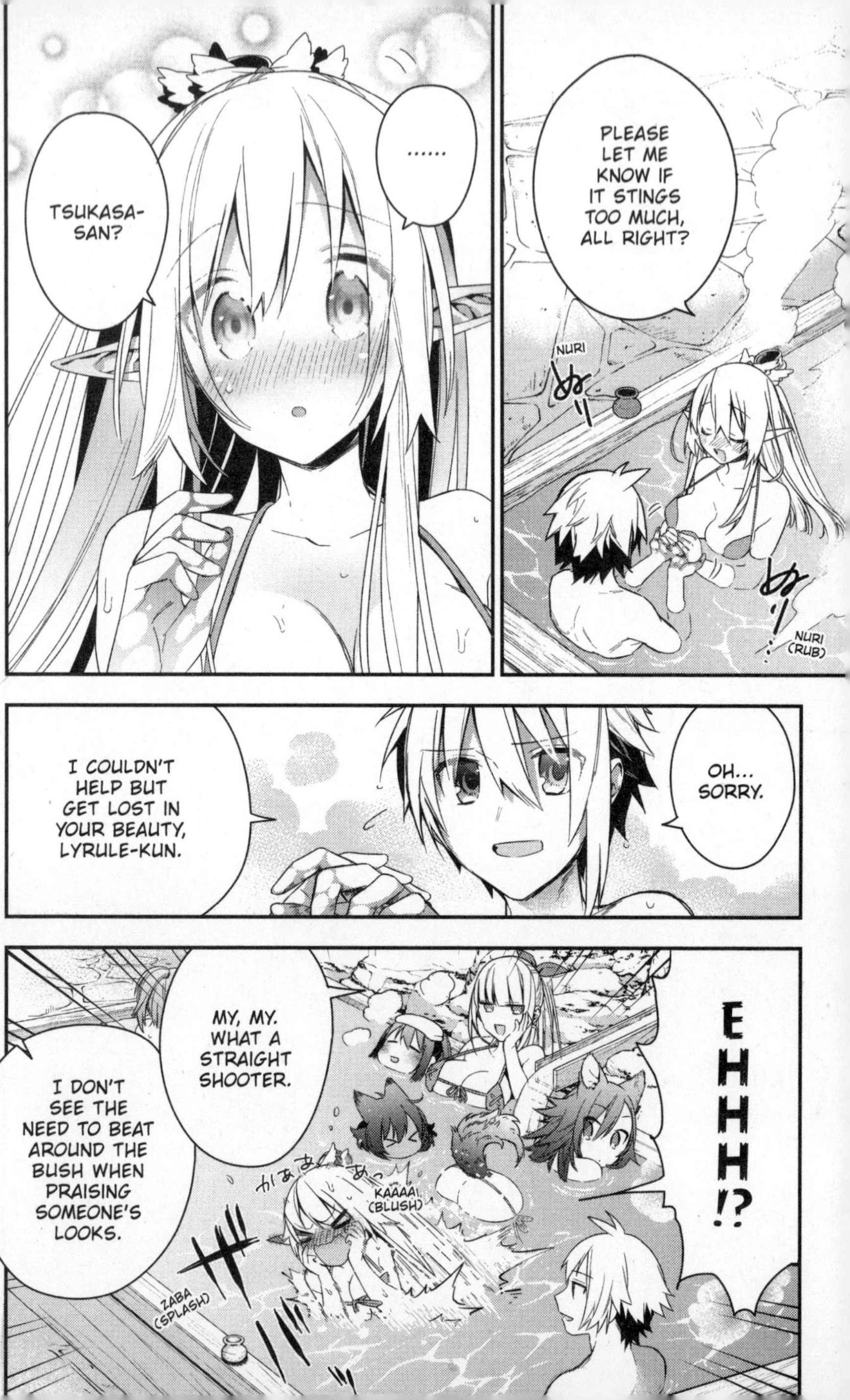
PLEASE LET ME KNOW IF IT STINGS TOO MUCH, ALL RIGHT?
NURI
NURI (RUB)
......
TSUKASA-SAN?
OH... SORRY.
I COULDN'T HELP BUT GET LOST IN YOUR BEAUTY, LYRULE-KUN.
EHHHH!?
MY, MY. WHAT A STRAIGHT SHOOTER.
KAAAA (BLUSH)
I DON'T SEE THE NEED TO BEAT AROUND THE BUSH WHEN PRAISING SOMEONE'S LOOKS.
ZABA (SPLASH)

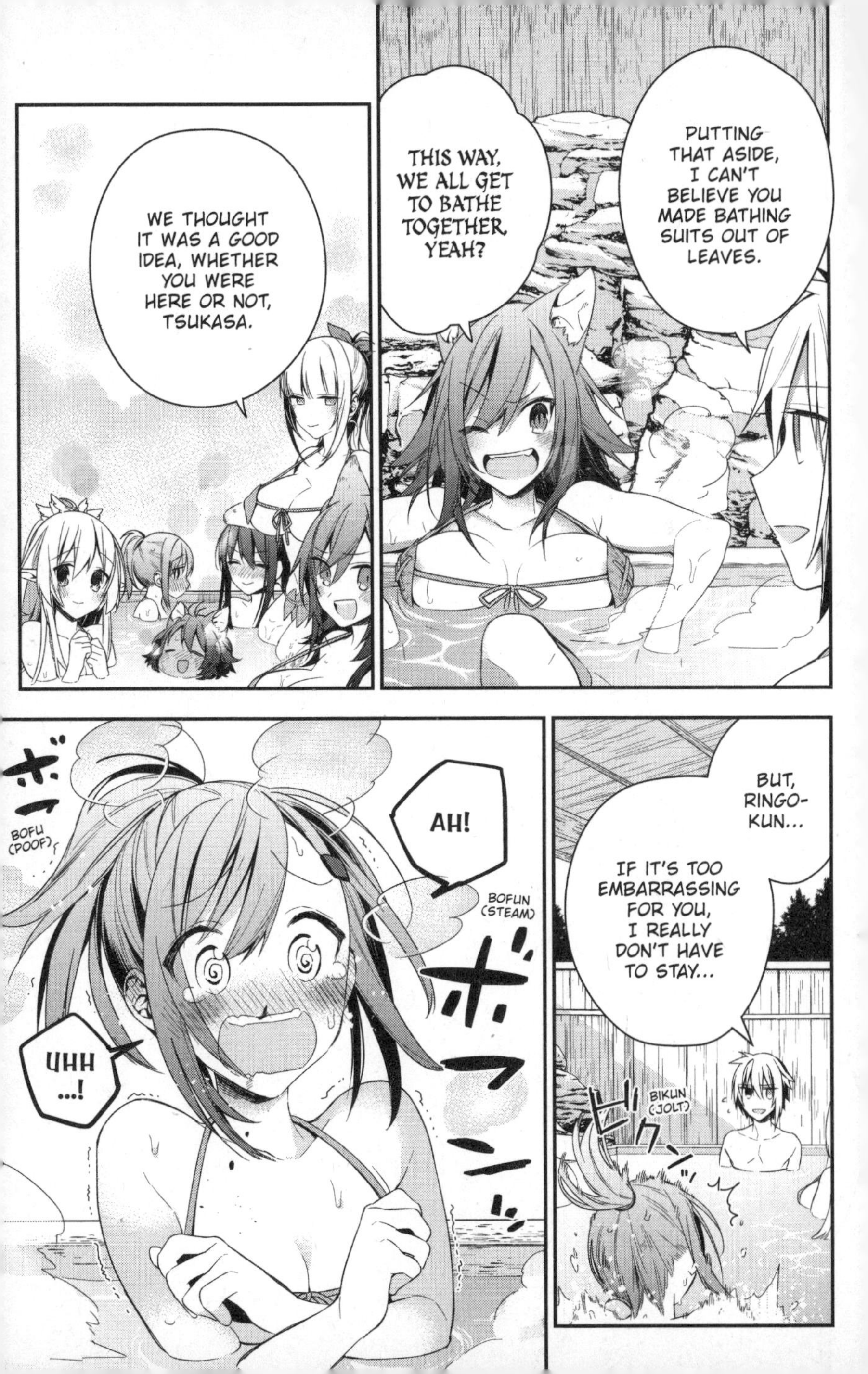
PUTTING THAT ASIDE, I CAN'T BELIEVE YOU MADE BATHING SUITS OUT OF LEAVES.
THIS WAY, WE ALL GET TO BATHE TOGETHER, YEAH?
WE THOUGHT IT WAS A GOOD IDEA, WHETHER YOU WERE HERE OR NOT, TSUKASA.
BUT, RINGO-KUN...
IF IT'S TOO EMBARRASSING FOR YOU, I REALLY DON'T HAVE TO STAY...
BIKUN (JOLT)
AH!
BOFUN (STEAM)
BOFU (POOF)
UHH ...!

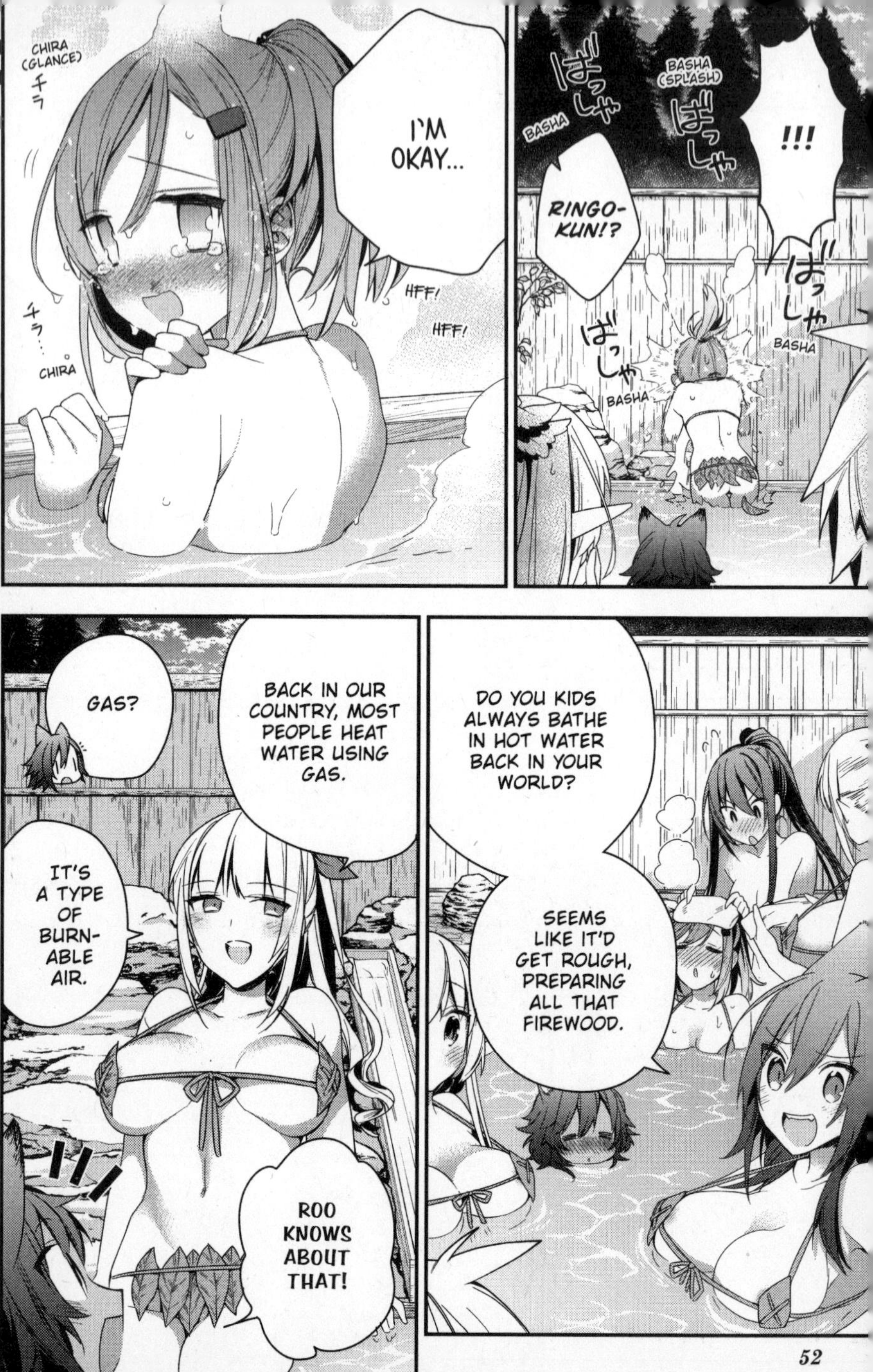
!!!
BASHA (SPLASH)
ばっしゃ
ばっしゃ
BASHA
RINGO-KUN!?
ばっしゃ
BASHA
ばっしゃ
BASHA
I'M OKAY...
CHIRA (GLANCE)
チラ
HFF!
HFF!
チラ…
CHIRA
DO YOU KIDS ALWAYS BATHE IN HOT WATER BACK IN YOUR WORLD?
SEEMS LIKE IT'D GET ROUGH, PREPARING ALL THAT FIREWOOD.
BACK IN OUR COUNTRY, MOST PEOPLE HEAT WATER USING GAS.
GAS?
IT'S A TYPE OF BURN-ABLE AIR.
ROO KNOWS ABOUT THAT!

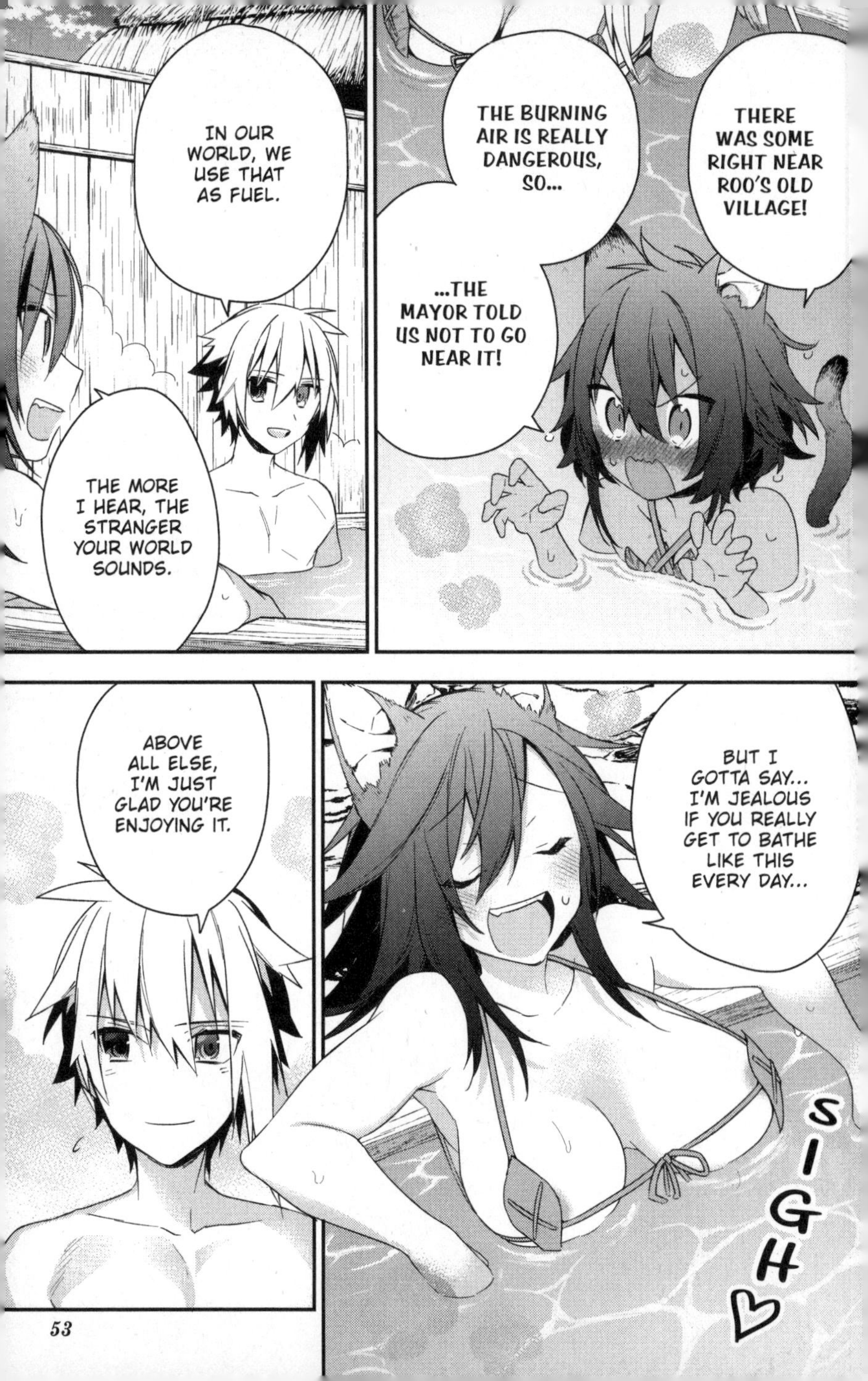
THERE WAS SOME RIGHT NEAR ROO'S OLD VILLAGE!
THE BURNING AIR IS REALLY DANGEROUS, SO...
...THE MAYOR TOLD US NOT TO GO NEAR IT!
IN OUR WORLD, WE USE THAT AS FUEL.
THE MORE I HEAR, THE STRANGER YOUR WORLD SOUNDS.
BUT I GOTTA SAY... I'M JEALOUS IF YOU REALLY GET TO BATHE LIKE THIS EVERY DAY...
SIGH ♡
ABOVE ALL ELSE, I'M JUST GLAD YOU'RE ENJOYING IT.

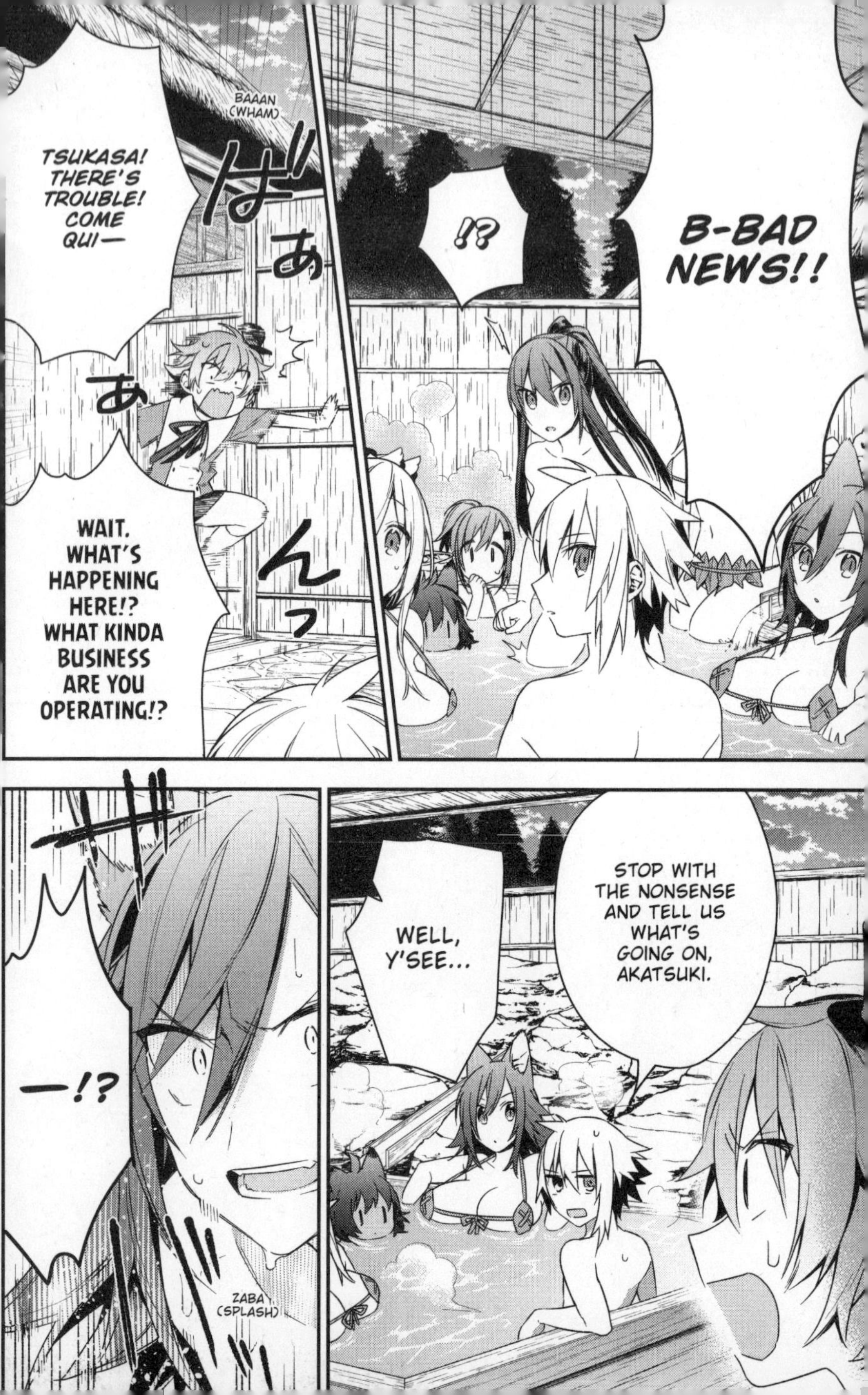
B-BAD NEWS!!
!?
BAAAN (WHAM)
TSUKASA! THERE'S TROUBLE! COME QUI—
WAIT. WHAT'S HAPPENING HERE!? WHAT KINDA BUSINESS ARE YOU OPERATING!?
STOP WITH THE NONSENSE AND TELL US WHAT'S GOING ON, AKATSUKI.
WELL, Y'SEE...
—!?
ZABA (SPLASH)

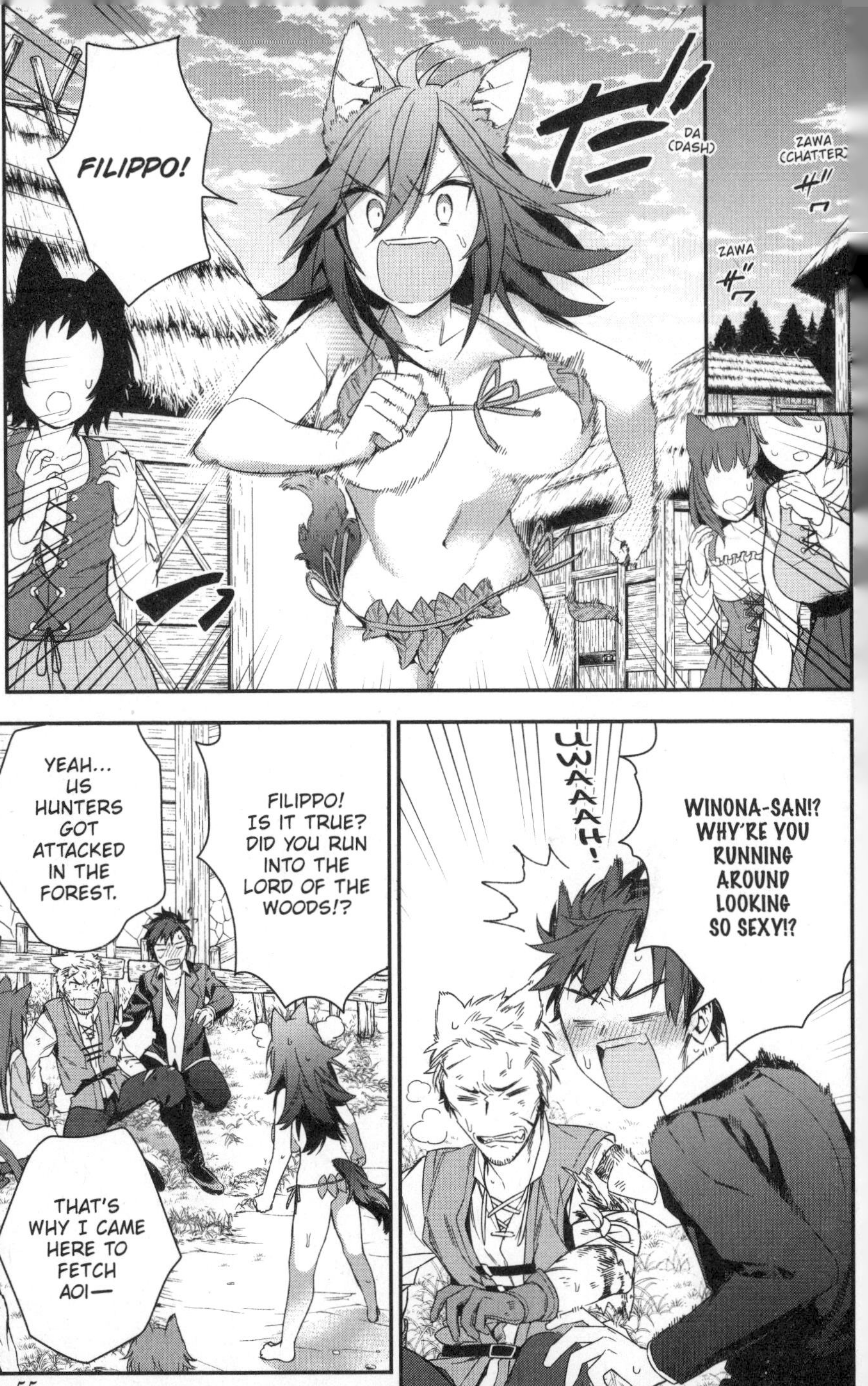
ZAWA (CHATTER)
ZAWA
DA (DASH)
FILIPPO!
WINONA-SAN!? WHY'RE YOU RUNNING AROUND LOOKING SO SEXY!?
UWAAAAH!
FILIPPO! IS IT TRUE? DID YOU RUN INTO THE LORD OF THE WOODS!?
YEAH... US HUNTERS GOT ATTACKED IN THE FOREST.
THAT'S WHY I CAME HERE TO FETCH AOI—

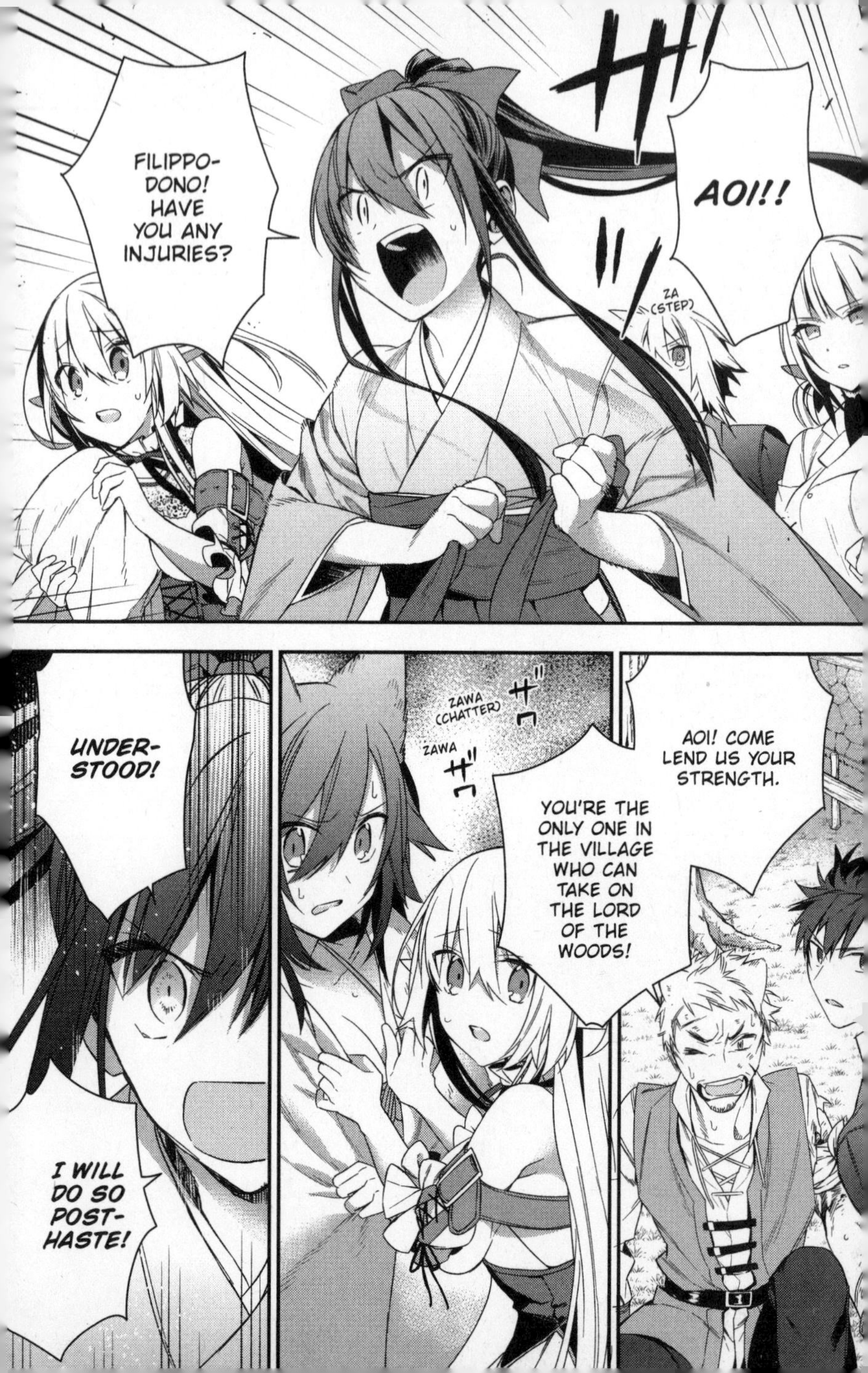
AOI!!
ZA (STEP)
FILIPPO-DONO! HAVE YOU ANY INJURIES?
AOI! COME LEND US YOUR STRENGTH.
YOU'RE THE ONLY ONE IN THE VILLAGE WHO CAN TAKE ON THE LORD OF THE WOODS!
ZAWA (CHATTER)
ZAWA
UNDER-STOOD!
I WILL DO SO POST-HASTE!

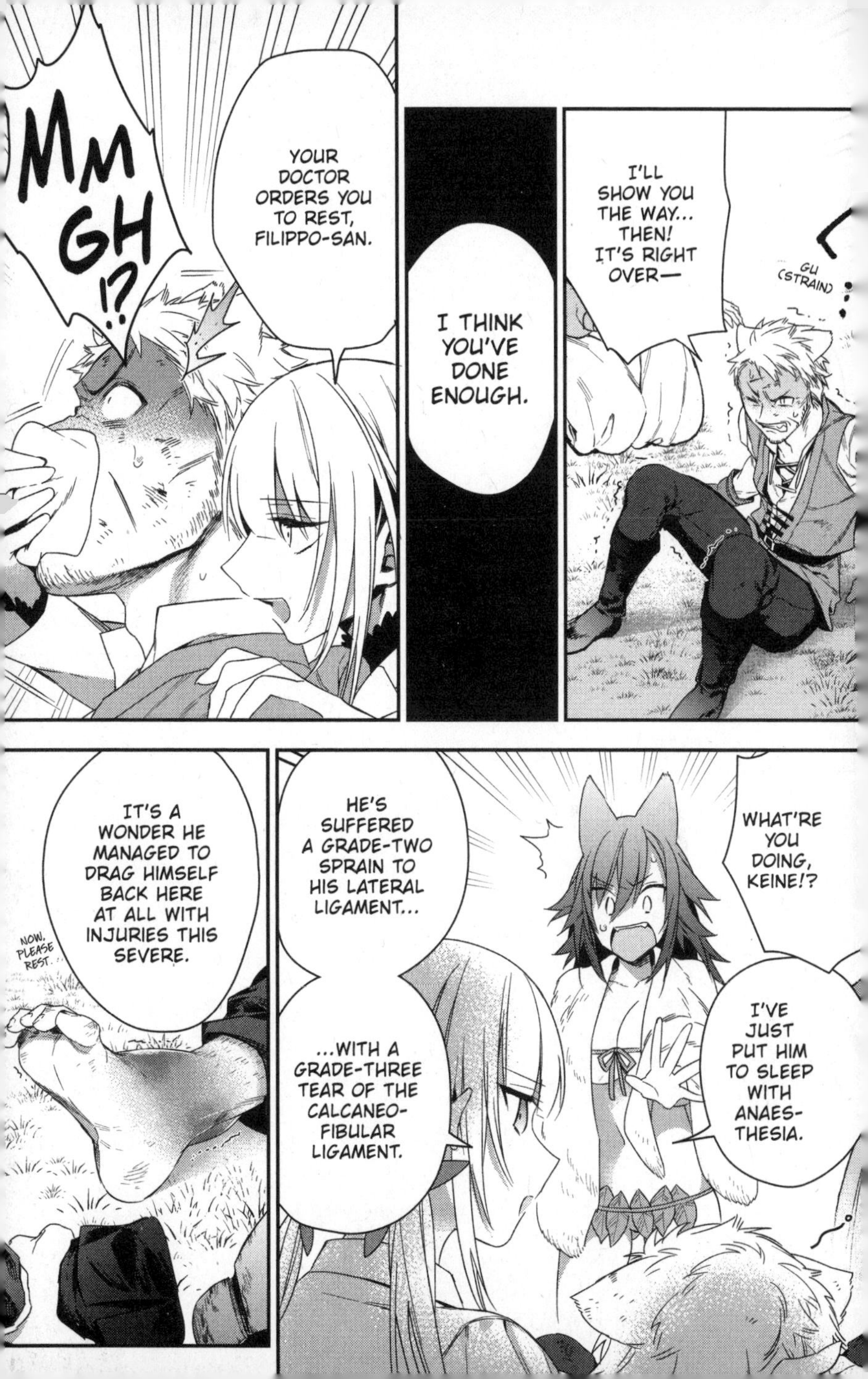
I'LL SHOW YOU THE WAY... THEN! IT'S RIGHT OVER—
GU (STRAIN)
I THINK YOU'VE DONE ENOUGH.
YOUR DOCTOR ORDERS YOU TO REST, FILIPPO-SAN.
MMGH!?
WHAT'RE YOU DOING, KEINE!?
I'VE JUST PUT HIM TO SLEEP WITH ANAES-THESIA.
HE'S SUFFERED A GRADE-TWO SPRAIN TO HIS LATERAL LIGAMENT...
...WITH A GRADE-THREE TEAR OF THE CALCANEO-FIBULAR LIGAMENT.
IT'S A WONDER HE MANAGED TO DRAG HIMSELF BACK HERE AT ALL WITH INJURIES THIS SEVERE.
NOW, PLEASE REST.

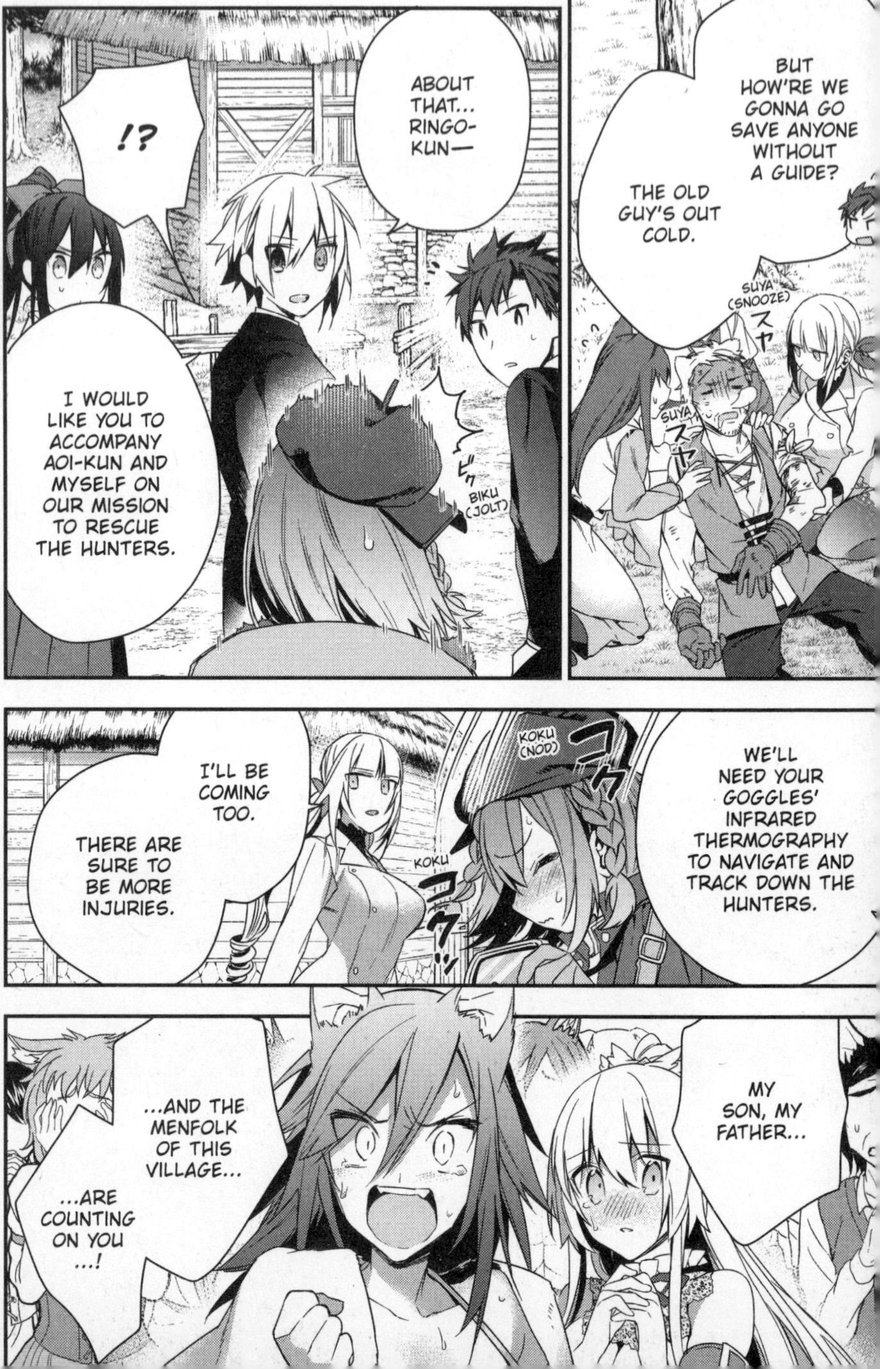
BUT HOW'RE WE GONNA GO SAVE ANYONE WITHOUT A GUIDE?
THE OLD GUY'S OUT COLD.
SUYA (SNOOZE)
SUYA
ABOUT THAT... RINGO-KUN—
!?
BIKU (JOLT)
I WOULD LIKE YOU TO ACCOMPANY AOI-KUN AND MYSELF ON OUR MISSION TO RESCUE THE HUNTERS.
WE'LL NEED YOUR GOGGLES' INFRARED THERMOGRAPHY TO NAVIGATE AND TRACK DOWN THE HUNTERS.
KOKU (NOD)
KOKU
I'LL BE COMING TOO.
THERE ARE SURE TO BE MORE INJURIES.
MY SON, MY FATHER...
...AND THE MENFOLK OF THIS VILLAGE...
...ARE COUNTING ON YOU ...!

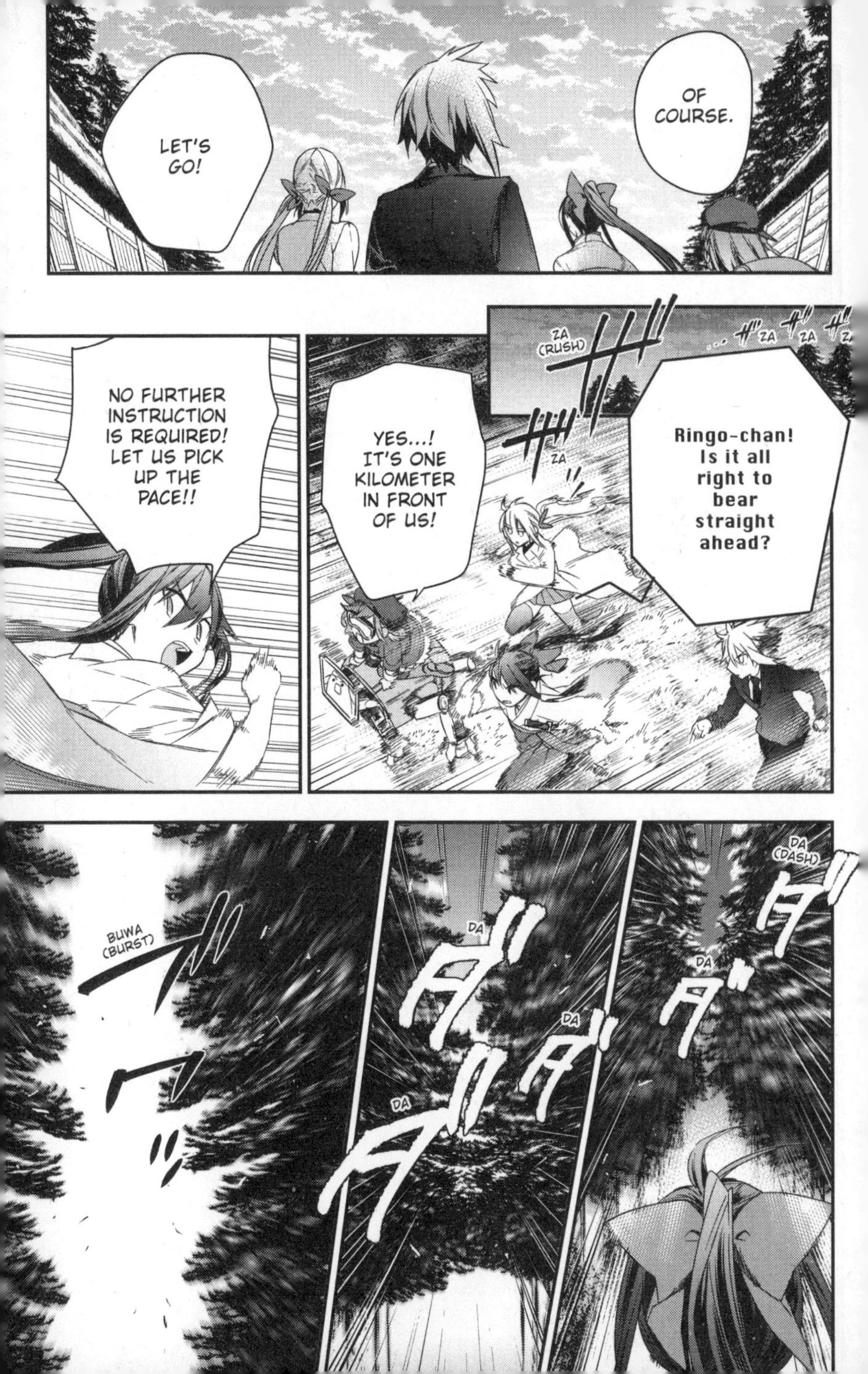
OF COURSE.
LET'S GO!
ZA (RUSH)
ZA
ZA
ZA
Ringo-chan! Is it all right to bear straight ahead?
ZA
YES...! IT'S ONE KILOMETER IN FRONT OF US!
NO FURTHER INSTRUCTION IS REQUIRED! LET US PICK UP THE PACE!!
DA (DASH)
DA
DA
DA
DA
BUWA (BURST)

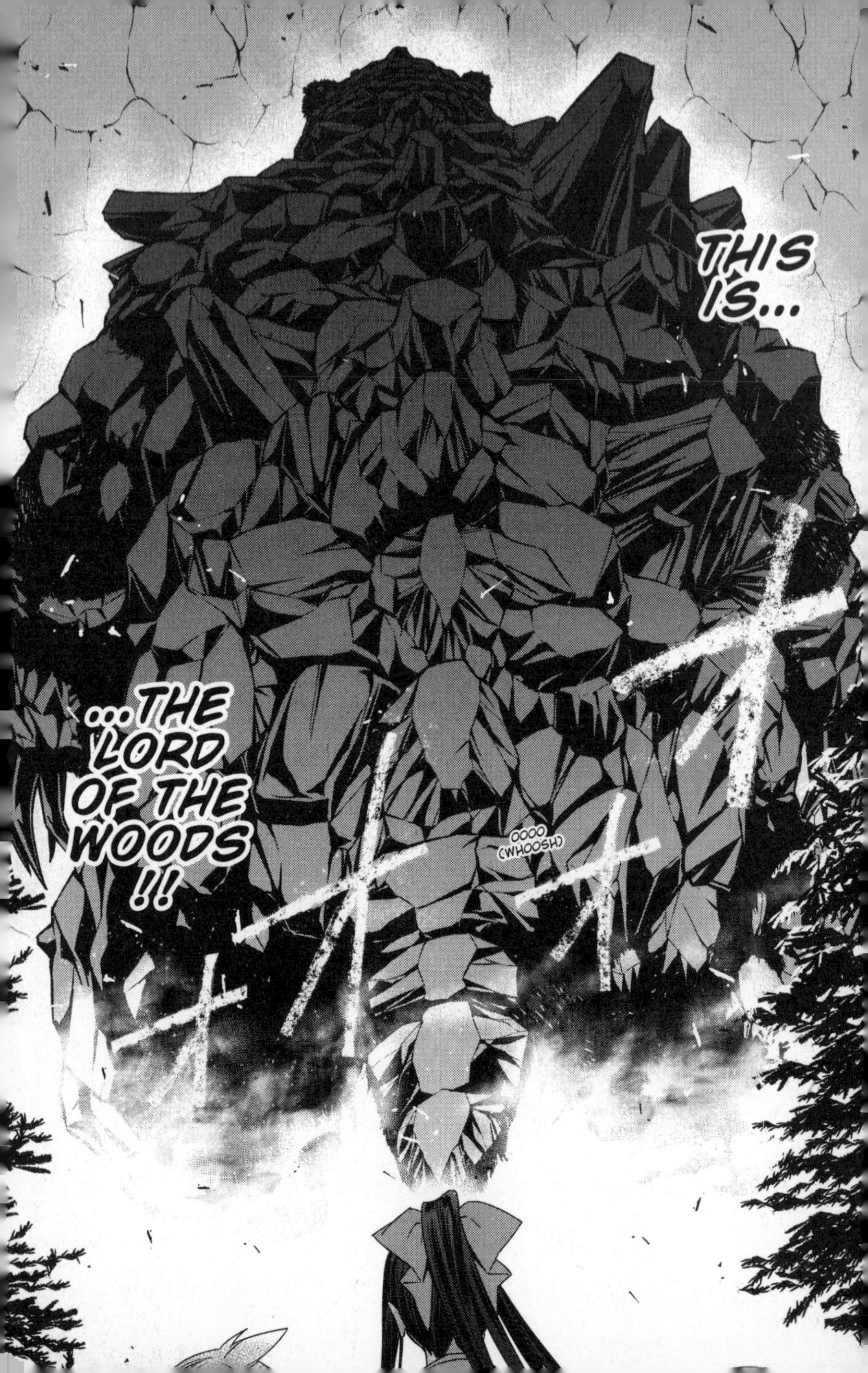
THIS IS...
...THE LORD OF THE WOODS!!
OOOO (WHOOSH)

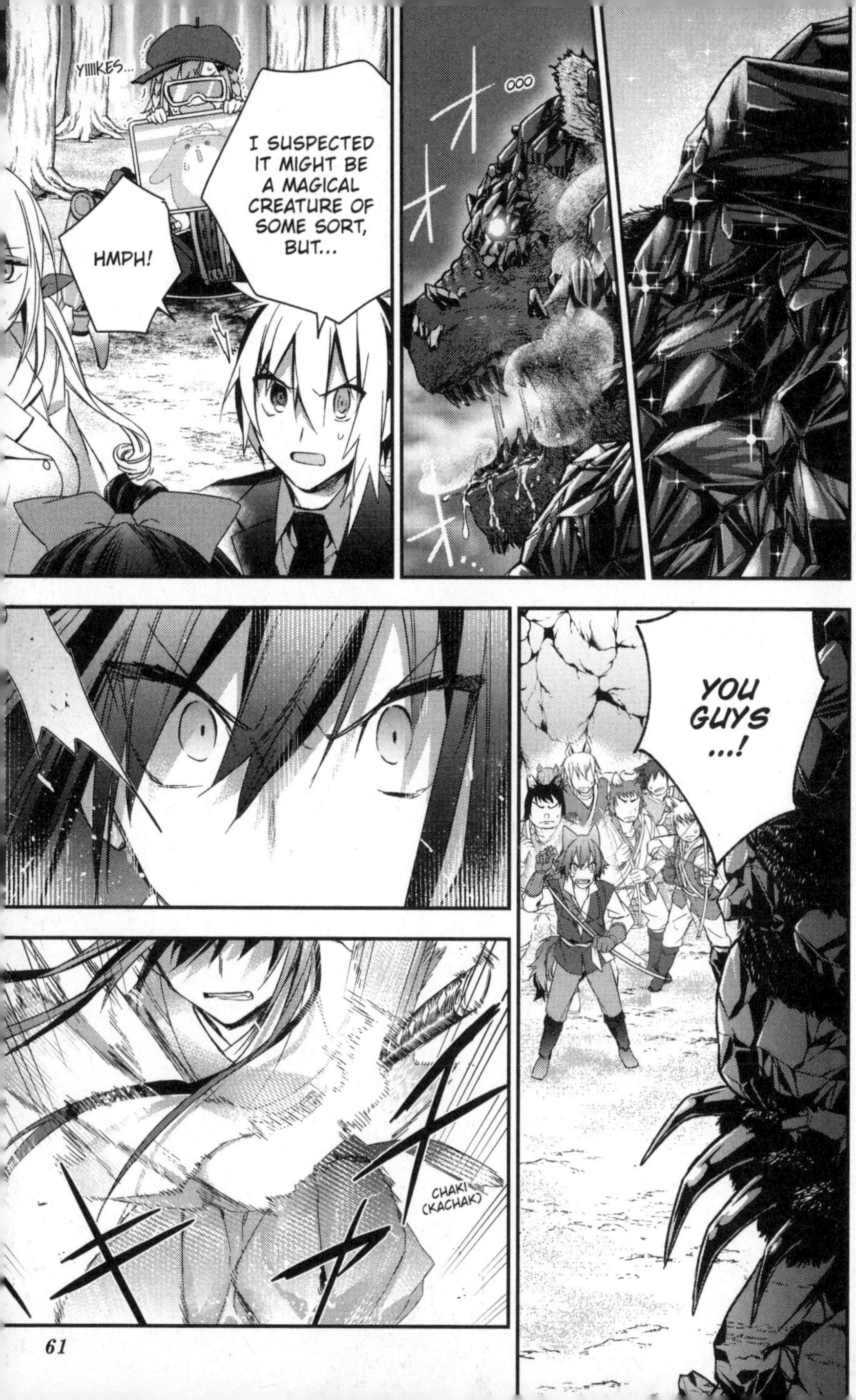
オオオ
OOO
I SUSPECTED IT MIGHT BE A MAGICAL CREATURE OF SOME SORT, BUT...
YIIIIKES...
HMPH!
YOU GUYS ...!
CHAKI (KACHAK)

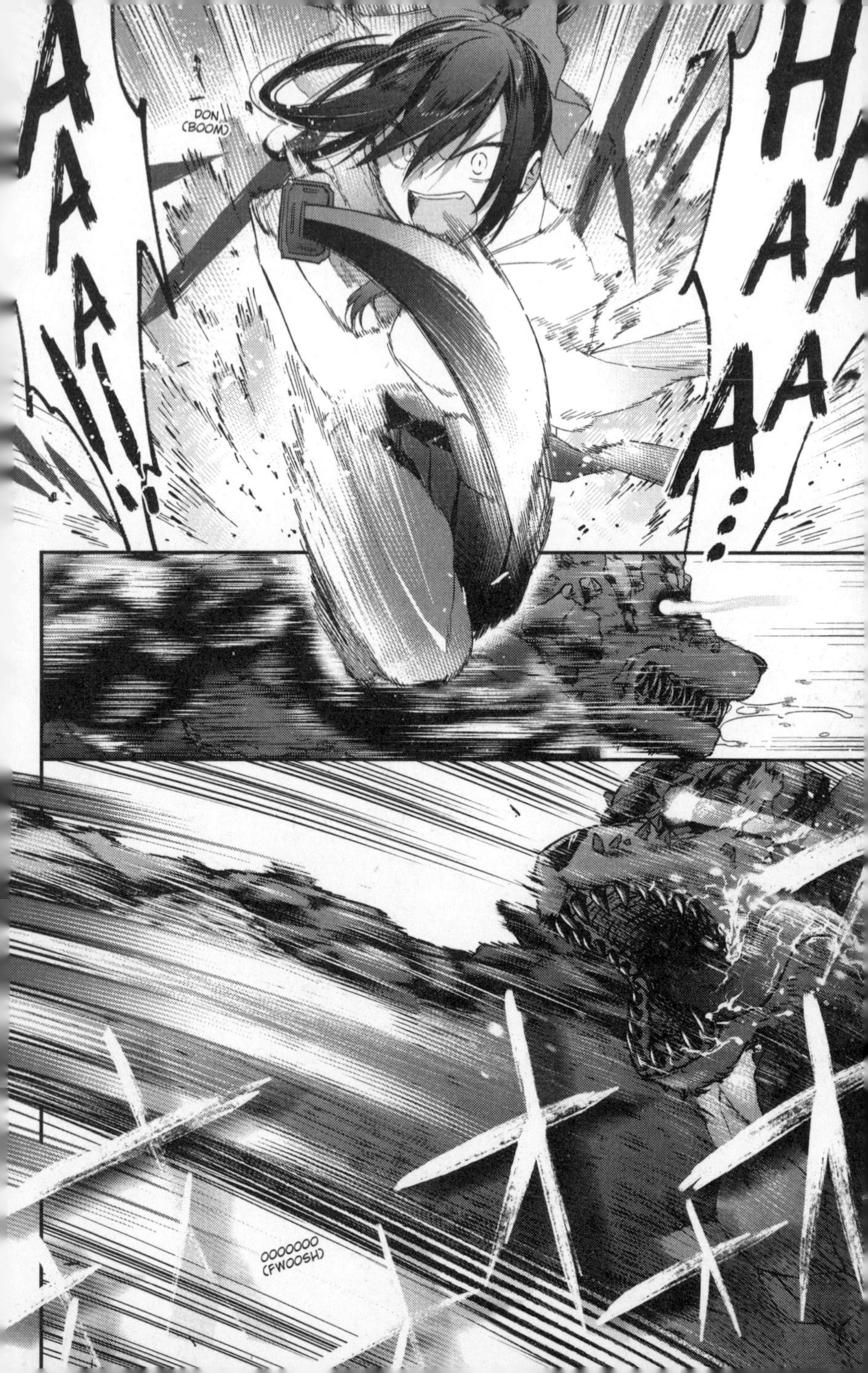
HAAAAAAA...
AAAA!!!
DON (BOOM)
OOOOOOO (FWOOSH)

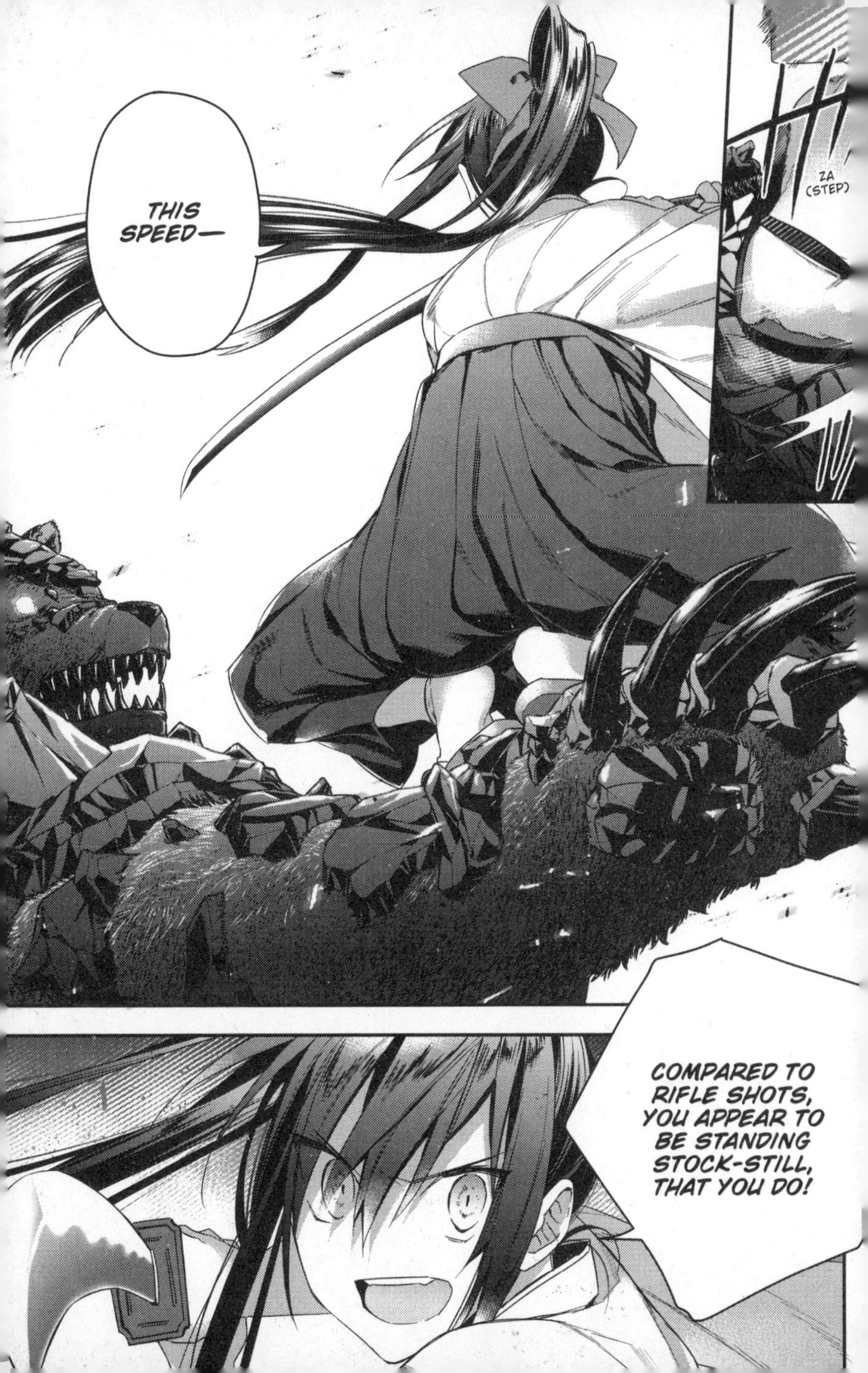
ZA (STEP)
THIS SPEED—
COMPARED TO RIFLE SHOTS, YOU APPEAR TO BE STANDING STOCK-STILL, THAT YOU DO!

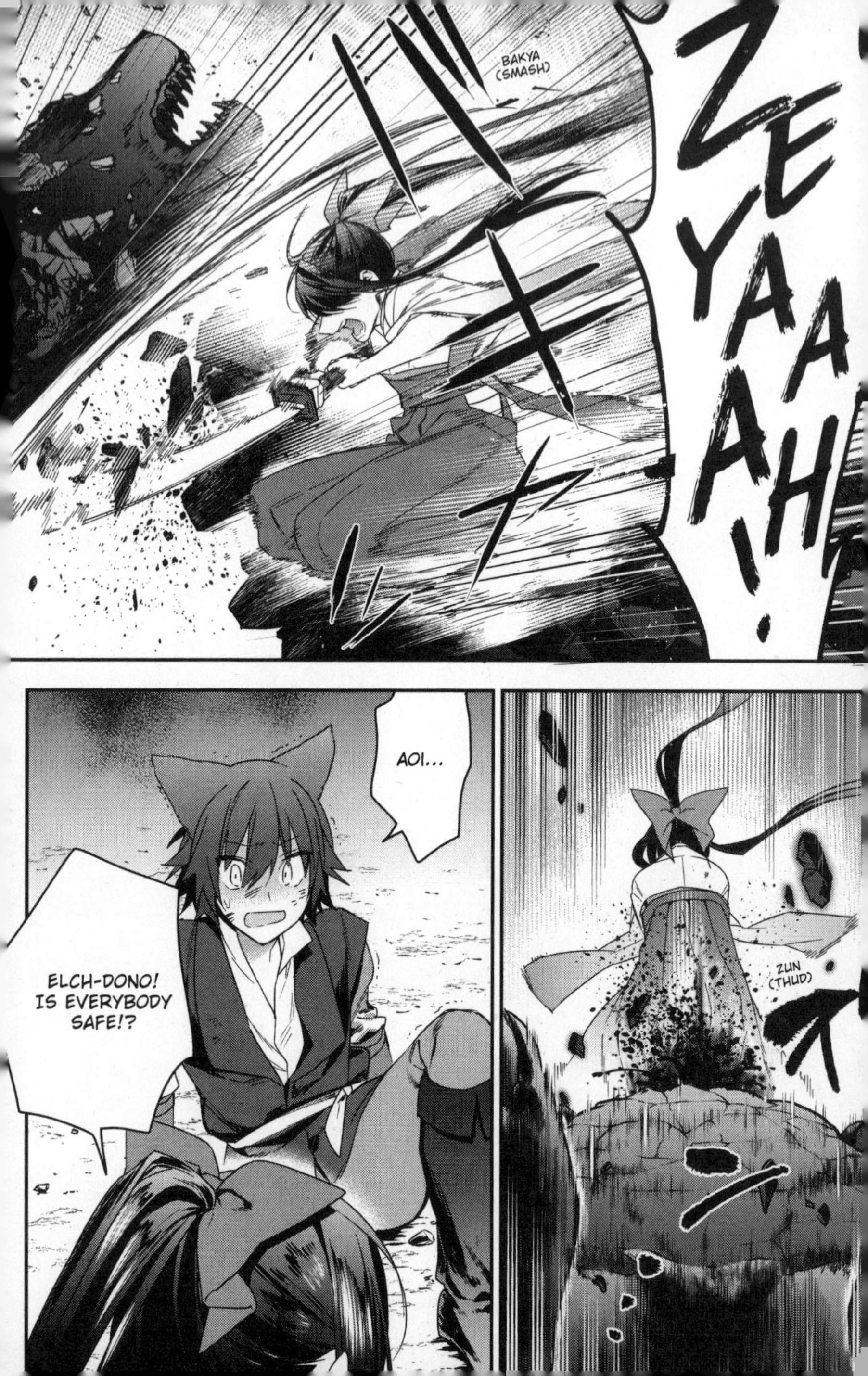
ZEYAAAAH!!
BAKYA (SMASH)
ZUN (THUD)
AOI...
ELCH-DONO! IS EVERYBODY SAFE!?

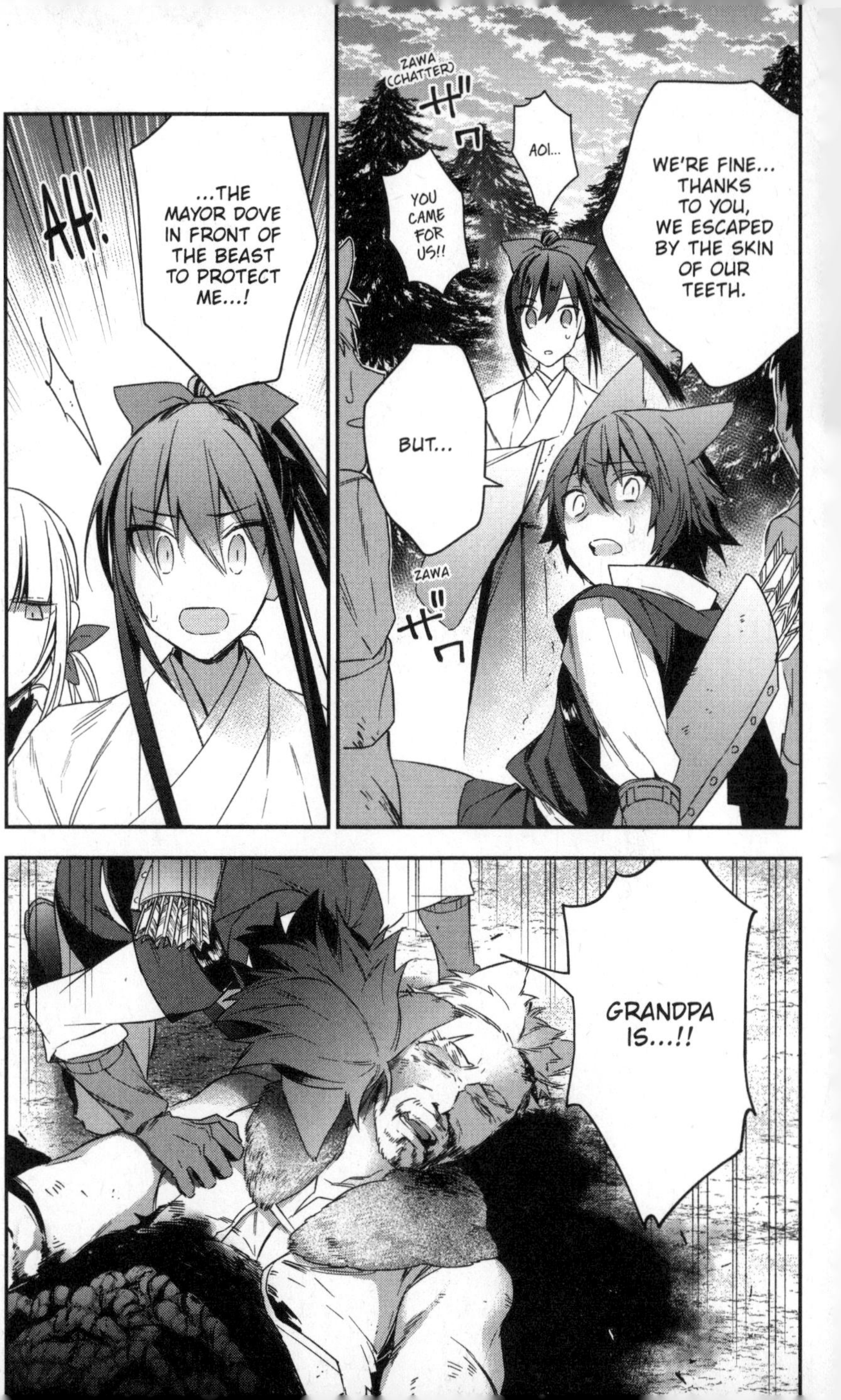
ZAWA (CHATTER)
ザワ
AOI...
WE'RE FINE... THANKS TO YOU, WE ESCAPED BY THE SKIN OF OUR TEETH.
YOU CAME FOR US!!
BUT...
ZAWA
ザワ
...THE MAYOR DOVE IN FRONT OF THE BEAST TO PROTECT ME...!
AH!
GRANDPA IS...!!

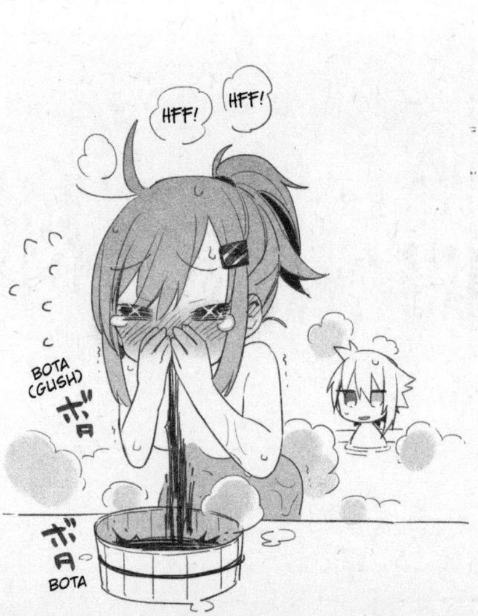
HFF!
HFF!
BOTA (GUSH)
ボタ
ボタ
BOTA

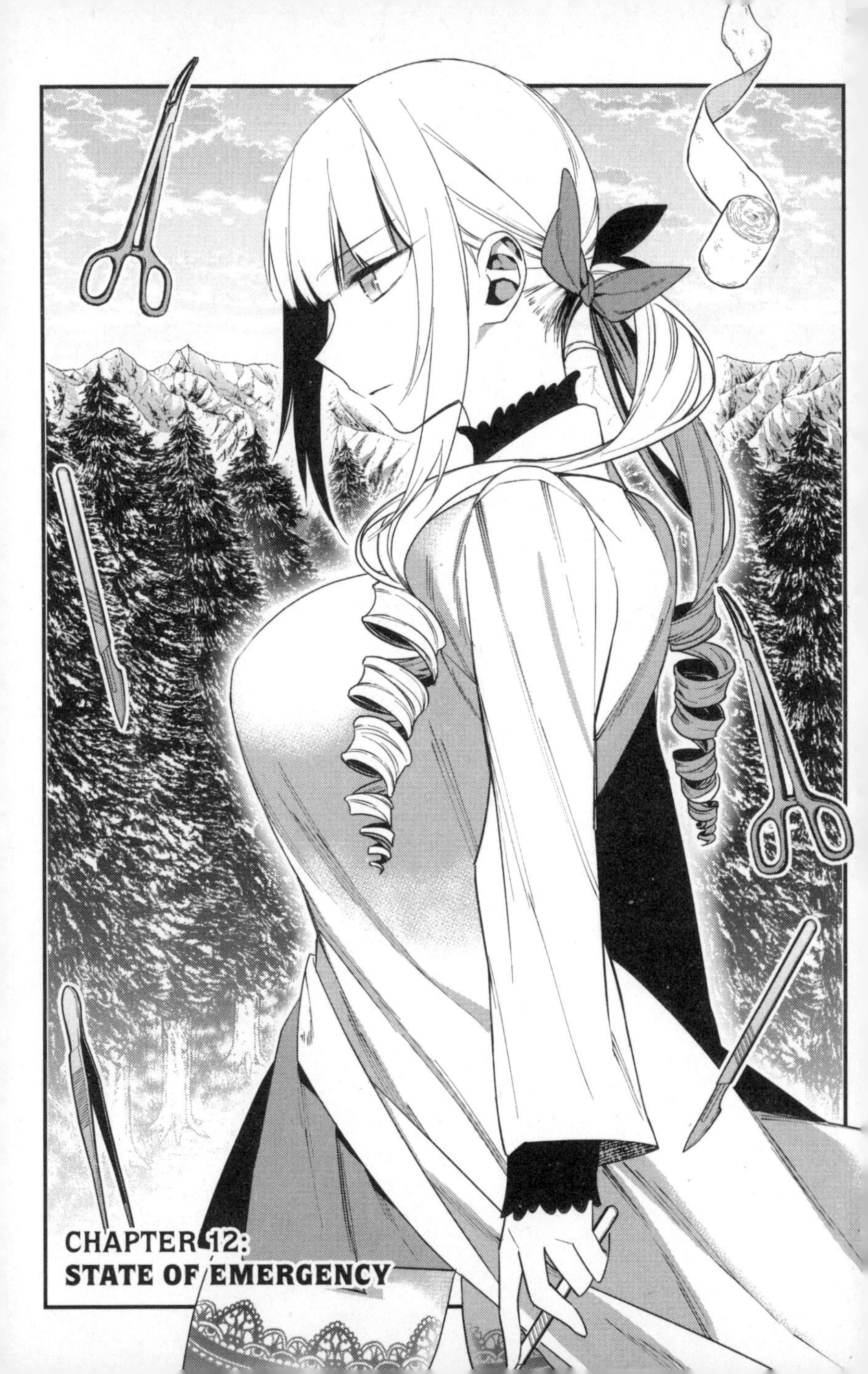
CHAPTER 12:
STATE OF EMERGENCY

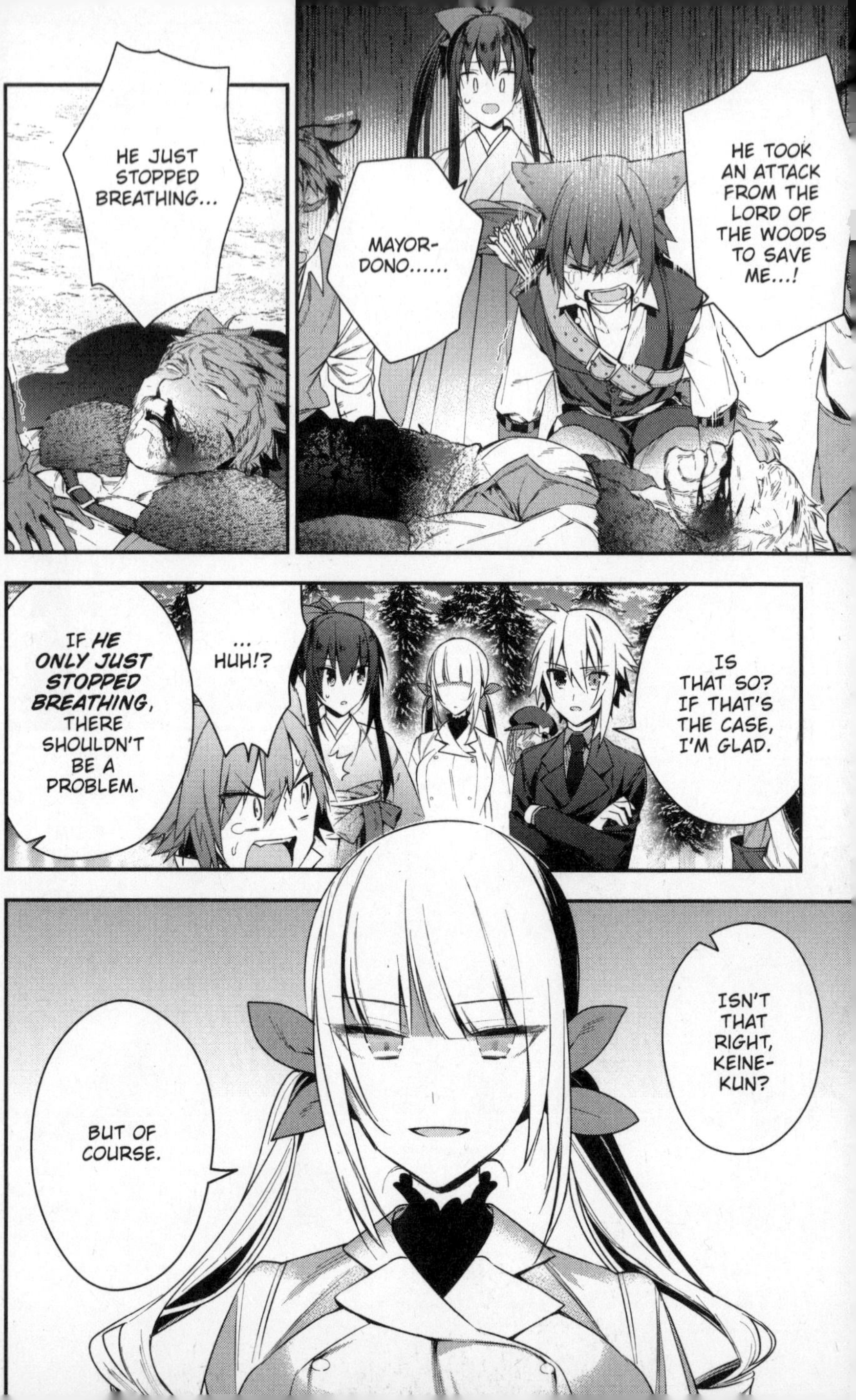
HE TOOK AN ATTACK FROM THE LORD OF THE WOODS TO SAVE ME...!
MAYOR-DONO......
HE JUST STOPPED BREATHING...
IS THAT SO? IF THAT'S THE CASE, I'M GLAD.
... HUH!?
IF *HE ONLY JUST STOPPED BREATHING*, THERE SHOULDN'T BE A PROBLEM.
ISN'T THAT RIGHT, KEINE-KUN?
BUT OF COURSE.

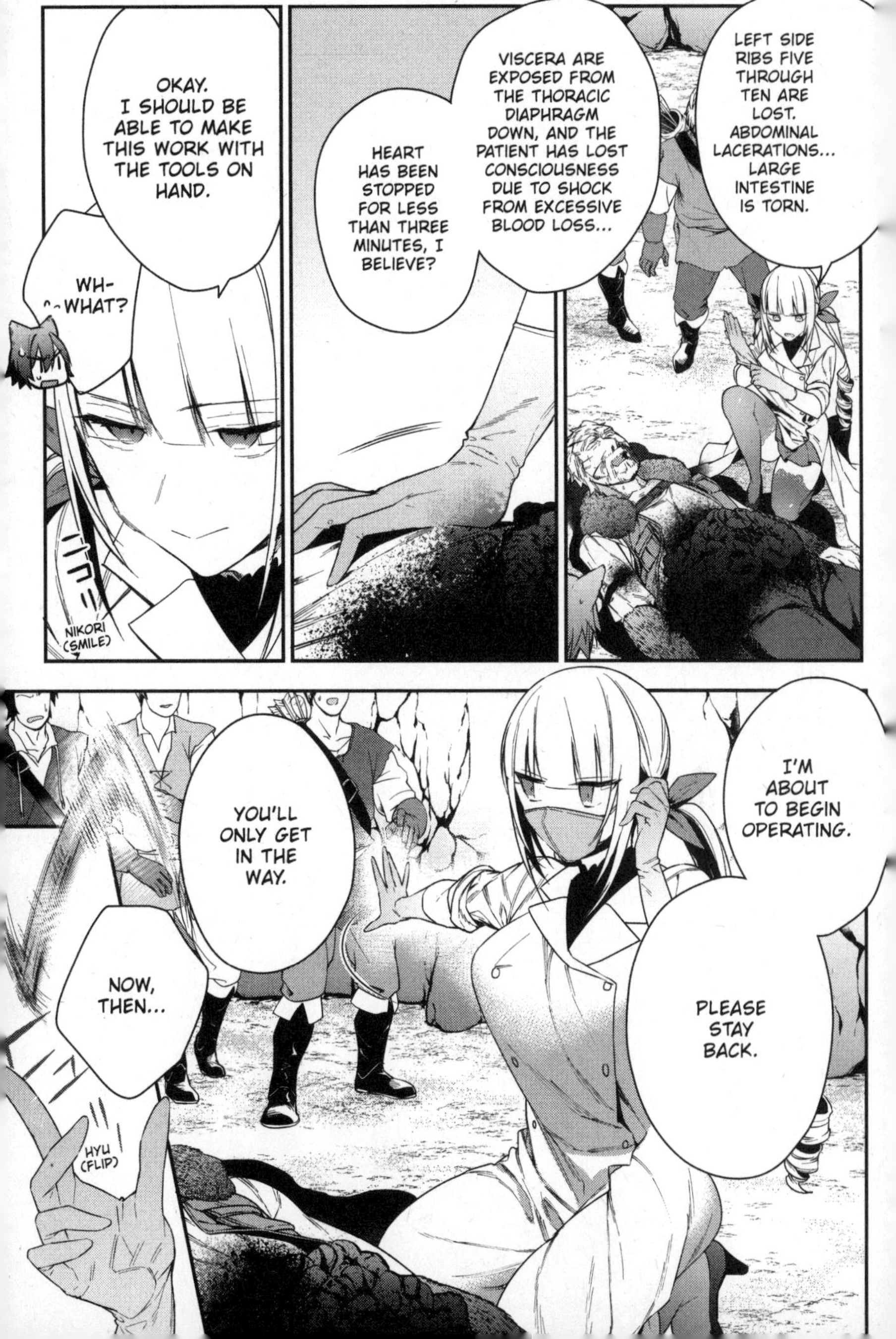
LEFT SIDE RIBS FIVE THROUGH TEN ARE LOST. ABDOMINAL LACERATIONS... LARGE INTESTINE IS TORN.
VISCERA ARE EXPOSED FROM THE THORACIC DIAPHRAGM DOWN, AND THE PATIENT HAS LOST CONSCIOUSNESS DUE TO SHOCK FROM EXCESSIVE BLOOD LOSS...
HEART HAS BEEN STOPPED FOR LESS THAN THREE MINUTES, I BELIEVE?
OKAY. I SHOULD BE ABLE TO MAKE THIS WORK WITH THE TOOLS ON HAND.
WH- W-WHAT?
NIKORI (SMILE)
I'M ABOUT TO BEGIN OPERATING.
PLEASE STAY BACK.
YOU'LL ONLY GET IN THE WAY.
NOW, THEN...
HYU (FLIP)

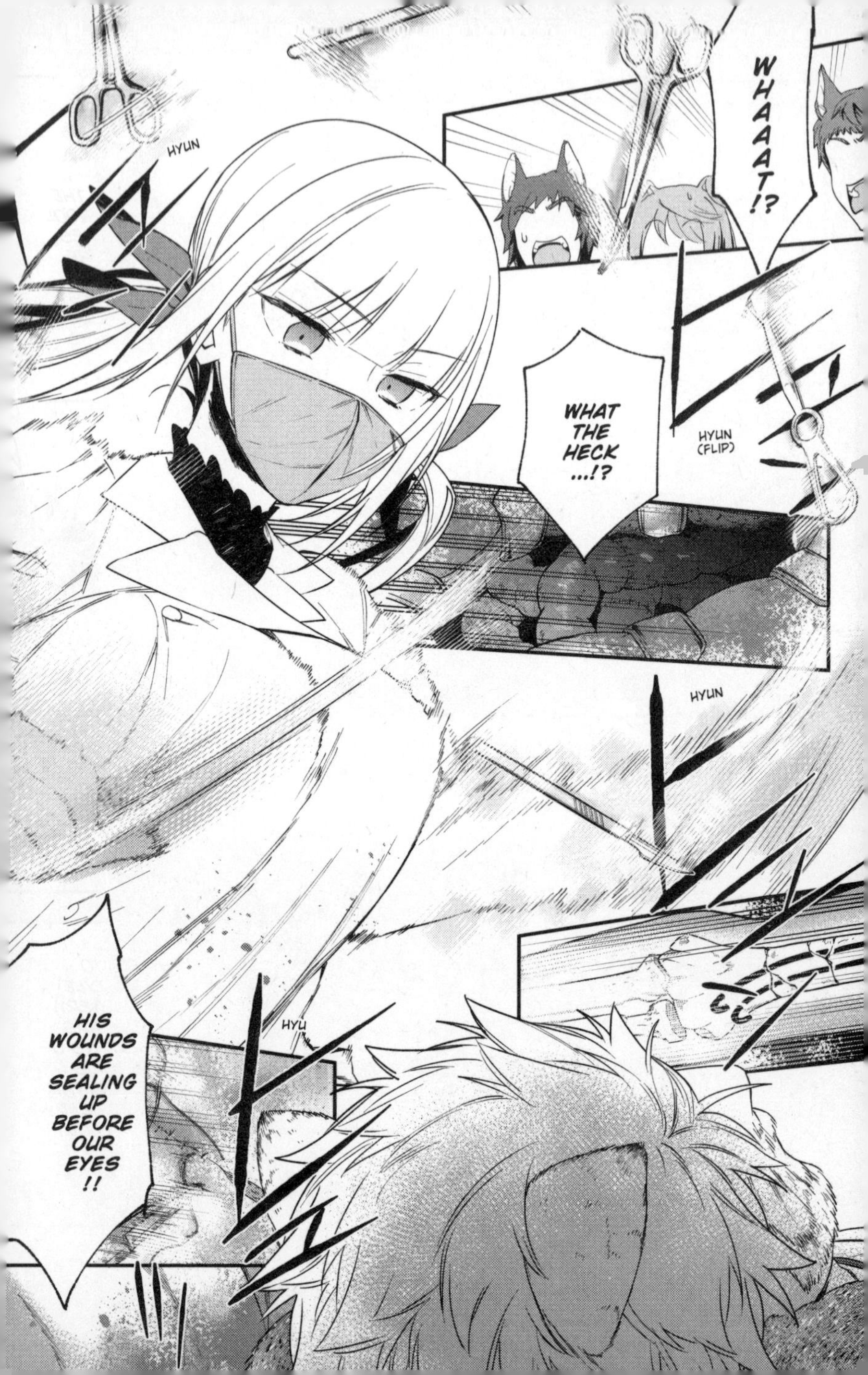
WHAAAAT!?
WHAT THE HECK...!?
HYUN (FLIP)
HYUN
HYUN
HYU
HIS WOUNDS ARE SEALING UP BEFORE OUR EYES!!

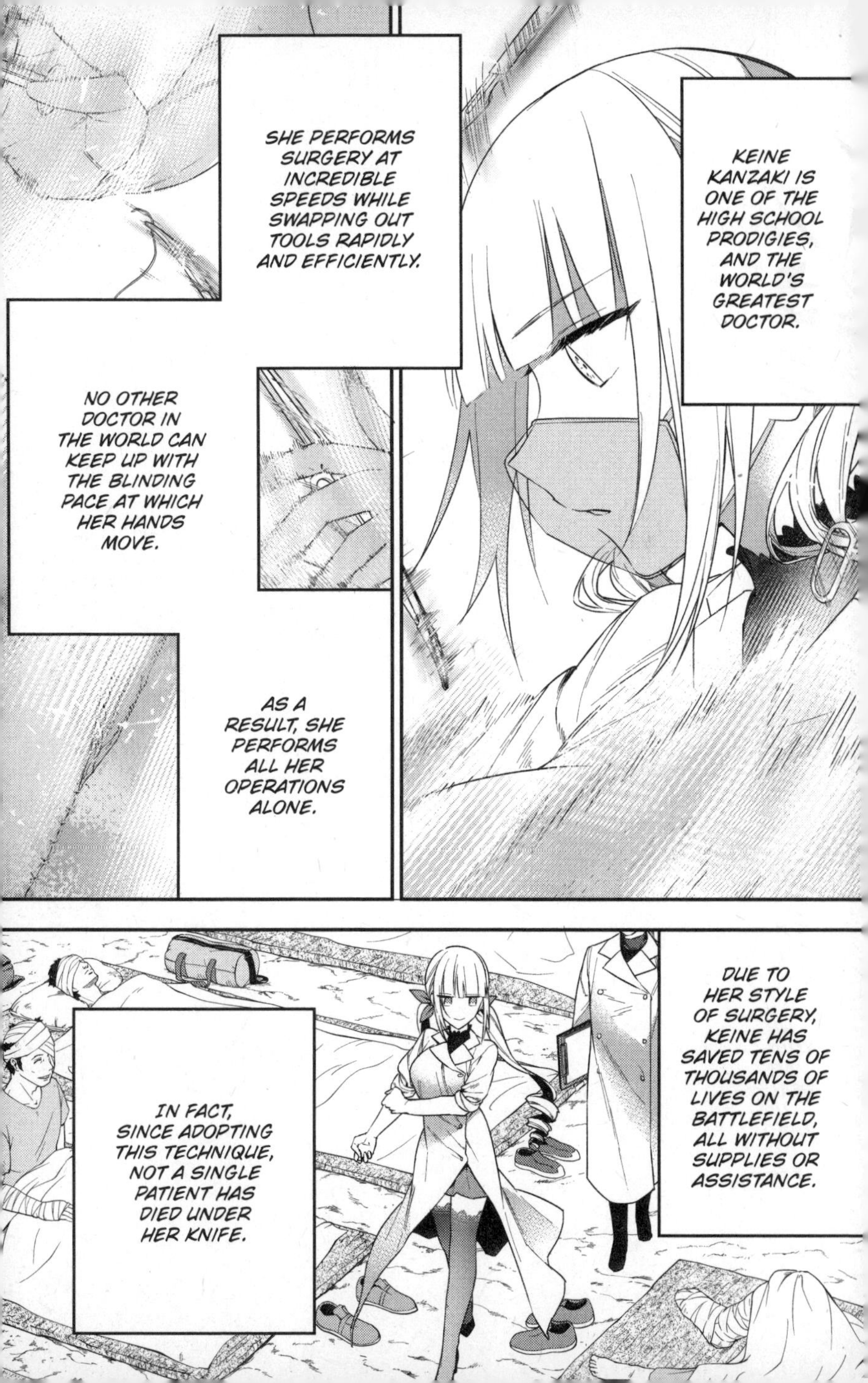
KEINE KANZAKI IS ONE OF THE HIGH SCHOOL PRODIGIES, AND THE WORLD'S GREATEST DOCTOR.
SHE PERFORMS SURGERY AT INCREDIBLE SPEEDS WHILE SWAPPING OUT TOOLS RAPIDLY AND EFFICIENTLY.
NO OTHER DOCTOR IN THE WORLD CAN KEEP UP WITH THE BLINDING PACE AT WHICH HER HANDS MOVE.
AS A RESULT, SHE PERFORMS ALL HER OPERATIONS ALONE.
DUE TO HER STYLE OF SURGERY, KEINE HAS SAVED TENS OF THOUSANDS OF LIVES ON THE BATTLEFIELD, ALL WITHOUT SUPPLIES OR ASSISTANCE.
IN FACT, SINCE ADOPTING THIS TECHNIQUE, NOT A SINGLE PATIENT HAS DIED UNDER HER KNIFE.

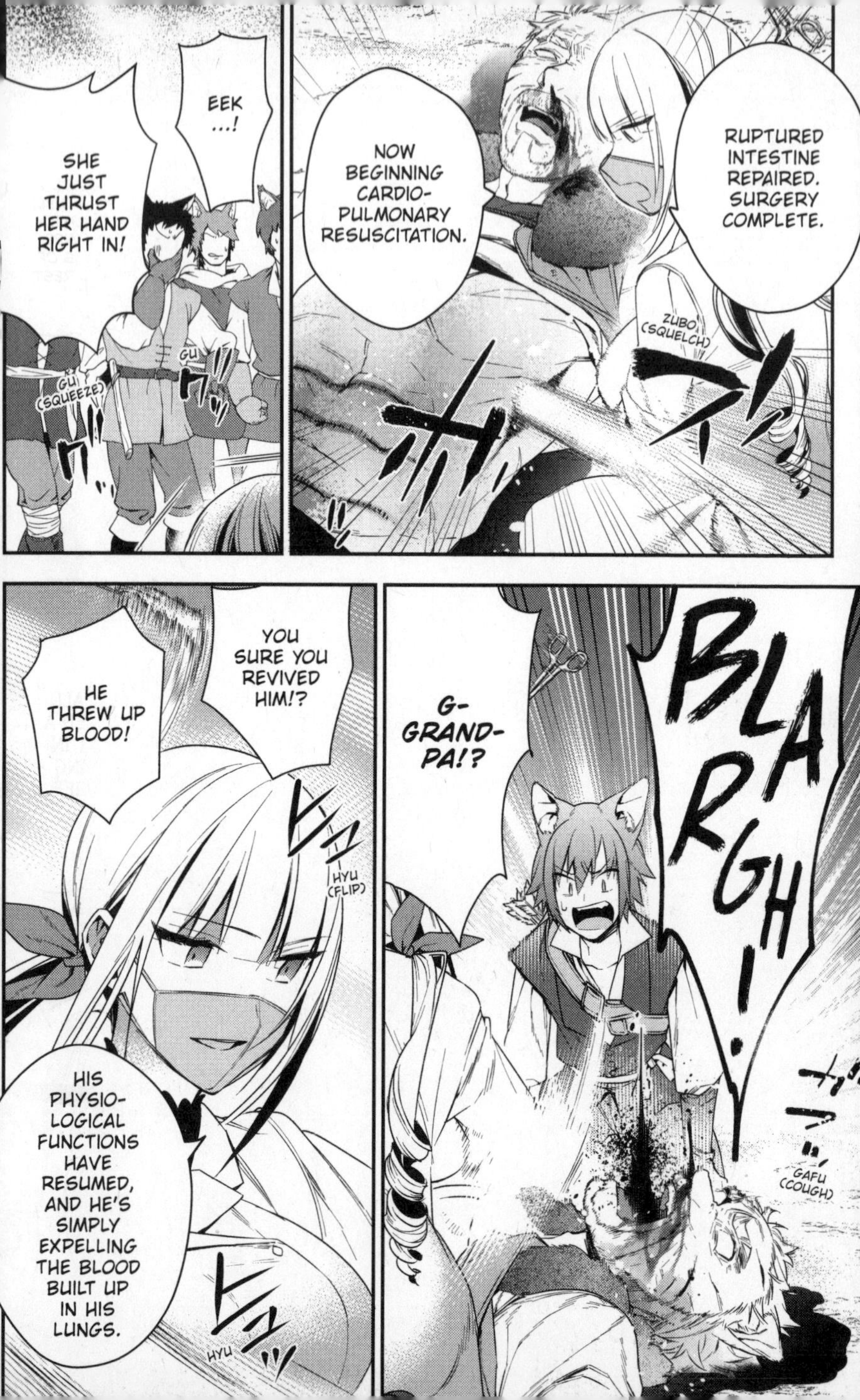
RUPTURED INTESTINE REPAIRED. SURGERY COMPLETE.
NOW BEGINNING CARDIO-PULMONARY RESUSCITATION.
ZUBO (SQUELCH)
EEK ...!
SHE JUST THRUST HER HAND RIGHT IN!
GU (SQUEEZE)
BLARGH!
G-GRANDPA!?
GAFU (COUGH)
YOU SURE YOU REVIVED HIM!?
HE THREW UP BLOOD!
HYU (FLIP)
HIS PHYSIO-LOGICAL FUNCTIONS HAVE RESUMED, AND HE'S SIMPLY EXPELLING THE BLOOD BUILT UP IN HIS LUNGS.
HYU

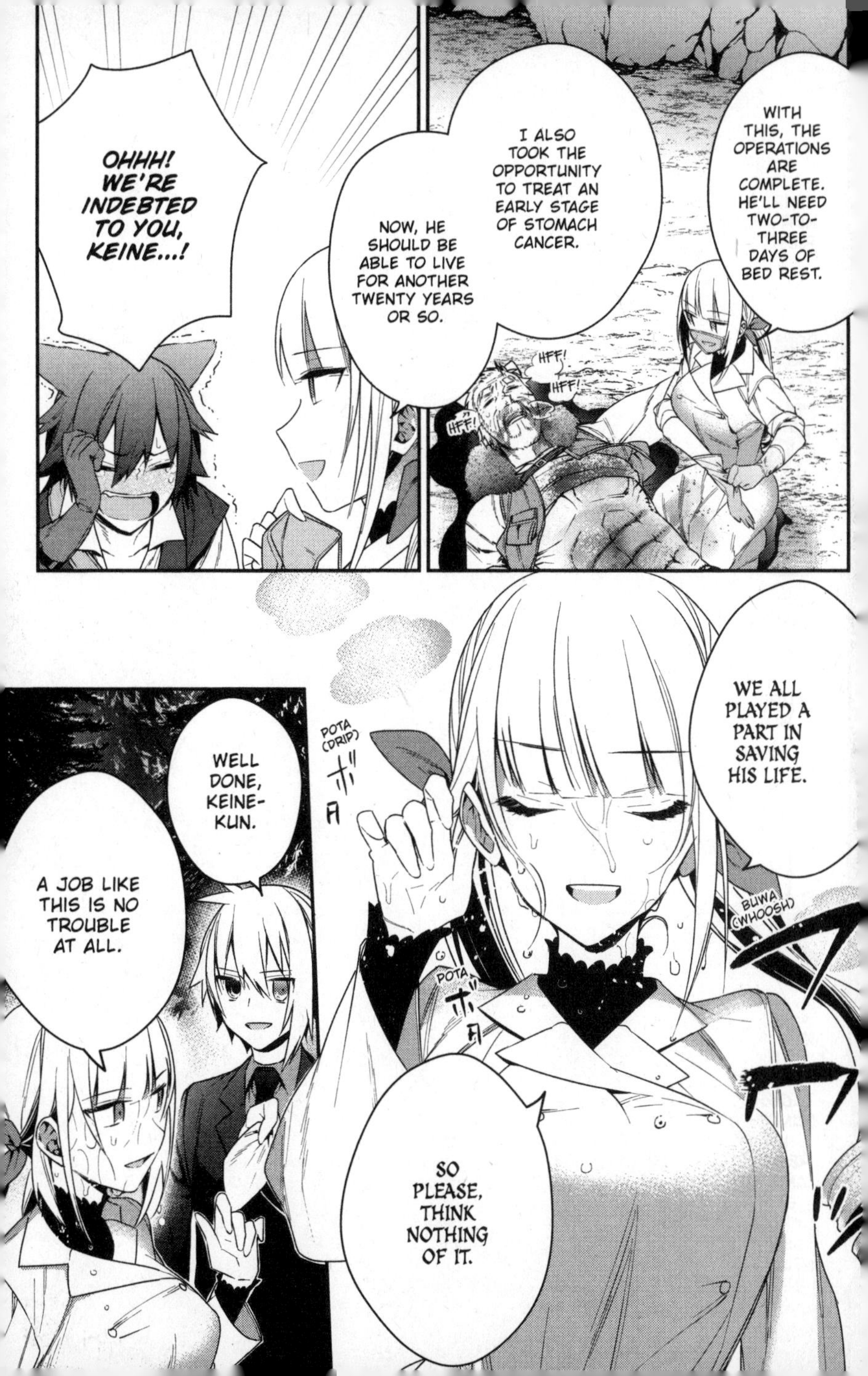
WITH THIS, THE OPERATIONS ARE COMPLETE. HE'LL NEED TWO-TO-THREE DAYS OF BED REST.
I ALSO TOOK THE OPPORTUNITY TO TREAT AN EARLY STAGE OF STOMACH CANCER.
HFF!
HFF!
HFF!
NOW, HE SHOULD BE ABLE TO LIVE FOR ANOTHER TWENTY YEARS OR SO.
OHHH! WE'RE INDEBTED TO YOU, KEINE...!
WE ALL PLAYED A PART IN SAVING HIS LIFE.
BUWA (WHOOSH)
POTA (DRIP)
POTA
SO PLEASE, THINK NOTHING OF IT.
WELL DONE, KEINE-KUN.
A JOB LIKE THIS IS NO TROUBLE AT ALL.

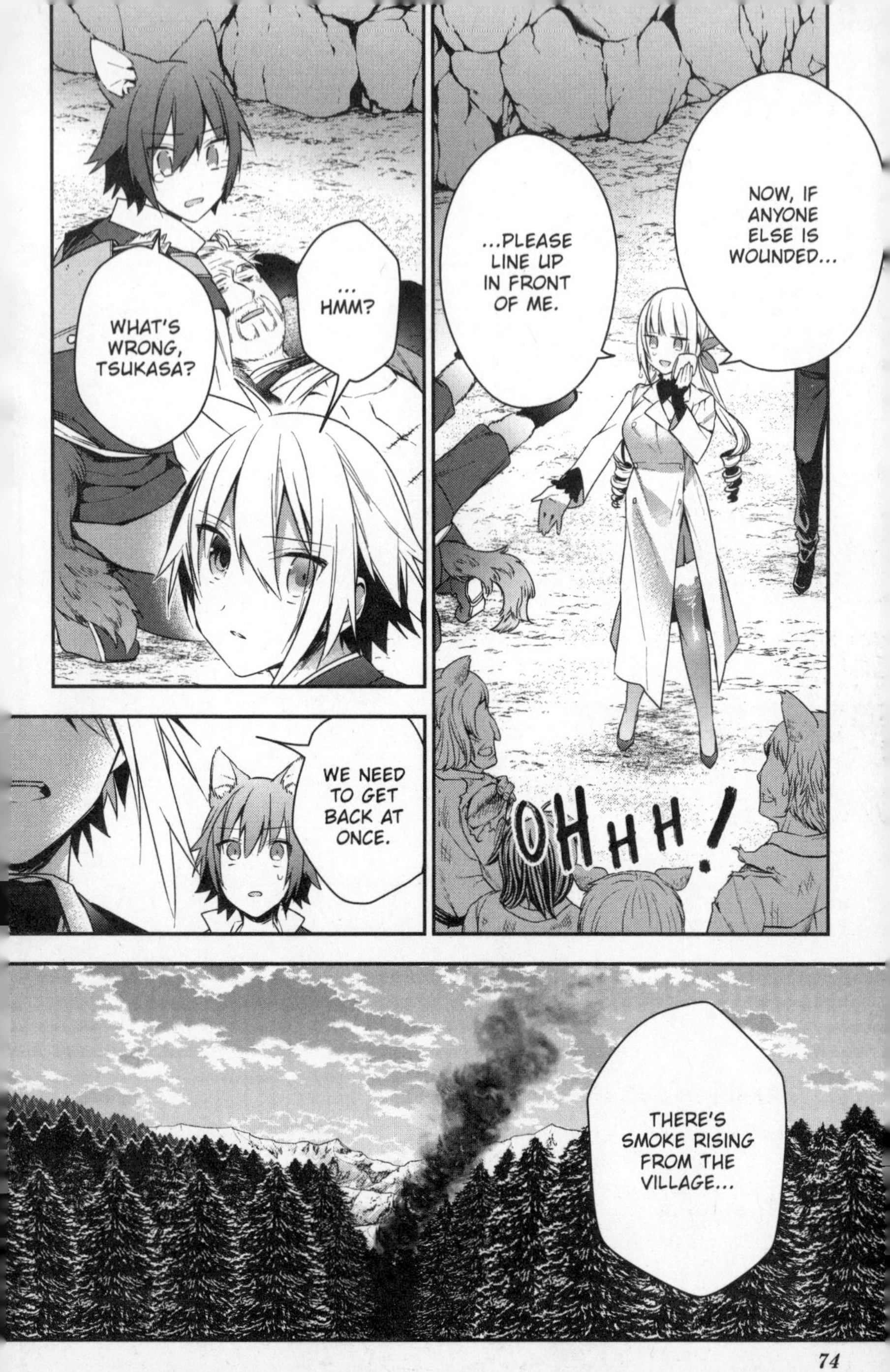
NOW, IF ANYONE ELSE IS WOUNDED...
...PLEASE LINE UP IN FRONT OF ME.
OHHH!
... HMM?
WHAT'S WRONG, TSUKASA?
WE NEED TO GET BACK AT ONCE.
THERE'S SMOKE RISING FROM THE VILLAGE...

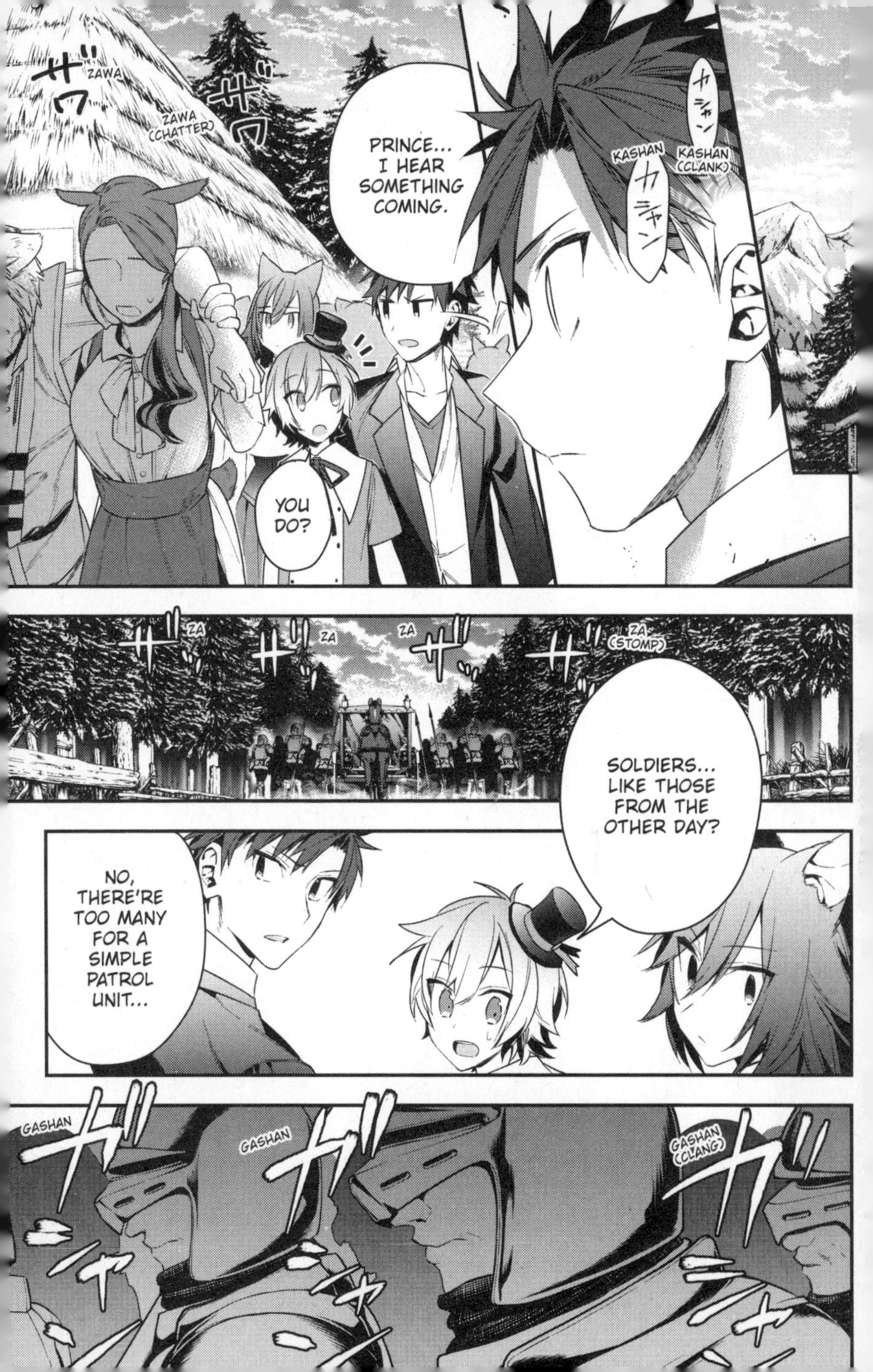
カシャン
KASHAN KASHAN (CLANK)
カシャン
PRINCE... I HEAR SOMETHING COMING.
ザワ
ZAWA ZAWA (CHATTER)
ザワ
YOU DO?
ZA (STOMP)
ZA
ZA
ZA
SOLDIERS... LIKE THOSE FROM THE OTHER DAY?
NO, THERE'RE TOO MANY FOR A SIMPLE PATROL UNIT...
GASHAN (CLANG)
GASHAN
GASHAN

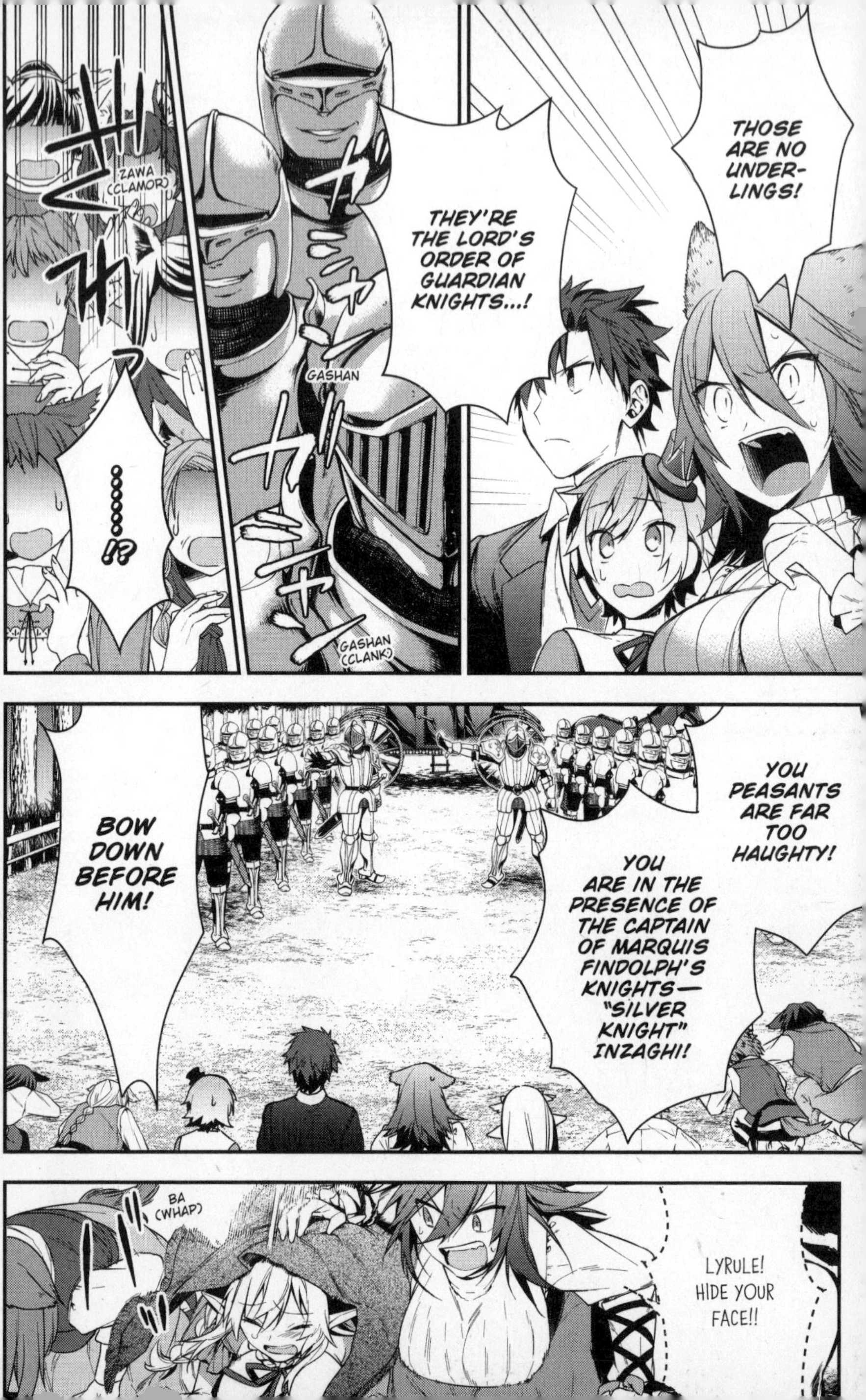
THOSE ARE NO UNDER-LINGS!
THEY'RE THE LORD'S ORDER OF GUARDIAN KNIGHTS...!
GASHAN
GASHAN (CLANK)
ZAWA (CLAMOR)
......!?
YOU PEASANTS ARE FAR TOO HAUGHTY!
YOU ARE IN THE PRESENCE OF THE CAPTAIN OF MARQUIS FINDOLPH'S KNIGHTS—"SILVER KNIGHT" INZAGHI!
BOW DOWN BEFORE HIM!
LYRULE! HIDE YOUR FACE!!
BA (WHAP)

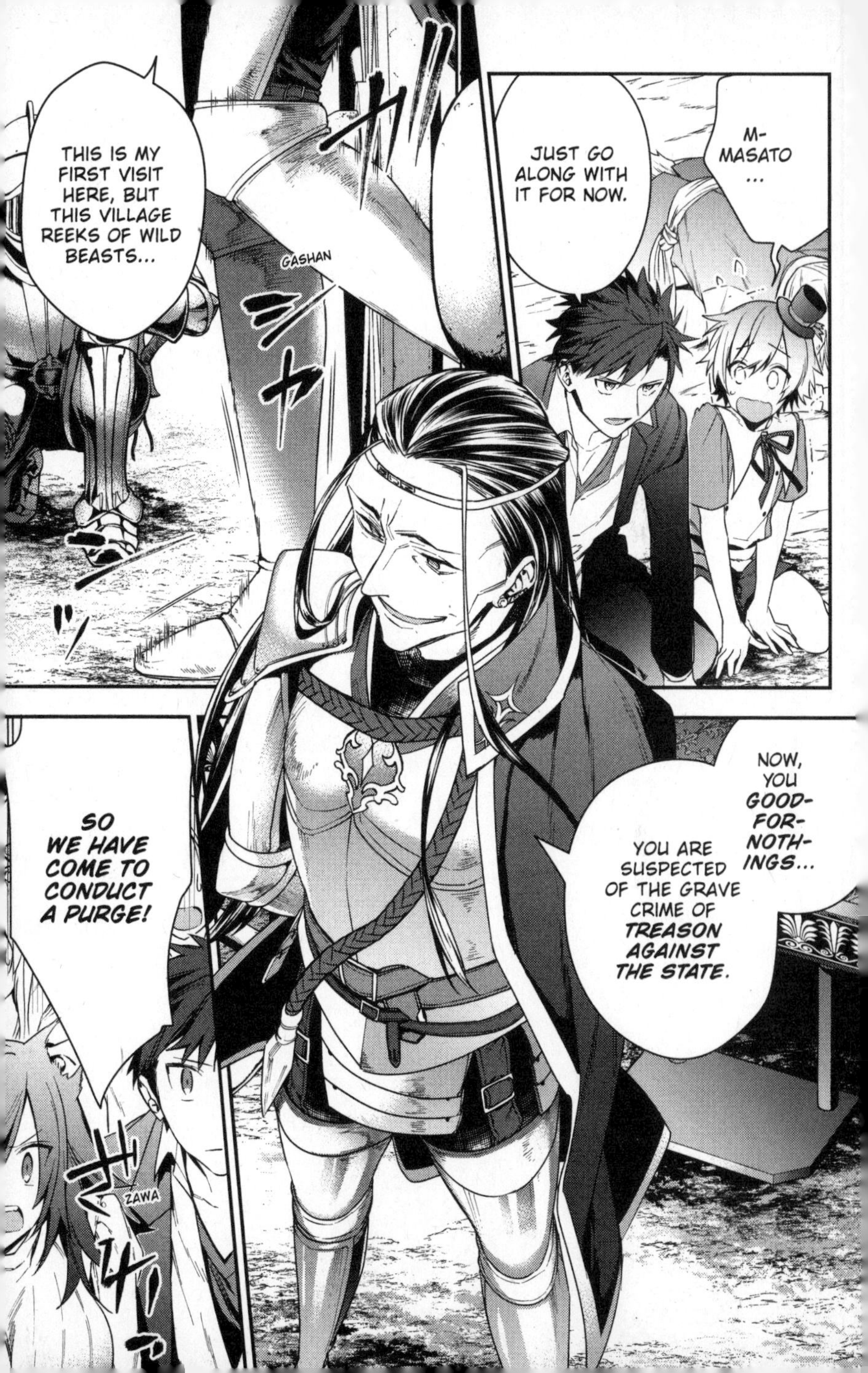
M-MASATO...
JUST GO ALONG WITH IT FOR NOW.
THIS IS MY FIRST VISIT HERE, BUT THIS VILLAGE REEKS OF WILD BEASTS...
GASHAN
NOW, YOU GOOD-FOR-NOTHINGS...
YOU ARE SUSPECTED OF THE GRAVE CRIME OF TREASON AGAINST THE STATE.
SO WE HAVE COME TO CONDUCT A PURGE!
ZAWA

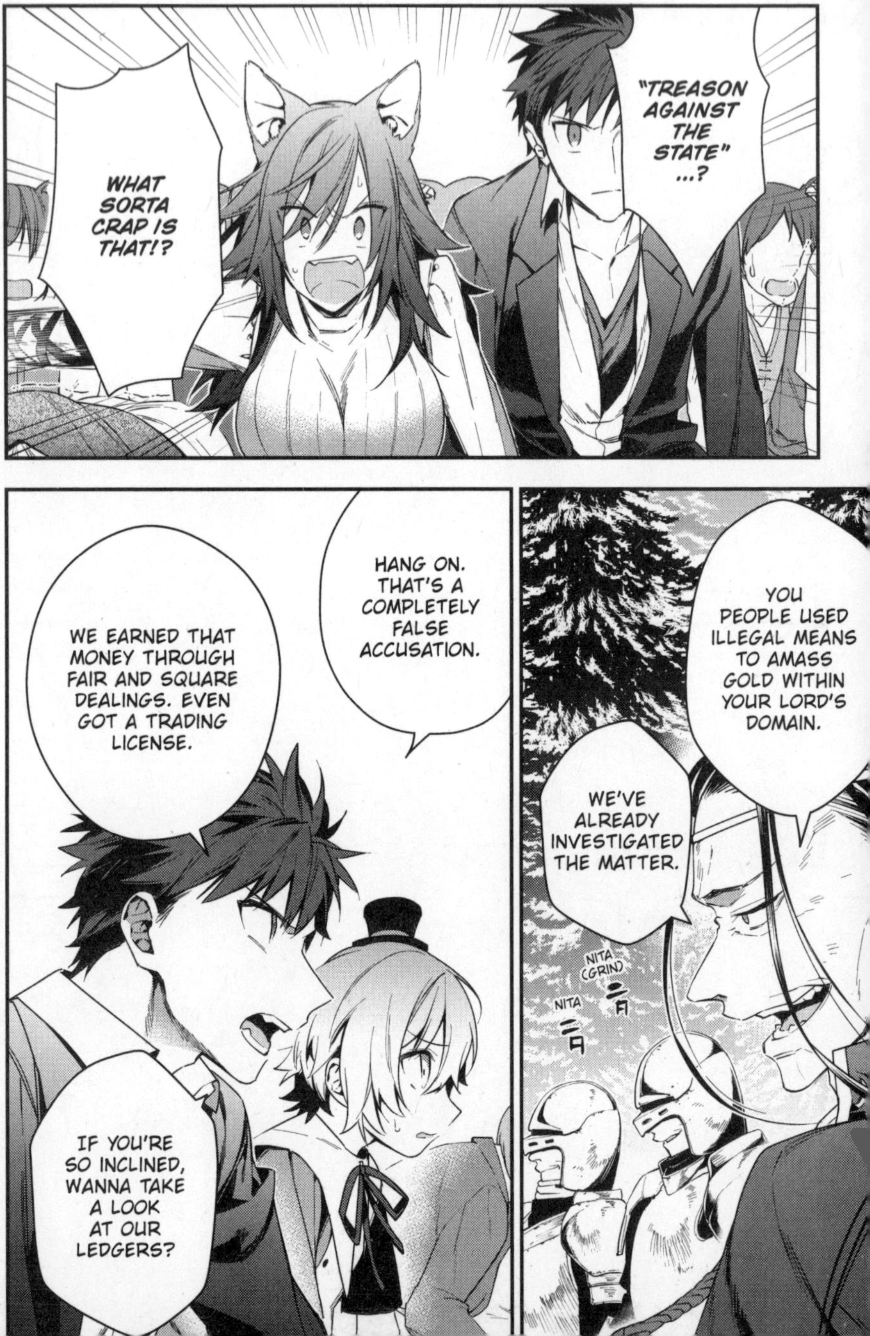
"TREASON AGAINST THE STATE"...?
WHAT SORTA CRAP IS THAT!?
YOU PEOPLE USED ILLEGAL MEANS TO AMASS GOLD WITHIN YOUR LORD'S DOMAIN.
WE'VE ALREADY INVESTIGATED THE MATTER.
NITA (GRIN)
NITA
HANG ON. THAT'S A COMPLETELY FALSE ACCUSATION.
WE EARNED THAT MONEY THROUGH FAIR AND SQUARE DEALINGS. EVEN GOT A TRADING LICENSE.
IF YOU'RE SO INCLINED, WANNA TAKE A LOOK AT OUR LEDGERS?

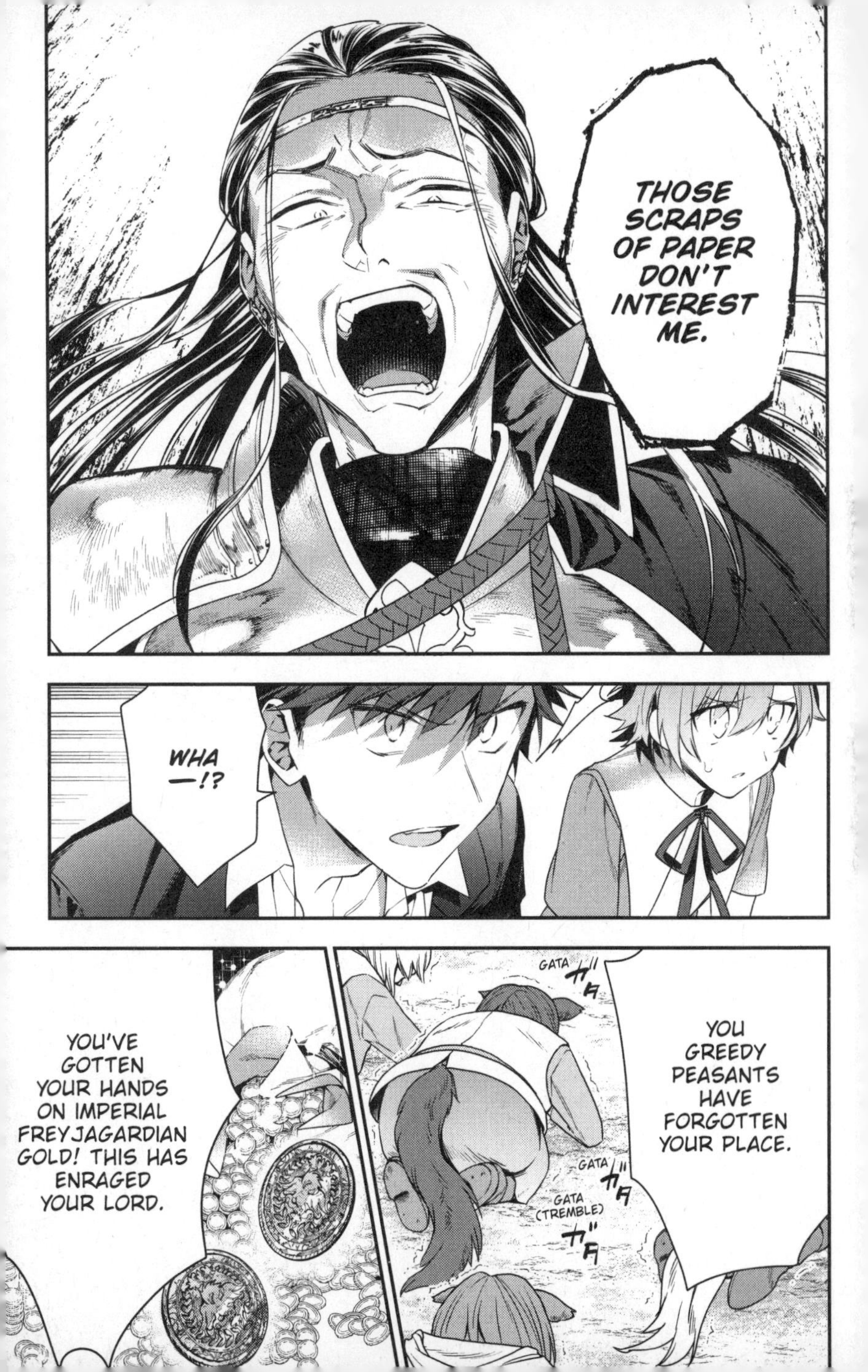
THOSE SCRAPS OF PAPER DON'T INTEREST ME.
WHA—!?
YOU GREEDY PEASANTS HAVE FORGOTTEN YOUR PLACE.
GATA
GATA
GATA (TREMBLE)
YOU'VE GOTTEN YOUR HANDS ON IMPERIAL FREYJAGARDIAN GOLD! THIS HAS ENRAGED YOUR LORD.

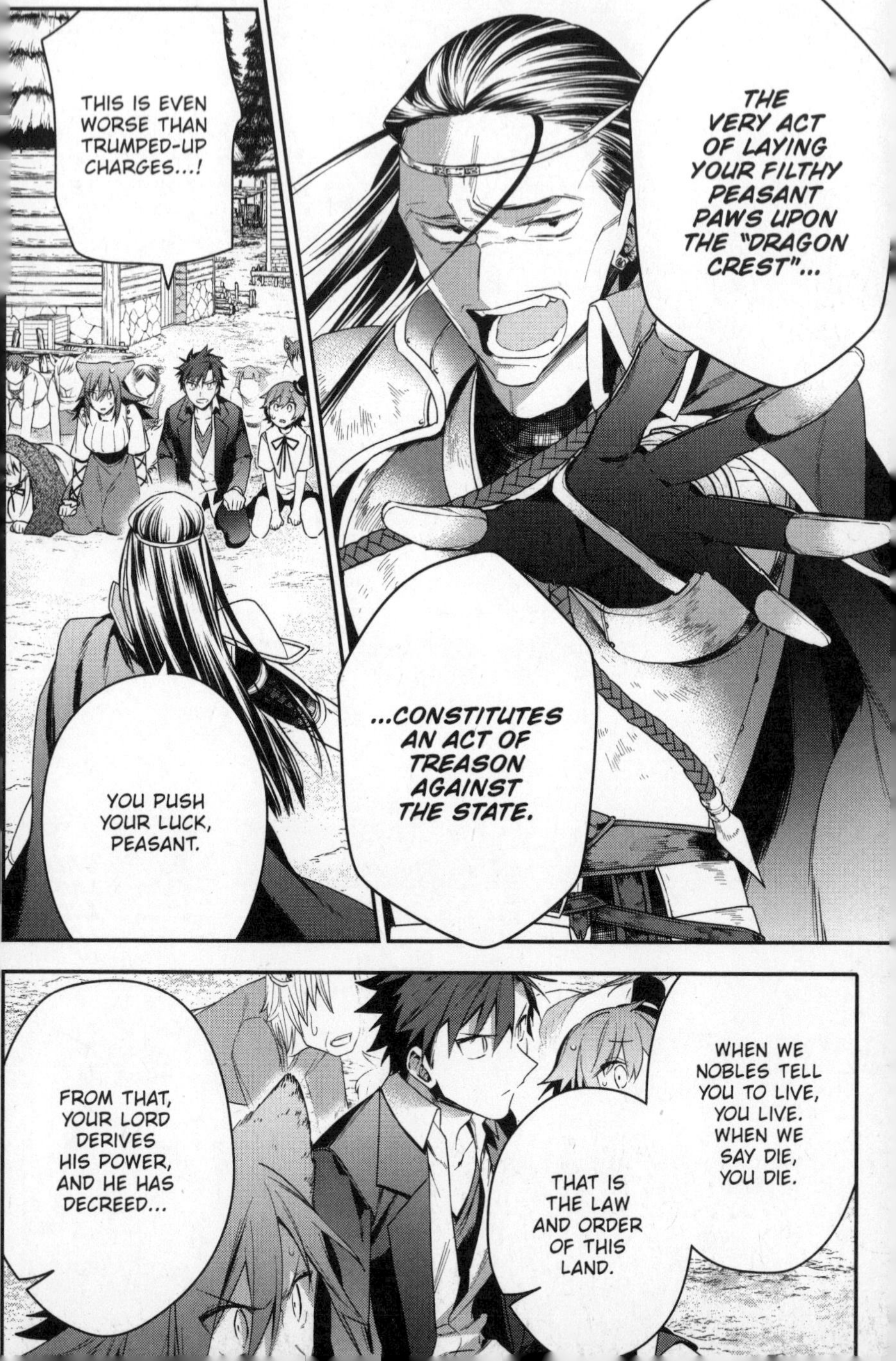
THE VERY ACT OF LAYING YOUR FILTHY PEASANT PAWS UPON THE "DRAGON CREST"...
...CONSTITUTES AN ACT OF TREASON AGAINST THE STATE.
THIS IS EVEN WORSE THAN TRUMPED-UP CHARGES...!
YOU PUSH YOUR LUCK, PEASANT.
WHEN WE NOBLES TELL YOU TO LIVE, YOU LIVE. WHEN WE SAY DIE, YOU DIE.
THAT IS THE LAW AND ORDER OF THIS LAND.
FROM THAT, YOUR LORD DERIVES HIS POWER, AND HE HAS DECREED...

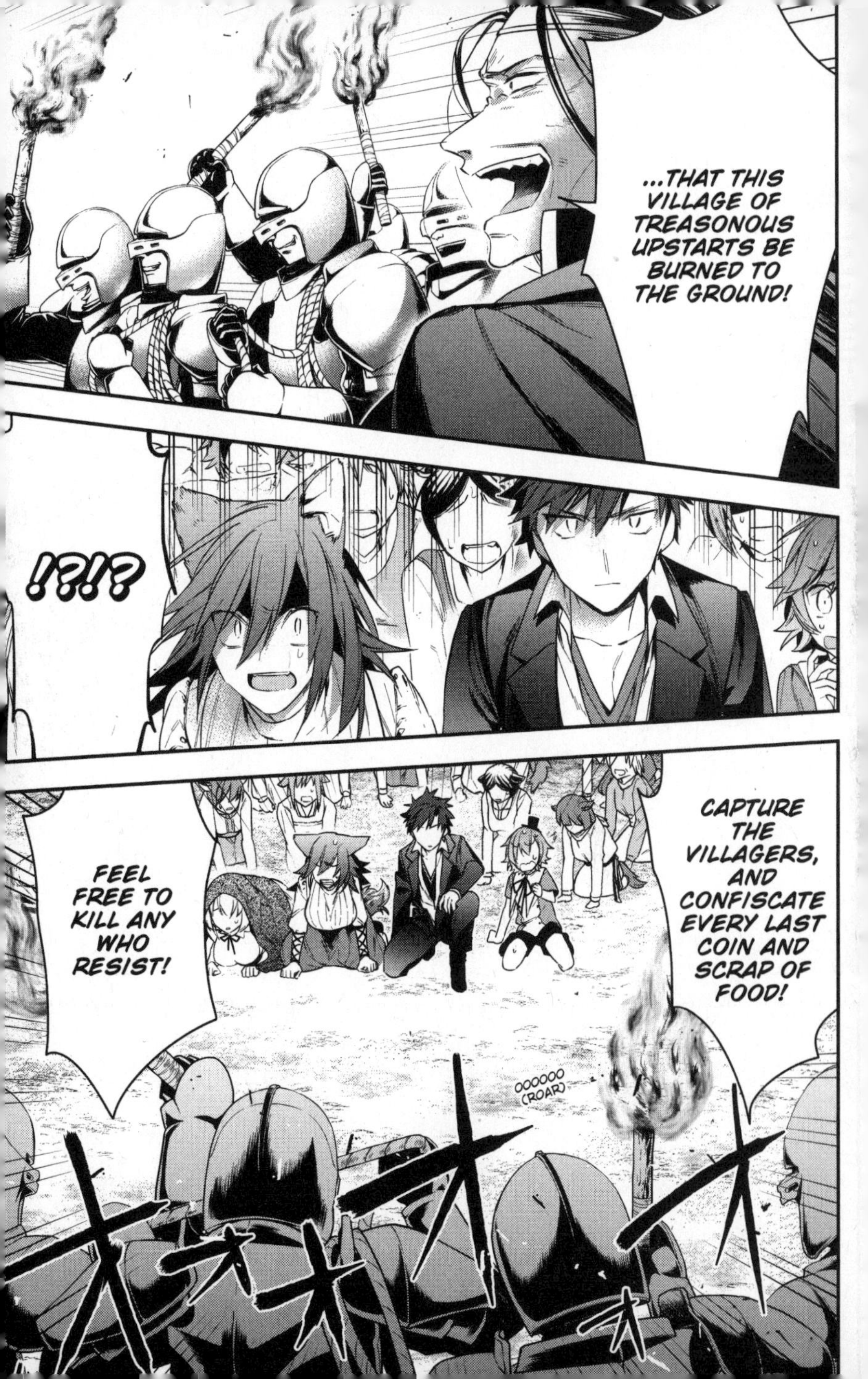
...THAT THIS VILLAGE OF TREASONOUS UPSTARTS BE BURNED TO THE GROUND!
!?!?
CAPTURE THE VILLAGERS, AND CONFISCATE EVERY LAST COIN AND SCRAP OF FOOD!
FEEL FREE TO KILL ANY WHO RESIST!
OOOOOO (ROAR)

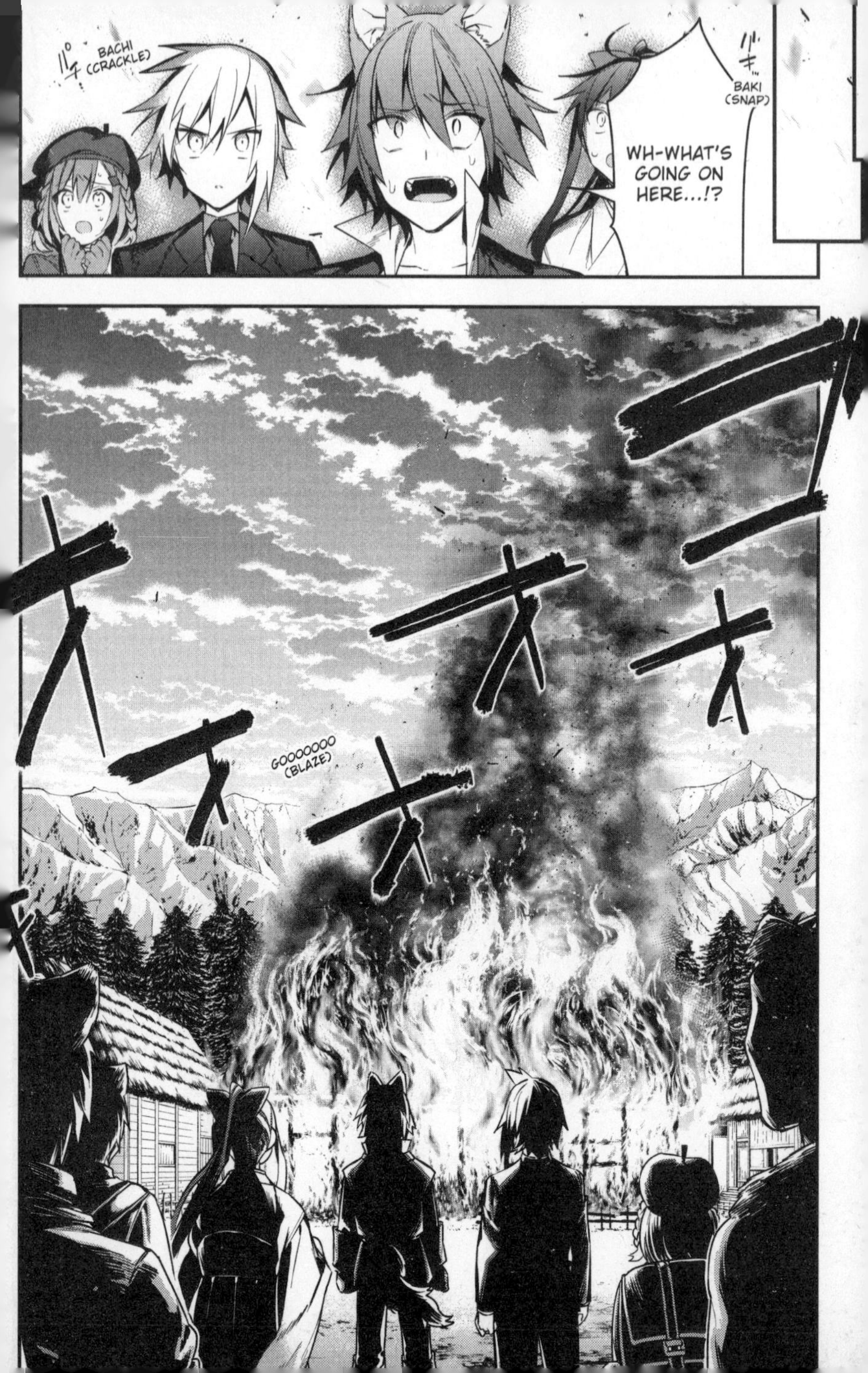
BAKI (SNAP)
WH-WHAT'S GOING ON HERE...!?
BACHI (CRACKLE)
GOOOOOOO (BLAZE)

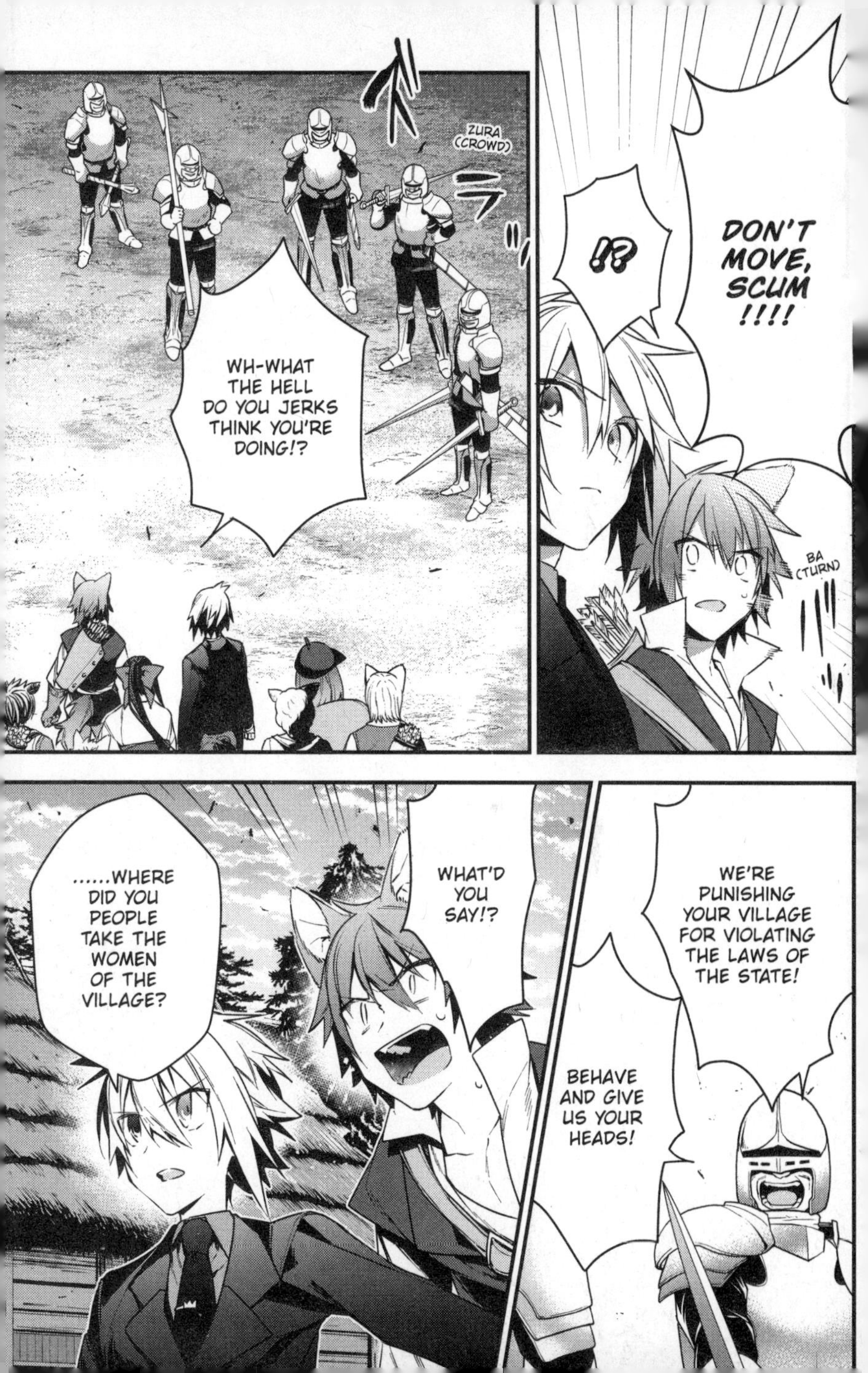
DON'T MOVE, SCUM!!!!
!?
BA (TURN)
ZURA (CROWD)
WH-WHAT THE HELL DO YOU JERKS THINK YOU'RE DOING!?
WE'RE PUNISHING YOUR VILLAGE FOR VIOLATING THE LAWS OF THE STATE!
BEHAVE AND GIVE US YOUR HEADS!
WHAT'D YOU SAY!?
......WHERE DID YOU PEOPLE TAKE THE WOMEN OF THE VILLAGE?

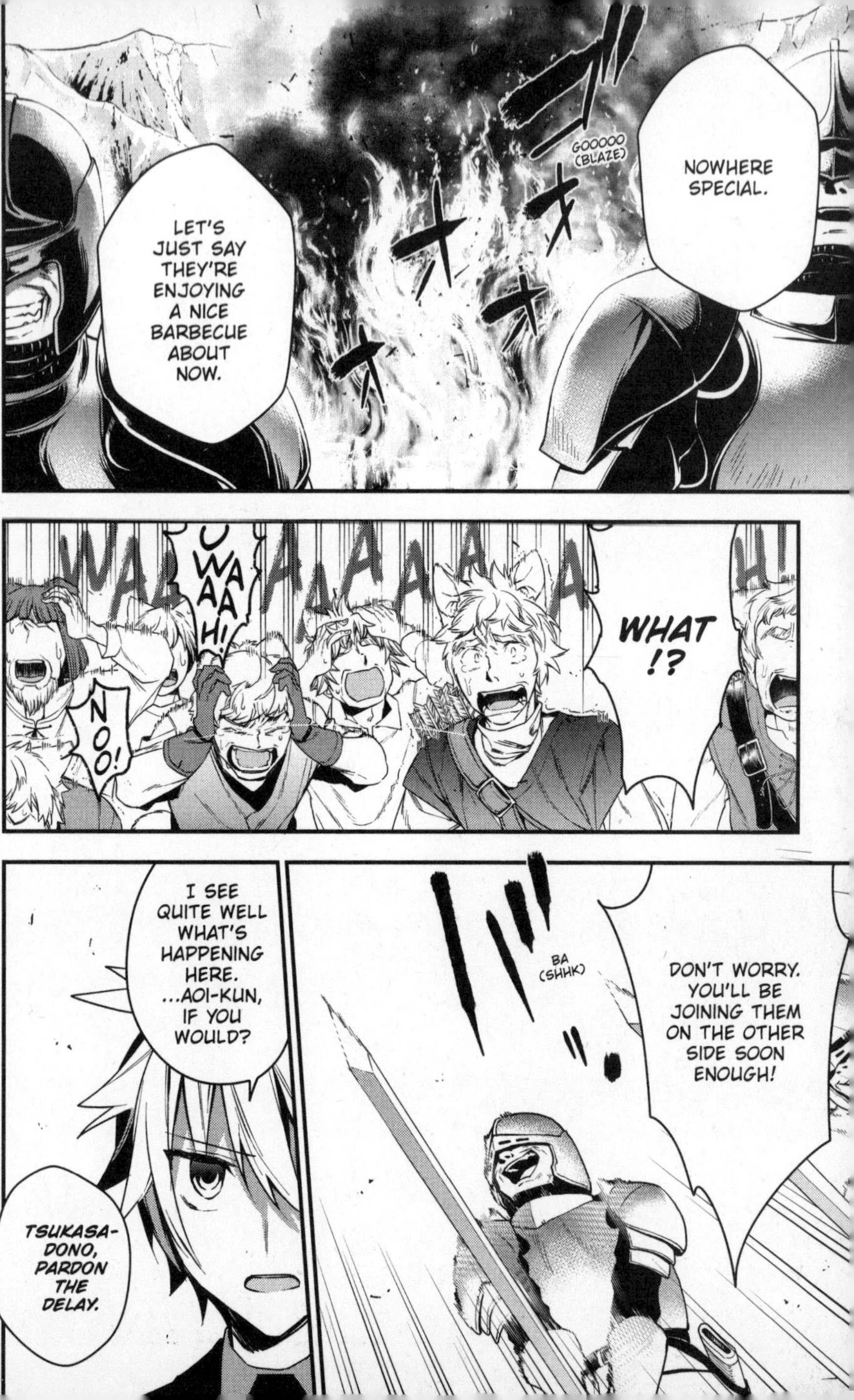
NOWHERE SPECIAL.
GOOOOO (BLAZE)
LET'S JUST SAY THEY'RE ENJOYING A NICE BARBECUE ABOUT NOW.
WHAT !?
NOO!
DON'T WORRY. YOU'LL BE JOINING THEM ON THE OTHER SIDE SOON ENOUGH!
BA (SHHK)
I SEE QUITE WELL WHAT'S HAPPENING HERE. ...AOI-KUN, IF YOU WOULD?
TSUKASA-DONO, PARDON THE DELAY.

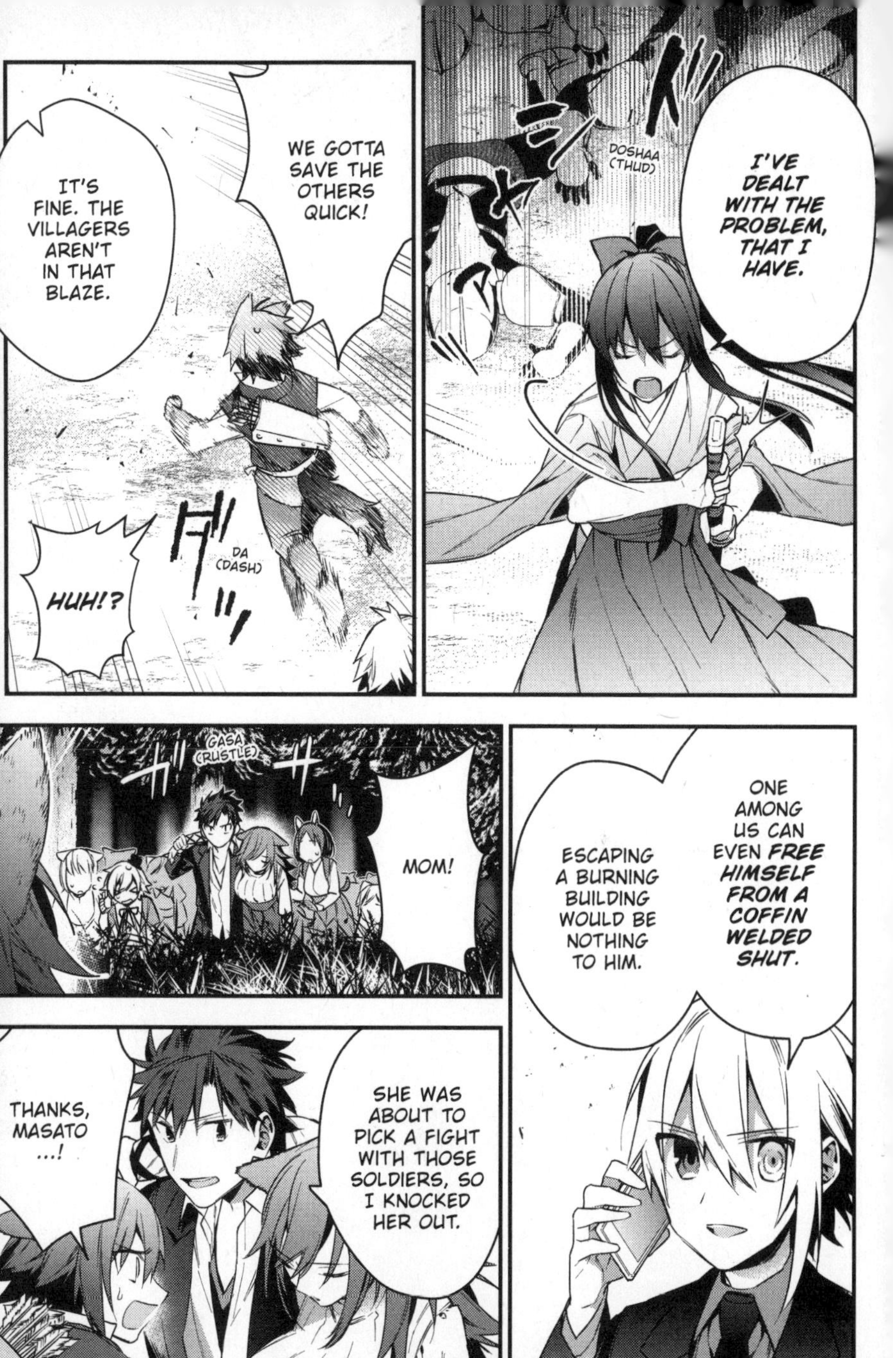
I'VE DEALT WITH THE PROBLEM, THAT I HAVE.
DOSHAA (THUD)
WE GOTTA SAVE THE OTHERS QUICK!
IT'S FINE. THE VILLAGERS AREN'T IN THAT BLAZE.
DA (DASH)
HUH!?
ONE AMONG US CAN EVEN FREE HIMSELF FROM A COFFIN WELDED SHUT.
ESCAPING A BURNING BUILDING WOULD BE NOTHING TO HIM.
GASA (RUSTLE)
MOM!
SHE WAS ABOUT TO PICK A FIGHT WITH THOSE SOLDIERS, SO I KNOCKED HER OUT.
THANKS, MASATO ...!

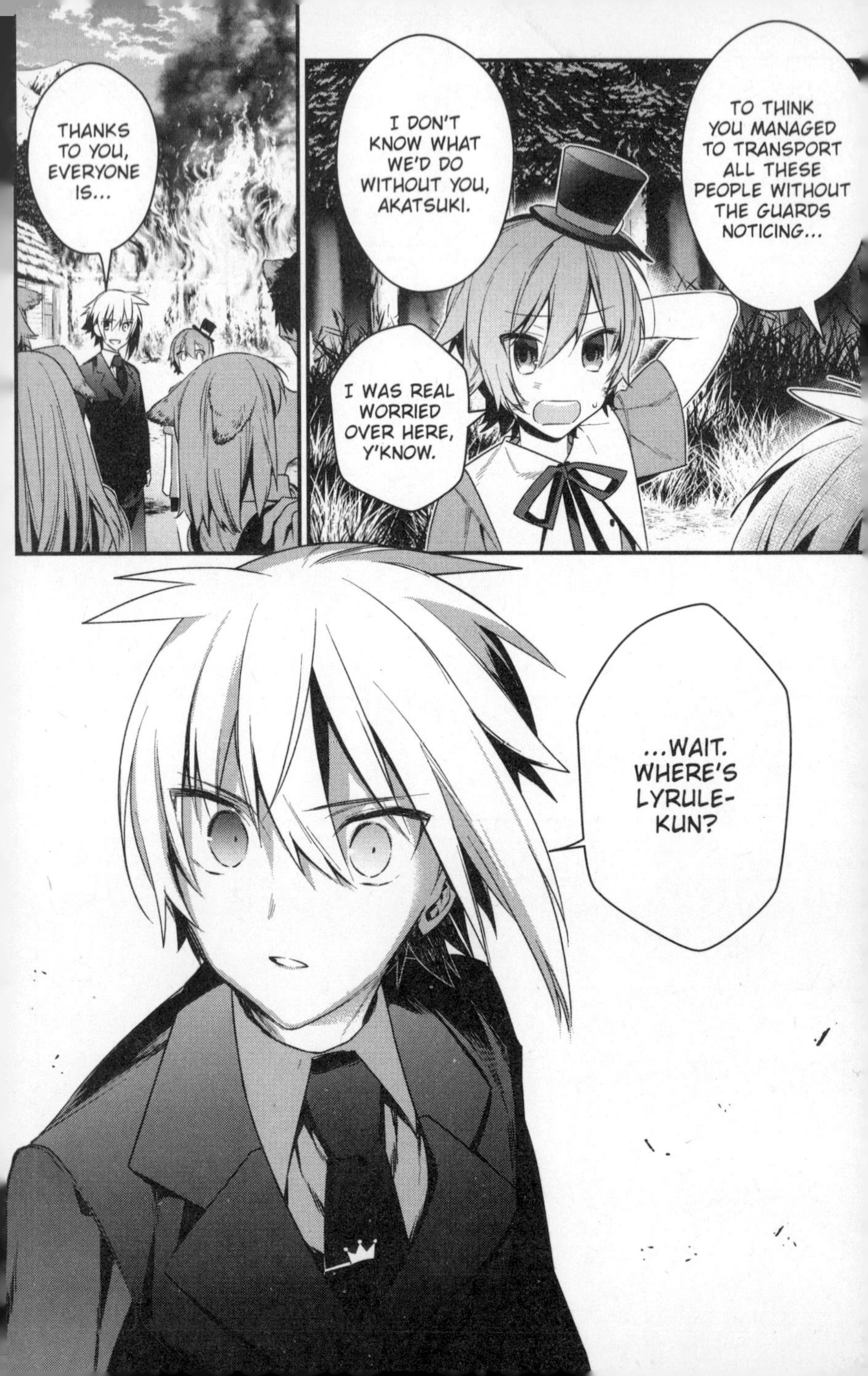
TO THINK YOU MANAGED TO TRANSPORT ALL THESE PEOPLE WITHOUT THE GUARDS NOTICING...
I DON'T KNOW WHAT WE'D DO WITHOUT YOU, AKATSUKI.
I WAS REAL WORRIED OVER HERE, Y'KNOW.
THANKS TO YOU, EVERYONE IS...
...WAIT. WHERE'S LYRULE-KUN?

HIGH SCHOOL
PRODIGIES HAVE
IT EASY EVEN IN
ANOTHER
WORLD!

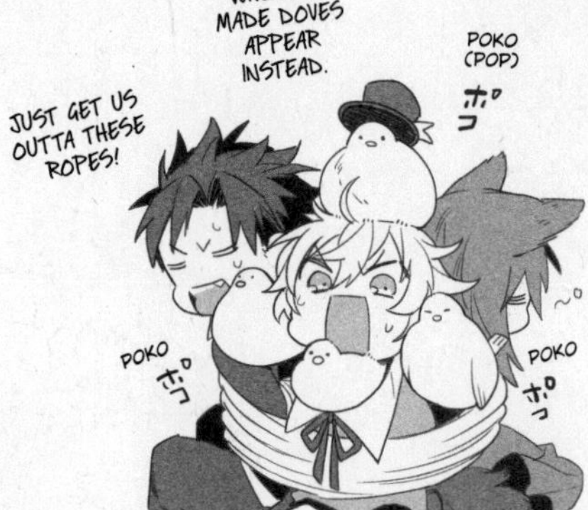
POKO (POP)
ポコ
WHOOPS! MADE DOVES APPEAR INSTEAD.
JUST GET US OUTTA THESE ROPES!
POKO
ポコ
POKO
ポコ

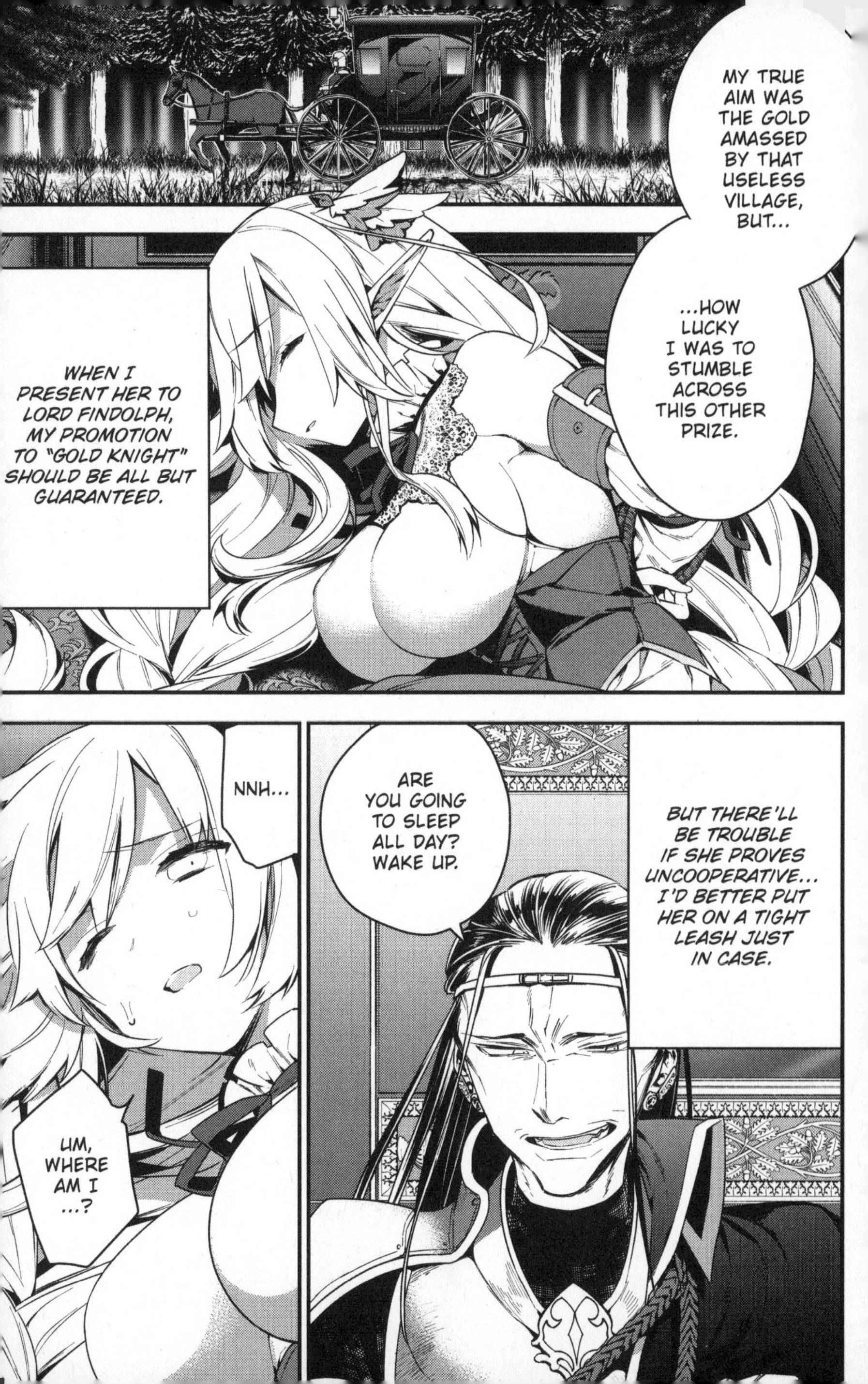
MY TRUE AIM WAS THE GOLD AMASSED BY THAT USELESS VILLAGE, BUT...
...HOW LUCKY I WAS TO STUMBLE ACROSS THIS OTHER PRIZE.
WHEN I PRESENT HER TO LORD FINDOLPH, MY PROMOTION TO "GOLD KNIGHT" SHOULD BE ALL BUT GUARANTEED.
BUT THERE'LL BE TROUBLE IF SHE PROVES UNCOOPERATIVE... I'D BETTER PUT HER ON A TIGHT LEASH JUST IN CASE.
ARE YOU GOING TO SLEEP ALL DAY? WAKE UP.
NNH...
UM, WHERE AM I ...?

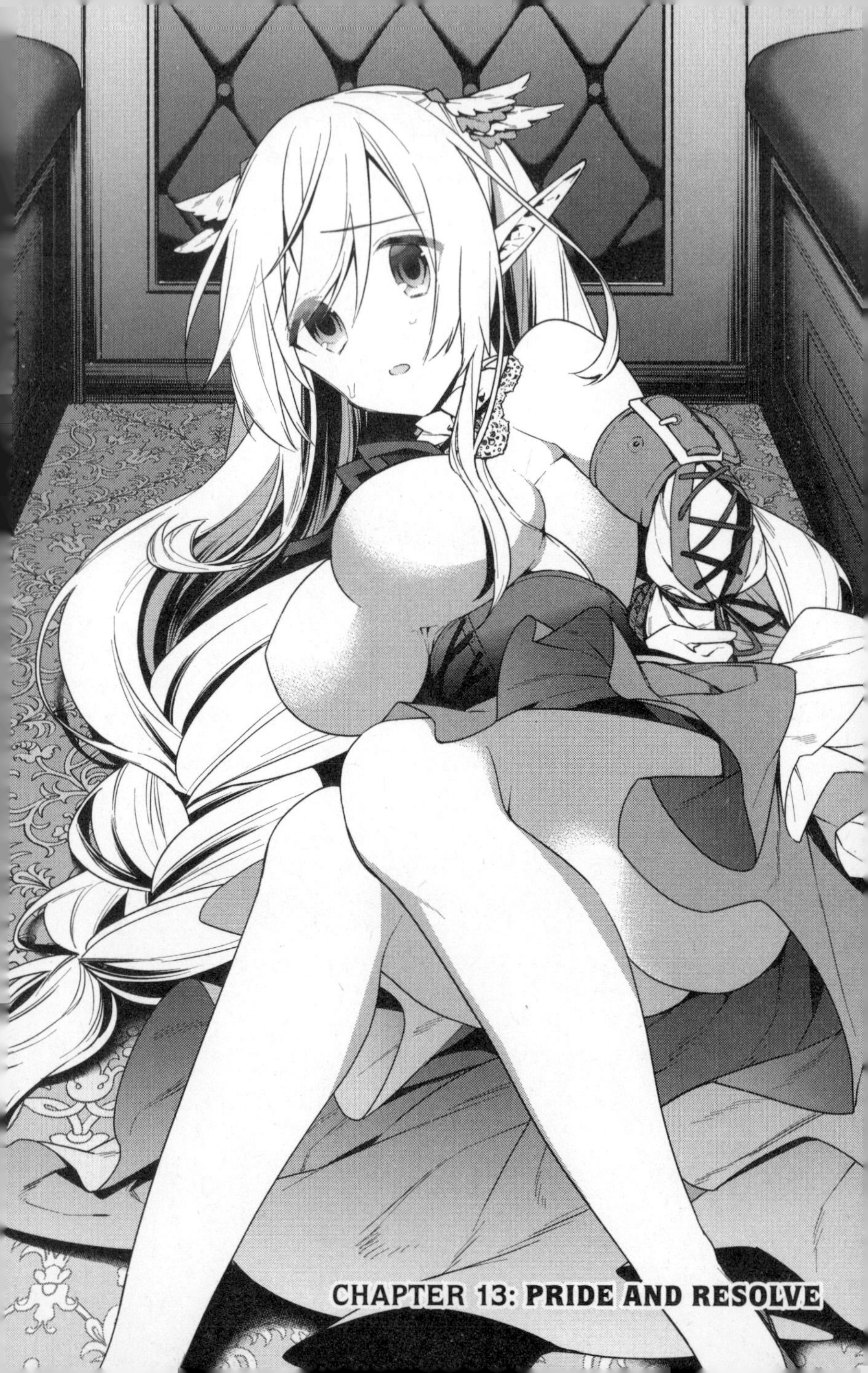

CHAPTER 13: PRIDE AND RESOLVE

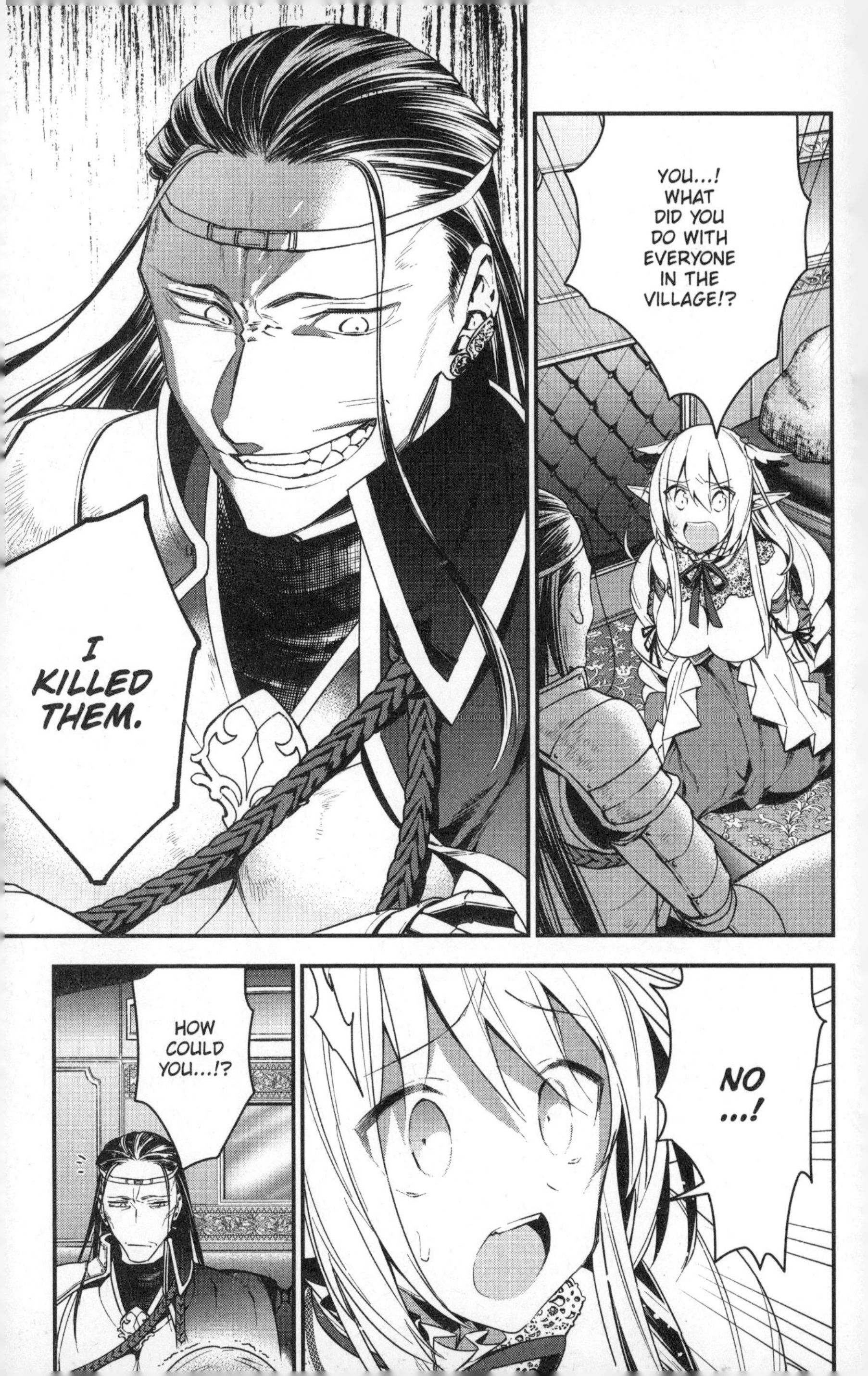
YOU...! WHAT DID YOU DO WITH EVERYONE IN THE VILLAGE!?
I KILLED THEM.
NO ...!
HOW COULD YOU...!?

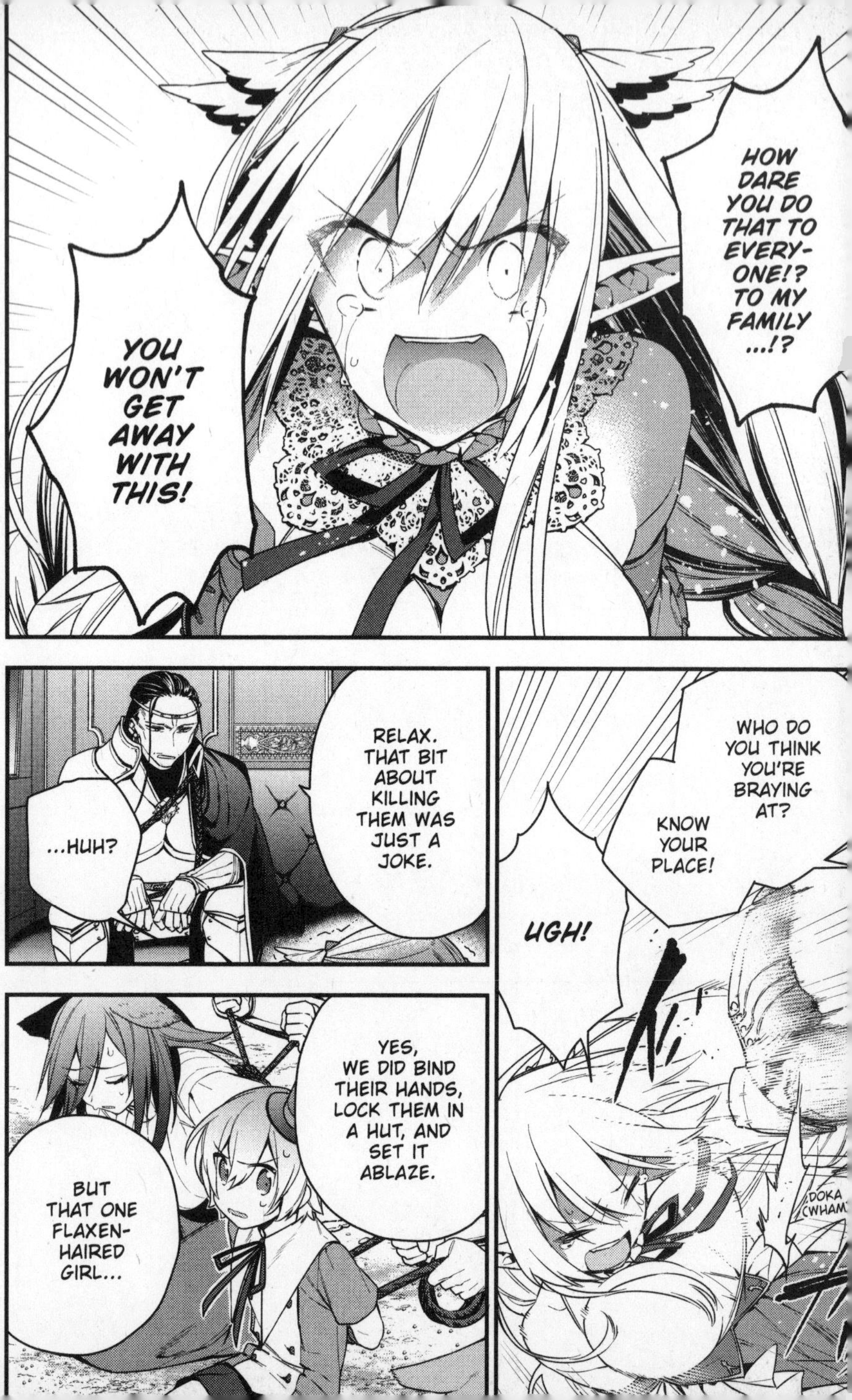
HOW DARE YOU DO THAT TO EVERYONE!? TO MY FAMILY...!?
YOU WON'T GET AWAY WITH THIS!
WHO DO YOU THINK YOU'RE BRAYING AT?
KNOW YOUR PLACE!
UGH!
DOKA (WHAM
RELAX. THAT BIT ABOUT KILLING THEM WAS JUST A JOKE.
...HUH?
YES, WE DID BIND THEIR HANDS, LOCK THEM IN A HUT, AND SET IT ABLAZE.
BUT THAT ONE FLAXEN-HAIRED GIRL...

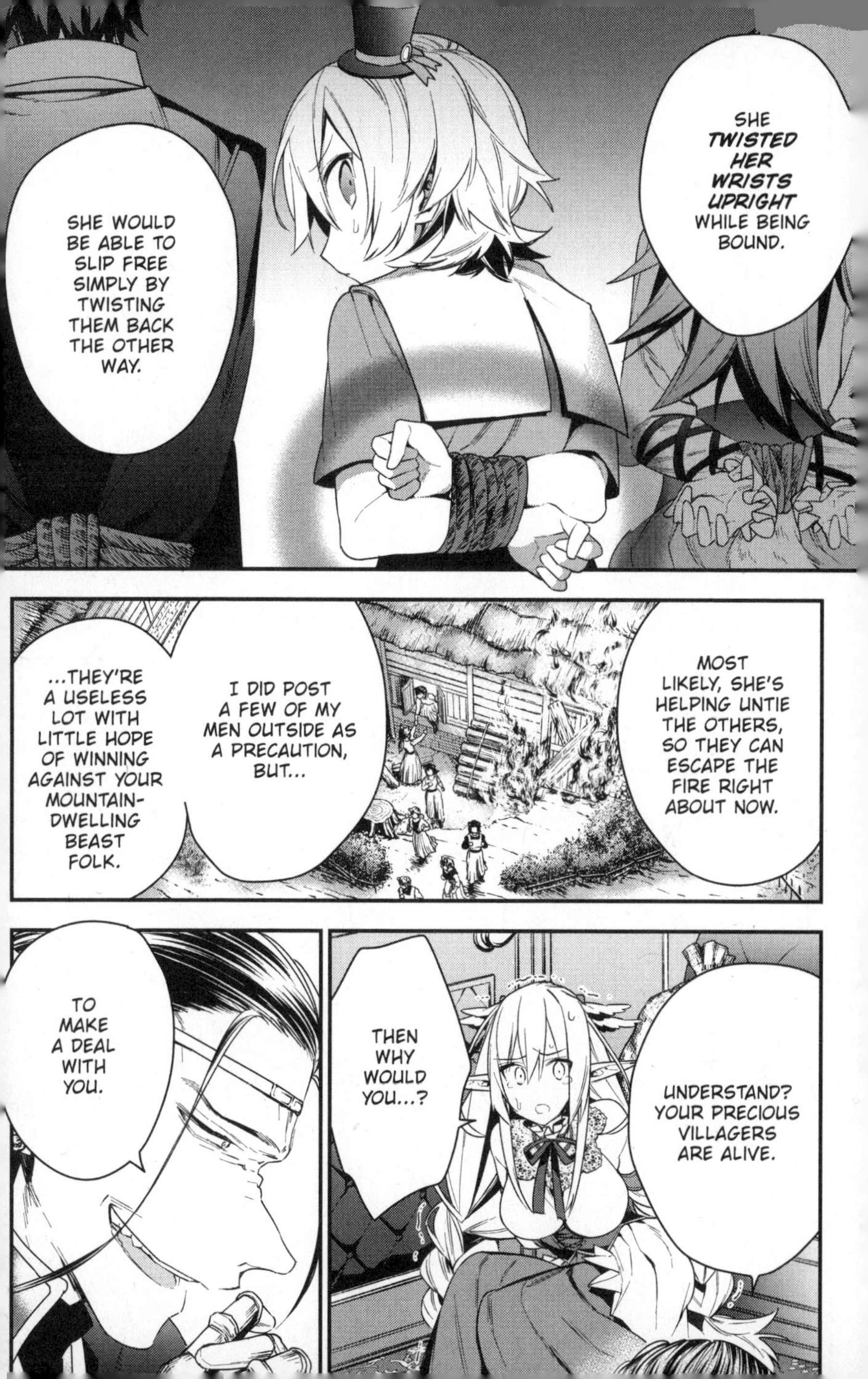
SHE TWISTED HER WRISTS UPRIGHT WHILE BEING BOUND.
SHE WOULD BE ABLE TO SLIP FREE SIMPLY BY TWISTING THEM BACK THE OTHER WAY.
MOST LIKELY, SHE'S HELPING UNTIE THE OTHERS, SO THEY CAN ESCAPE THE FIRE RIGHT ABOUT NOW.
I DID POST A FEW OF MY MEN OUTSIDE AS A PRECAUTION, BUT...
...THEY'RE A USELESS LOT WITH LITTLE HOPE OF WINNING AGAINST YOUR MOUNTAIN-DWELLING BEAST FOLK.
UNDERSTAND? YOUR PRECIOUS VILLAGERS ARE ALIVE.
THEN WHY WOULD YOU...?
TO MAKE A DEAL WITH YOU.

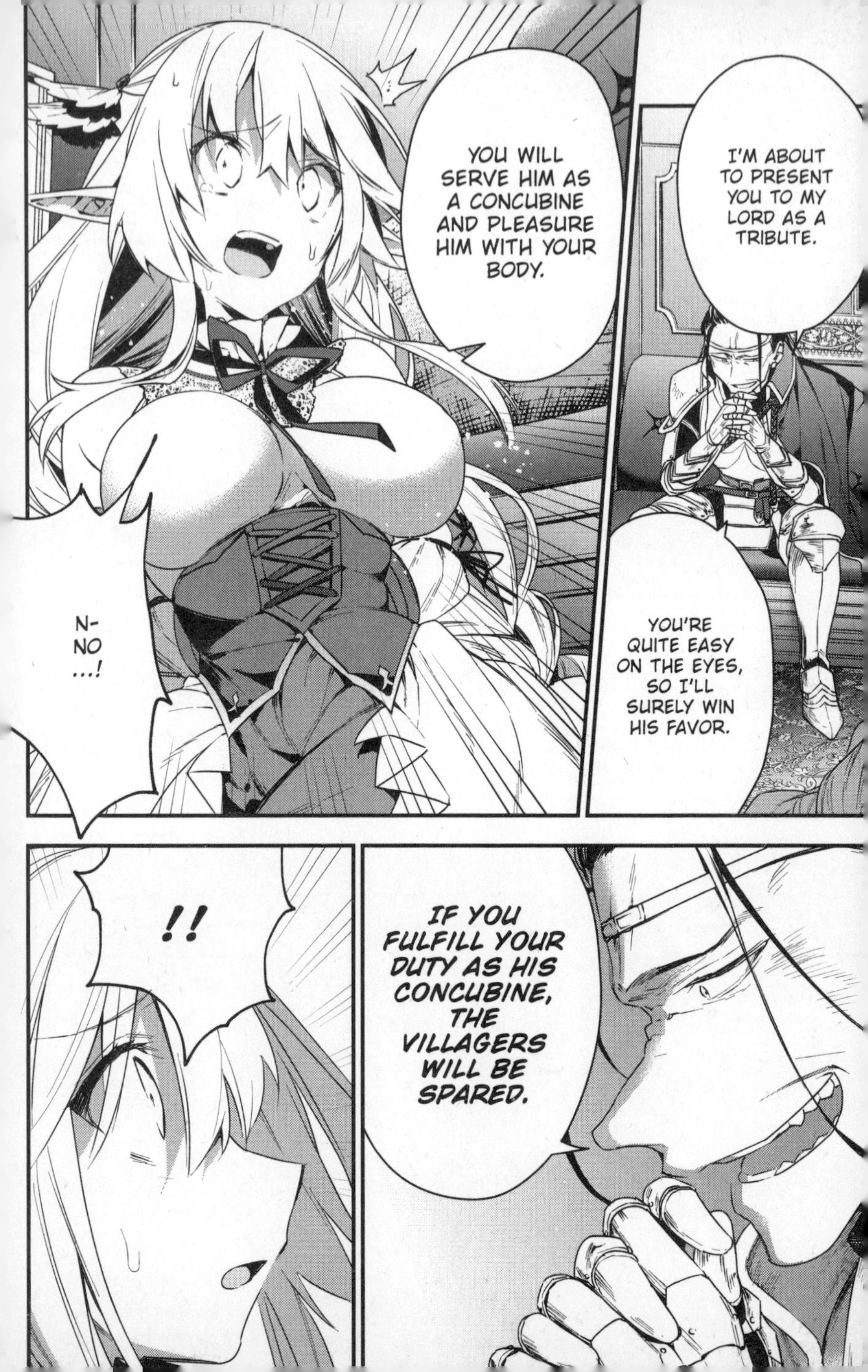
I'M ABOUT TO PRESENT YOU TO MY LORD AS A TRIBUTE.
YOU'RE QUITE EASY ON THE EYES, SO I'LL SURELY WIN HIS FAVOR.
YOU WILL SERVE HIM AS A CONCUBINE AND PLEASURE HIM WITH YOUR BODY.
N-NO ...!
IF YOU FULFILL YOUR DUTY AS HIS CONCUBINE, THE VILLAGERS WILL BE SPARED.
!!

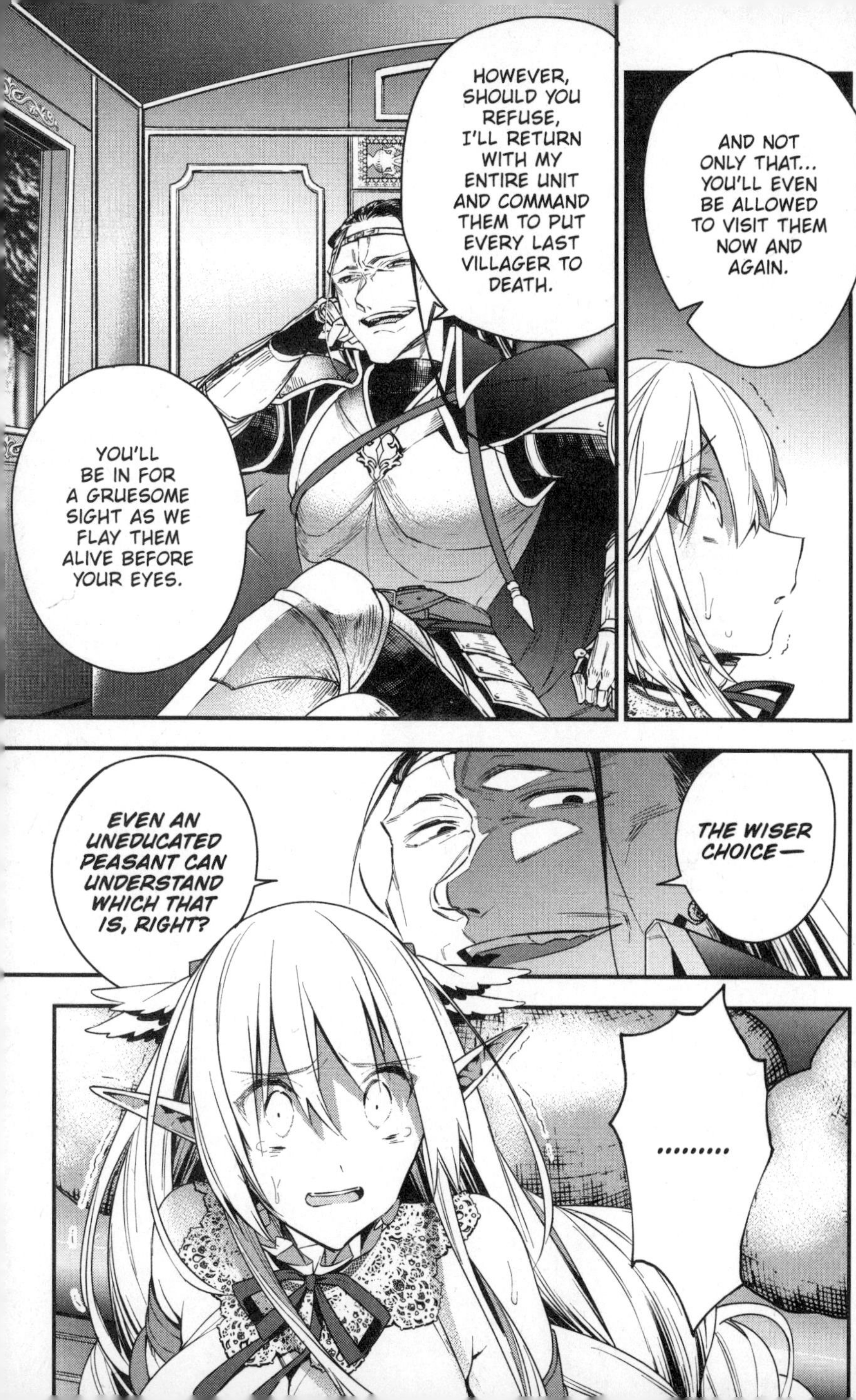
AND NOT ONLY THAT... YOU'LL EVEN BE ALLOWED TO VISIT THEM NOW AND AGAIN.
HOWEVER, SHOULD YOU REFUSE, I'LL RETURN WITH MY ENTIRE UNIT AND COMMAND THEM TO PUT EVERY LAST VILLAGER TO DEATH.
YOU'LL BE IN FOR A GRUESOME SIGHT AS WE FLAY THEM ALIVE BEFORE YOUR EYES.
THE WISER CHOICE—
EVEN AN UNEDUCATED PEASANT CAN UNDERSTAND WHICH THAT IS, RIGHT?
....

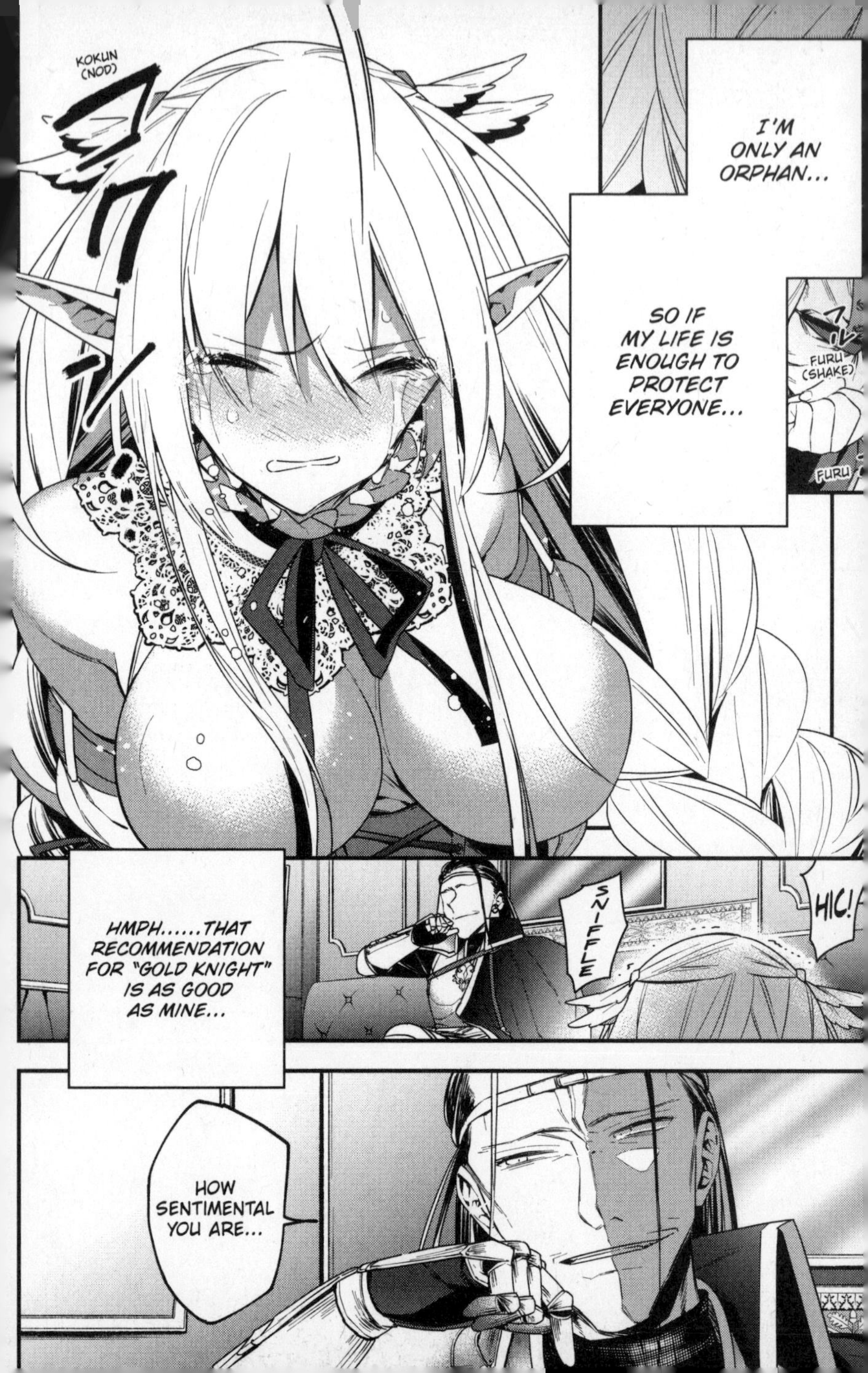
I'M ONLY AN ORPHAN...
SO IF MY LIFE IS ENOUGH TO PROTECT EVERYONE...
FURU (SHAKE)
FURU
KOKUN (NOD)
HIC!
SNIFFLE
HMPH......THAT RECOMMENDATION FOR "GOLD KNIGHT" IS AS GOOD AS MINE...
HOW SENTIMENTAL YOU ARE...

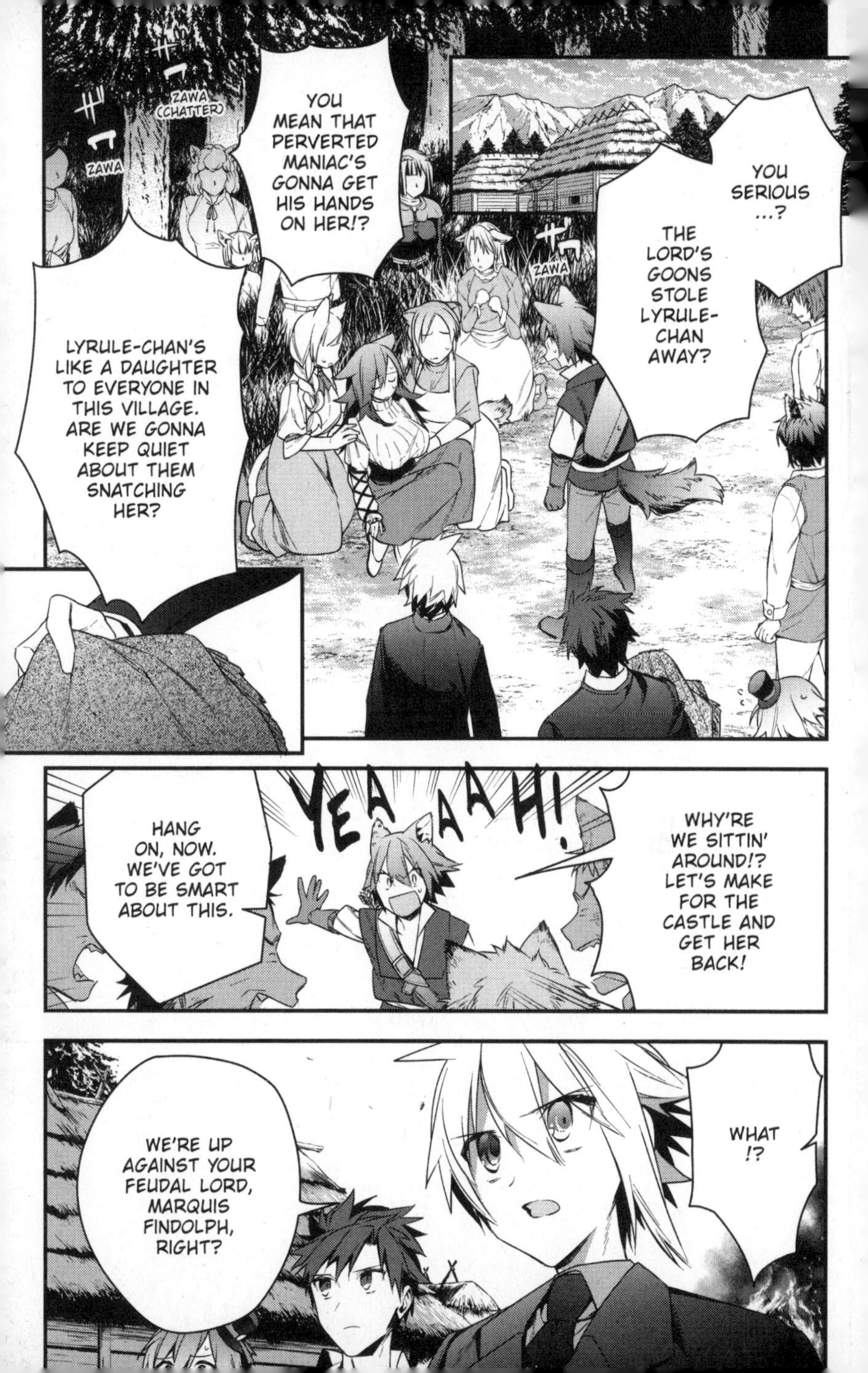
YOU SERIOUS ...?
THE LORD'S GOONS STOLE LYRULE-CHAN AWAY?
ZAWA
ZAWA (CHATTER)
ZAWA
YOU MEAN THAT PERVERTED MANIAC'S GONNA GET HIS HANDS ON HER!?
LYRULE-CHAN'S LIKE A DAUGHTER TO EVERYONE IN THIS VILLAGE. ARE WE GONNA KEEP QUIET ABOUT THEM SNATCHING HER?
WHY'RE WE SITTIN' AROUND!? LET'S MAKE FOR THE CASTLE AND GET HER BACK!
YEAAAH!
HANG ON, NOW. WE'VE GOT TO BE SMART ABOUT THIS.
WHAT!?
WE'RE UP AGAINST YOUR FEUDAL LORD, MARQUIS FINDOLPH, RIGHT?

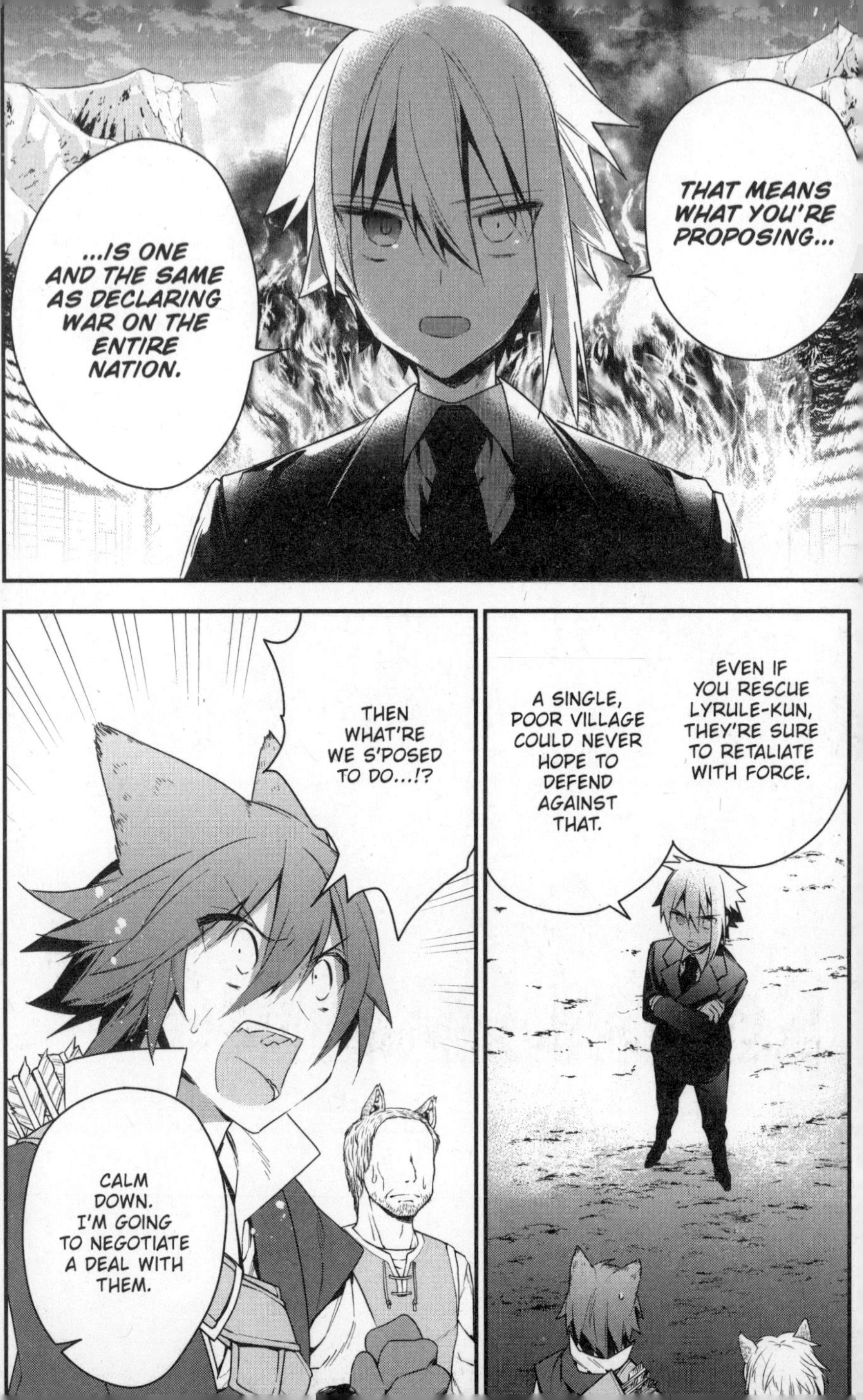
THAT MEANS WHAT YOU'RE PROPOSING...
...IS ONE AND THE SAME AS DECLARING WAR ON THE ENTIRE NATION.
EVEN IF YOU RESCUE LYRULE-KUN, THEY'RE SURE TO RETALIATE WITH FORCE.
A SINGLE, POOR VILLAGE COULD NEVER HOPE TO DEFEND AGAINST THAT.
THEN WHAT'RE WE S'POSED TO DO...!?
CALM DOWN. I'M GOING TO NEGOTIATE A DEAL WITH THEM.

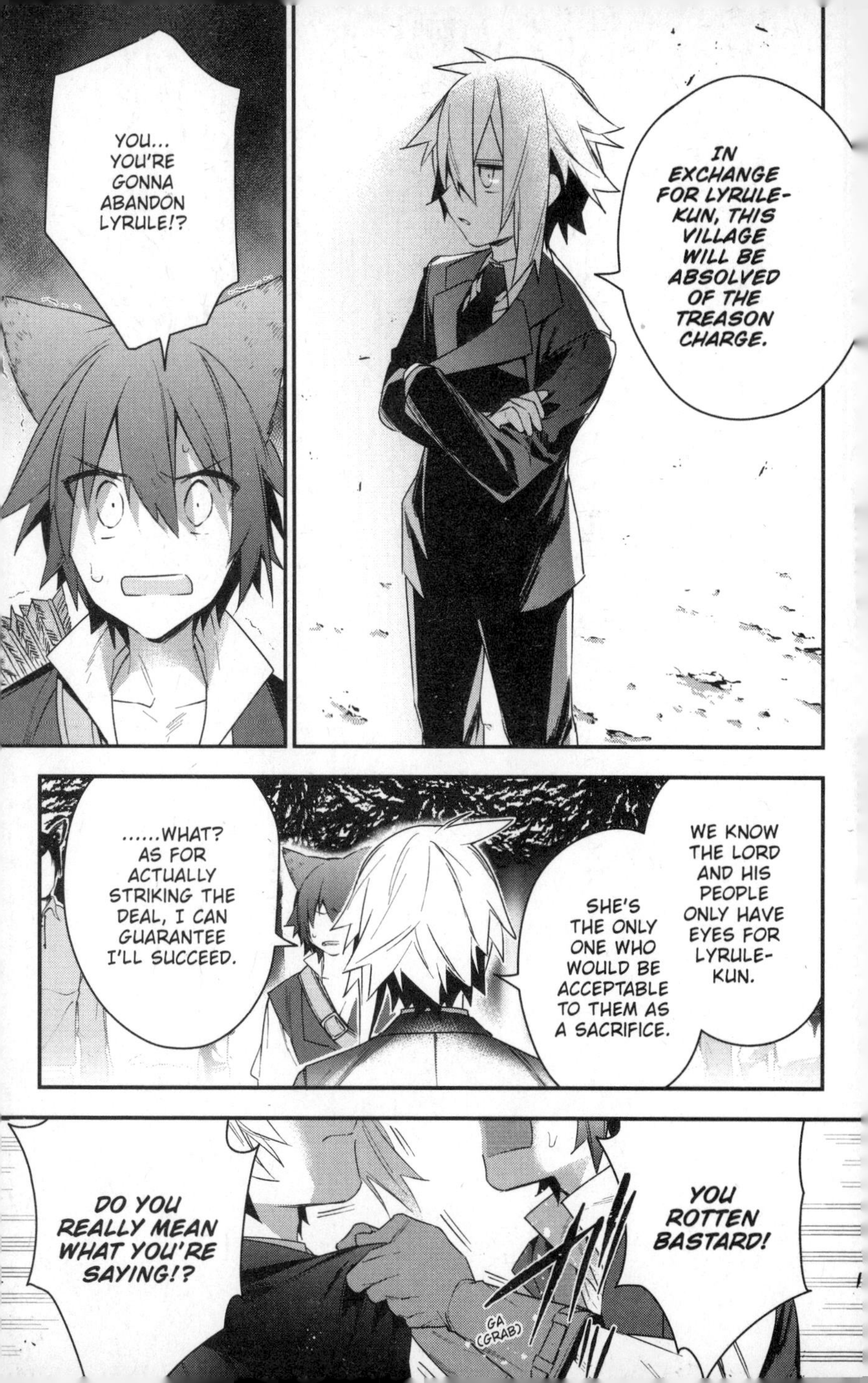
IN EXCHANGE FOR LYRULE-KUN, THIS VILLAGE WILL BE ABSOLVED OF THE TREASON CHARGE.
YOU... YOU'RE GONNA ABANDON LYRULE!?
WE KNOW THE LORD AND HIS PEOPLE ONLY HAVE EYES FOR LYRULE-KUN.
SHE'S THE ONLY ONE WHO WOULD BE ACCEPTABLE TO THEM AS A SACRIFICE.
......WHAT? AS FOR ACTUALLY STRIKING THE DEAL, I CAN GUARANTEE I'LL SUCCEED.
YOU ROTTEN BASTARD!
GA (GRAB)
DO YOU REALLY MEAN WHAT YOU'RE SAYING!?

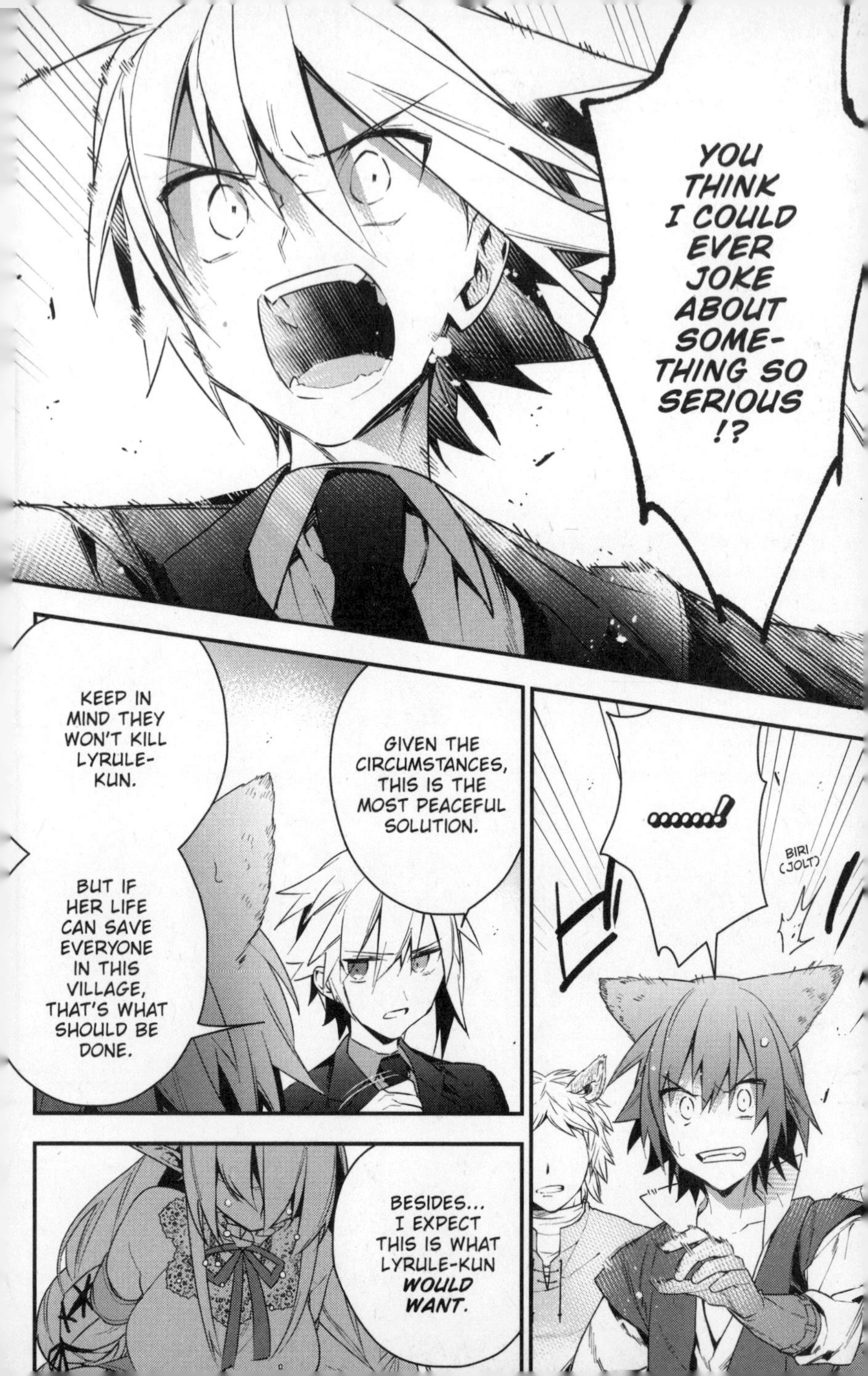
YOU THINK I COULD EVER JOKE ABOUT SOME-THING SO SERIOUS !?
......!
BIRI (JOLT)
GIVEN THE CIRCUMSTANCES, THIS IS THE MOST PEACEFUL SOLUTION.
KEEP IN MIND THEY WON'T KILL LYRULE-KUN.
BUT IF HER LIFE CAN SAVE EVERYONE IN THIS VILLAGE, THAT'S WHAT SHOULD BE DONE.
BESIDES... I EXPECT THIS IS WHAT LYRULE-KUN *WOULD WANT*.

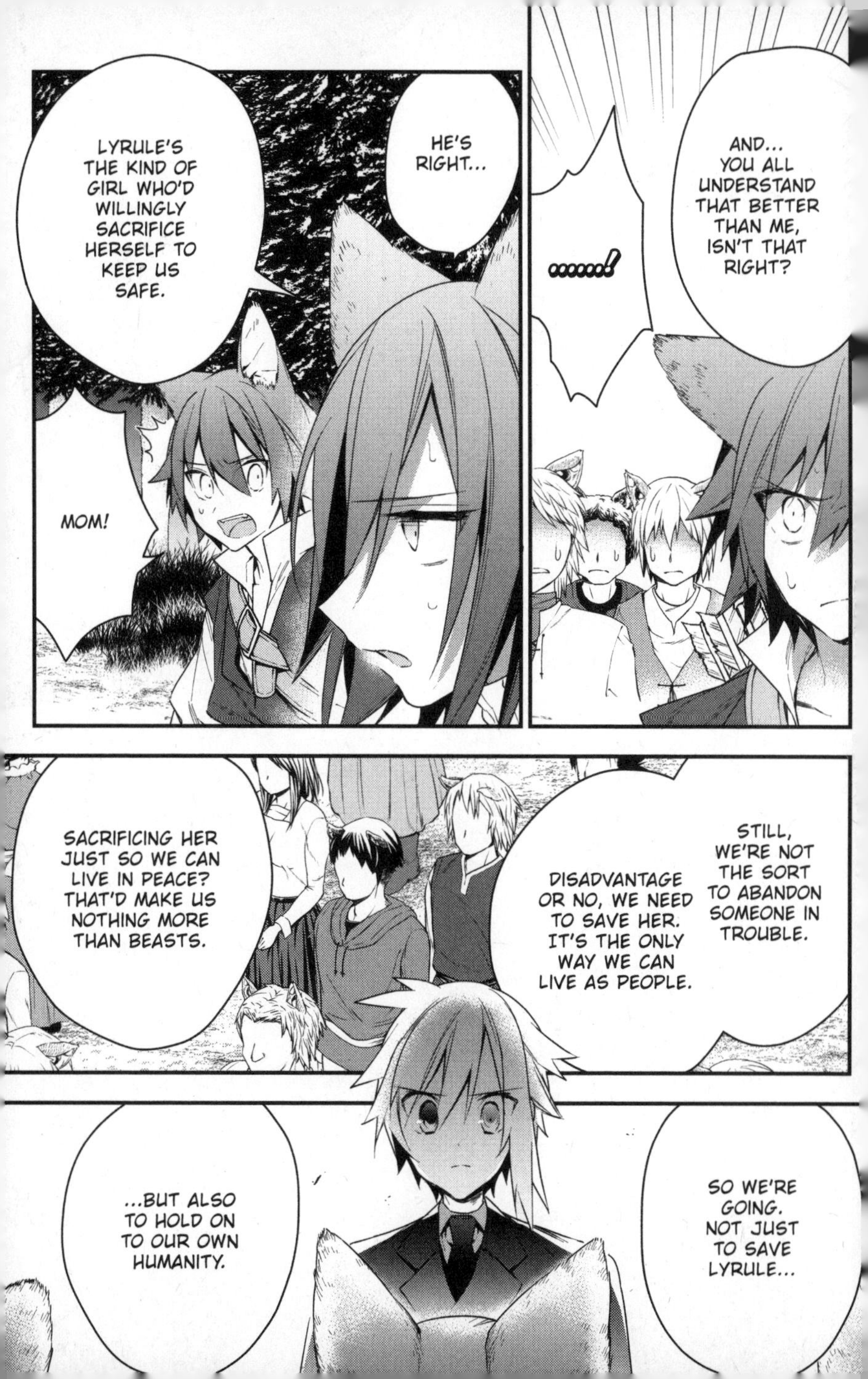
AND... YOU ALL UNDERSTAND THAT BETTER THAN ME, ISN'T THAT RIGHT?
......!
HE'S RIGHT...
LYRULE'S THE KIND OF GIRL WHO'D WILLINGLY SACRIFICE HERSELF TO KEEP US SAFE.
MOM!
STILL, WE'RE NOT THE SORT TO ABANDON SOMEONE IN TROUBLE.
DISADVANTAGE OR NO, WE NEED TO SAVE HER. IT'S THE ONLY WAY WE CAN LIVE AS PEOPLE.
SACRIFICING HER JUST SO WE CAN LIVE IN PEACE? THAT'D MAKE US NOTHING MORE THAN BEASTS.
SO WE'RE GOING. NOT JUST TO SAVE LYRULE...
...BUT ALSO TO HOLD ON TO OUR OWN HUMANITY.

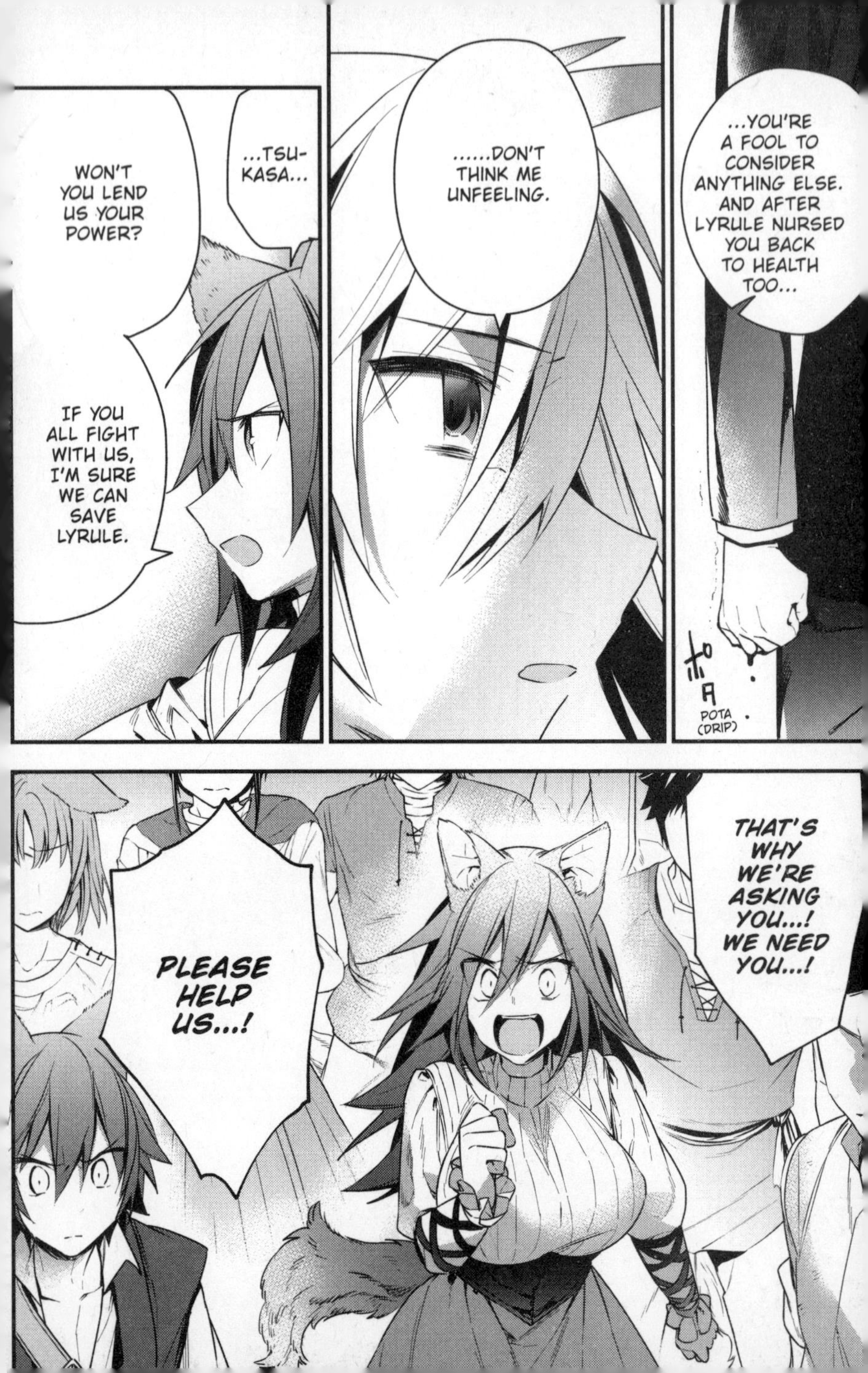
...YOU'RE A FOOL TO CONSIDER ANYTHING ELSE. AND AFTER LYRULE NURSED YOU BACK TO HEALTH TOO...
POTA (DRIP)
......DON'T THINK ME UNFEELING.
...TSU-KASA...
WON'T YOU LEND US YOUR POWER?
IF YOU ALL FIGHT WITH US, I'M SURE WE CAN SAVE LYRULE.
THAT'S WHY WE'RE ASKING YOU...! WE NEED YOU...!
PLEASE HELP US...!

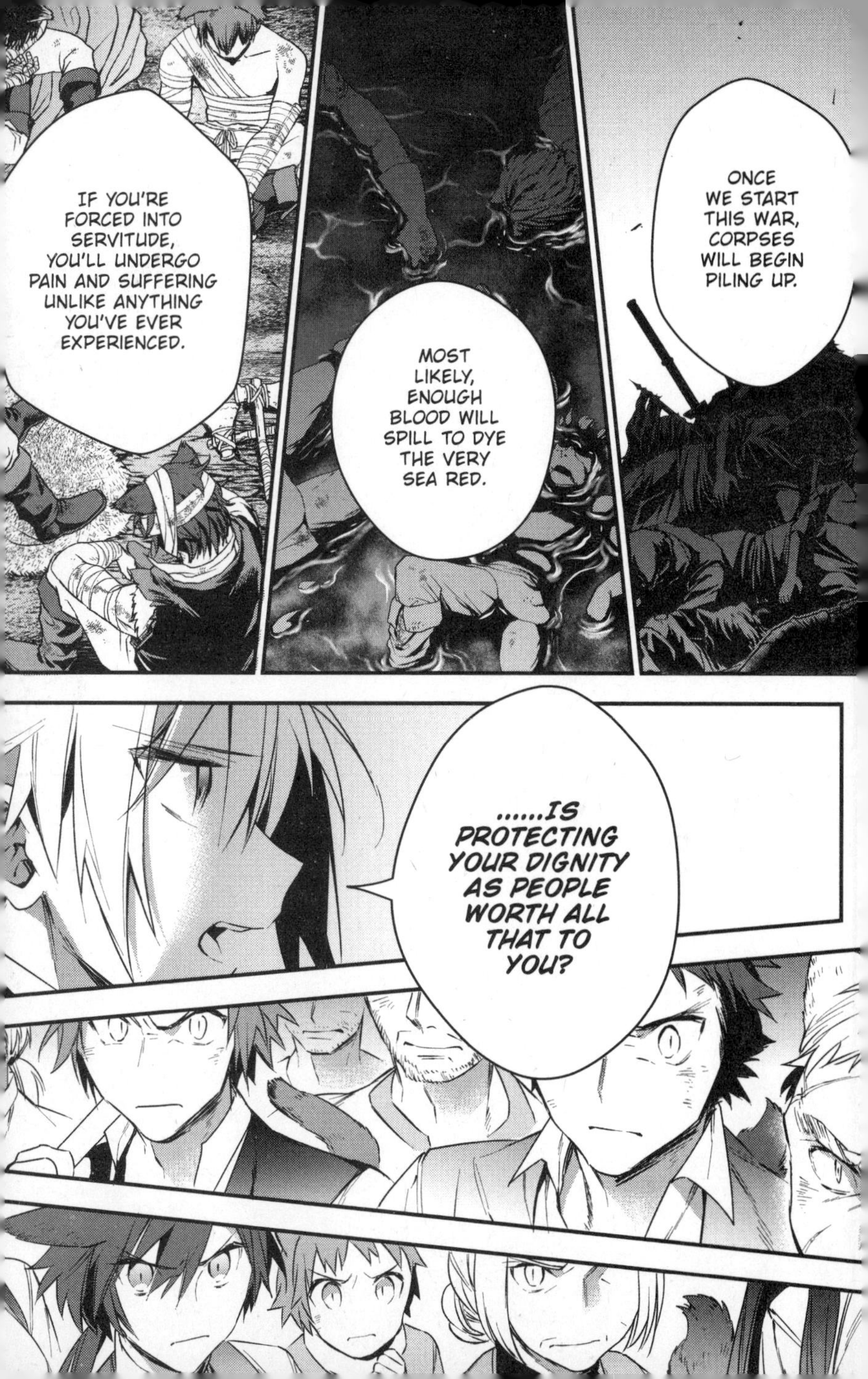
ONCE WE START THIS WAR, CORPSES WILL BEGIN PILING UP.
MOST LIKELY, ENOUGH BLOOD WILL SPILL TO DYE THE VERY SEA RED.
IF YOU'RE FORCED INTO SERVITUDE, YOU'LL UNDERGO PAIN AND SUFFERING UNLIKE ANYTHING YOU'VE EVER EXPERIENCED.
......IS PROTECTING YOUR DIGNITY AS PEOPLE WORTH ALL THAT TO YOU?

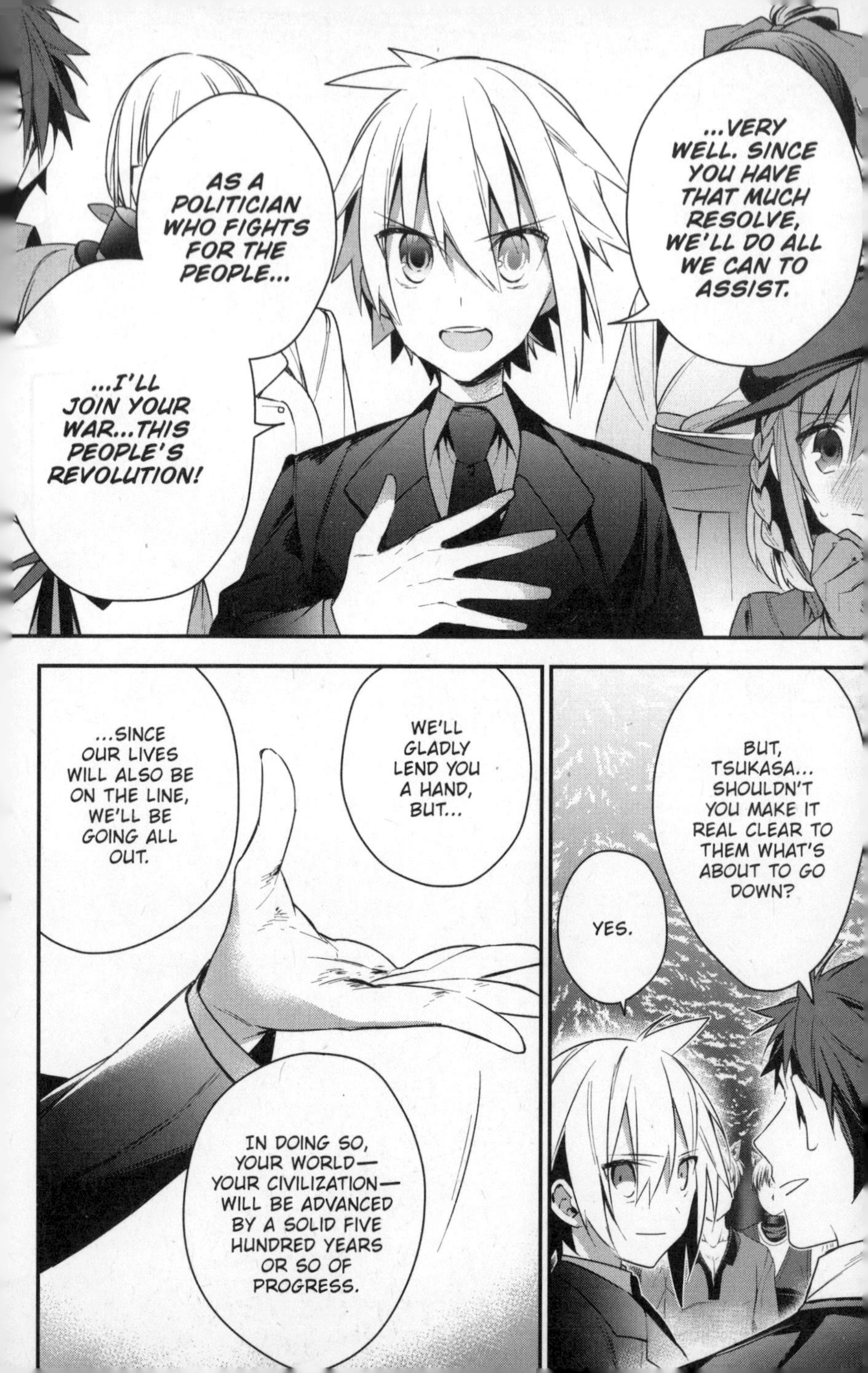
AS A POLITICIAN WHO FIGHTS FOR THE PEOPLE...
...I'LL JOIN YOUR WAR...THIS PEOPLE'S REVOLUTION!
...VERY WELL. SINCE YOU HAVE THAT MUCH RESOLVE, WE'LL DO ALL WE CAN TO ASSIST.
BUT, TSUKASA... SHOULDN'T YOU MAKE IT REAL CLEAR TO THEM WHAT'S ABOUT TO GO DOWN?
YES.
WE'LL GLADLY LEND YOU A HAND, BUT...
...SINCE OUR LIVES WILL ALSO BE ON THE LINE, WE'LL BE GOING ALL OUT.
IN DOING SO, YOUR WORLD—YOUR CIVILIZATION—WILL BE ADVANCED BY A SOLID FIVE HUNDRED YEARS OR SO OF PROGRESS.

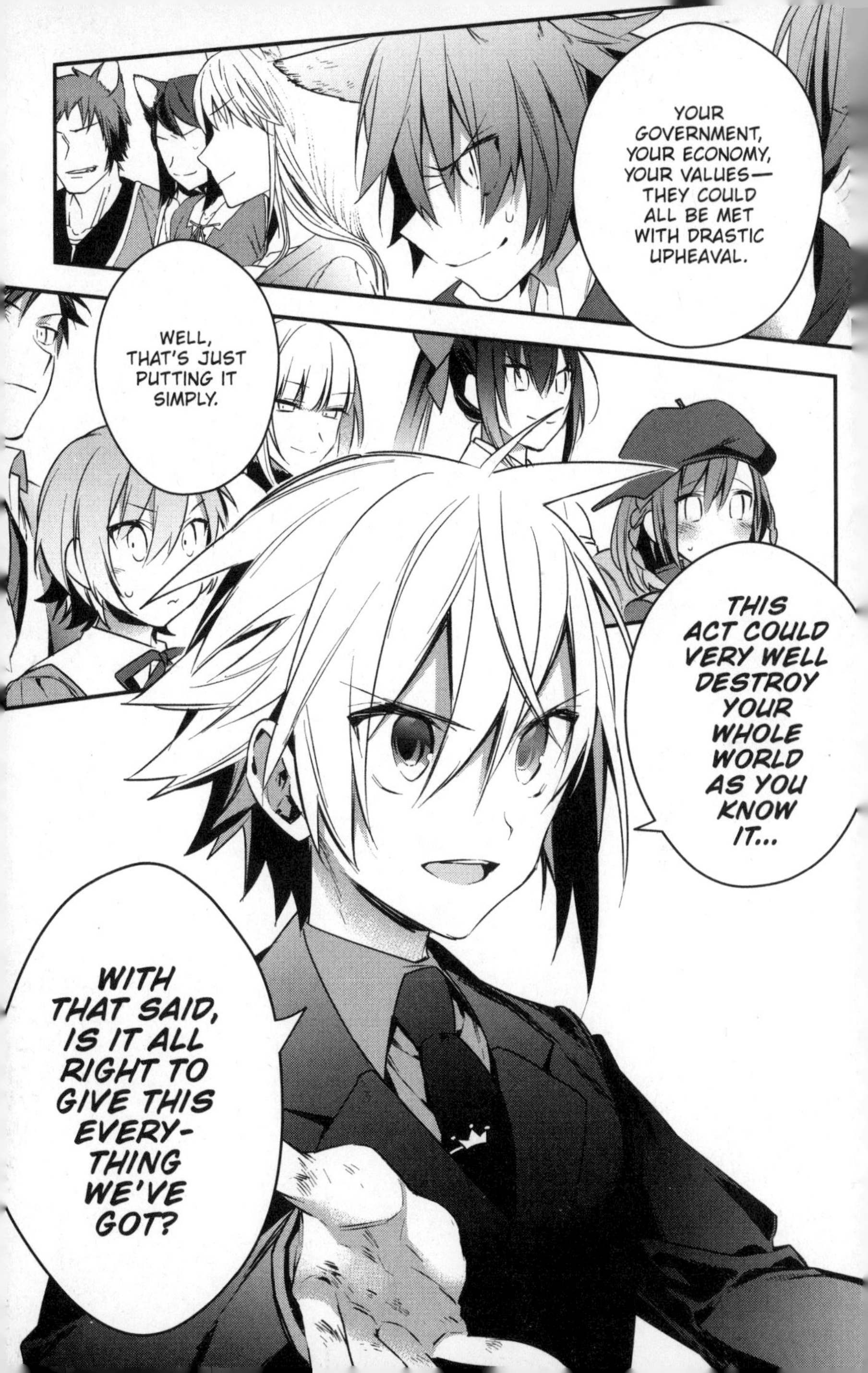
YOUR GOVERNMENT, YOUR ECONOMY, YOUR VALUES— THEY COULD ALL BE MET WITH DRASTIC UPHEAVAL.
WELL, THAT'S JUST PUTTING IT SIMPLY.
THIS ACT COULD VERY WELL DESTROY YOUR WHOLE WORLD AS YOU KNOW IT...
WITH THAT SAID, IS IT ALL RIGHT TO GIVE THIS EVERY-THING WE'VE GOT?

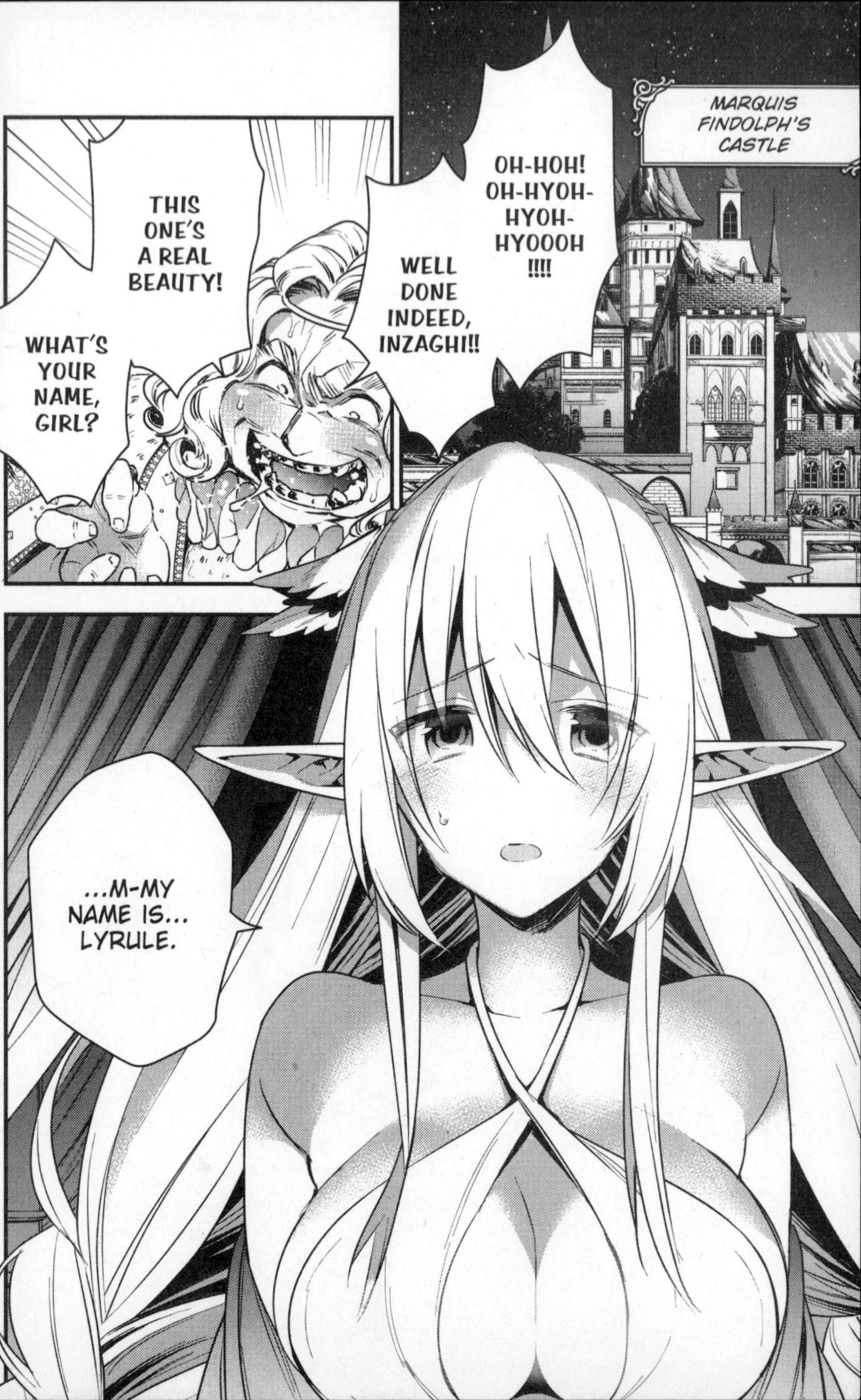
MARQUIS FINDOLPH'S CASTLE
OH-HOH! OH-HYOH-HYOH-HYOOOH!!!!
WELL DONE INDEED, INZAGHI!!
THIS ONE'S A REAL BEAUTY!
WHAT'S YOUR NAME, GIRL?
...M-MY NAME IS... LYRULE.

HIGH SCHOOL
PRODIGIES HAVE
IT EASY EVEN IN
ANOTHER
WORLD!

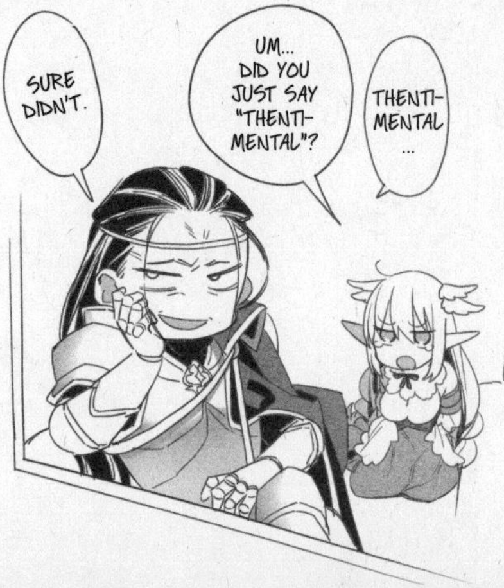
THENTI-MENTAL ...
UM... DID YOU JUST SAY "THENTI-MENTAL"?
SURE DIDN'T.

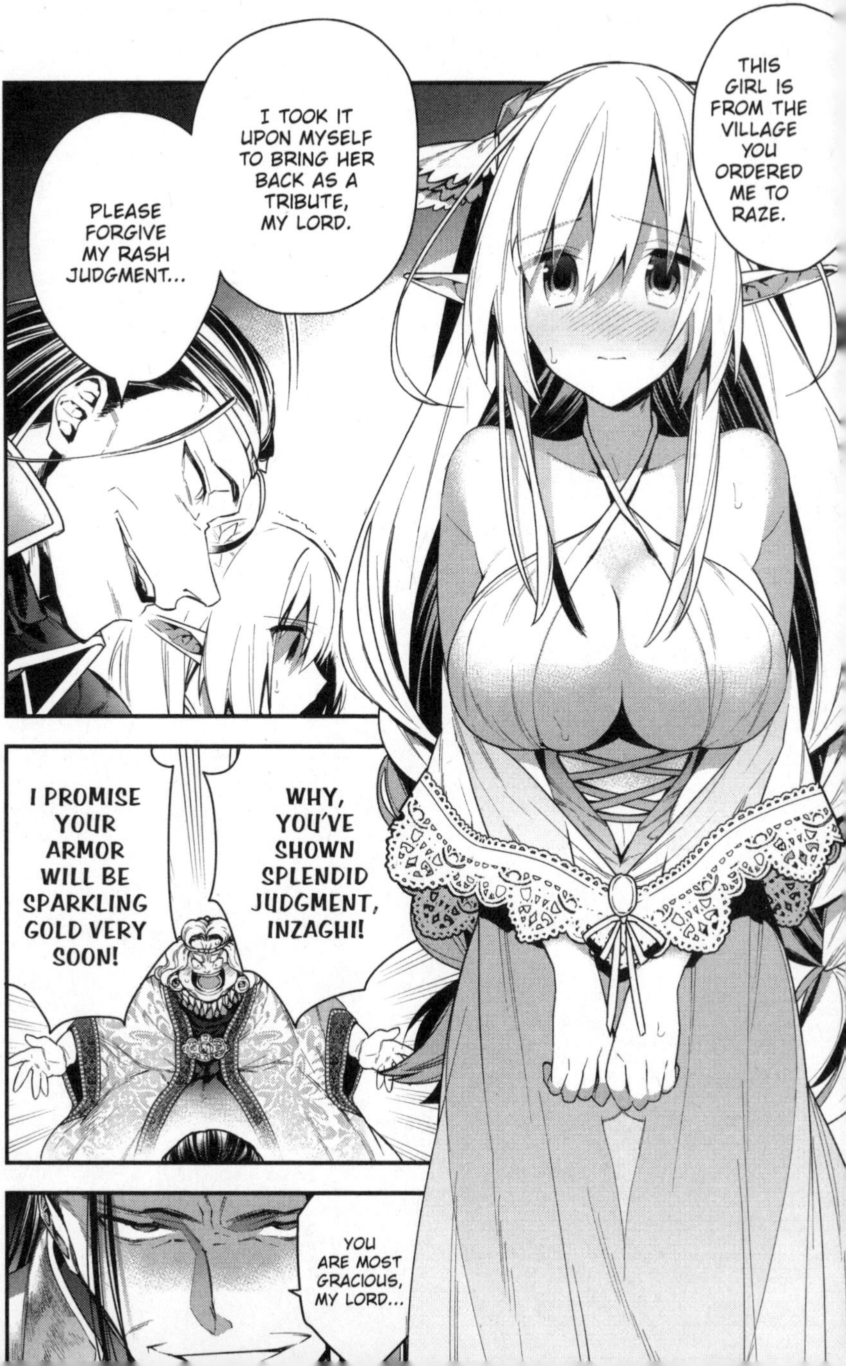
THIS GIRL IS FROM THE VILLAGE YOU ORDERED ME TO RAZE.
I TOOK IT UPON MYSELF TO BRING HER BACK AS A TRIBUTE, MY LORD.
PLEASE FORGIVE MY RASH JUDGMENT...
WHY, YOU'VE SHOWN SPLENDID JUDGMENT, INZAGHI!
I PROMISE YOUR ARMOR WILL BE SPARKLING GOLD VERY SOON!
YOU ARE MOST GRACIOUS, MY LORD...

CHAPTER 14: THE PEOPLE'S REVOLUTION AND THE HIGH SCHOOL PRODIGIES

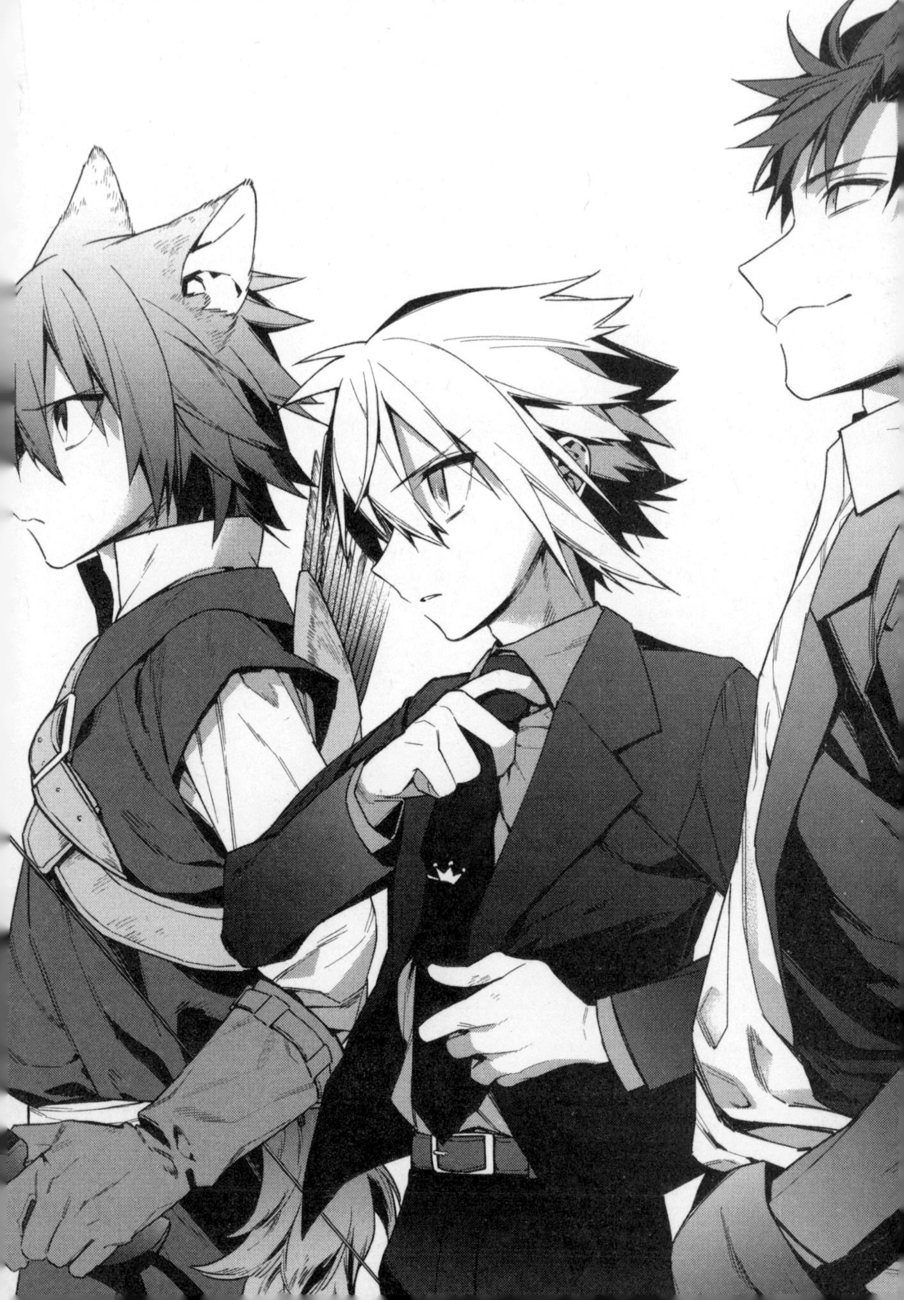

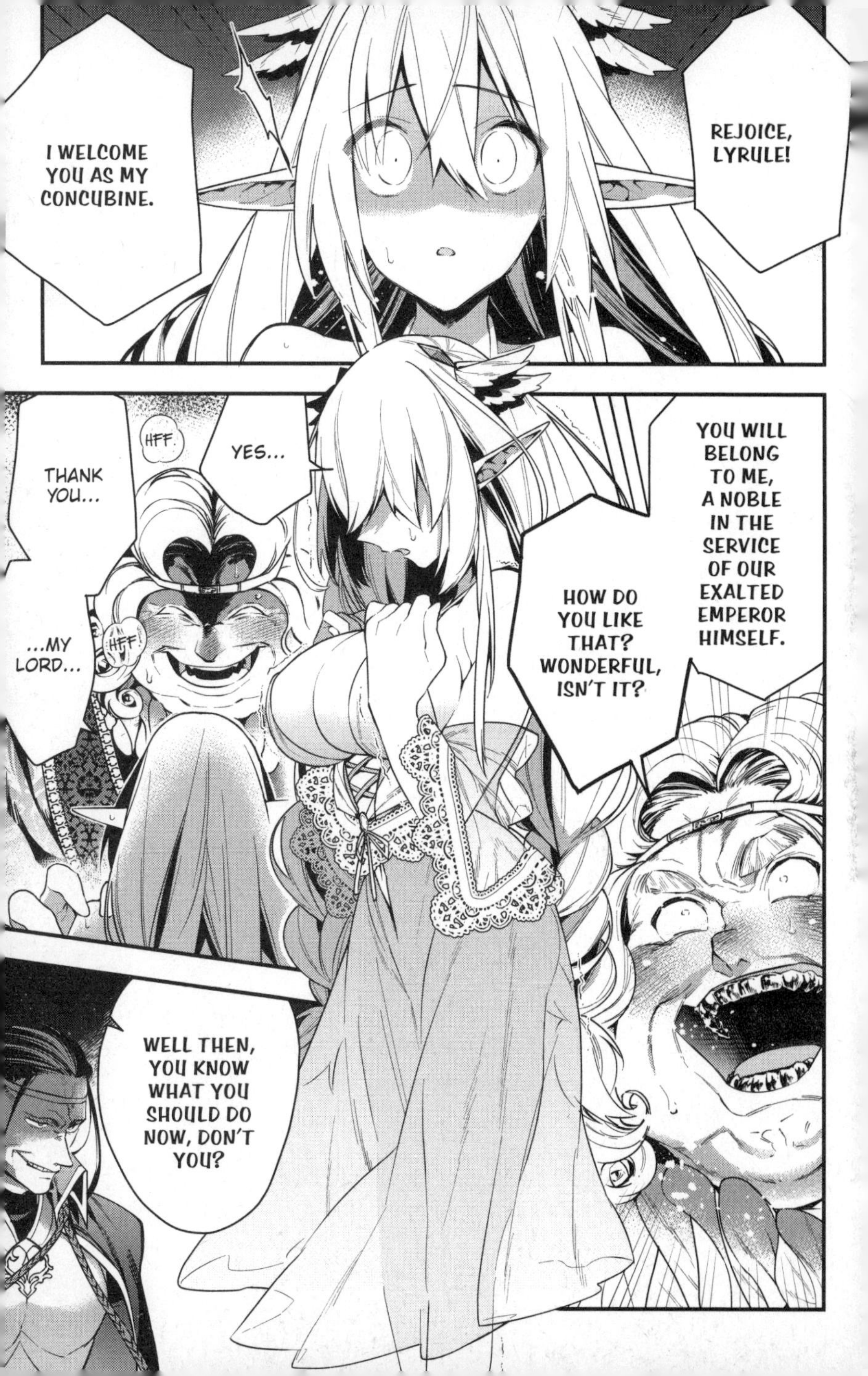
REJOICE, LYRULE!
I WELCOME YOU AS MY CONCUBINE.
YOU WILL BELONG TO ME, A NOBLE IN THE SERVICE OF OUR EXALTED EMPEROR HIMSELF.
HOW DO YOU LIKE THAT? WONDERFUL, ISN'T IT?
YES...
HFF.
THANK YOU...
HFF.
...MY LORD...
WELL THEN, YOU KNOW WHAT YOU SHOULD DO NOW, DON'T YOU?

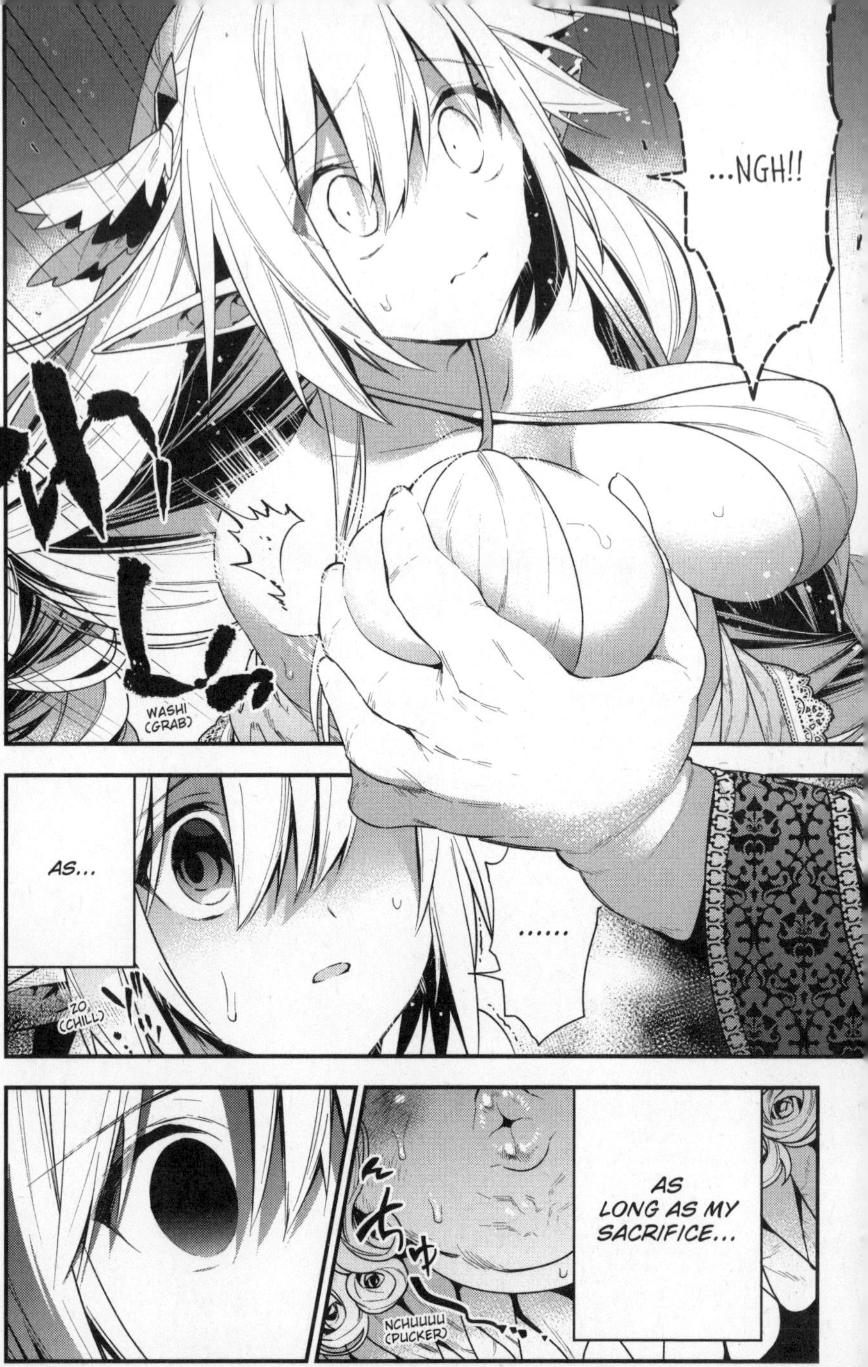
...NGH!!
WASHI (GRAB)
......
AS...
ZO (CHILL)
AS LONG AS MY SACRIFICE...
NCHUUUU (PUCKER)

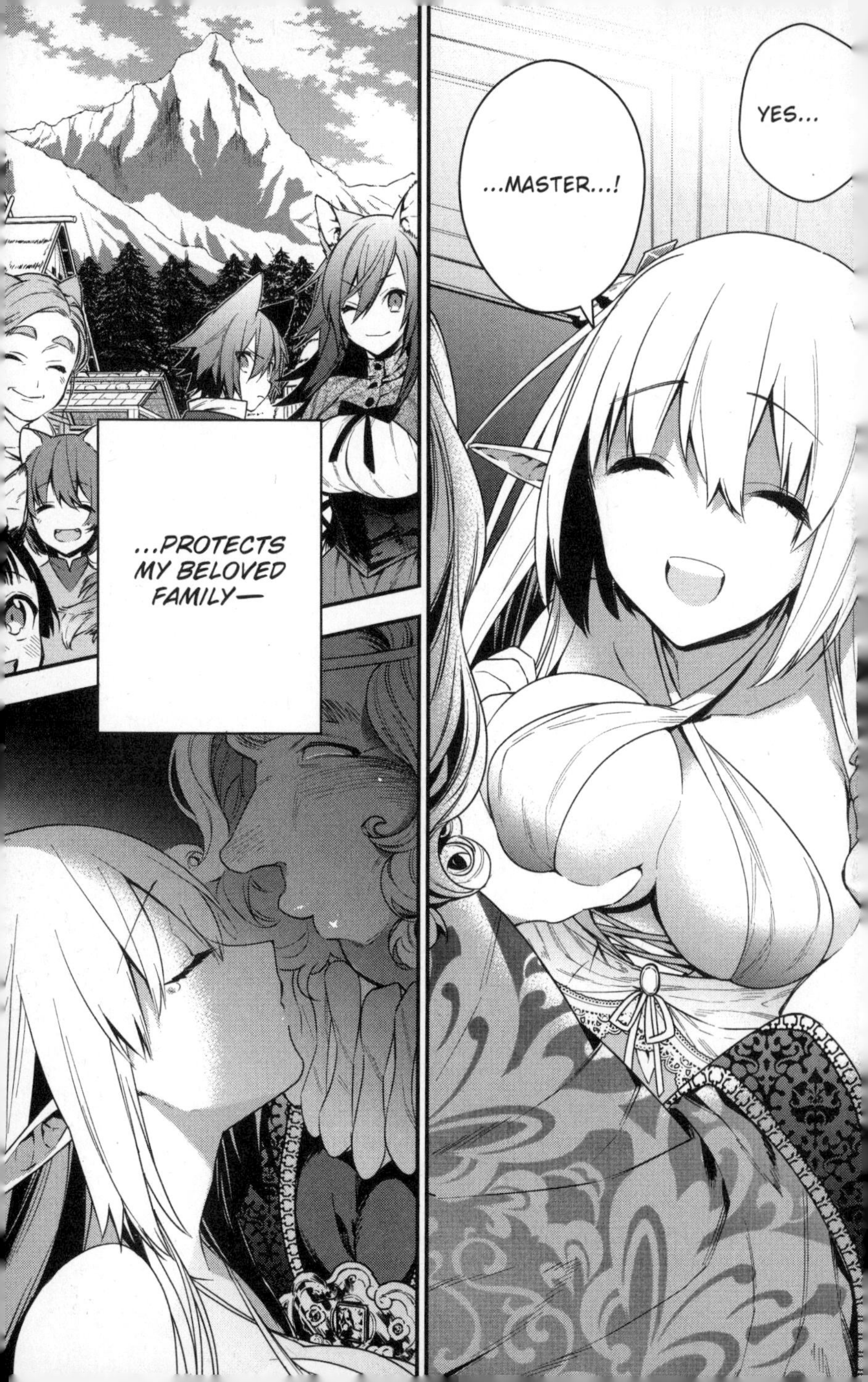
YES...
...MASTER...!
...PROTECTS MY BELOVED FAMILY—

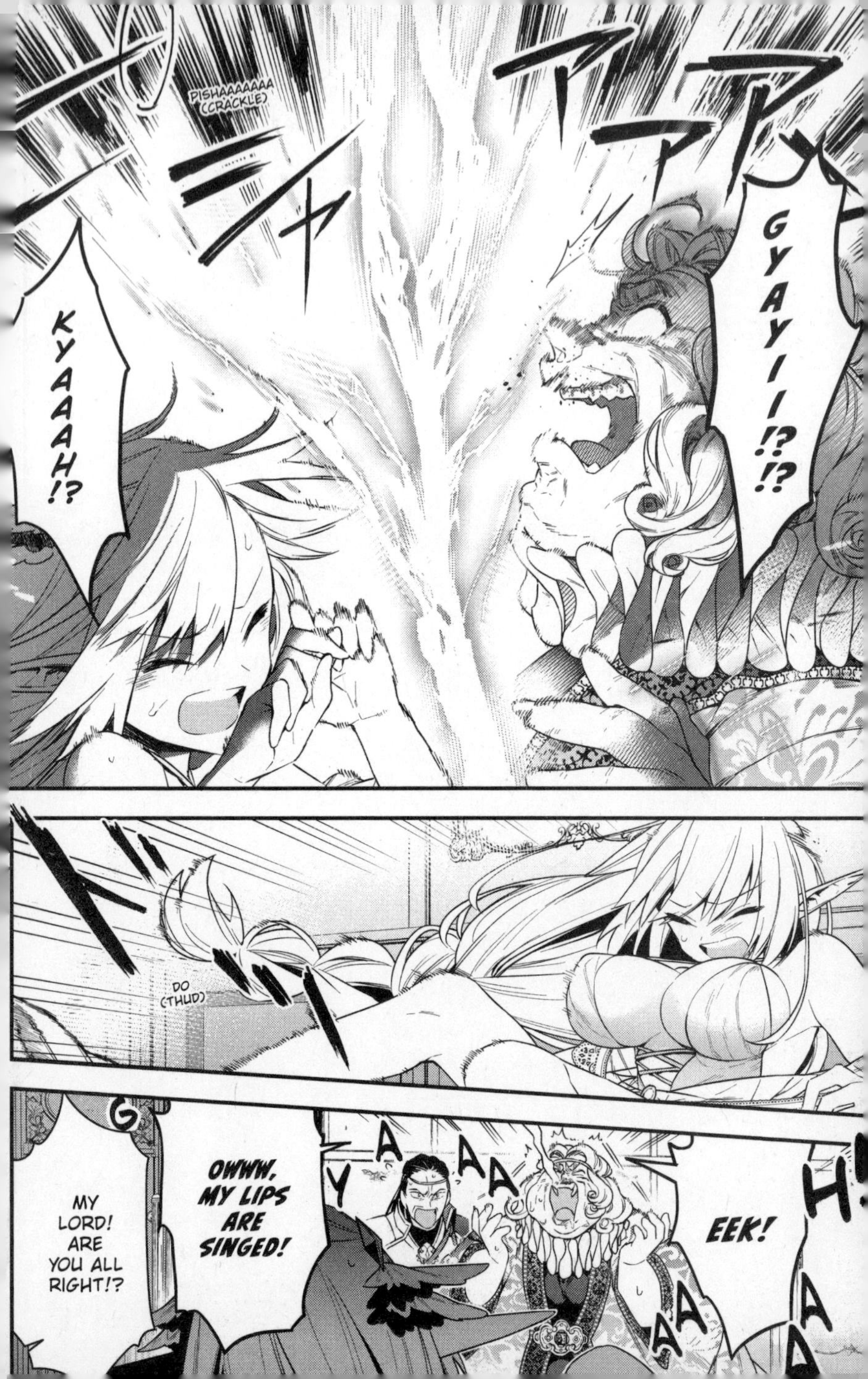
GYAYIII!?!?
PISHAAAAAAA (CRACKLE)
KYAAAAH!?
DO (THUD)
EEK!
OWWW, MY LIPS ARE SINGED!
MY LORD! ARE YOU ALL RIGHT!?

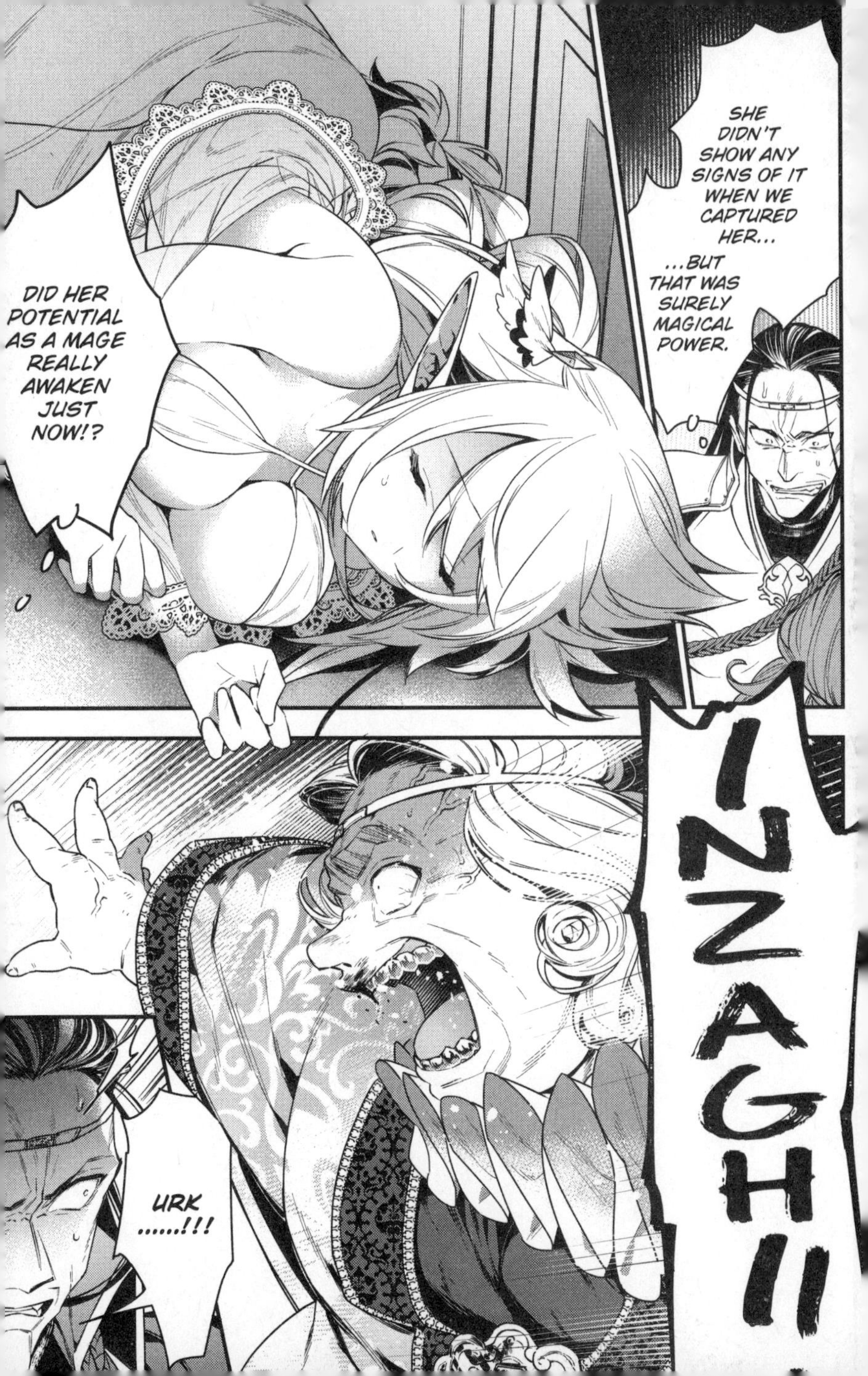
SHE DIDN'T SHOW ANY SIGNS OF IT WHEN WE CAPTURED HER...
...BUT THAT WAS SURELY MAGICAL POWER.
DID HER POTENTIAL AS A MAGE REALLY AWAKEN JUST NOW!?
INZAGH!!
URK ......!!!

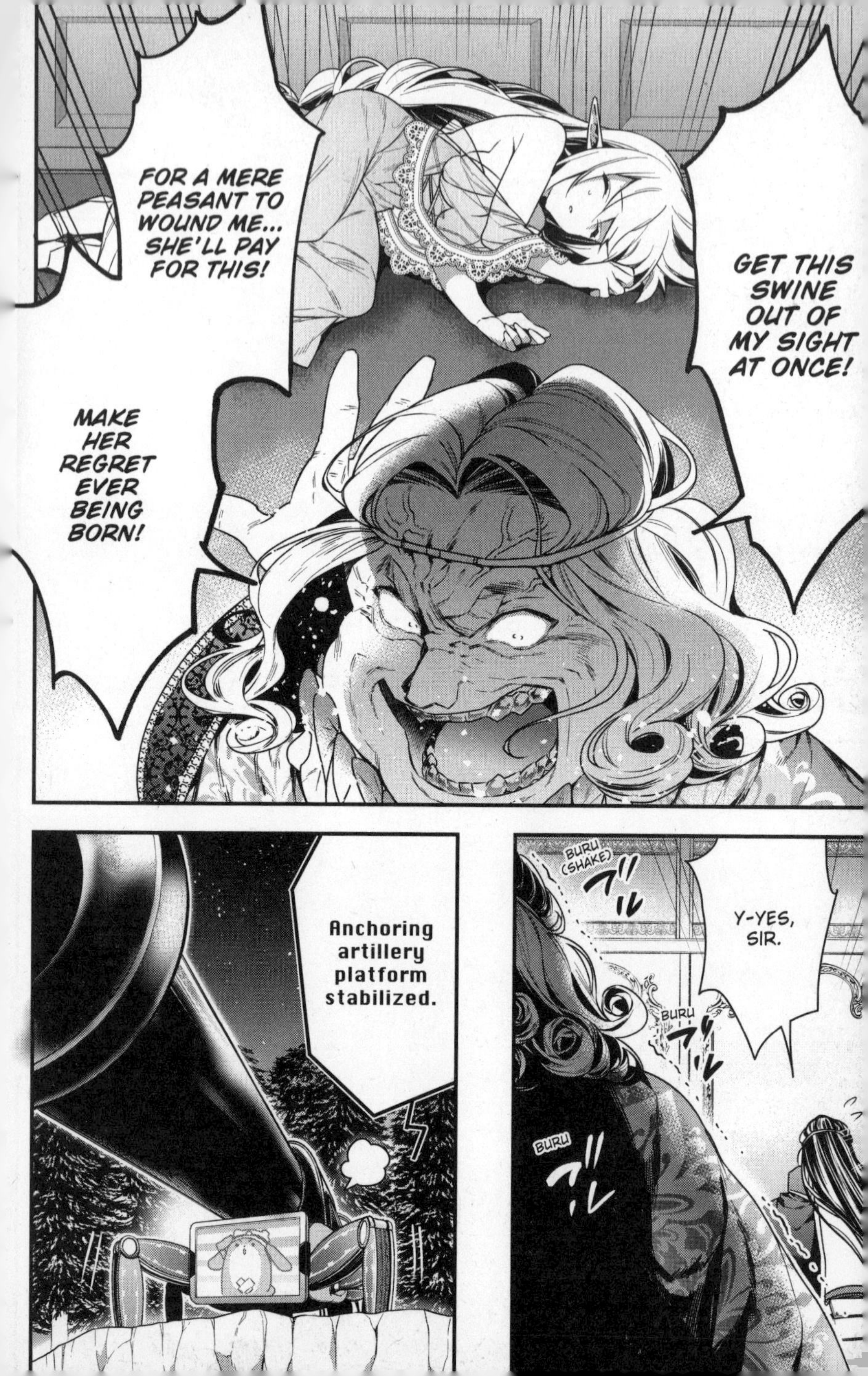
FOR A MERE PEASANT TO WOUND ME... SHE'LL PAY FOR THIS!
GET THIS SWINE OUT OF MY SIGHT AT ONCE!
MAKE HER REGRET EVER BEING BORN!
BURU (SHAKE)
ブル
Y-YES, SIR.
BURU
ブル
BURU
ブル
Anchoring artillery platform stabilized.

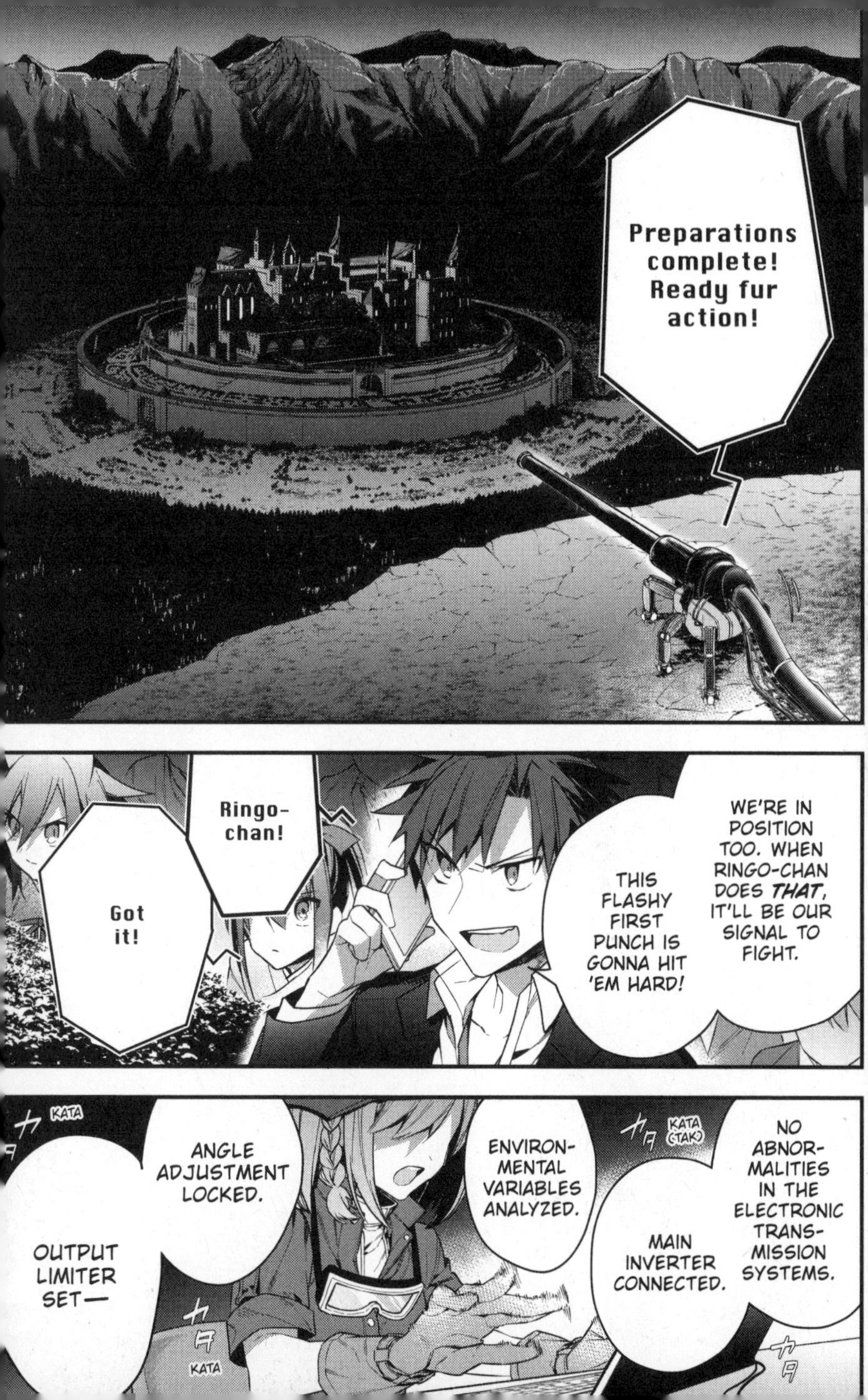
Preparations complete! Ready fur action!
WE'RE IN POSITION TOO. WHEN RINGO-CHAN DOES *THAT*, IT'LL BE OUR SIGNAL TO FIGHT.
THIS FLASHY FIRST PUNCH IS GONNA HIT 'EM HARD!
Ringo-chan!
Got it!
NO ABNORMALITIES IN THE ELECTRONIC TRANSMISSION SYSTEMS.
KATA (TAK)
MAIN INVERTER CONNECTED.
ENVIRONMENTAL VARIABLES ANALYZED.
ANGLE ADJUSTMENT LOCKED.
KATA
OUTPUT LIMITER SET—
KATA

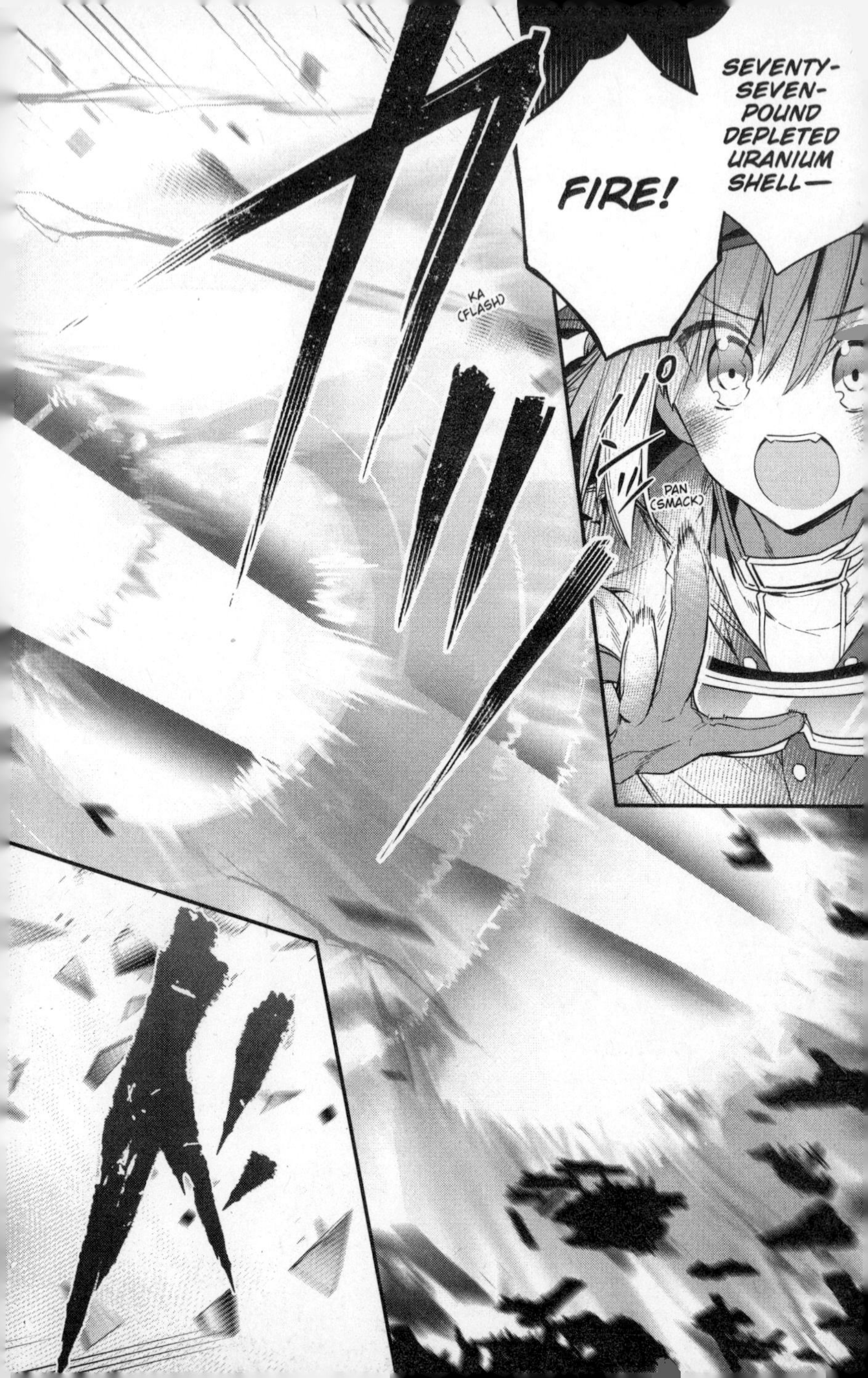
SEVENTY-SEVEN-POUND DEPLETED URANIUM SHELL—
FIRE!
PAN (SMACK)
KA (FLASH)

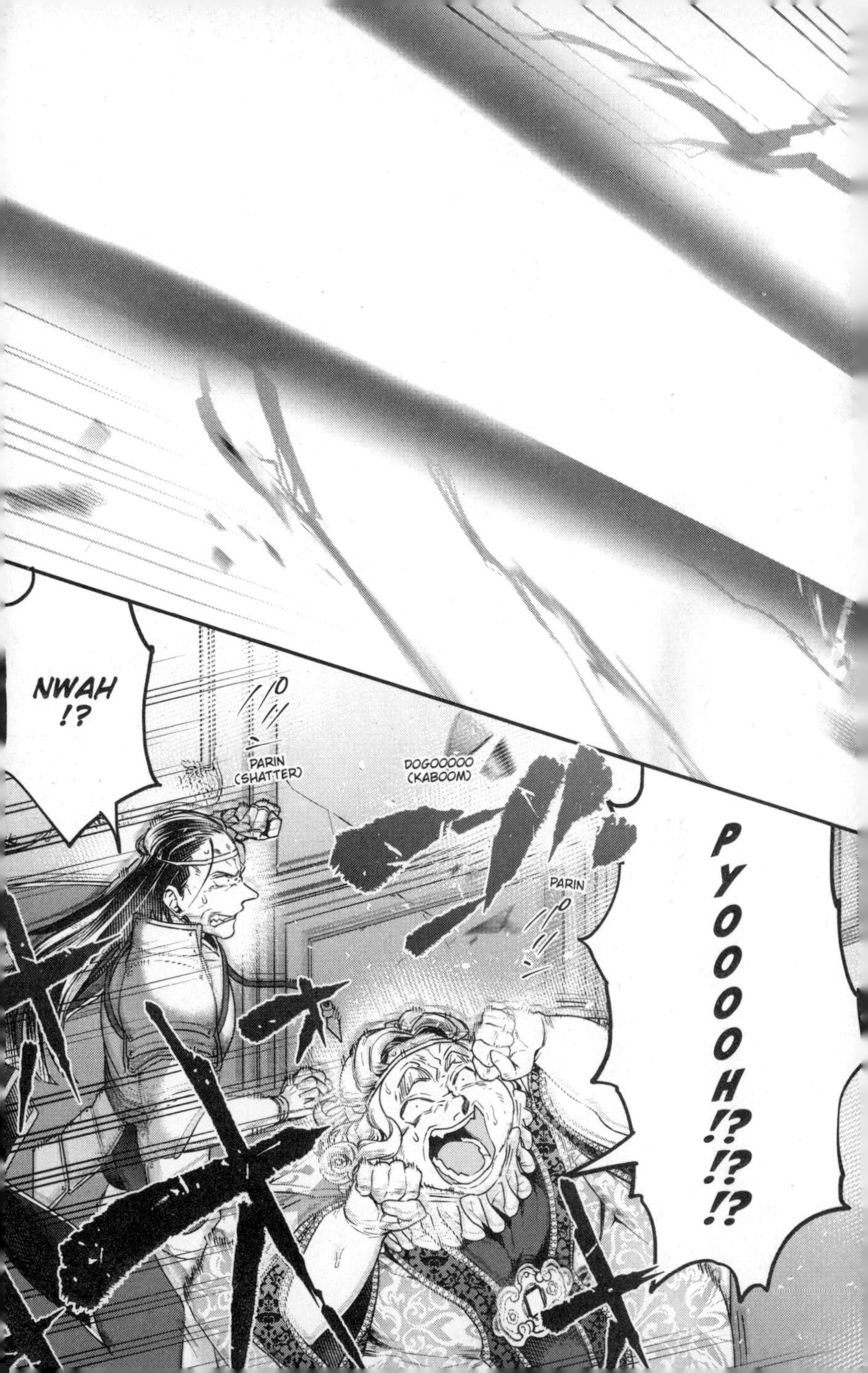
PYOOOOH!?!?!?
PARIN
DOGOOOOO (KABOOM)
PARIN (SHATTER)
NWAH!?

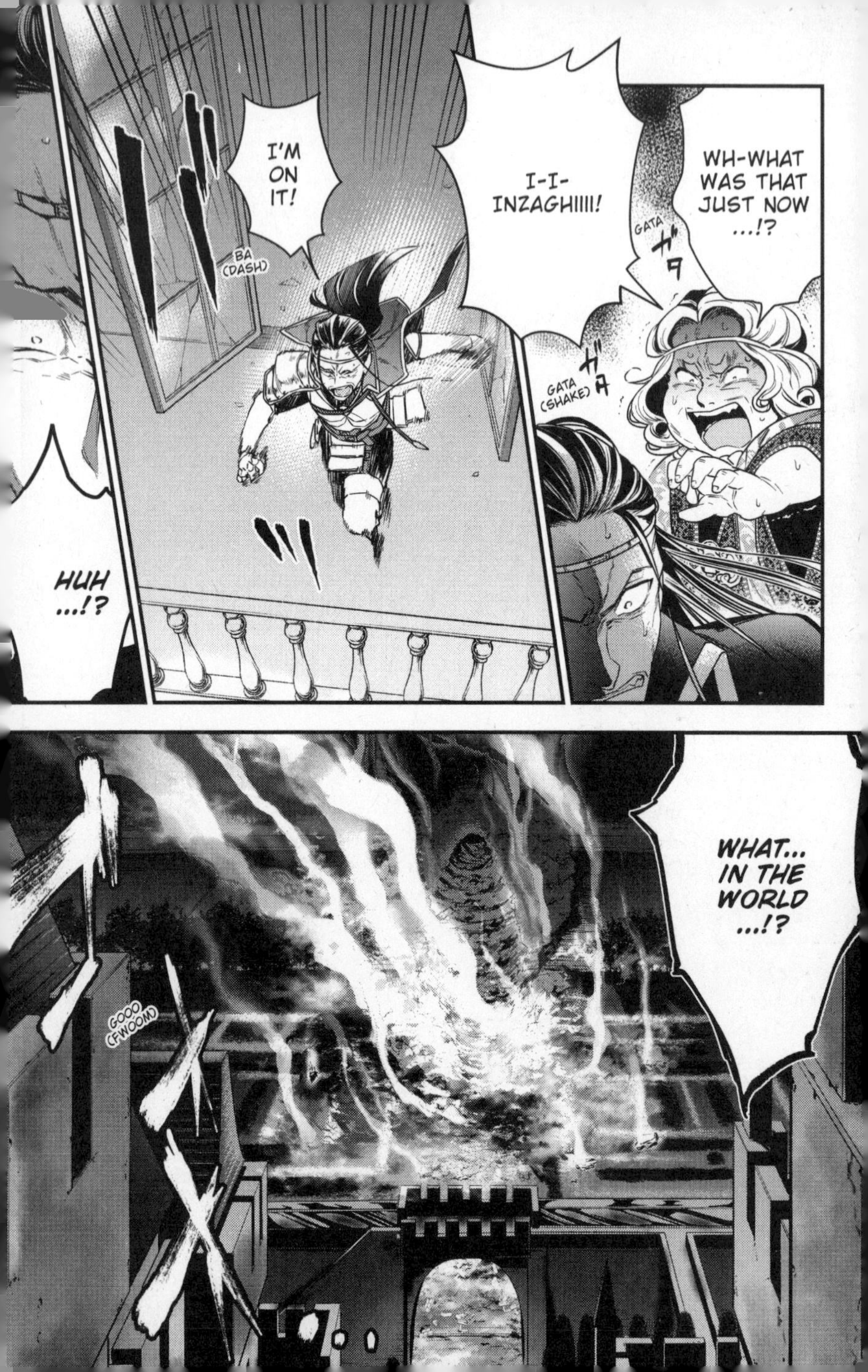
WH-WHAT WAS THAT JUST NOW ...!?
GATA
GATA (SHAKE)
I-I-INZAGHIIIII!
I'M ON IT!
BA (DASH)
HUH ...!?
WHAT... IN THE WORLD ...!?
GOOO (FWOOM)

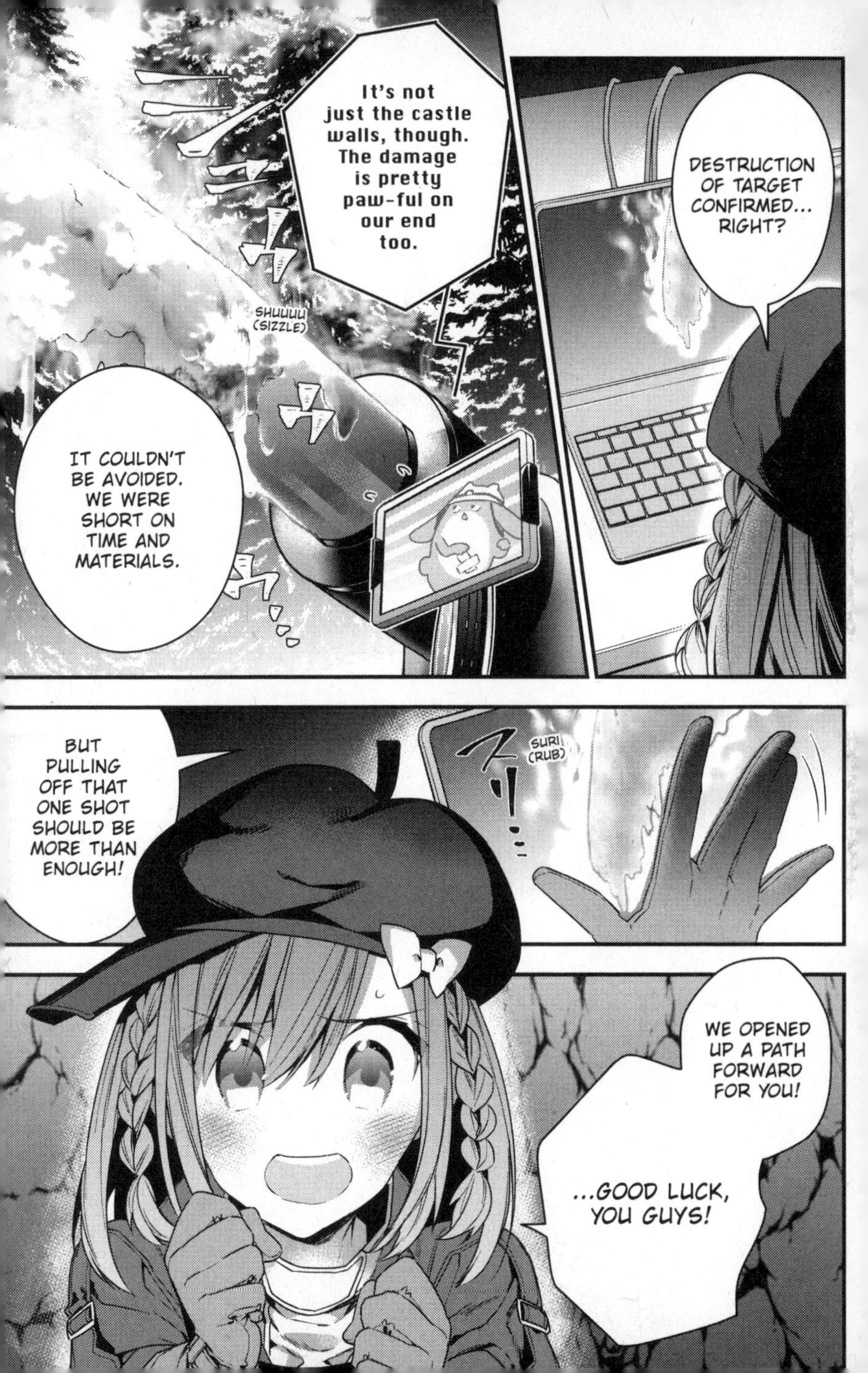
DESTRUCTION OF TARGET CONFIRMED... RIGHT?
It's not just the castle walls, though. The damage is pretty paw-ful on our end too.
SHUUUU (SIZZLE)
IT COULDN'T BE AVOIDED. WE WERE SHORT ON TIME AND MATERIALS.
SURI (RUB)
BUT PULLING OFF THAT ONE SHOT SHOULD BE MORE THAN ENOUGH!
WE OPENED UP A PATH FORWARD FOR YOU!
...GOOD LUCK, YOU GUYS!

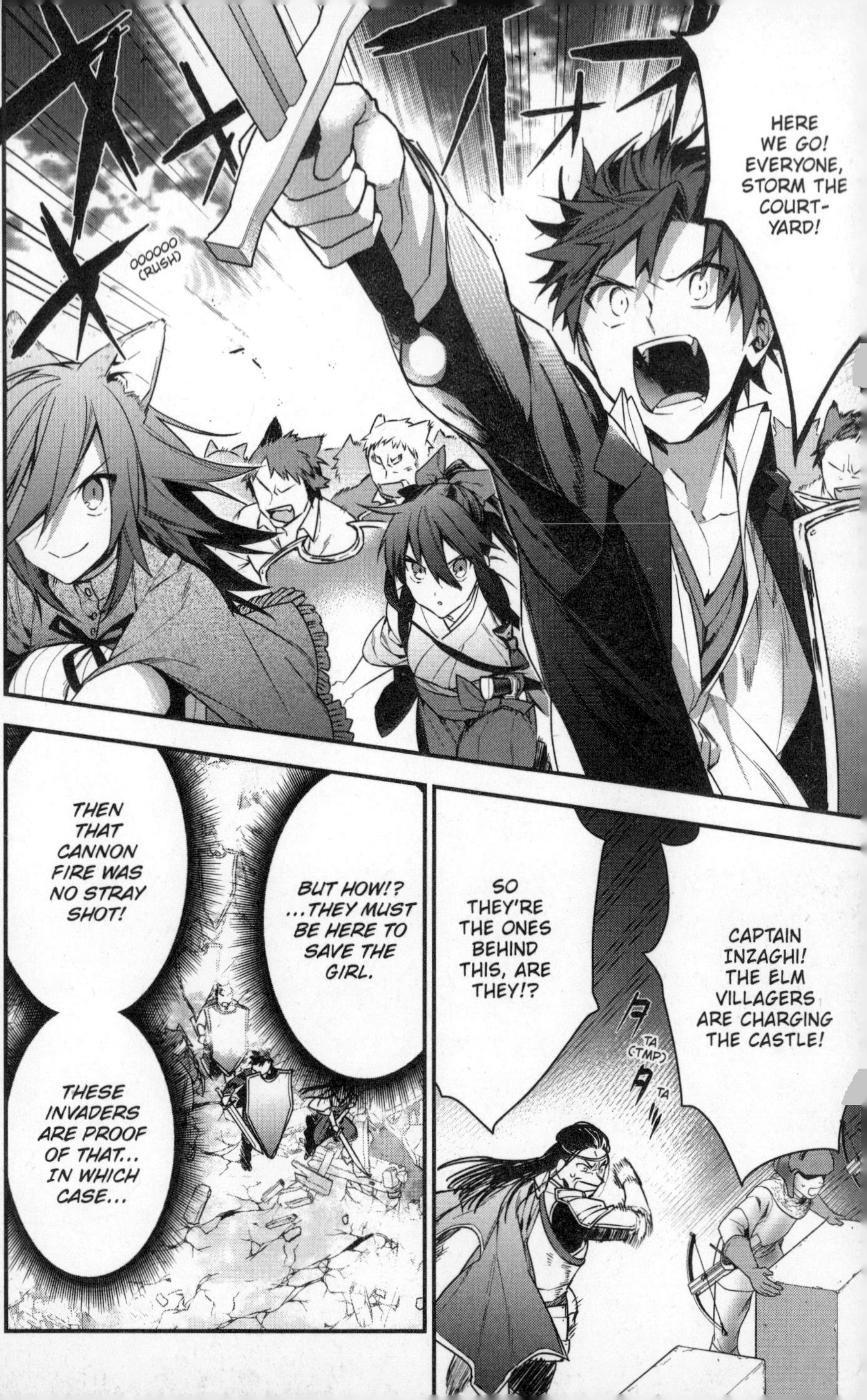
HERE WE GO! EVERYONE, STORM THE COURT-YARD!
OOOOOO (RUSH)
CAPTAIN INZAGHI! THE ELM VILLAGERS ARE CHARGING THE CASTLE!
TA (TMP) TA
SO THEY'RE THE ONES BEHIND THIS, ARE THEY!?
BUT HOW!? ...THEY MUST BE HERE TO SAVE THE GIRL.
THEN THAT CANNON FIRE WAS NO STRAY SHOT!
THESE INVADERS ARE PROOF OF THAT... IN WHICH CASE...

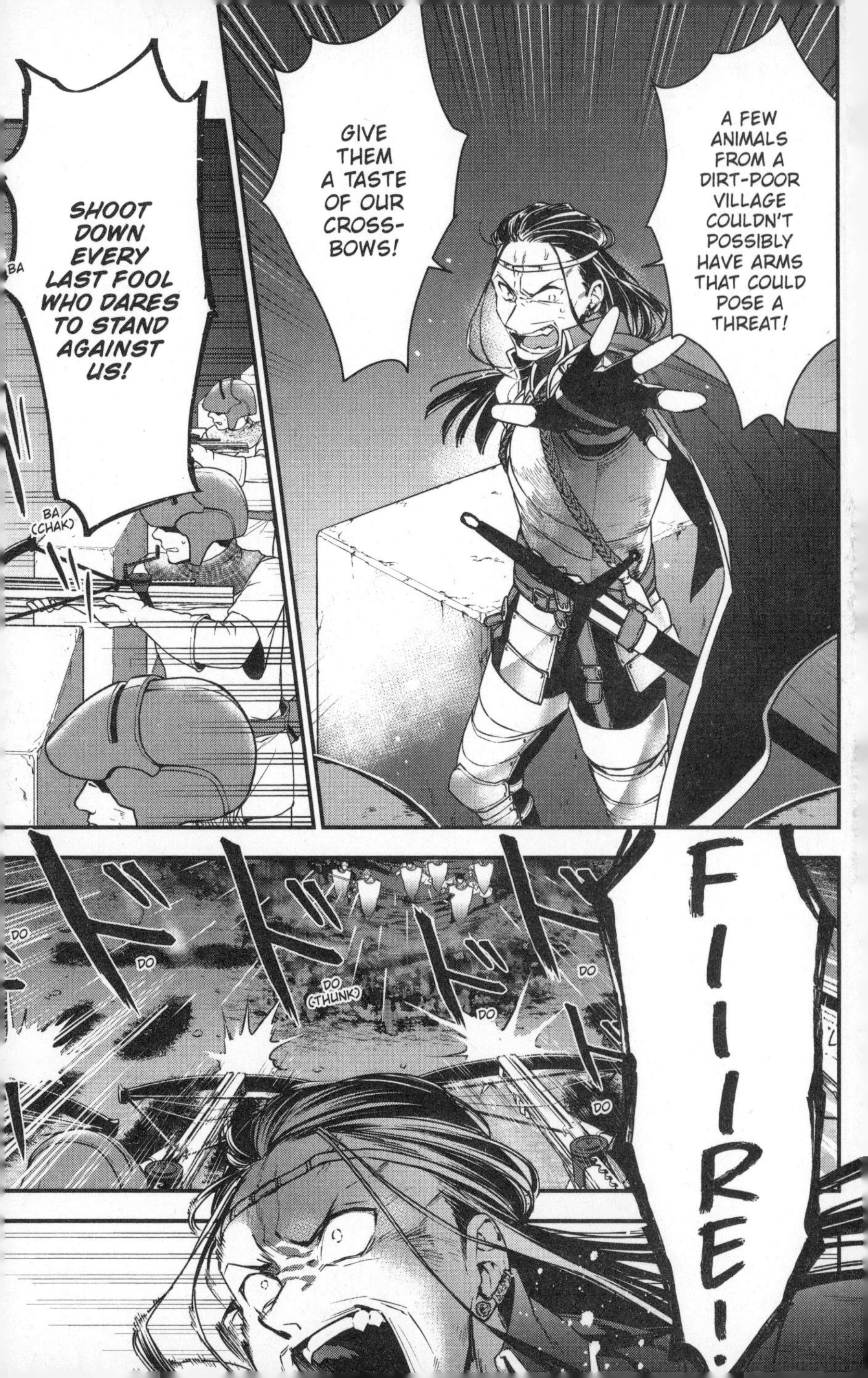
A FEW ANIMALS FROM A DIRT-POOR VILLAGE COULDN'T POSSIBLY HAVE ARMS THAT COULD POSE A THREAT!
GIVE THEM A TASTE OF OUR CROSS-BOWS!
SHOOT DOWN EVERY LAST FOOL WHO DARES TO STAND AGAINST US!
BA
BA (CHAK)
FIIIRE!
DO
DO
DO
DO (THUNK)
DO
DO

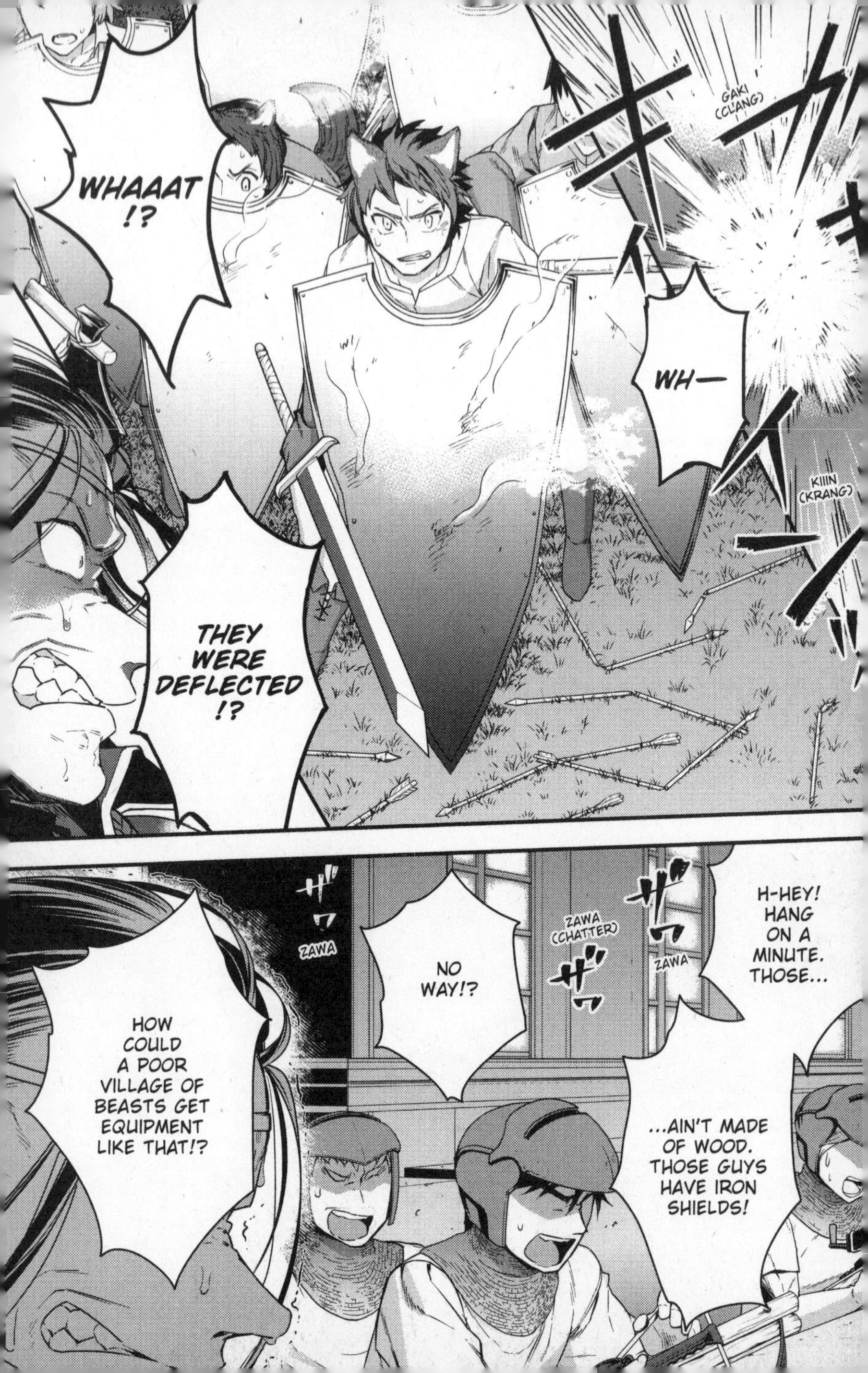
GAKI (CLANG)
WH—
KIIIN (KRANG)
WHAAAT!?
THEY WERE DEFLECTED!?
H-HEY! HANG ON A MINUTE. THOSE...
...AIN'T MADE OF WOOD. THOSE GUYS HAVE IRON SHIELDS!
ZAWA
ZAWA (CHATTER)
NO WAY!?
ZAWA
HOW COULD A POOR VILLAGE OF BEASTS GET EQUIPMENT LIKE THAT!?

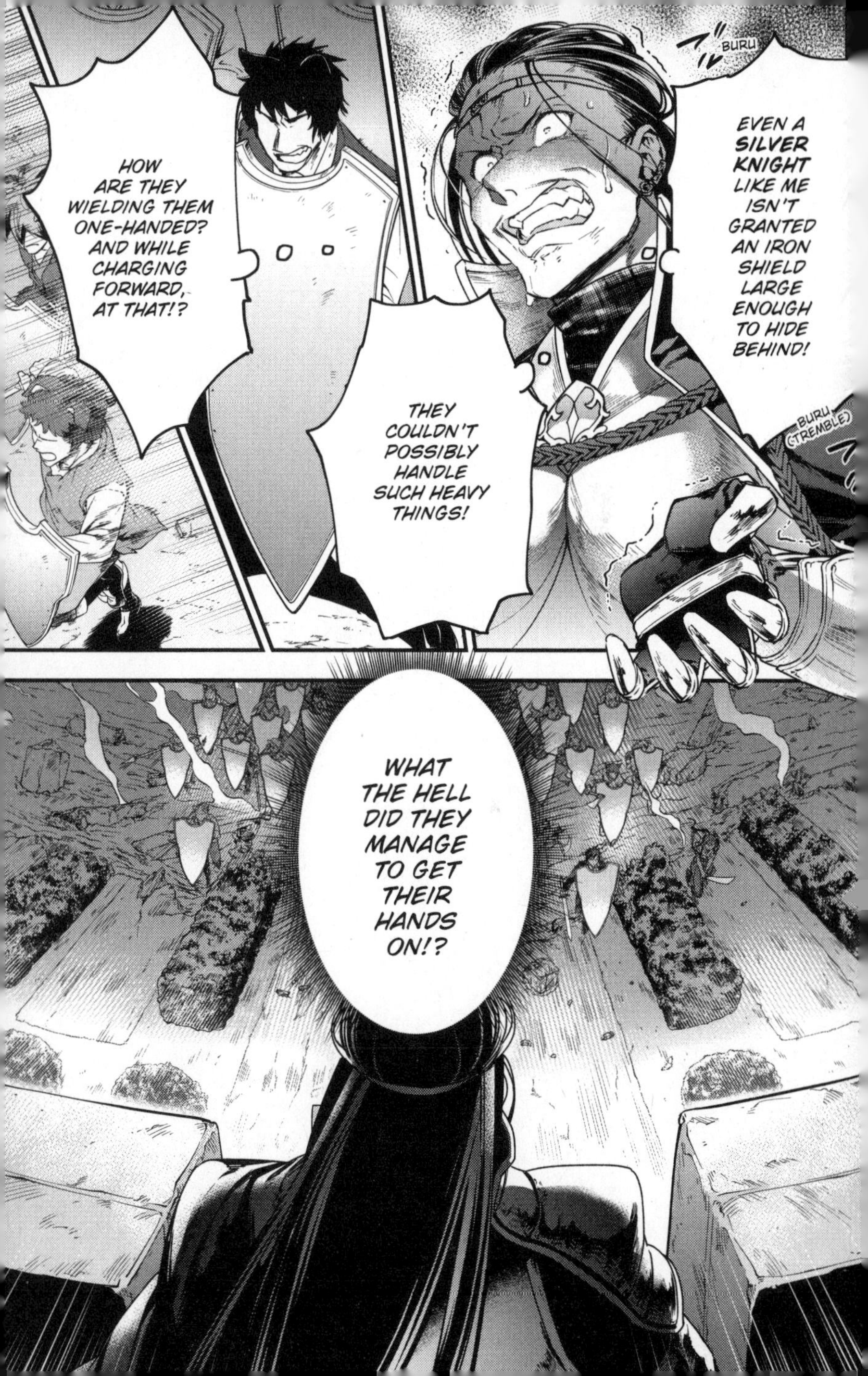
BURU
EVEN A SILVER KNIGHT LIKE ME ISN'T GRANTED AN IRON SHIELD LARGE ENOUGH TO HIDE BEHIND!
BURU (TREMBLE)
THEY COULDN'T POSSIBLY HANDLE SUCH HEAVY THINGS!
HOW ARE THEY WIELDING THEM ONE-HANDED? AND WHILE CHARGING FORWARD, AT THAT!?
WHAT THE HELL DID THEY MANAGE TO GET THEIR HANDS ON!?

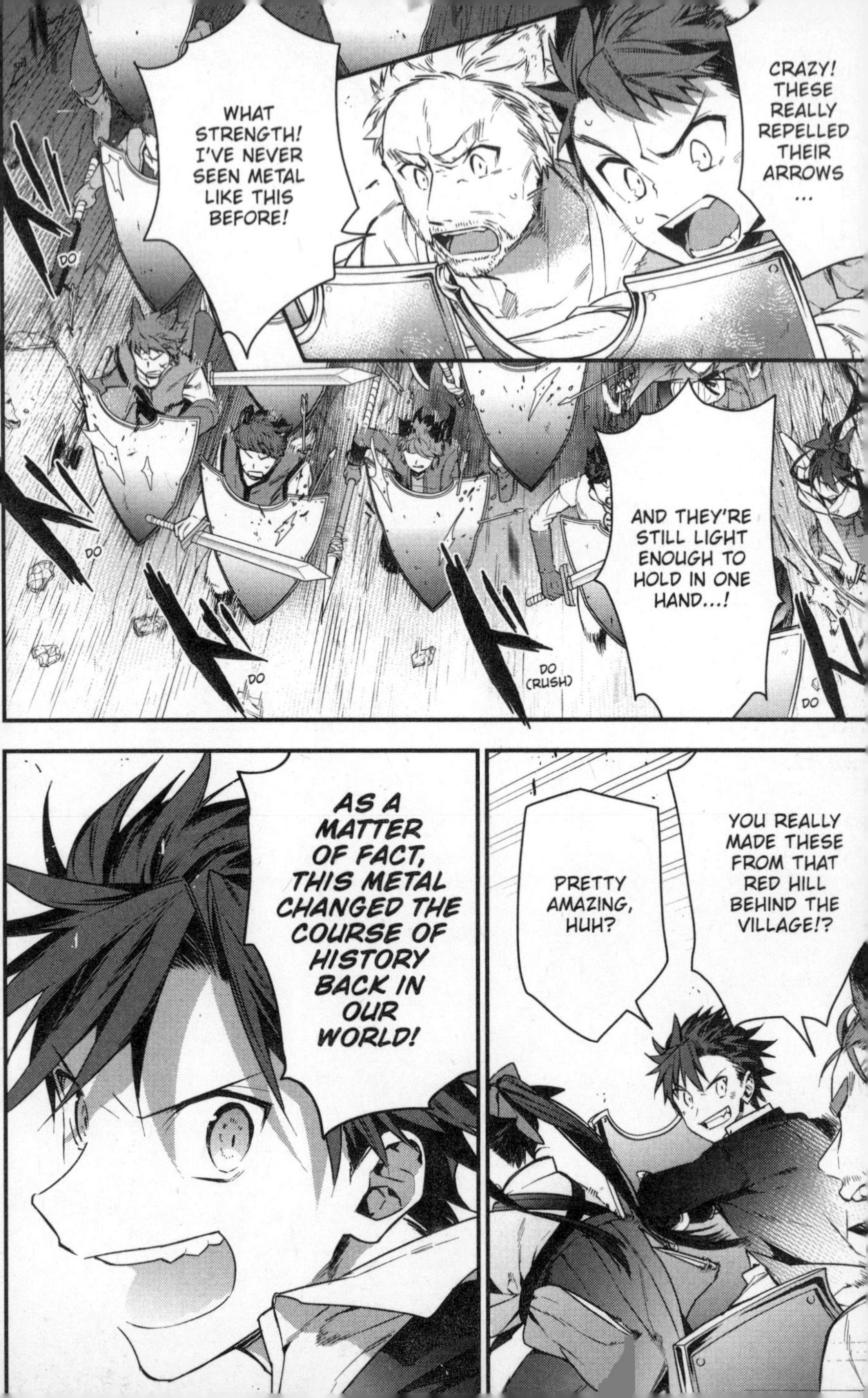
CRAZY! THESE REALLY REPELLED THEIR ARROWS...
WHAT STRENGTH! I'VE NEVER SEEN METAL LIKE THIS BEFORE!
DO
AND THEY'RE STILL LIGHT ENOUGH TO HOLD IN ONE HAND...!
DO
DO (RUSH)
DO
DO
YOU REALLY MADE THESE FROM THAT RED HILL BEHIND THE VILLAGE!?
PRETTY AMAZING, HUH?
AS A MATTER OF FACT, THIS METAL CHANGED THE COURSE OF HISTORY BACK IN OUR WORLD!

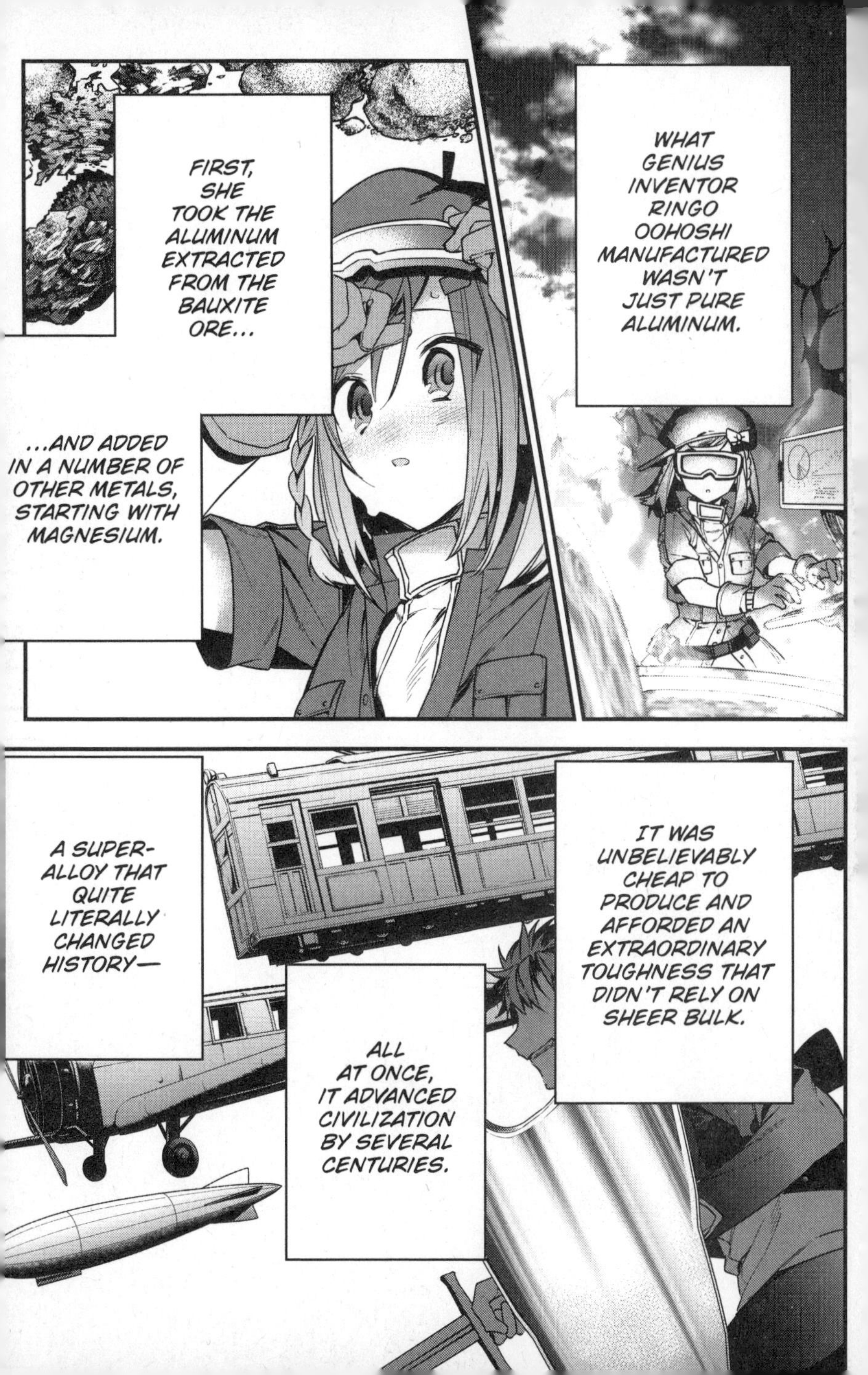
WHAT GENIUS INVENTOR RINGO OOHOSHI MANUFACTURED WASN'T JUST PURE ALUMINUM.
FIRST, SHE TOOK THE ALUMINUM EXTRACTED FROM THE BAUXITE ORE...
...AND ADDED IN A NUMBER OF OTHER METALS, STARTING WITH MAGNESIUM.
IT WAS UNBELIEVABLY CHEAP TO PRODUCE AND AFFORDED AN EXTRAORDINARY TOUGHNESS THAT DIDN'T RELY ON SHEER BULK.
A SUPER-ALLOY THAT QUITE LITERALLY CHANGED HISTORY—
ALL AT ONCE, IT ADVANCED CIVILIZATION BY SEVERAL CENTURIES.

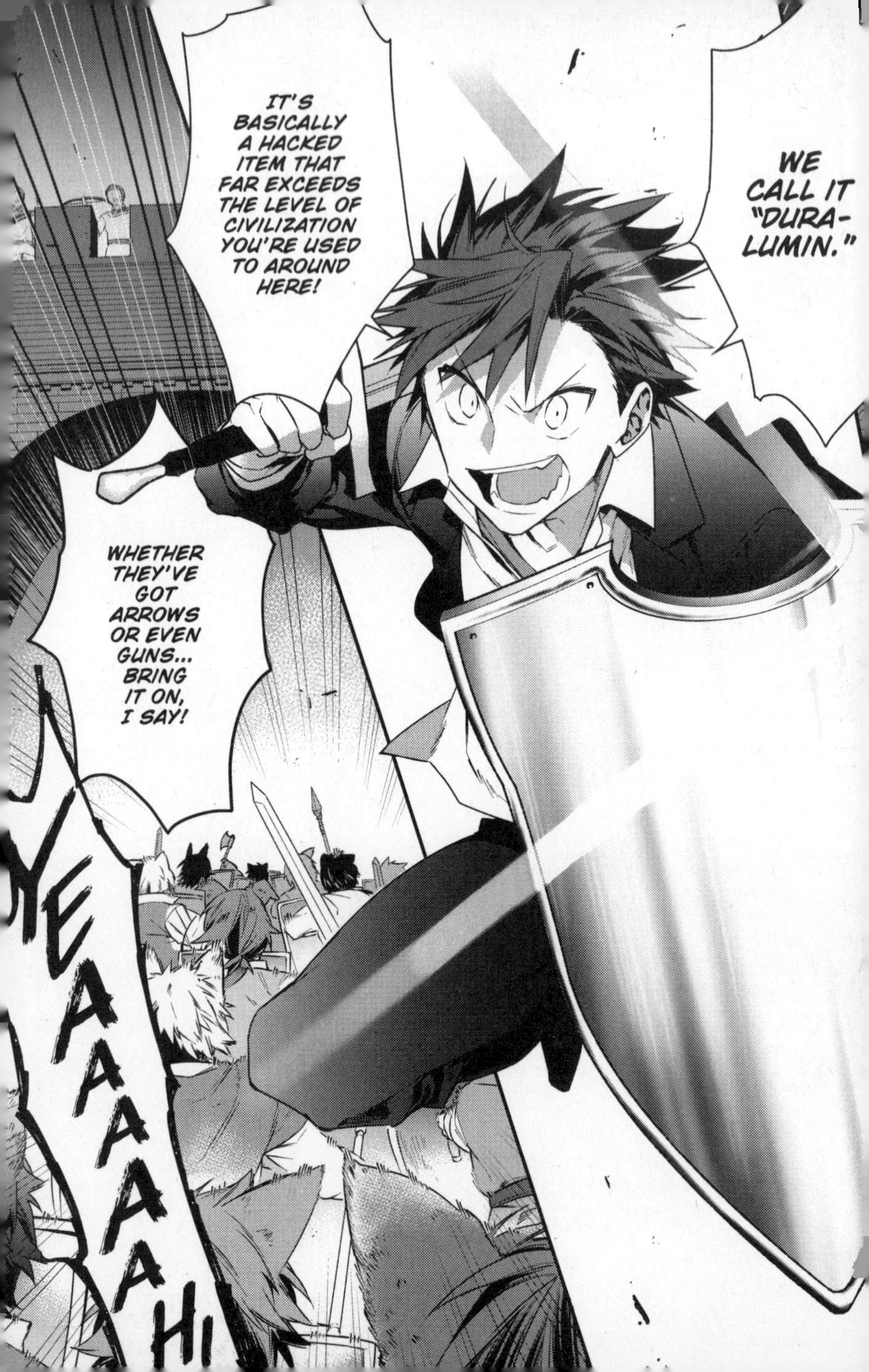
WE CALL IT "DURALUMIN."
IT'S BASICALLY A HACKED ITEM THAT FAR EXCEEDS THE LEVEL OF CIVILIZATION YOU'RE USED TO AROUND HERE!
WHETHER THEY'VE GOT ARROWS OR EVEN GUNS... BRING IT ON, I SAY!
YEAAAAAH!

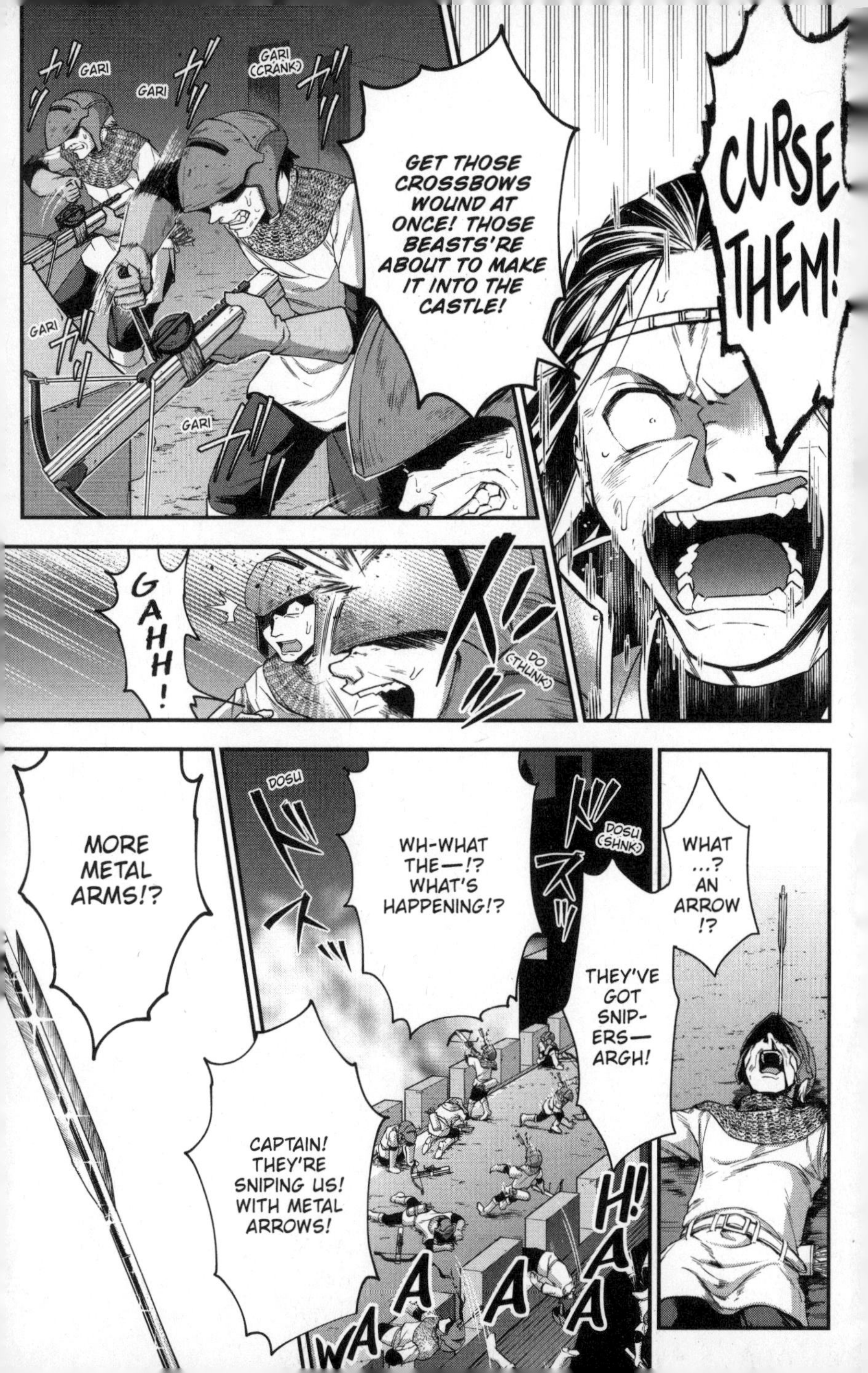
CURSE THEM!
GARI (CRANK)
GARI
GARI
GET THOSE CROSSBOWS WOUND AT ONCE! THOSE BEASTS'RE ABOUT TO MAKE IT INTO THE CASTLE!
GARI
GARI
DO (THUNK)
GAHH!
DOSU (SHNK)
WHAT ...? AN ARROW !?
THEY'VE GOT SNIP-ERS— ARGH!
DOSU
WH-WHAT THE—!? WHAT'S HAPPENING!?
CAPTAIN! THEY'RE SNIPING US! WITH METAL ARROWS!
WAAAAAH!
MORE METAL ARMS!?

CHAPTER 15:
EACH OF THEIR FEELINGS

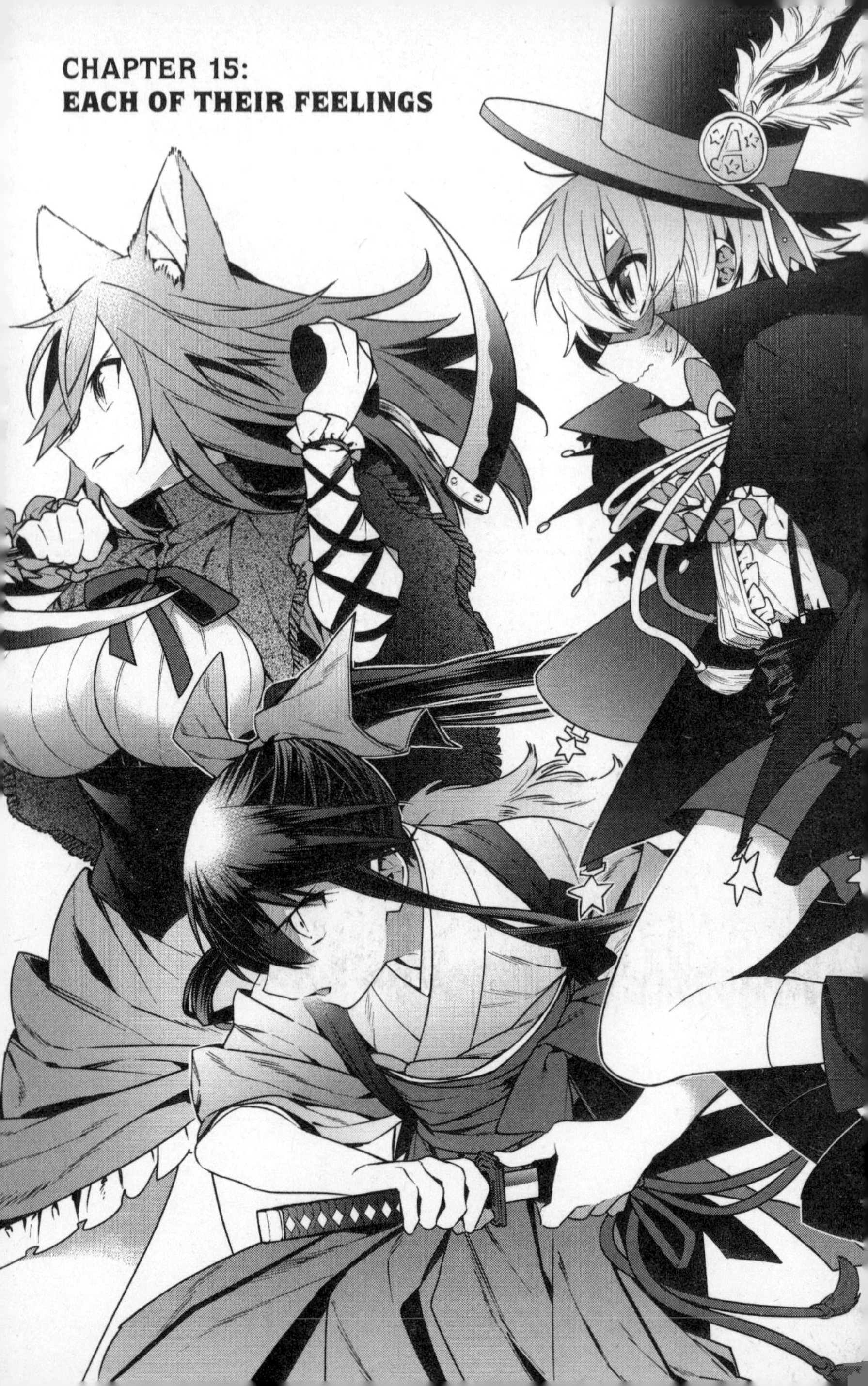

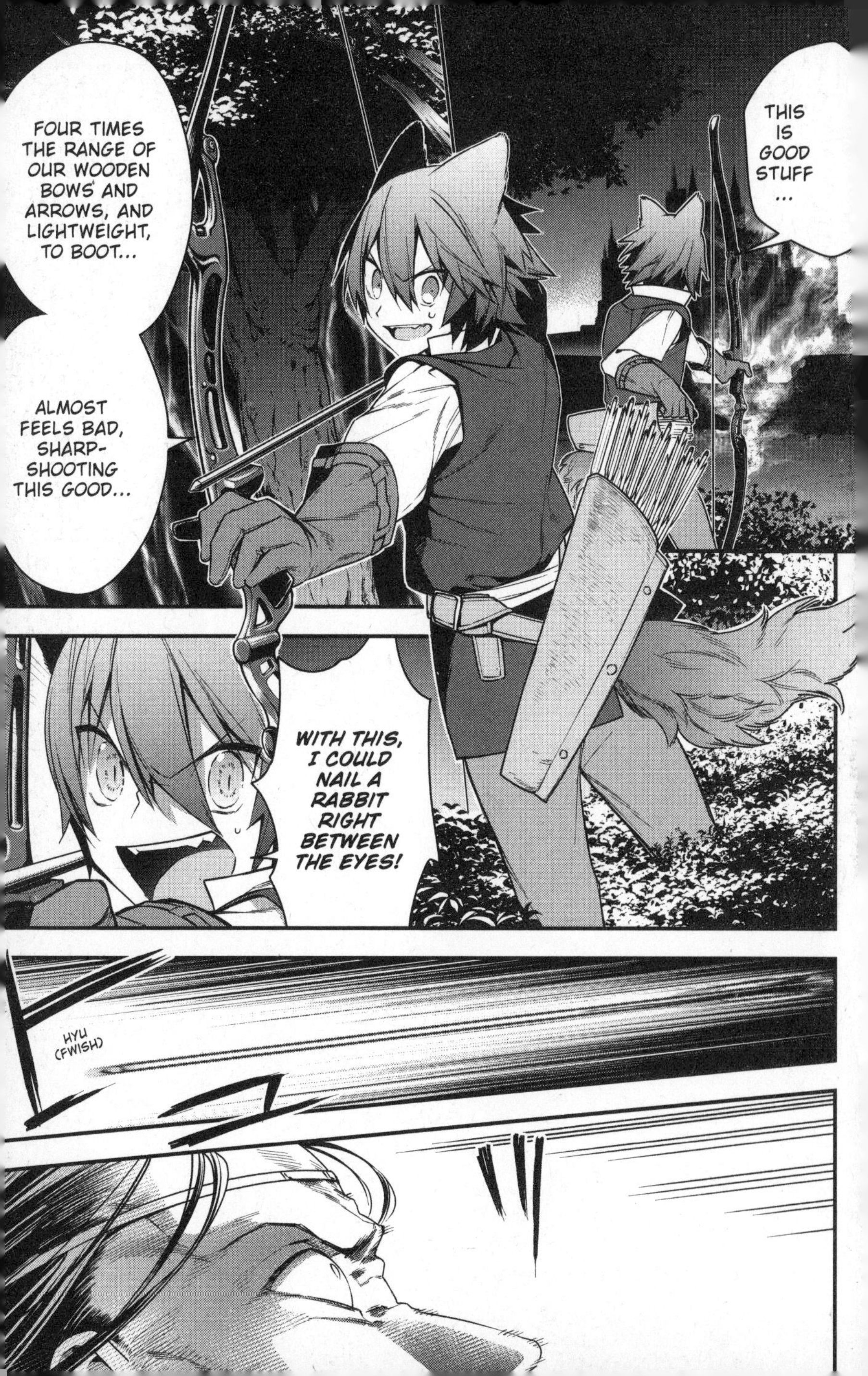
THIS IS GOOD STUFF...
FOUR TIMES THE RANGE OF OUR WOODEN BOWS AND ARROWS, AND LIGHTWEIGHT, TO BOOT...
ALMOST FEELS BAD, SHARP-SHOOTING THIS GOOD...
WITH THIS, I COULD NAIL A RABBIT RIGHT BETWEEN THE EYES!
HYU (FWISH)

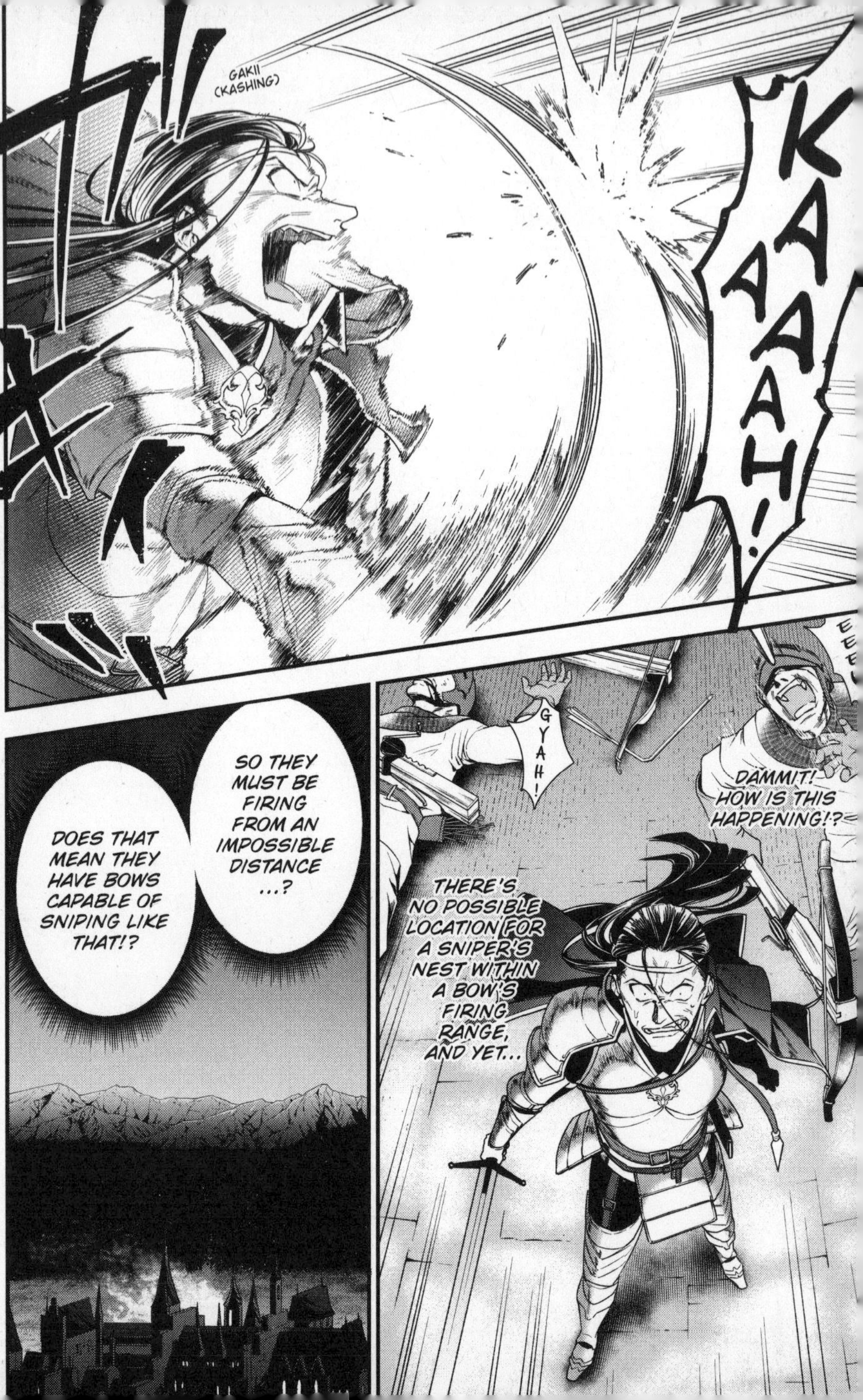
GAKII (KASHING)
KAAAAH!
EEE
GYAH!
DAMMIT! HOW IS THIS HAPPENING!?
THERE'S NO POSSIBLE LOCATION FOR A SNIPER'S NEST WITHIN A BOW'S FIRING RANGE, AND YET...
SO THEY MUST BE FIRING FROM AN IMPOSSIBLE DISTANCE ...?
DOES THAT MEAN THEY HAVE BOWS CAPABLE OF SNIPING LIKE THAT!?

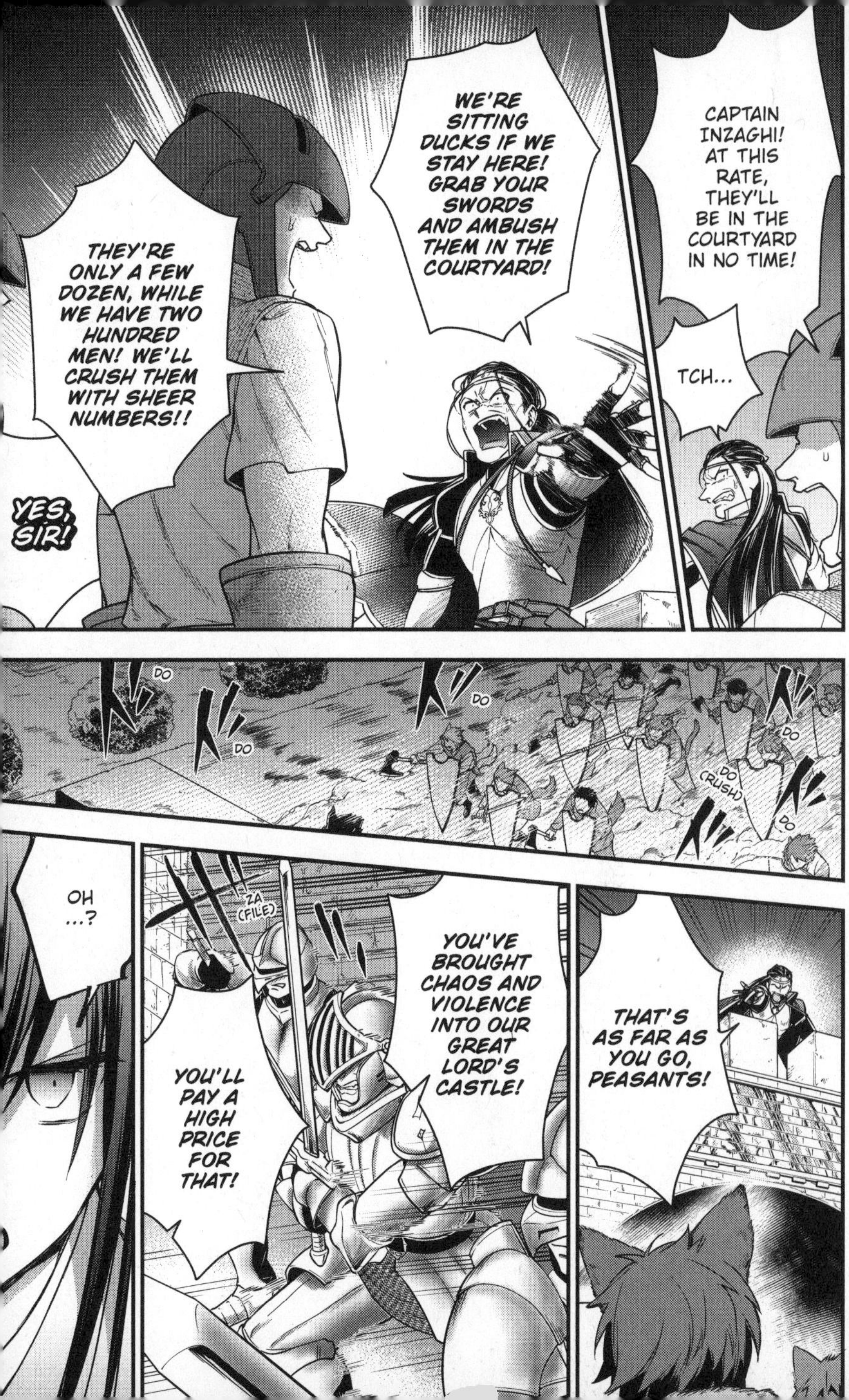
CAPTAIN INZAGHI! AT THIS RATE, THEY'LL BE IN THE COURTYARD IN NO TIME!
TCH...
WE'RE SITTING DUCKS IF WE STAY HERE! GRAB YOUR SWORDS AND AMBUSH THEM IN THE COURTYARD!
THEY'RE ONLY A FEW DOZEN, WHILE WE HAVE TWO HUNDRED MEN! WE'LL CRUSH THEM WITH SHEER NUMBERS!!
YES, SIR!
DO
DO (RUSH)
DO
DO
DO
DO
THAT'S AS FAR AS YOU GO, PEASANTS!
YOU'VE BROUGHT CHAOS AND VIOLENCE INTO OUR GREAT LORD'S CASTLE!
YOU'LL PAY A HIGH PRICE FOR THAT!
ZA (FILE)
OH ...?

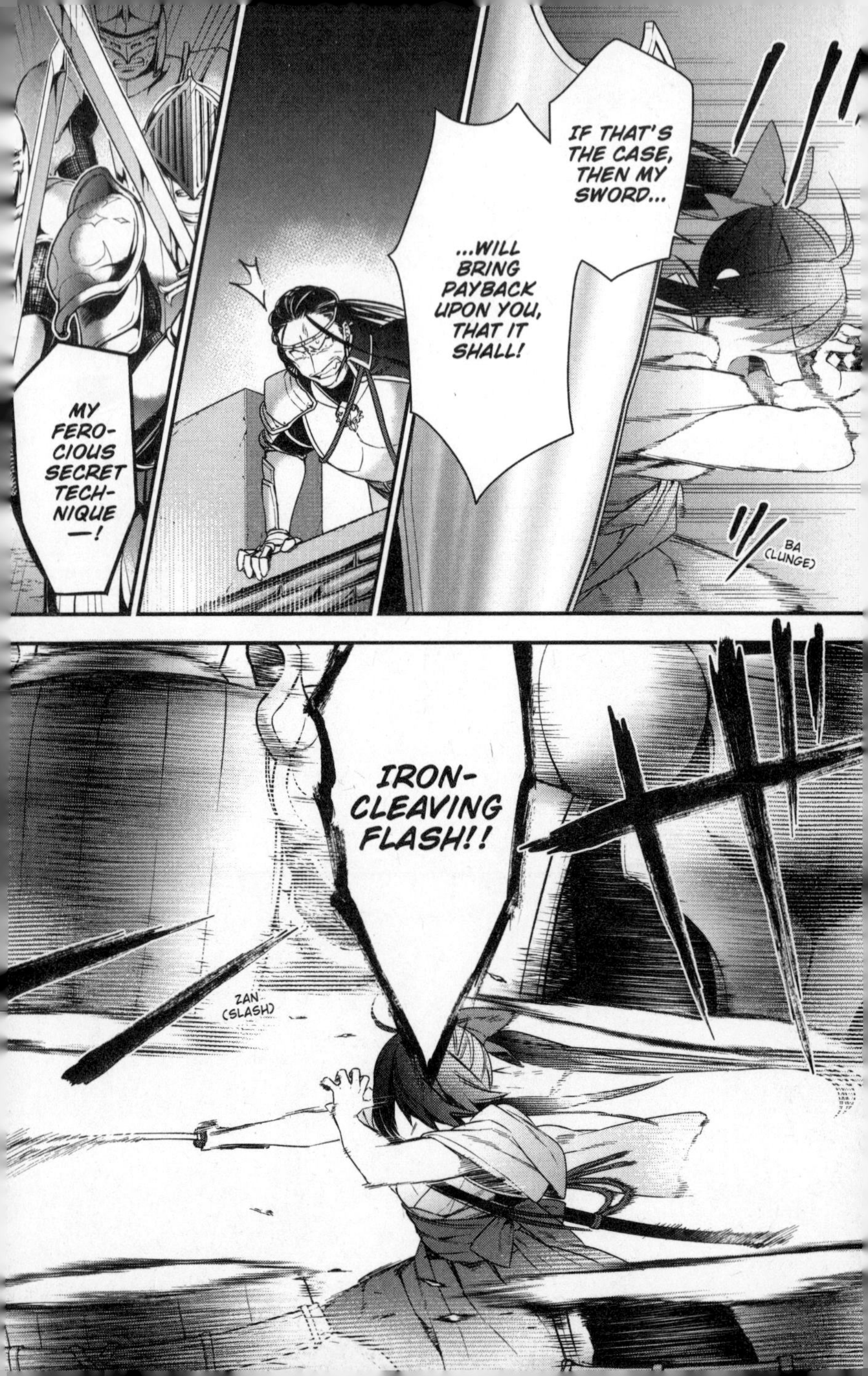
IF THAT'S THE CASE, THEN MY SWORD...
...WILL BRING PAYBACK UPON YOU, THAT IT SHALL!
BA (LUNGE)
MY FEROCIOUS SECRET TECHNIQUE—!
IRON-CLEAVING FLASH!!
ZAN (SLASH)

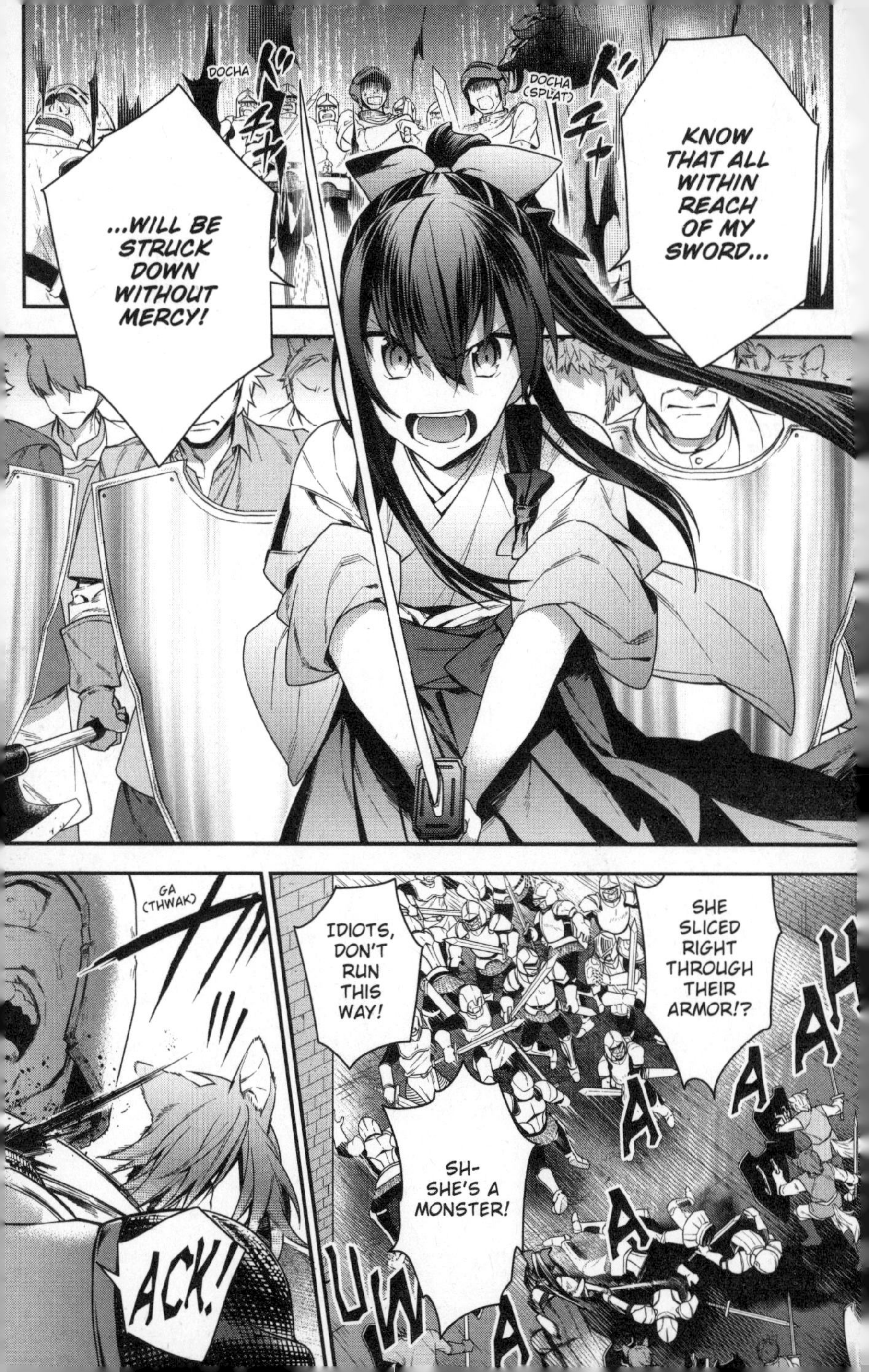
DOCHA (SPLAT)
DOCHA
KNOW THAT ALL WITHIN REACH OF MY SWORD...
...WILL BE STRUCK DOWN WITHOUT MERCY!
SHE SLICED RIGHT THROUGH THEIR ARMOR!?
IDIOTS, DON'T RUN THIS WAY!
SH- SHE'S A MONSTER!
UWAAAAAAH
GA (THWAK)
ACK!

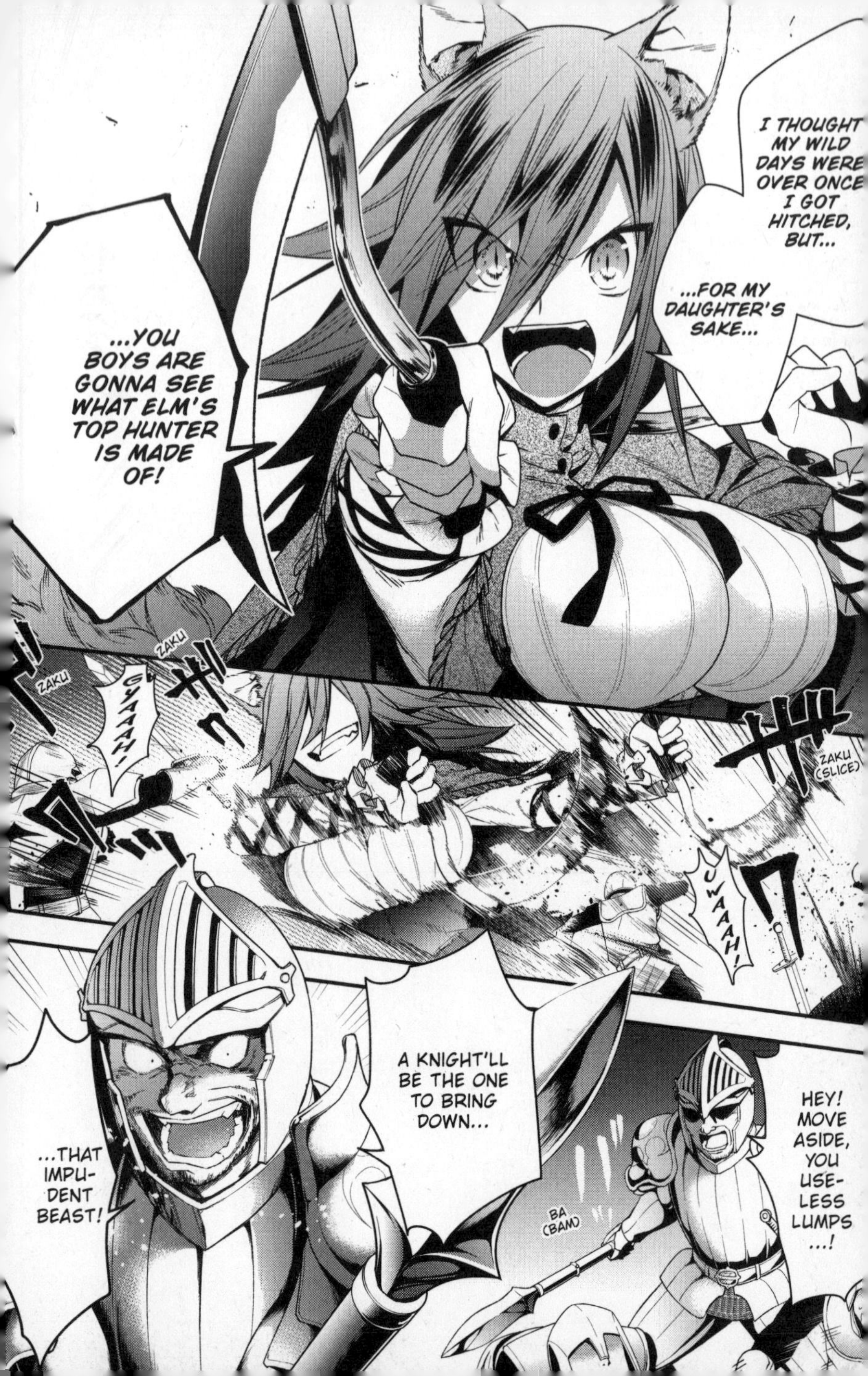
I THOUGHT MY WILD DAYS WERE OVER ONCE I GOT HITCHED, BUT...
...FOR MY DAUGHTER'S SAKE...
...YOU BOYS ARE GONNA SEE WHAT ELM'S TOP HUNTER IS MADE OF!
ZAKU (SLICE)
UWAAAH!
GYAAAH!
ZAKU
ZAKU
HEY! MOVE ASIDE, YOU USE-LESS LUMPS...!
BA (BAM)
A KNIGHT'LL BE THE ONE TO BRING DOWN...
...THAT IMPU-DENT BEAST!

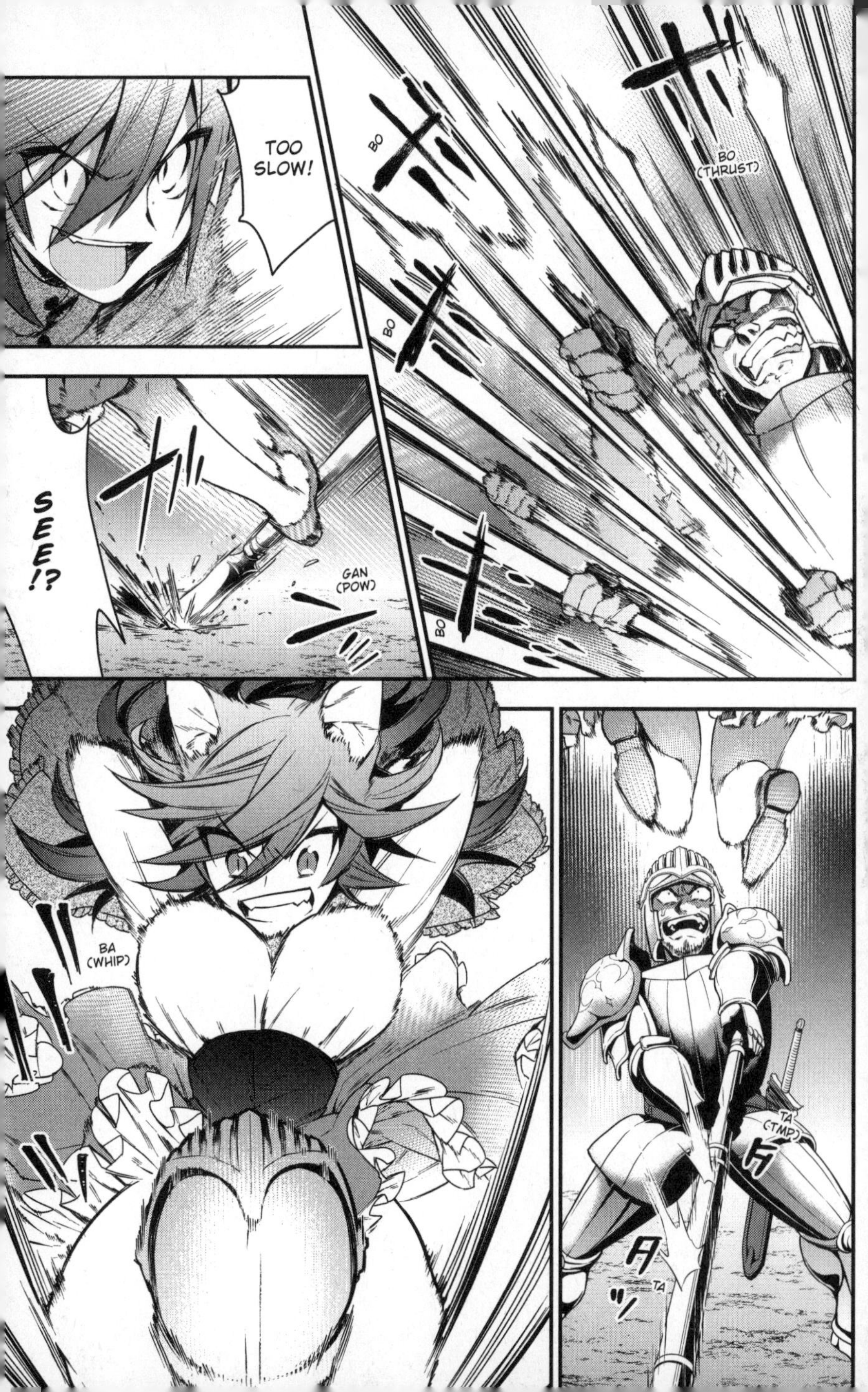
BO (THRUST)
BO
BO
BO
TOO SLOW!
SEE!?
GAN (POW)
TA (TMP)
TA
BA (WHIP)

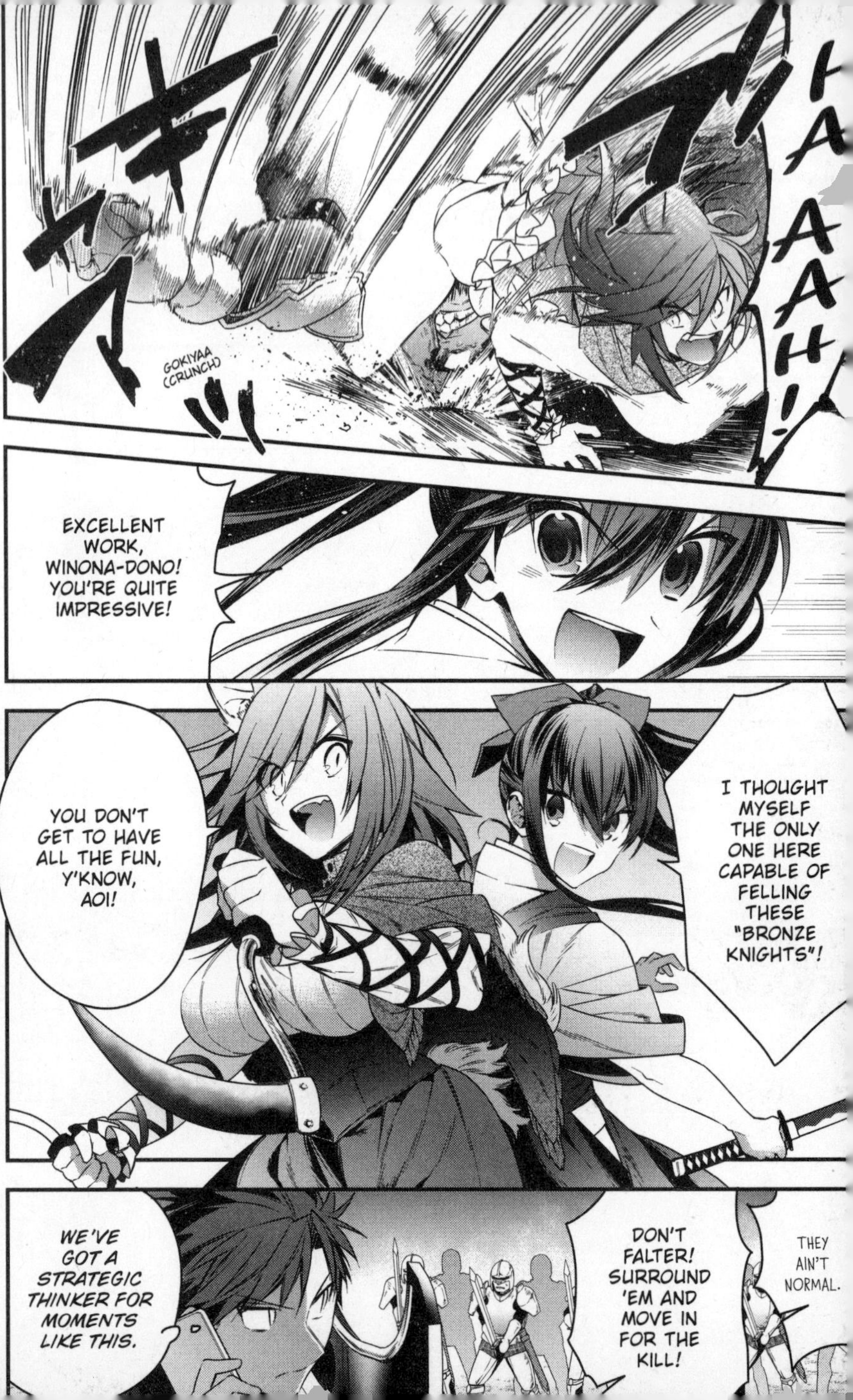
HAAAH!!
GOKIYAA (CRUNCH)
EXCELLENT WORK, WINONA-DONO! YOU'RE QUITE IMPRESSIVE!
I THOUGHT MYSELF THE ONLY ONE HERE CAPABLE OF FELLING THESE "BRONZE KNIGHTS"!
YOU DON'T GET TO HAVE ALL THE FUN, Y'KNOW, AOI!
THEY AIN'T NORMAL.
DON'T FALTER! SURROUND 'EM AND MOVE IN FOR THE KILL!
WE'VE GOT A STRATEGIC THINKER FOR MOMENTS LIKE THIS.

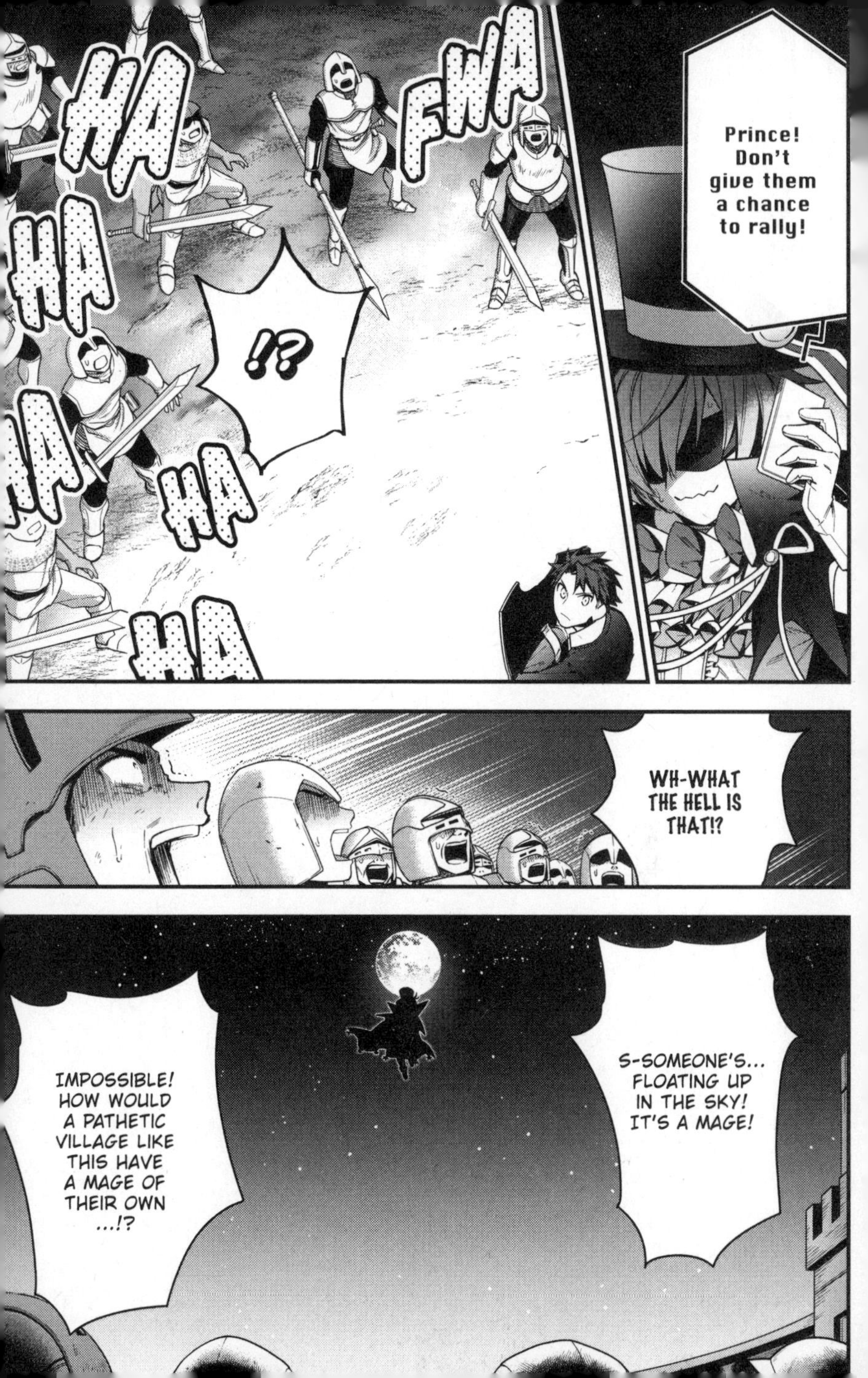
Prince! Don't give them a chance to rally!
FWA
HA
HA
HA
HA
HA
!?
WH-WHAT THE HELL IS THAT!?
S-SOMEONE'S... FLOATING UP IN THE SKY! IT'S A MAGE!
IMPOSSIBLE! HOW WOULD A PATHETIC VILLAGE LIKE THIS HAVE A MAGE OF THEIR OWN ...!?

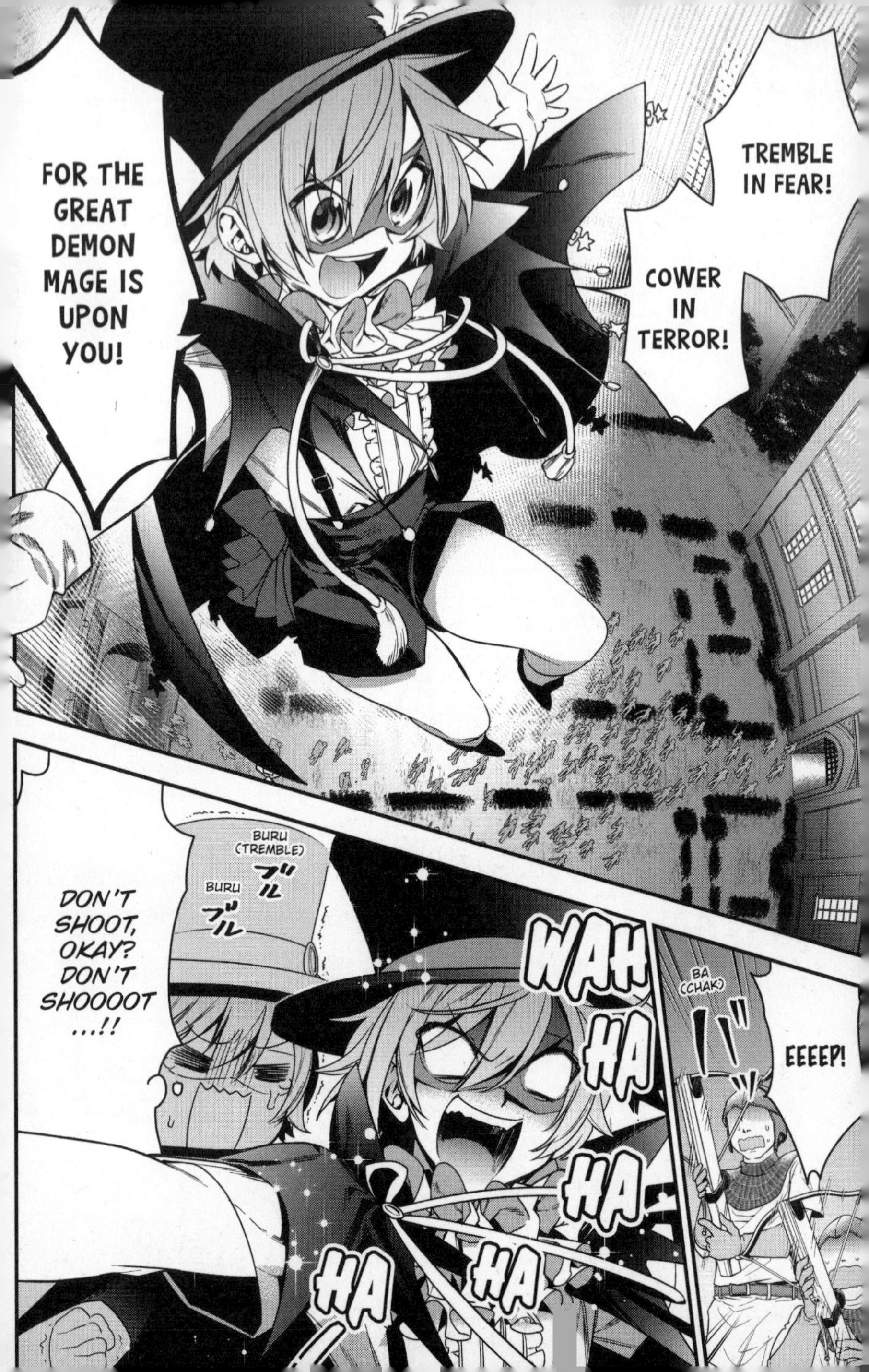
TREMBLE IN FEAR!
COWER IN TERROR!
FOR THE GREAT DEMON MAGE IS UPON YOU!
BA (CHAK)
EEEEP!
BURU (TREMBLE)
BURU
DON'T SHOOT, OKAY? DON'T SHOOOOT ...!!
WAH HA HA HA HA

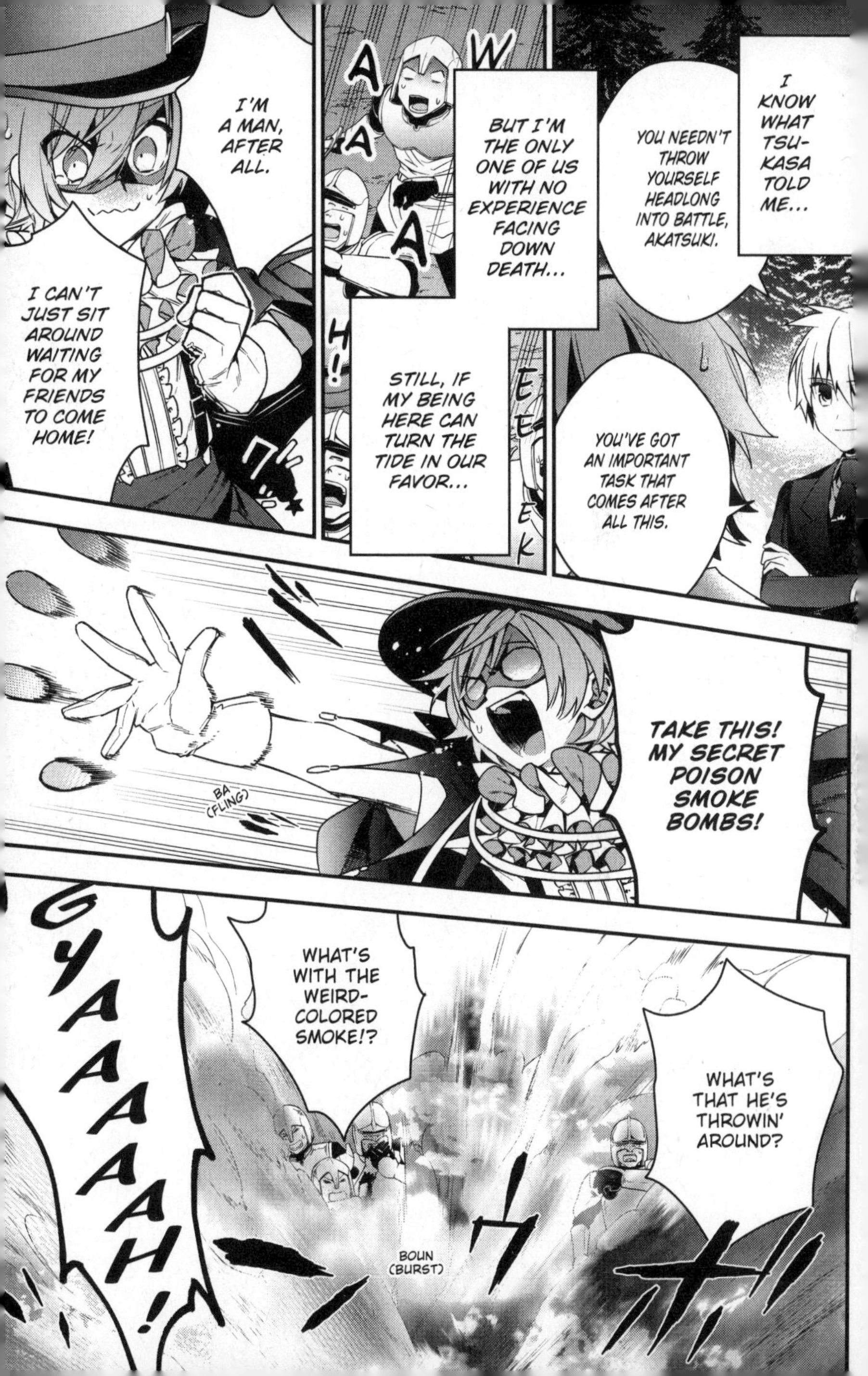
I KNOW WHAT TSU-KASA TOLD ME...
YOU NEEDN'T THROW YOURSELF HEADLONG INTO BATTLE, AKATSUKI.
YOU'VE GOT AN IMPORTANT TASK THAT COMES AFTER ALL THIS.
BUT I'M THE ONLY ONE OF US WITH NO EXPERIENCE FACING DOWN DEATH...
STILL, IF MY BEING HERE CAN TURN THE TIDE IN OUR FAVOR...
AWAAAH!
EEEK
I'M A MAN, AFTER ALL.
I CAN'T JUST SIT AROUND WAITING FOR MY FRIENDS TO COME HOME!
TAKE THIS! MY SECRET POISON SMOKE BOMBS!
BA (FLING)
WHAT'S THAT HE'S THROWIN' AROUND?
WHAT'S WITH THE WEIRD-COLORED SMOKE!?
BOUN (BURST)
GYAAAAAH!

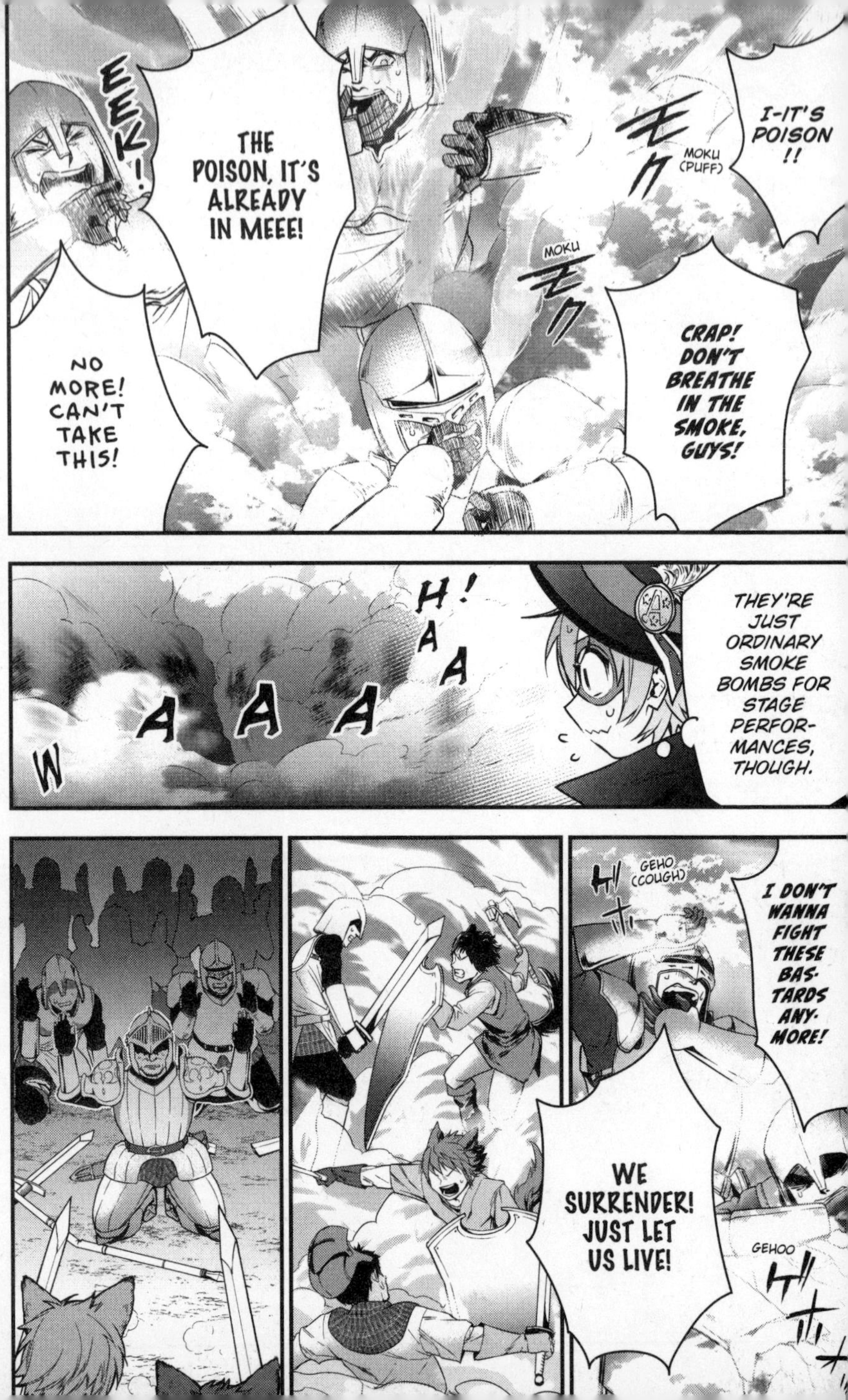

I-IT'S POISON!!
MOKU (PUFF)
THE POISON, IT'S ALREADY IN MEEE!
EEK!
MOKU
CRAP! DON'T BREATHE IN THE SMOKE, GUYS!
NO MORE! CAN'T TAKE THIS!
THEY'RE JUST ORDINARY SMOKE BOMBS FOR STAGE PERFORMANCES, THOUGH.
WAAAAAH!
GEHO (COUGH)
I DON'T WANNA FIGHT THESE BASTARDS ANYMORE!
WE SURRENDER! JUST LET US LIVE!
GEHOO

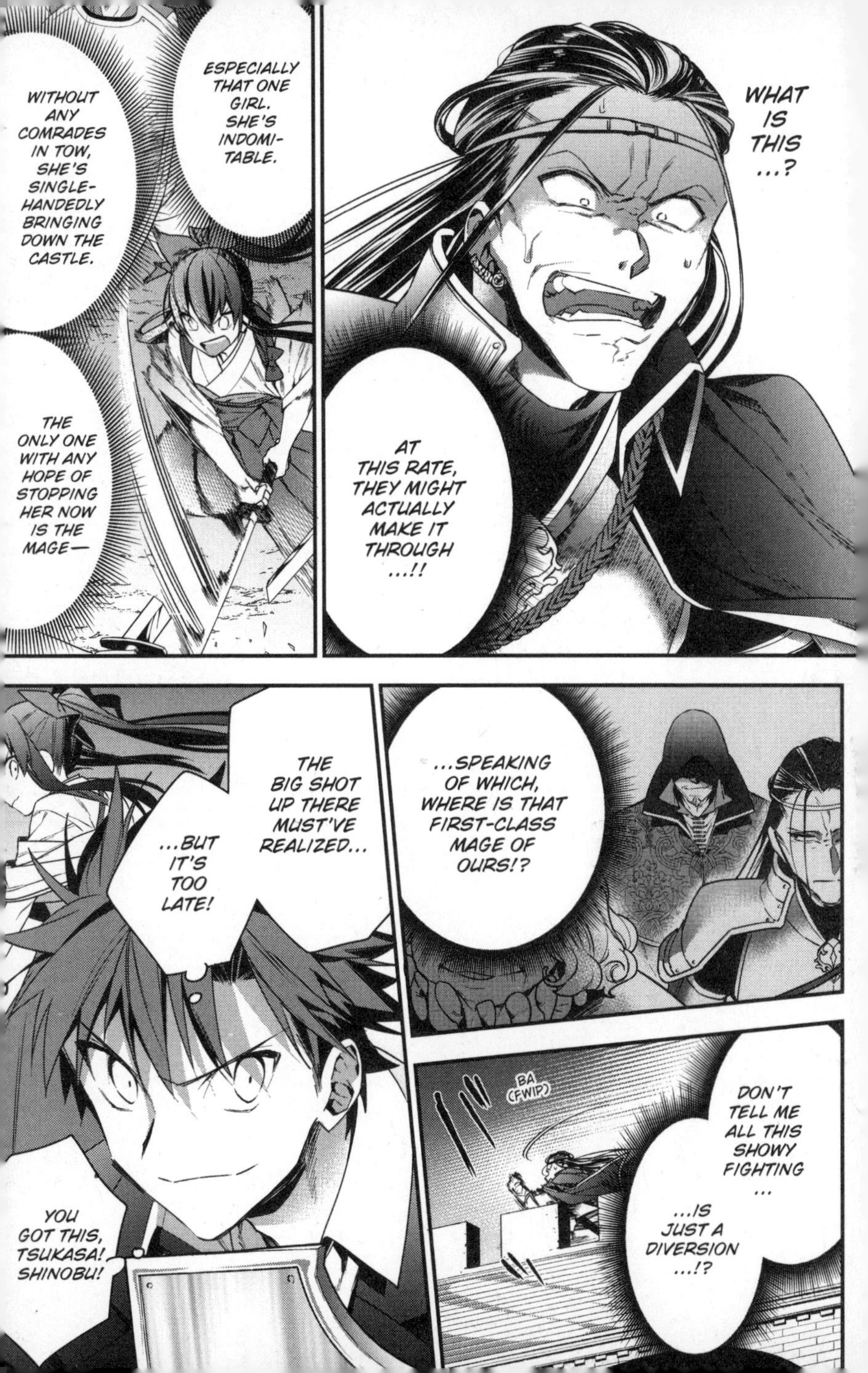
WHAT IS THIS ...?
AT THIS RATE, THEY MIGHT ACTUALLY MAKE IT THROUGH ...!!
ESPECIALLY THAT ONE GIRL. SHE'S INDOMITABLE.
WITHOUT ANY COMRADES IN TOW, SHE'S SINGLE-HANDEDLY BRINGING DOWN THE CASTLE.
THE ONLY ONE WITH ANY HOPE OF STOPPING HER NOW IS THE MAGE—
...SPEAKING OF WHICH, WHERE IS THAT FIRST-CLASS MAGE OF OURS!?
BA (FWIP)
DON'T TELL ME ALL THIS SHOWY FIGHTING ...
...IS JUST A DIVERSION ...!?
THE BIG SHOT UP THERE MUST'VE REALIZED...
...BUT IT'S TOO LATE!
YOU GOT THIS, TSUKASA! SHINOBU!

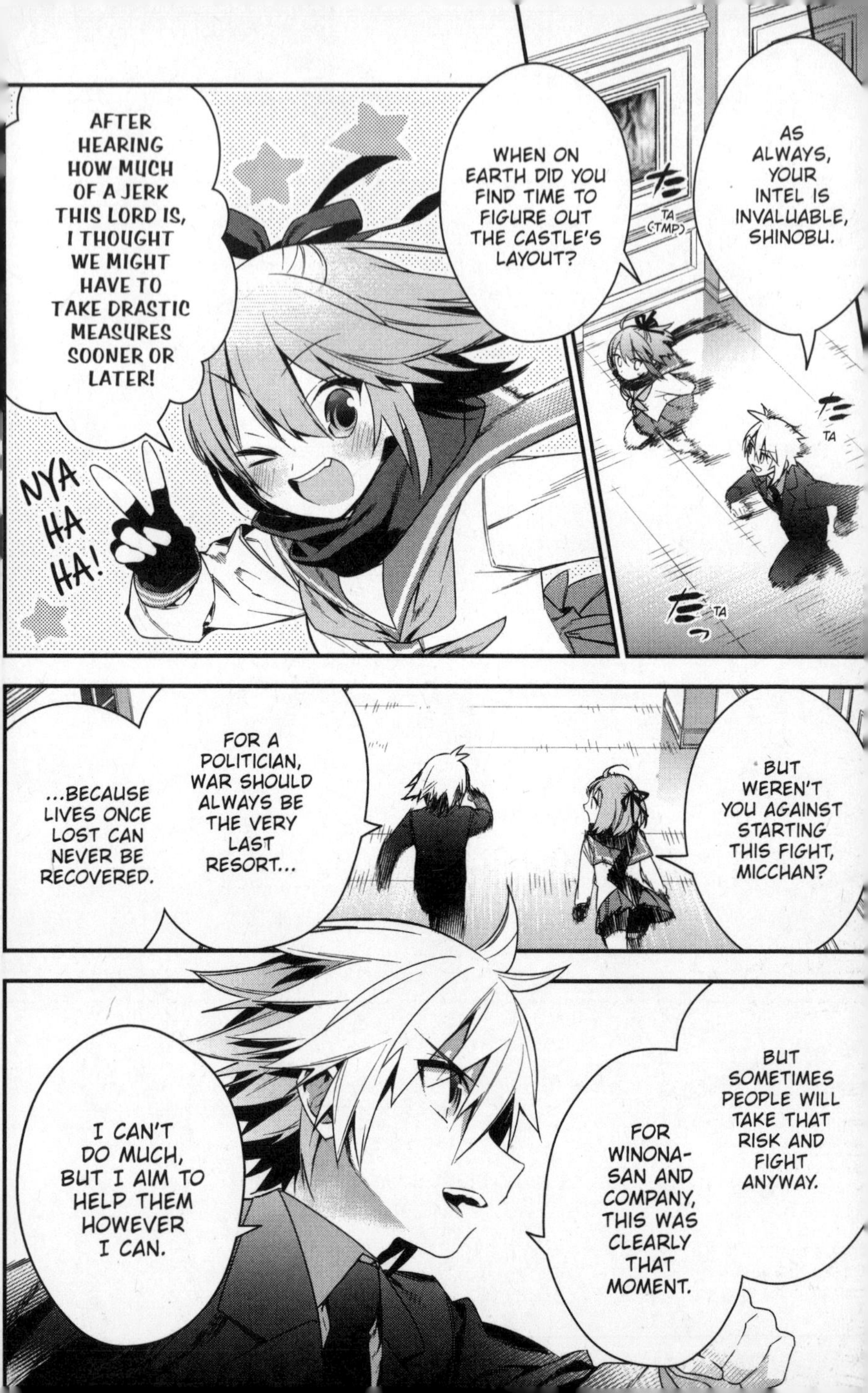
AS ALWAYS, YOUR INTEL IS INVALUABLE, SHINOBU.
WHEN ON EARTH DID YOU FIND TIME TO FIGURE OUT THE CASTLE'S LAYOUT?
TA (TMP)
TA
TA
AFTER HEARING HOW MUCH OF A JERK THIS LORD IS, I THOUGHT WE MIGHT HAVE TO TAKE DRASTIC MEASURES SOONER OR LATER!
NYA HA HA!
BUT WEREN'T YOU AGAINST STARTING THIS FIGHT, MICCHAN?
FOR A POLITICIAN, WAR SHOULD ALWAYS BE THE VERY LAST RESORT...
...BECAUSE LIVES ONCE LOST CAN NEVER BE RECOVERED.
BUT SOMETIMES PEOPLE WILL TAKE THAT RISK AND FIGHT ANYWAY.
FOR WINONA-SAN AND COMPANY, THIS WAS CLEARLY THAT MOMENT.
I CAN'T DO MUCH, BUT I AIM TO HELP THEM HOWEVER I CAN.

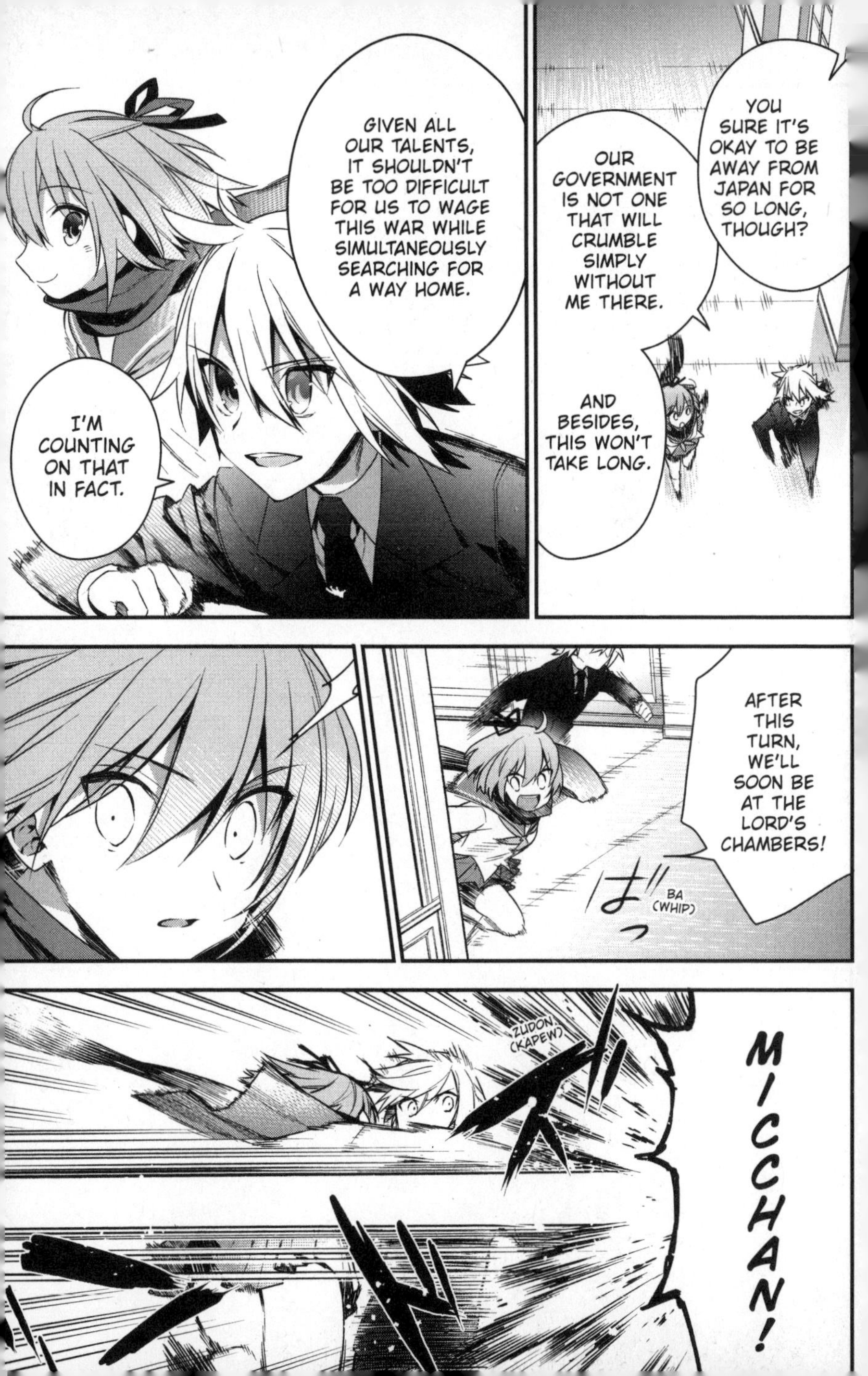
YOU SURE IT'S OKAY TO BE AWAY FROM JAPAN FOR SO LONG, THOUGH?
OUR GOVERNMENT IS NOT ONE THAT WILL CRUMBLE SIMPLY WITHOUT ME THERE.
AND BESIDES, THIS WON'T TAKE LONG.
GIVEN ALL OUR TALENTS, IT SHOULDN'T BE TOO DIFFICULT FOR US TO WAGE THIS WAR WHILE SIMULTANEOUSLY SEARCHING FOR A WAY HOME.
I'M COUNTING ON THAT IN FACT.
AFTER THIS TURN, WE'LL SOON BE AT THE LORD'S CHAMBERS!
BA (WHIP)
MICCHAN!
ZUDON (KAPEW)

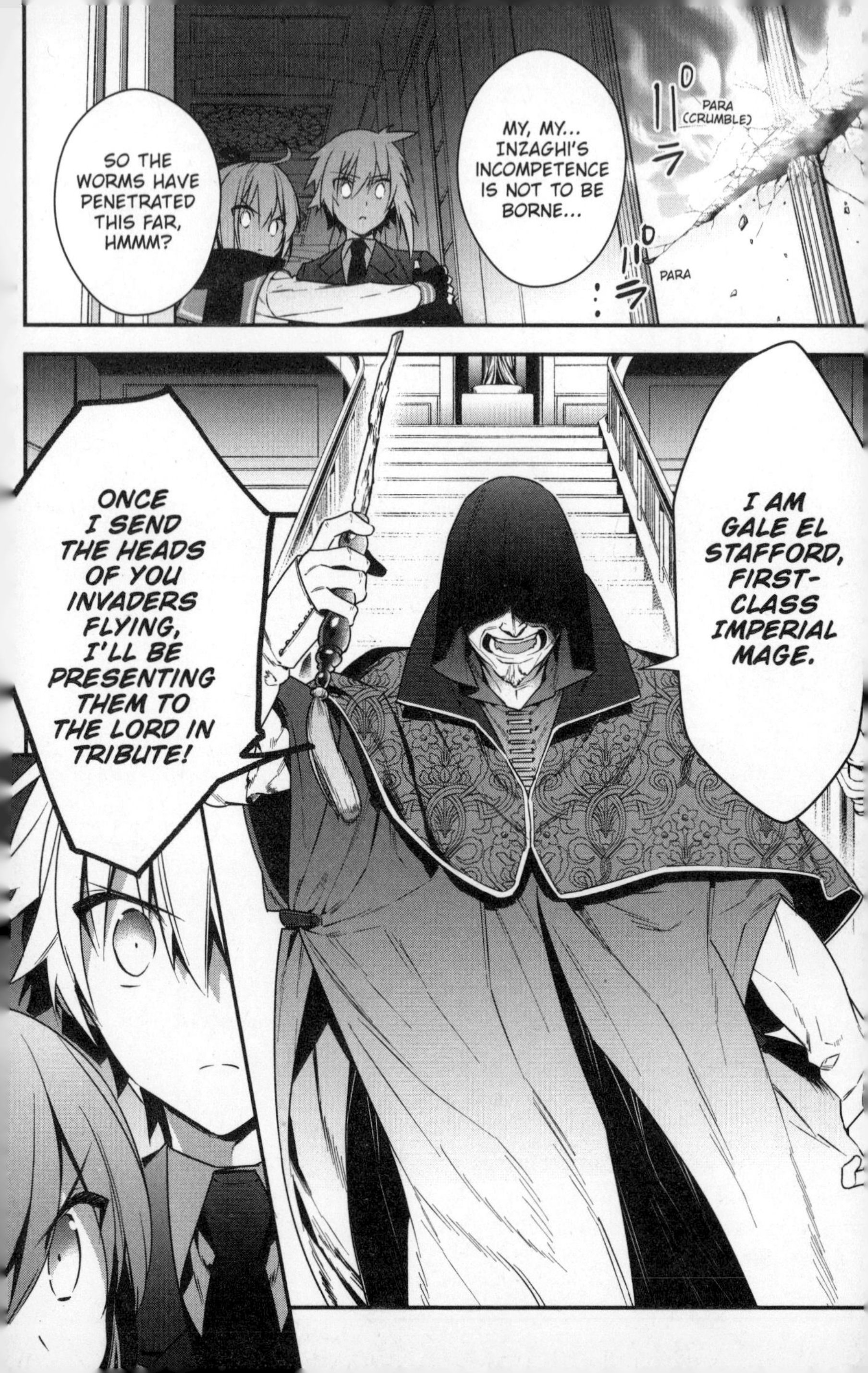
PARA (CRUMBLE)
PARA
MY, MY... INZAGHI'S INCOMPETENCE IS NOT TO BE BORNE...
SO THE WORMS HAVE PENETRATED THIS FAR, HMMM?
I AM GALE EL STAFFORD, FIRST-CLASS IMPERIAL MAGE.
ONCE I SEND THE HEADS OF YOU INVADERS FLYING, I'LL BE PRESENTING THEM TO THE LORD IN TRIBUTE!

HIGH SCHOOL PRODIGIES HAVE IT EASY EVEN IN ANOTHER WORLD!

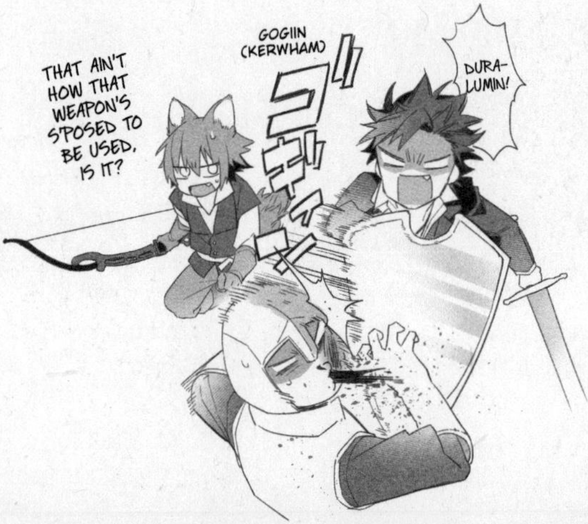
DURA-LUMIN!
GOGIIN (KERWHAM)
THAT AIN'T HOW THAT WEAPON'S S'POSED TO BE USED, IS IT?

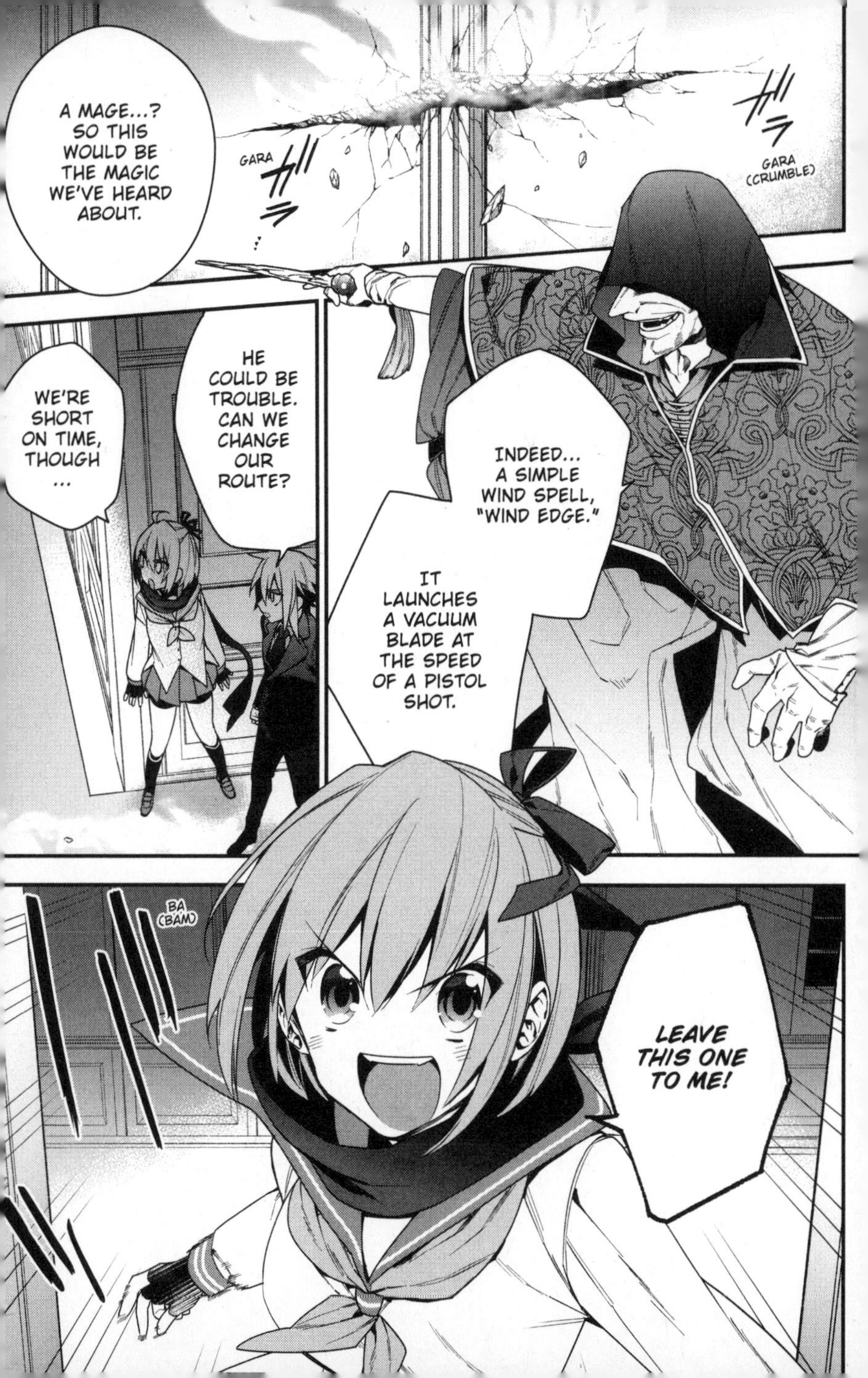
GARA (CRUMBLE)
GARA
A MAGE...? SO THIS WOULD BE THE MAGIC WE'VE HEARD ABOUT.
INDEED... A SIMPLE WIND SPELL, "WIND EDGE."
IT LAUNCHES A VACUUM BLADE AT THE SPEED OF A PISTOL SHOT.
HE COULD BE TROUBLE. CAN WE CHANGE OUR ROUTE?
WE'RE SHORT ON TIME, THOUGH...
LEAVE THIS ONE TO ME!
BA (BAM)

CHAPTER 16: WILL OF THE PEOPLE

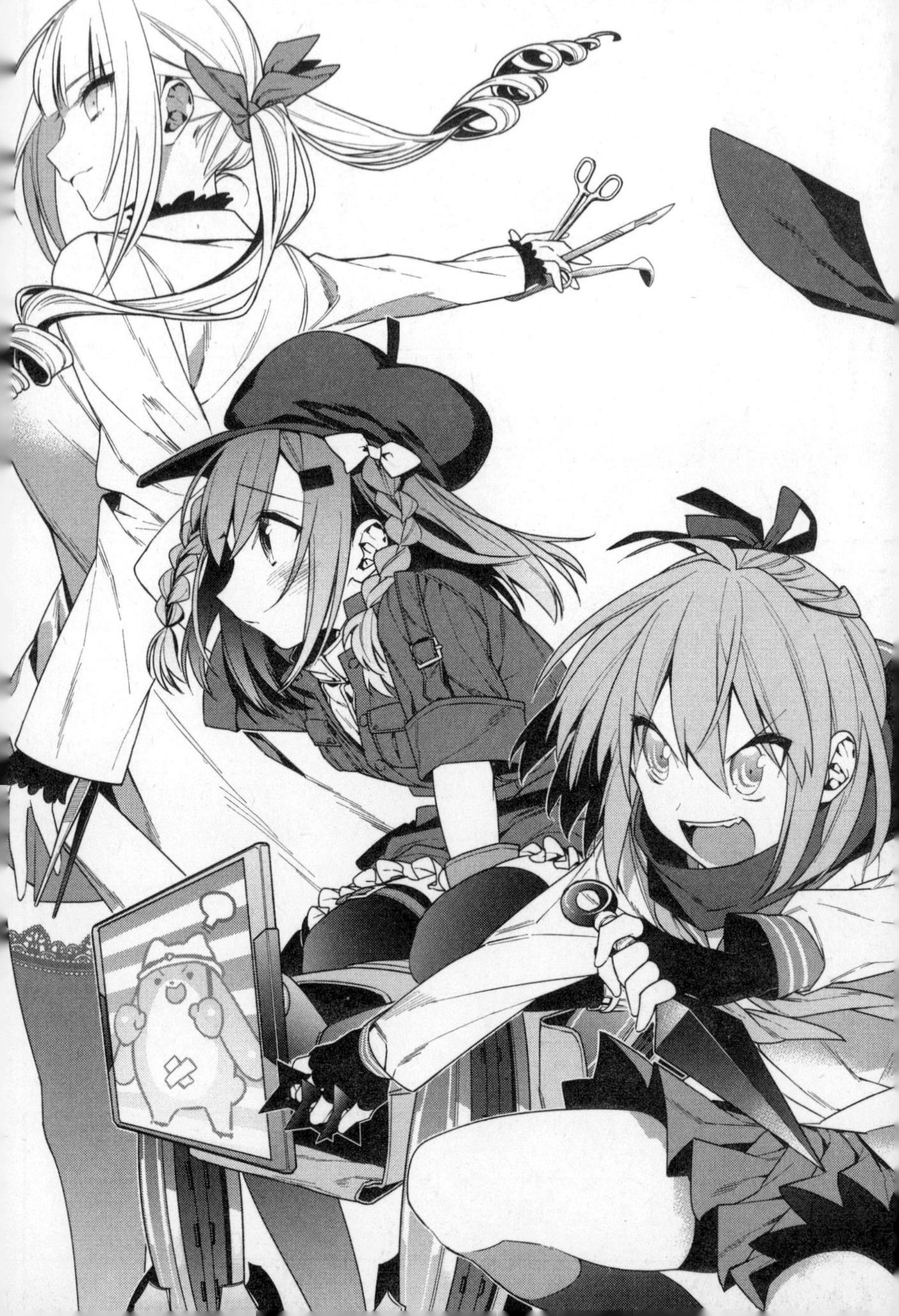

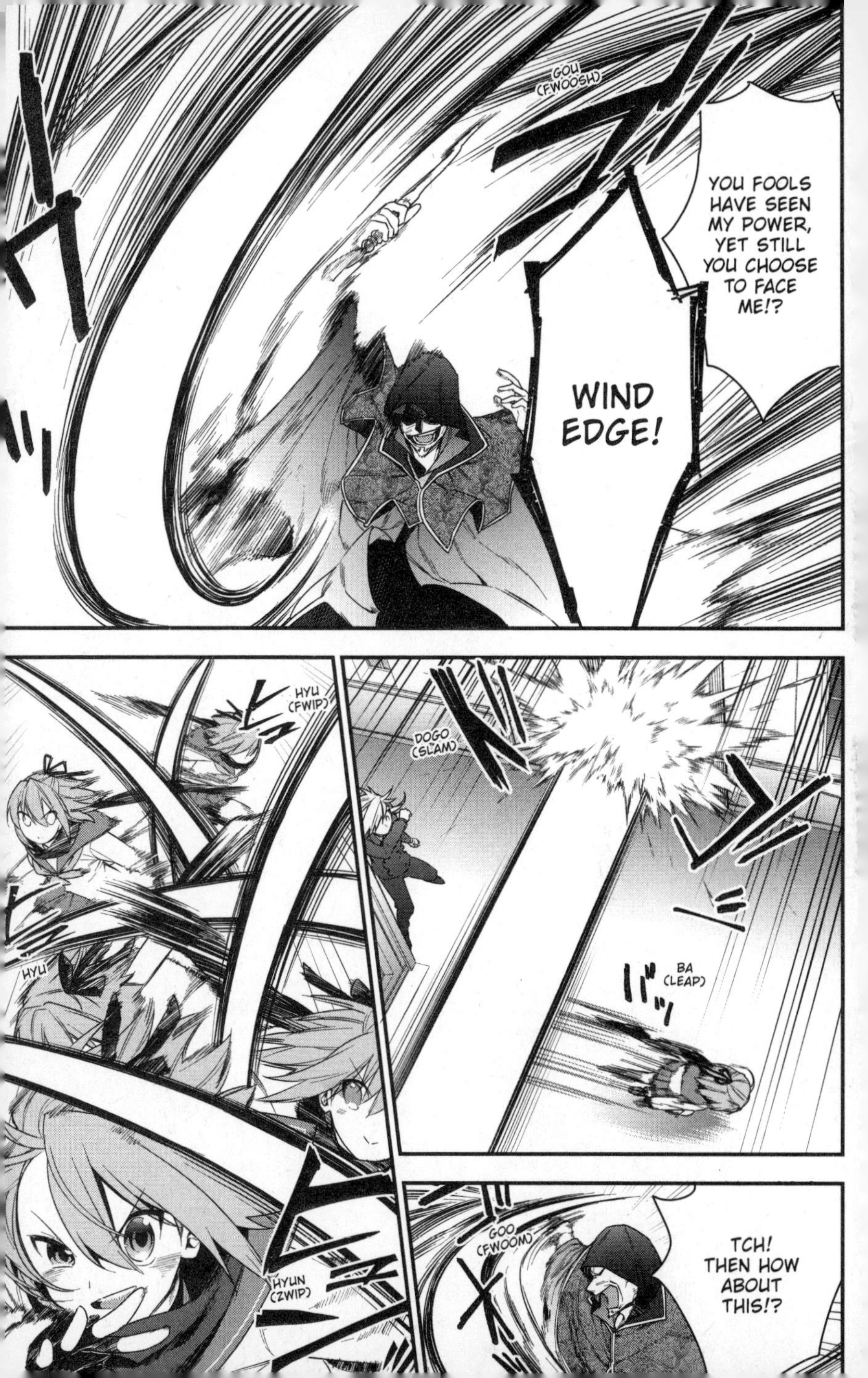
YOU FOOLS HAVE SEEN MY POWER, YET STILL YOU CHOOSE TO FACE ME!?
WIND EDGE!
GOU (FWOOSH)
DOGO (SLAM)
BA (LEAP)
TCH! THEN HOW ABOUT THIS!?
GOO (FWOOM)
HYU (FWIP)
HYU
HYUN (ZWIP)

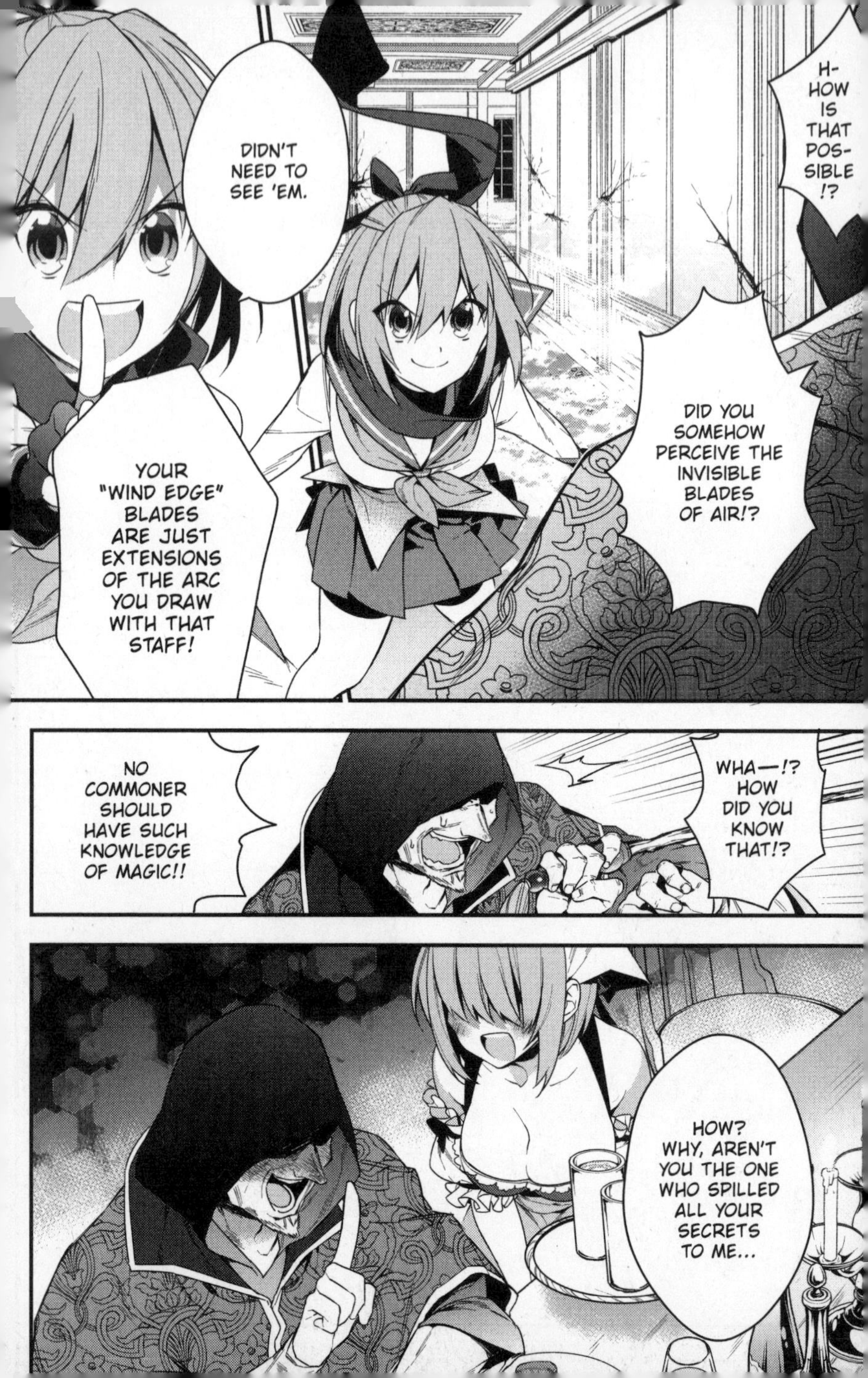
H-HOW IS THAT POS-SIBLE!?
DID YOU SOMEHOW PERCEIVE THE INVISIBLE BLADES OF AIR!?
DIDN'T NEED TO SEE 'EM.
YOUR "WIND EDGE" BLADES ARE JUST EXTENSIONS OF THE ARC YOU DRAW WITH THAT STAFF!
WHA—!? HOW DID YOU KNOW THAT!?
NO COMMONER SHOULD HAVE SUCH KNOWLEDGE OF MAGIC!!
HOW? WHY, AREN'T YOU THE ONE WHO SPILLED ALL YOUR SECRETS TO ME...

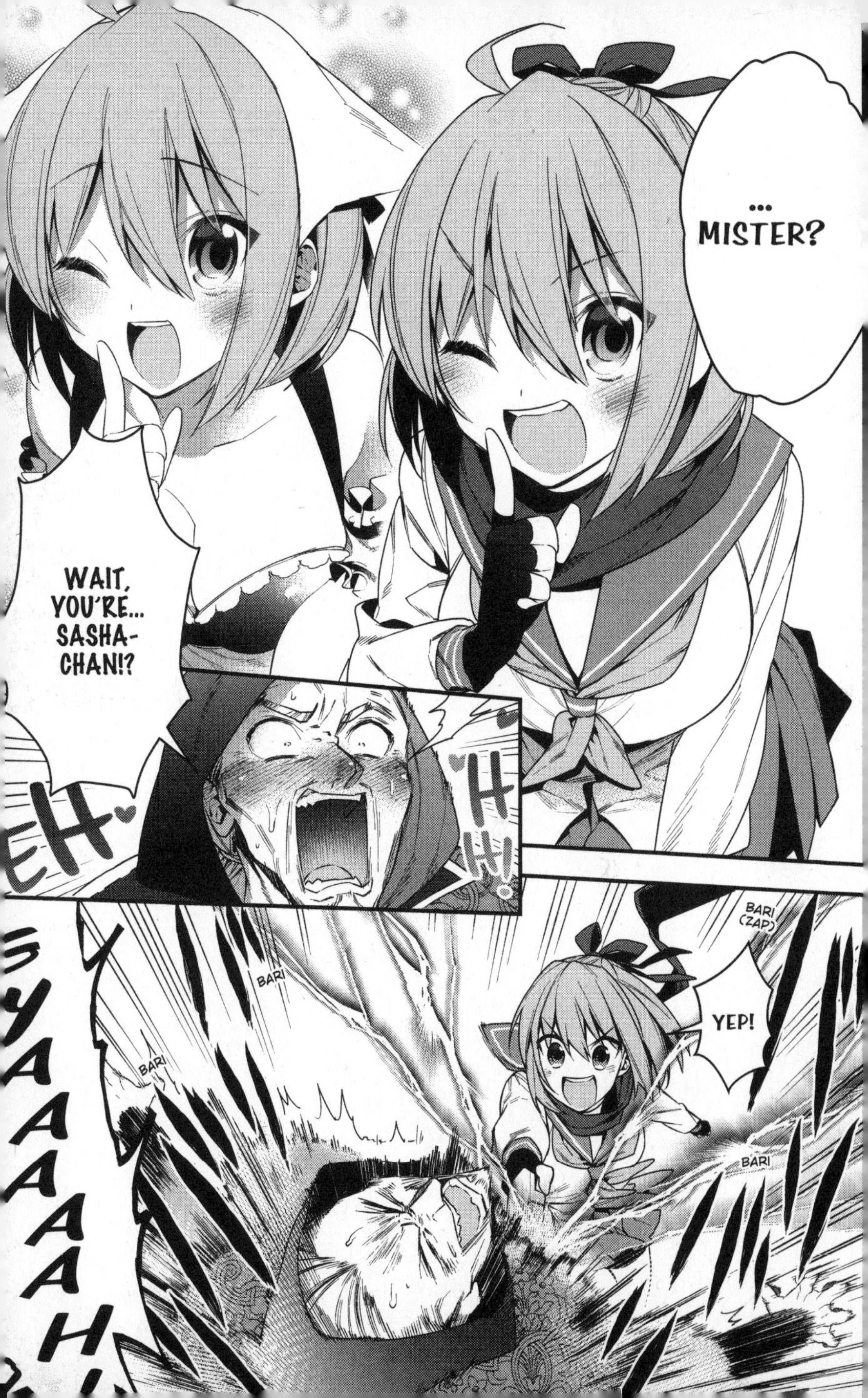
...MISTER?
WAIT, YOU'RE... SASHA-CHAN!?
EH♥
HH!
BARI (ZAP)
YEP!
BARI
BARI
BARI
BARI
YAAAAAAH!

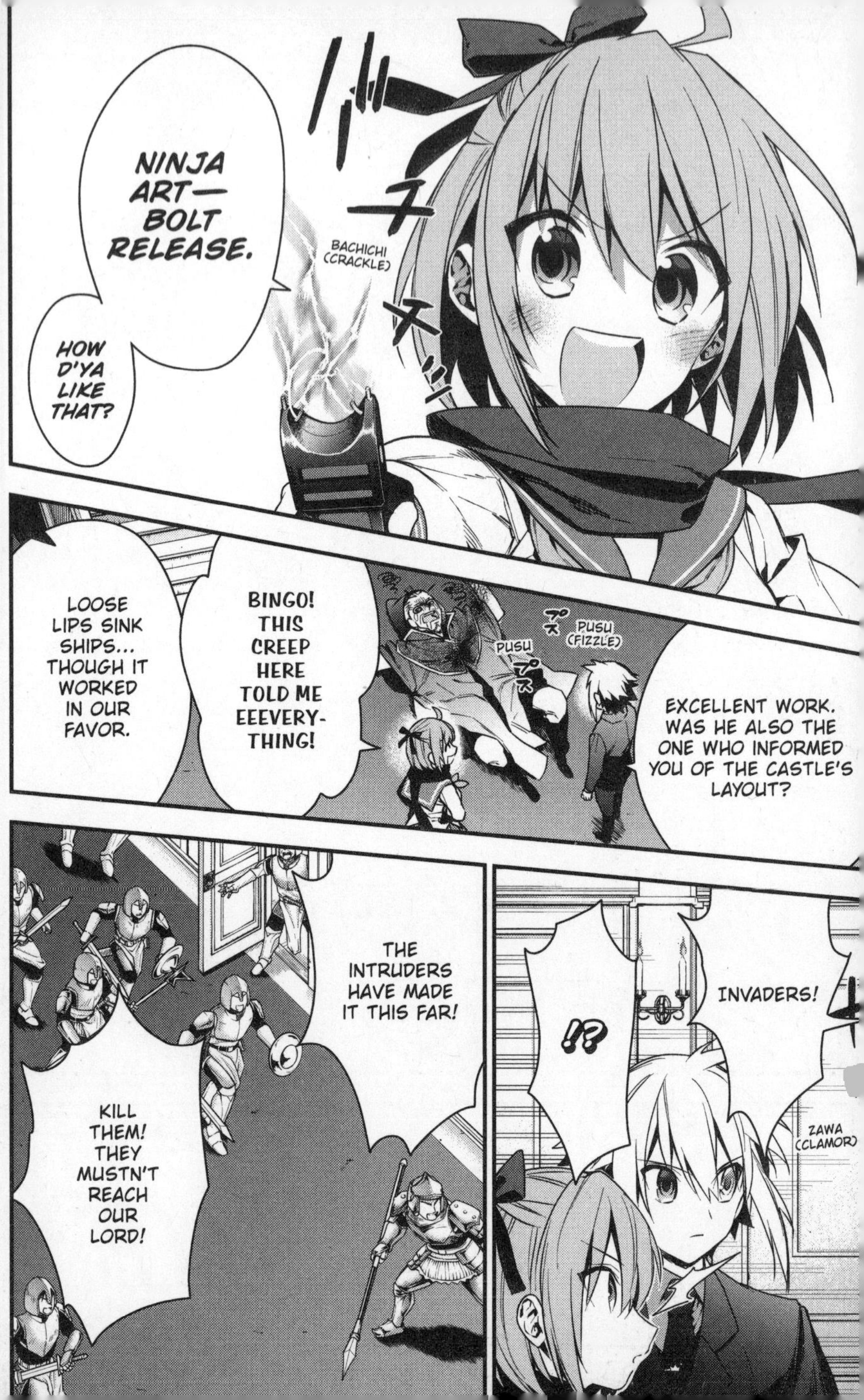
NINJA ART—BOLT RELEASE.
BACHICHI (CRACKLE)
HOW D'YA LIKE THAT?
EXCELLENT WORK. WAS HE ALSO THE ONE WHO INFORMED YOU OF THE CASTLE'S LAYOUT?
PUSU (FIZZLE)
PUSU
BINGO! THIS CREEP HERE TOLD ME EEEVERY-THING!
LOOSE LIPS SINK SHIPS... THOUGH IT WORKED IN OUR FAVOR.
INVADERS!
!?
ZAWA (CLAMOR)
THE INTRUDERS HAVE MADE IT THIS FAR!
KILL THEM! THEY MUSTN'T REACH OUR LORD!

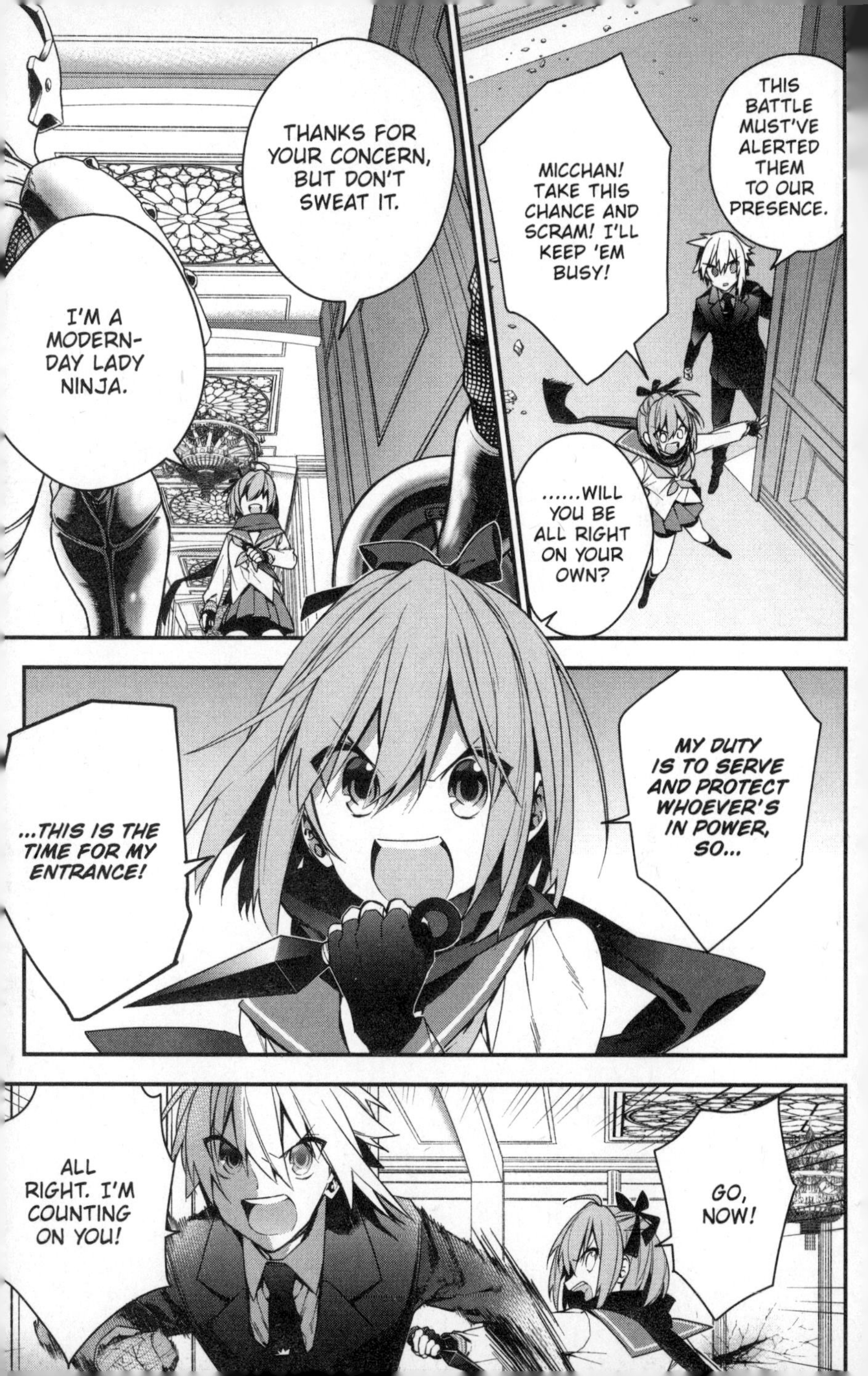
THIS BATTLE MUST'VE ALERTED THEM TO OUR PRESENCE.
MICCHAN! TAKE THIS CHANCE AND SCRAM! I'LL KEEP 'EM BUSY!
......WILL YOU BE ALL RIGHT ON YOUR OWN?
THANKS FOR YOUR CONCERN, BUT DON'T SWEAT IT.
I'M A MODERN-DAY LADY NINJA.
MY DUTY IS TO SERVE AND PROTECT WHOEVER'S IN POWER, SO...
...THIS IS THE TIME FOR MY ENTRANCE!
GO, NOW!
ALL RIGHT. I'M COUNTING ON YOU!

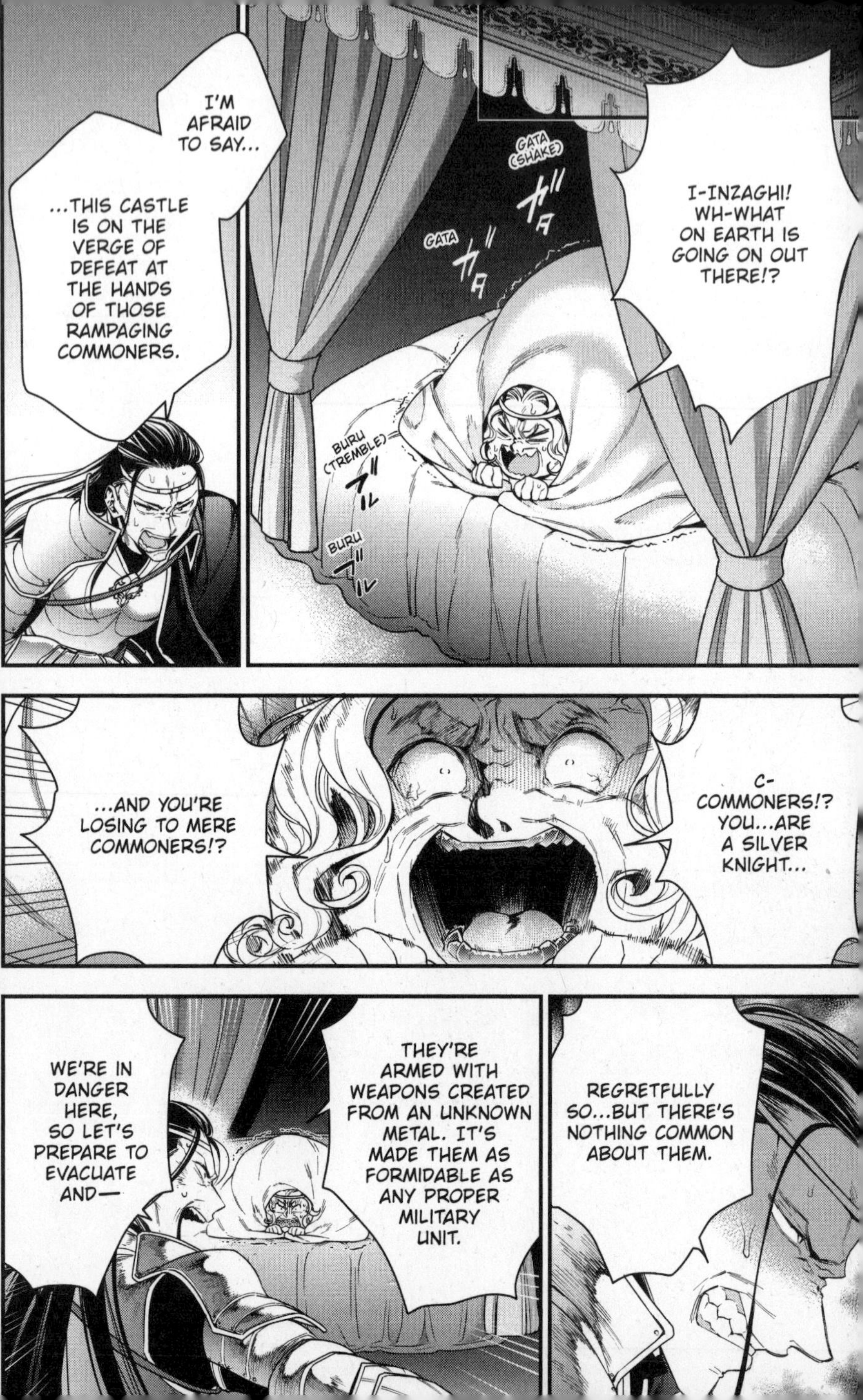
I-INZAGHI! WH-WHAT ON EARTH IS GOING ON OUT THERE!?
GATA (SHAKE)
GATA
BURU (TREMBLE)
BURU
I'M AFRAID TO SAY...
...THIS CASTLE IS ON THE VERGE OF DEFEAT AT THE HANDS OF THOSE RAMPAGING COMMONERS.
C- COMMONERS!? YOU...ARE A SILVER KNIGHT...
...AND YOU'RE LOSING TO MERE COMMONERS!?
REGRETFULLY SO...BUT THERE'S NOTHING COMMON ABOUT THEM.
THEY'RE ARMED WITH WEAPONS CREATED FROM AN UNKNOWN METAL. IT'S MADE THEM AS FORMIDABLE AS ANY PROPER MILITARY UNIT.
WE'RE IN DANGER HERE, SO LET'S PREPARE TO EVACUATE AND—

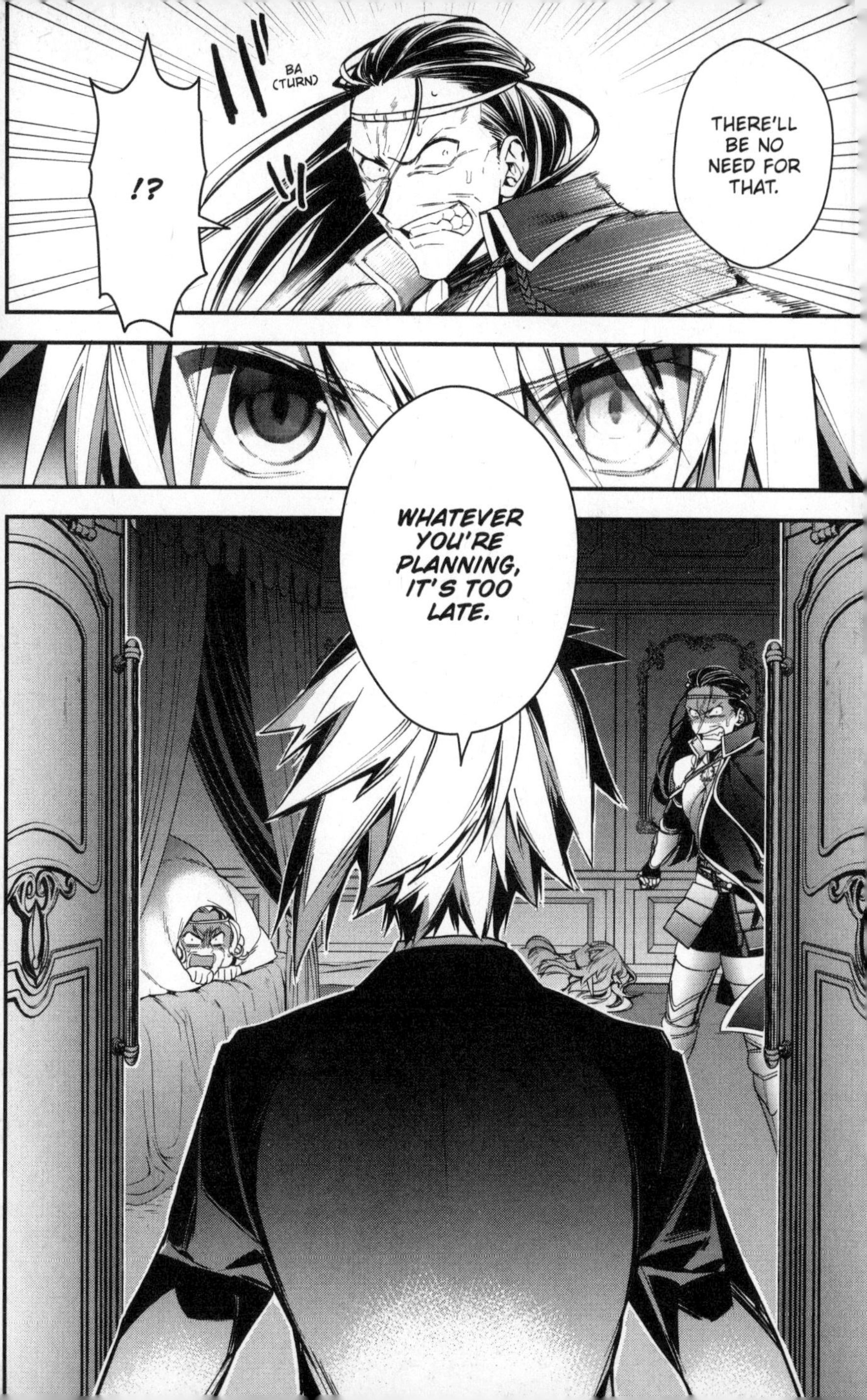
THERE'LL BE NO NEED FOR THAT.
BA (TURN)
!?
WHATEVER YOU'RE PLANNING, IT'S TOO LATE.

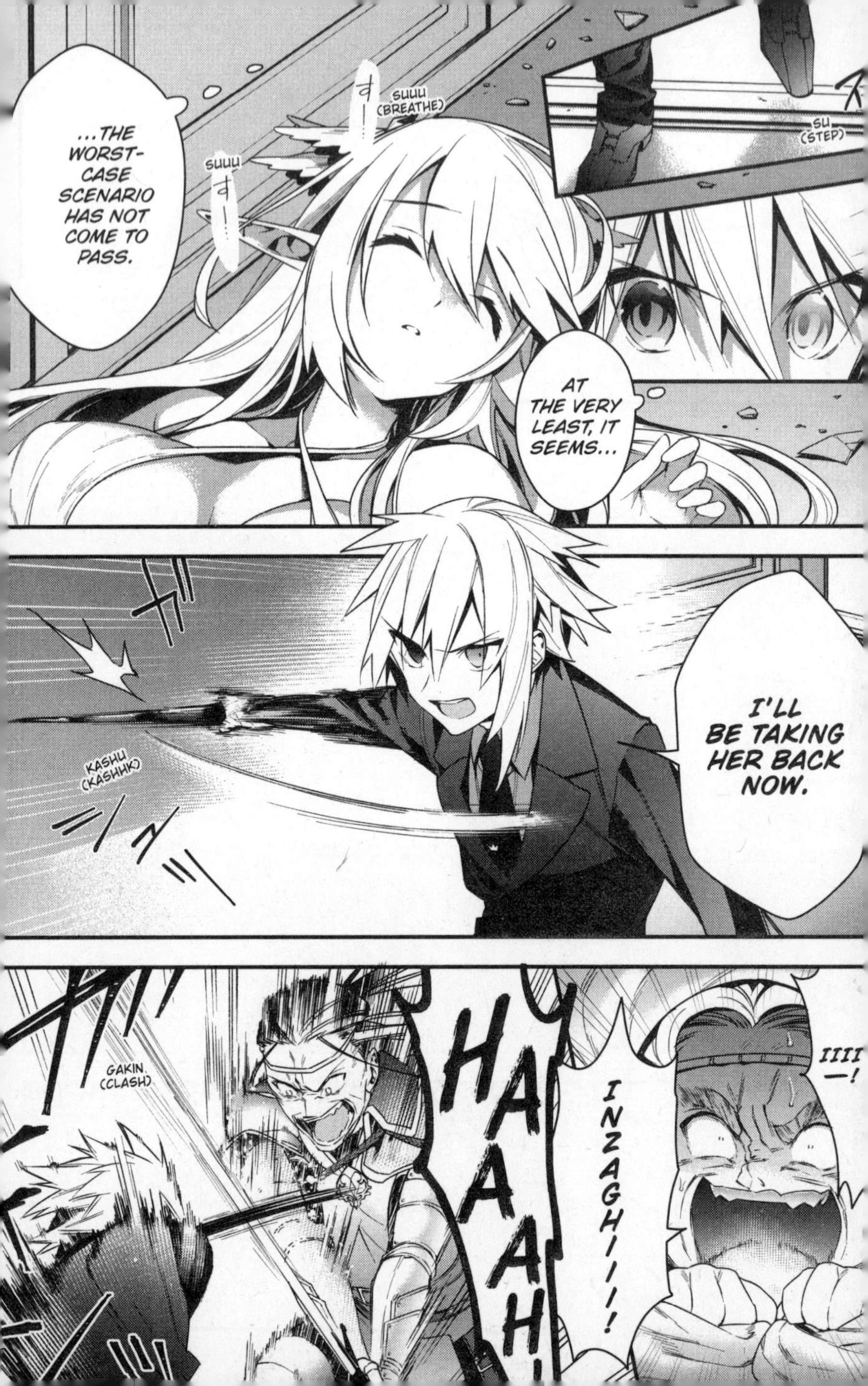
SU (STEP)
SUUU (BREATHE)
SUUU
AT THE VERY LEAST, IT SEEMS...
...THE WORST-CASE SCENARIO HAS NOT COME TO PASS.
I'LL BE TAKING HER BACK NOW.
KASHU (KASHHK)
IIII—!
INZAGHI!!!!
HAAAAH!
GAKIN (CLASH)

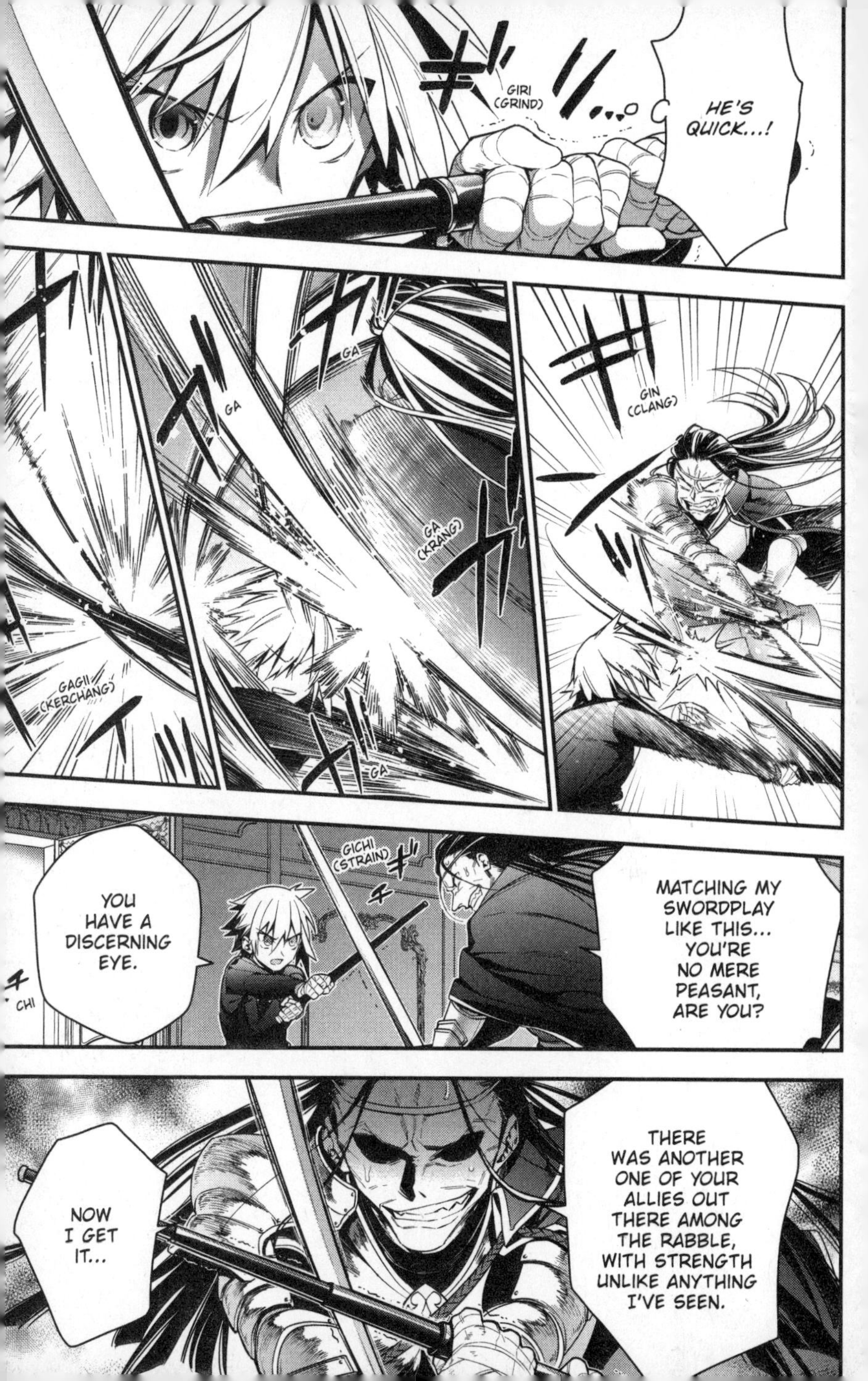
HE'S QUICK...!
GIRI (GRIND)
GIN (CLANG)
GA
GA (KRANG)
GA
GAGII (KERCHANG)
GA
MATCHING MY SWORDPLAY LIKE THIS... YOU'RE NO MERE PEASANT, ARE YOU?
GICHI (STRAIN)
YOU HAVE A DISCERNING EYE.
CHI
THERE WAS ANOTHER ONE OF YOUR ALLIES OUT THERE AMONG THE RABBLE, WITH STRENGTH UNLIKE ANYTHING I'VE SEEN.
NOW I GET IT...

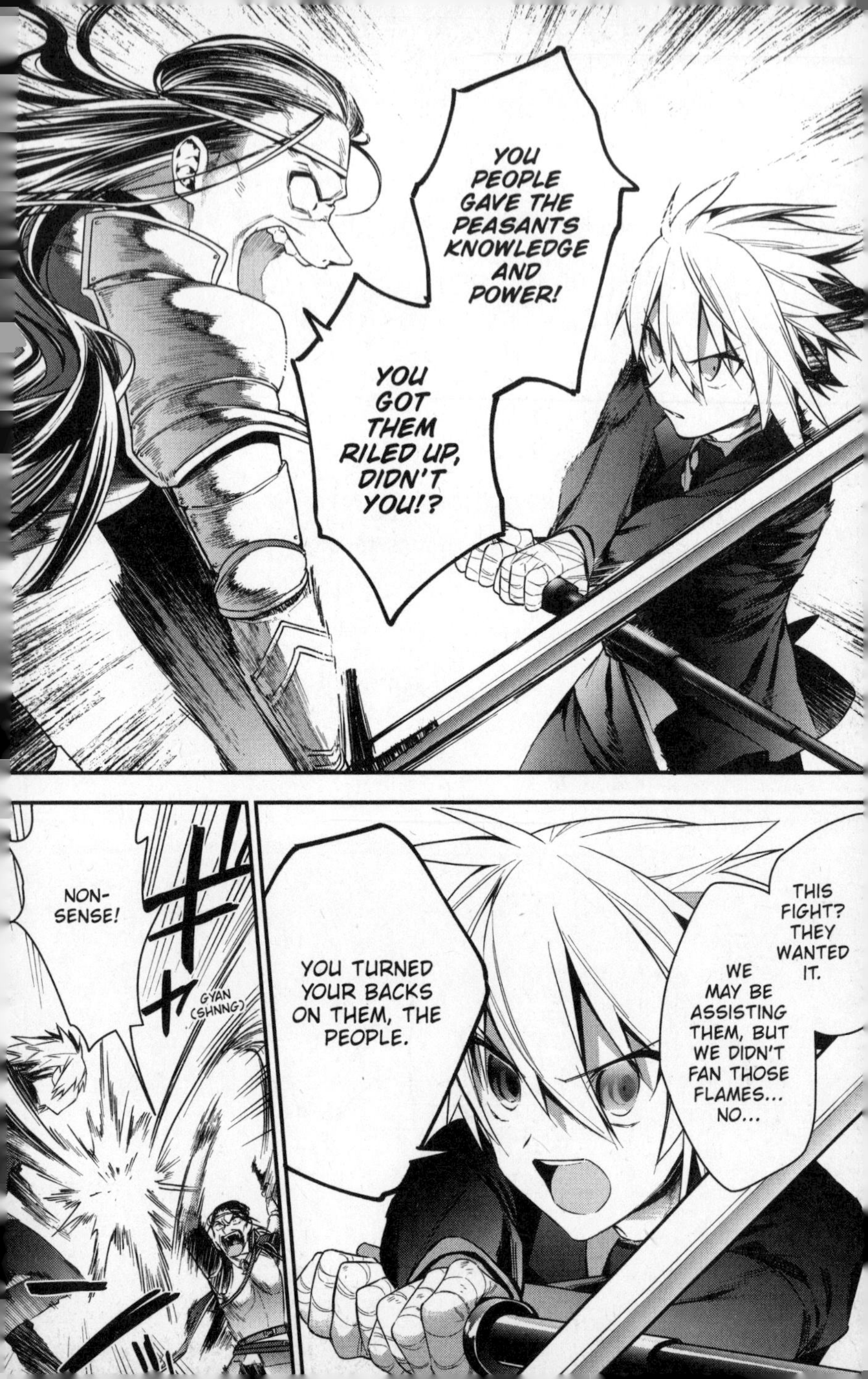
YOU PEOPLE GAVE THE PEASANTS KNOWLEDGE AND POWER!
YOU GOT THEM RILED UP, DIDN'T YOU!?
WE MAY BE ASSISTING THEM, BUT WE DIDN'T FAN THOSE FLAMES... NO...
THIS FIGHT? THEY WANTED IT.
YOU TURNED YOUR BACKS ON THEM, THE PEOPLE.
NON-SENSE!
GYAN (SHNNG)

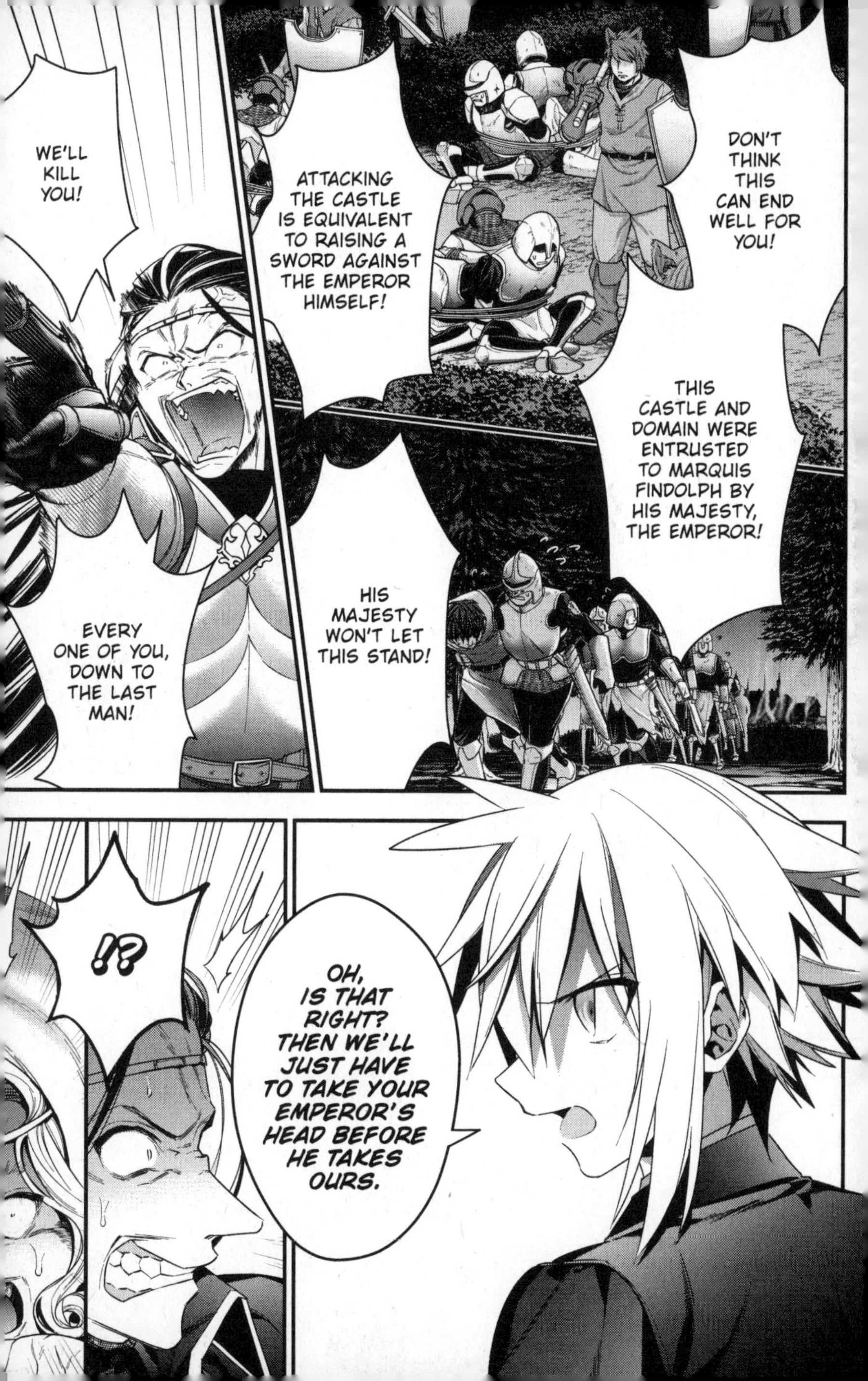
DON'T THINK THIS CAN END WELL FOR YOU!
ATTACKING THE CASTLE IS EQUIVALENT TO RAISING A SWORD AGAINST THE EMPEROR HIMSELF!
THIS CASTLE AND DOMAIN WERE ENTRUSTED TO MARQUIS FINDOLPH BY HIS MAJESTY, THE EMPEROR!
HIS MAJESTY WON'T LET THIS STAND!
WE'LL KILL YOU!
EVERY ONE OF YOU, DOWN TO THE LAST MAN!
OH, IS THAT RIGHT? THEN WE'LL JUST HAVE TO TAKE YOUR EMPEROR'S HEAD BEFORE HE TAKES OURS.
!?

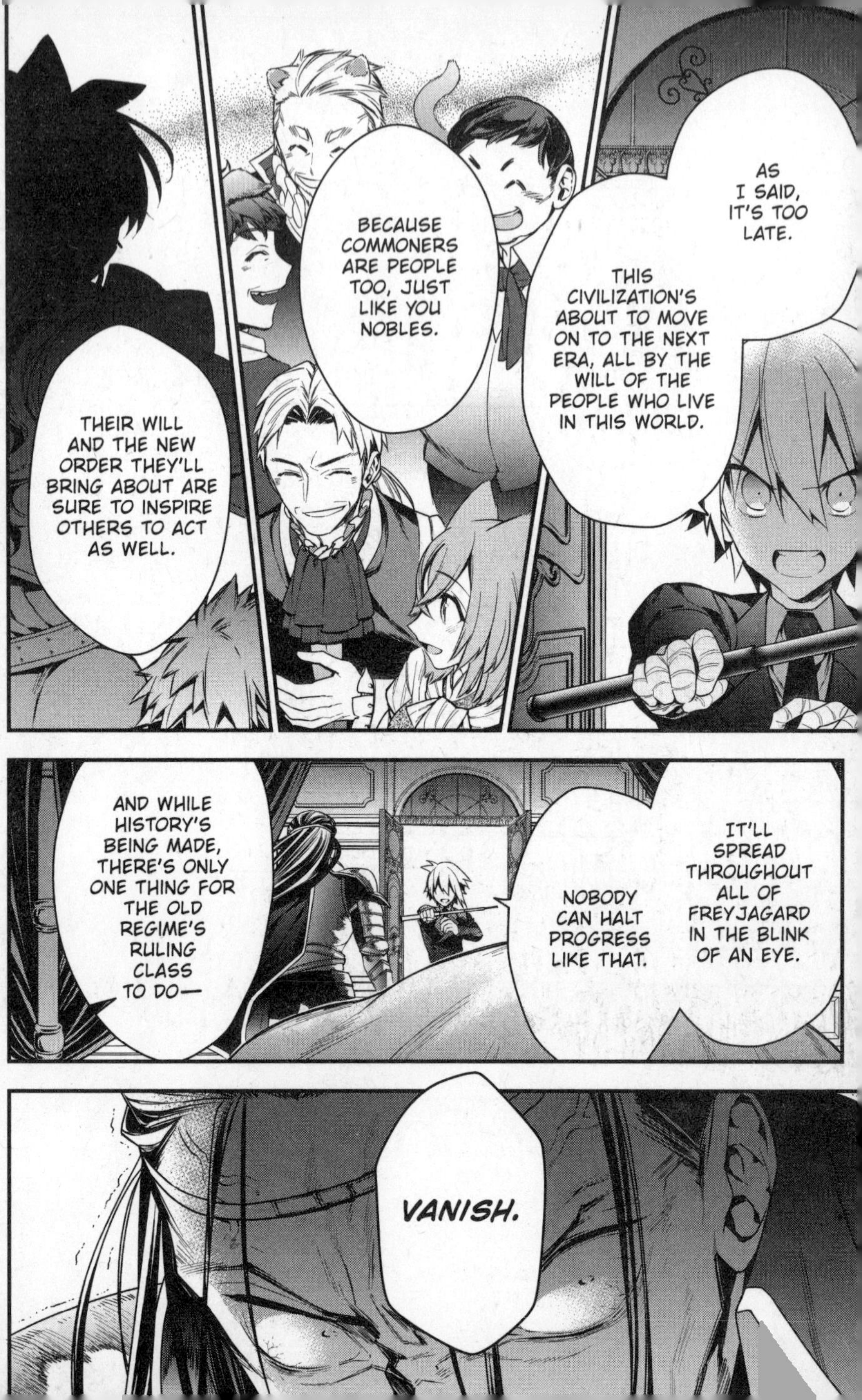
AS I SAID, IT'S TOO LATE.
THIS CIVILIZATION'S ABOUT TO MOVE ON TO THE NEXT ERA, ALL BY THE WILL OF THE PEOPLE WHO LIVE IN THIS WORLD.
BECAUSE COMMONERS ARE PEOPLE TOO, JUST LIKE YOU NOBLES.
THEIR WILL AND THE NEW ORDER THEY'LL BRING ABOUT ARE SURE TO INSPIRE OTHERS TO ACT AS WELL.
IT'LL SPREAD THROUGHOUT ALL OF FREYJAGARD IN THE BLINK OF AN EYE.
NOBODY CAN HALT PROGRESS LIKE THAT.
AND WHILE HISTORY'S BEING MADE, THERE'S ONLY ONE THING FOR THE OLD REGIME'S RULING CLASS TO DO—
VANISH.

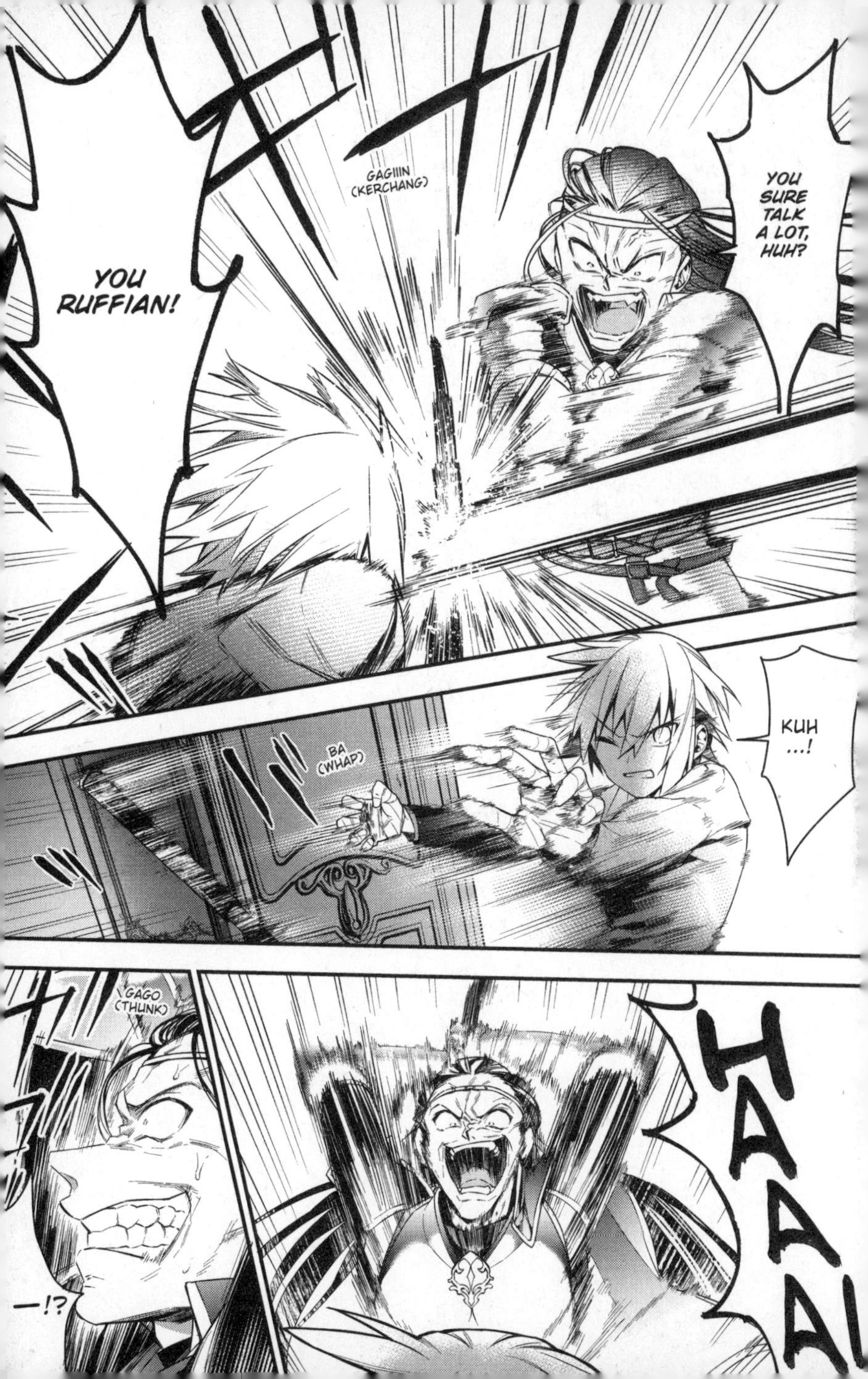
YOU SURE TALK A LOT, HUH?
GAGIIN (KERCHANG)
YOU RUFFIAN!
KUH ...!
BA (WHAP)
HAAA!
GAGO (THUNK)
—!?

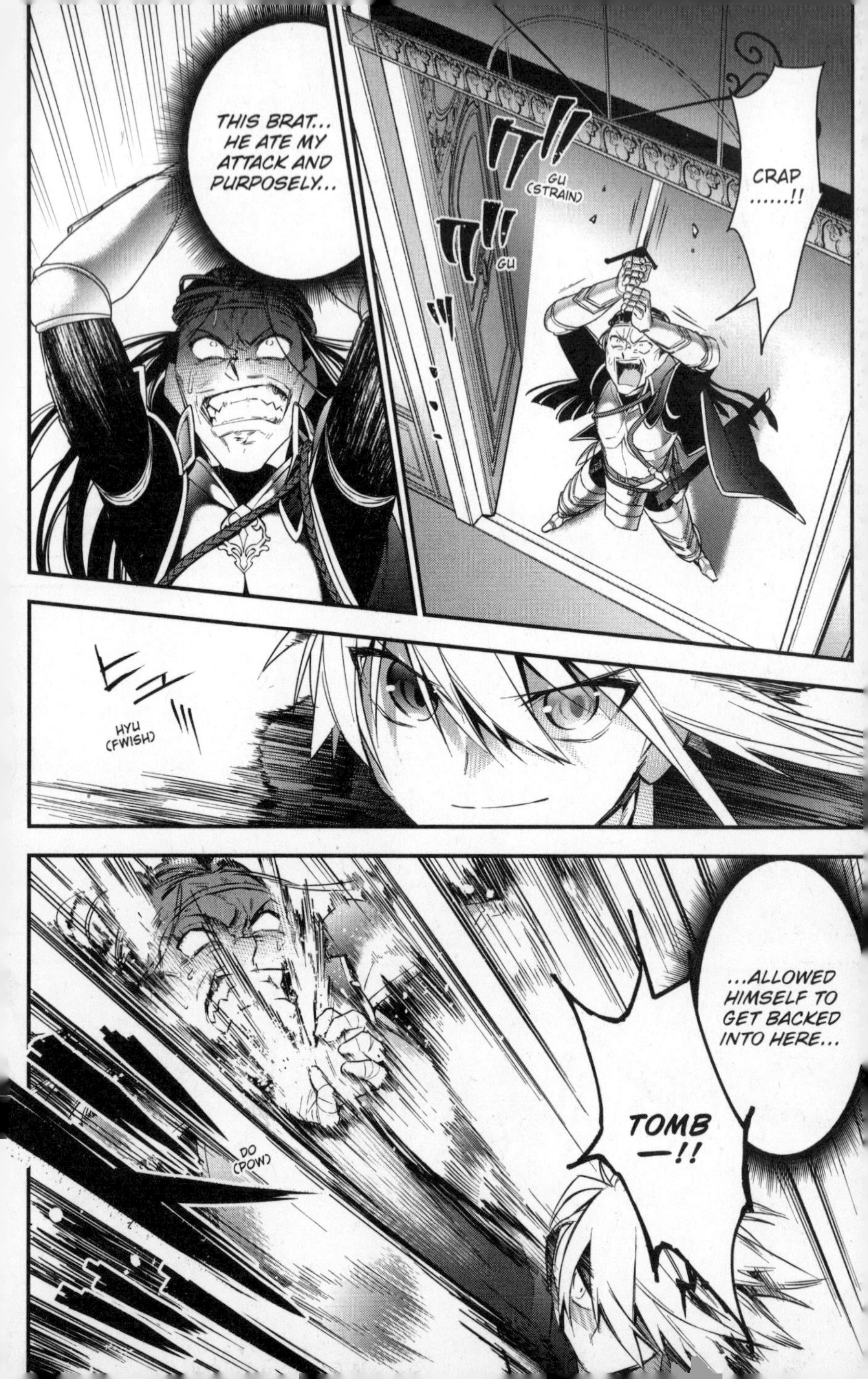
CRAP ......!!
GU (STRAIN)
GU
THIS BRAT... HE ATE MY ATTACK AND PURPOSELY...
HYU (FWISH)
...ALLOWED HIMSELF TO GET BACKED INTO HERE...
TOMB—!!
DO (POW)

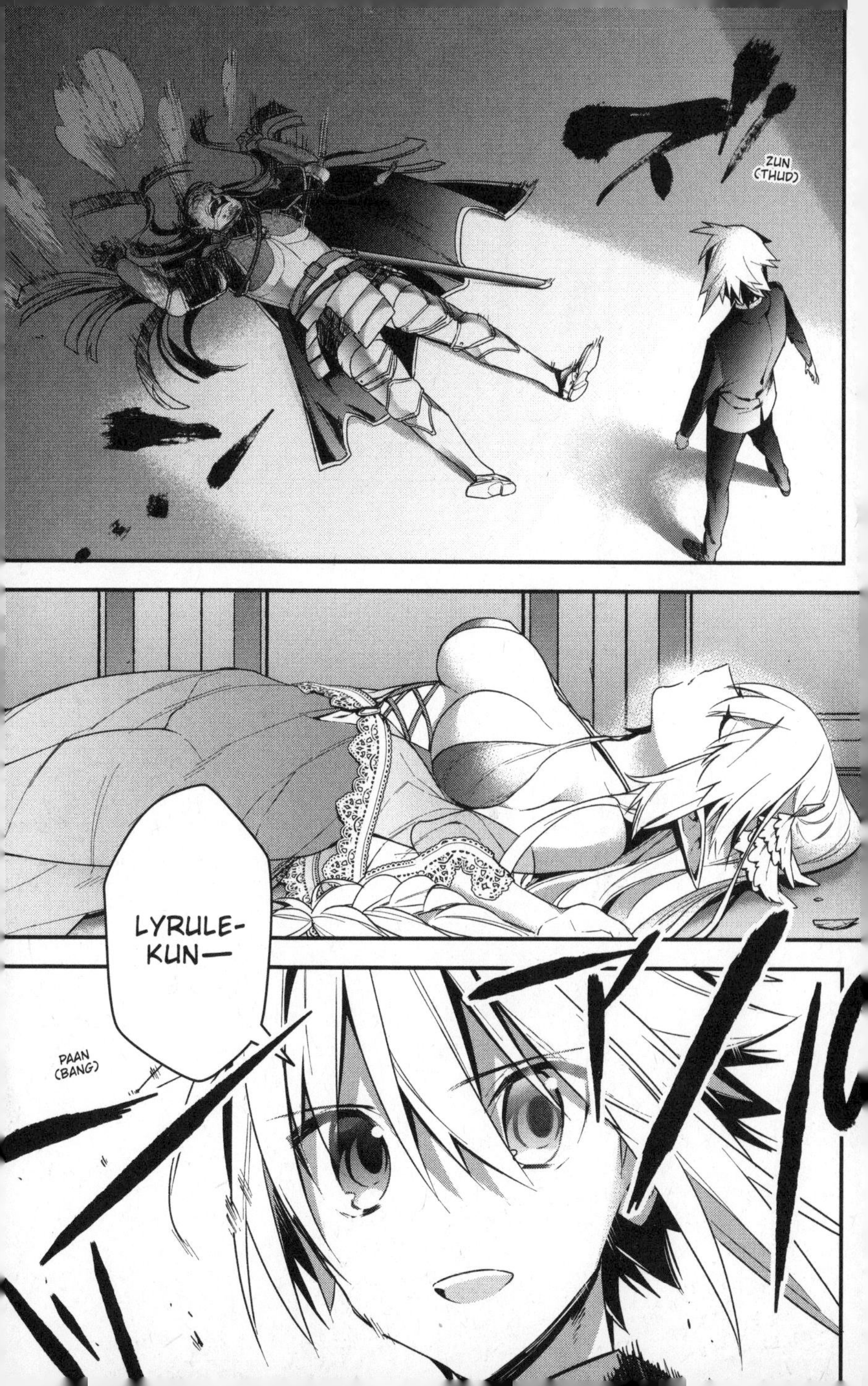
ZUN
(THUD)
LYRULE-KUN—
PAAN
(BANG)

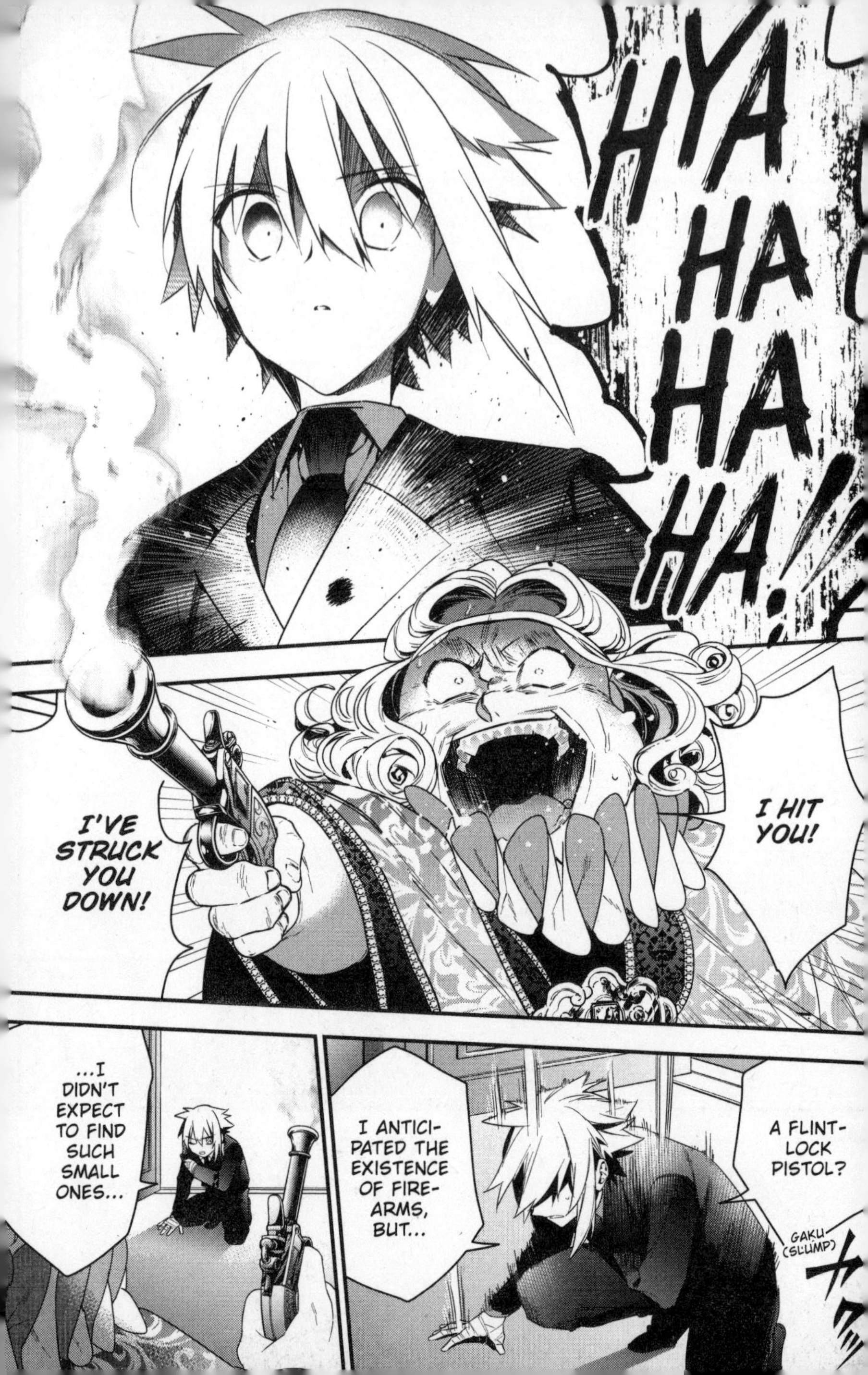
HYA HA HA HA!!
I HIT YOU!
I'VE STRUCK YOU DOWN!
A FLINT-LOCK PISTOL?
GAKU (SLUMP)
I ANTICI-PATED THE EXISTENCE OF FIRE-ARMS, BUT...
...I DIDN'T EXPECT TO FIND SUCH SMALL ONES...

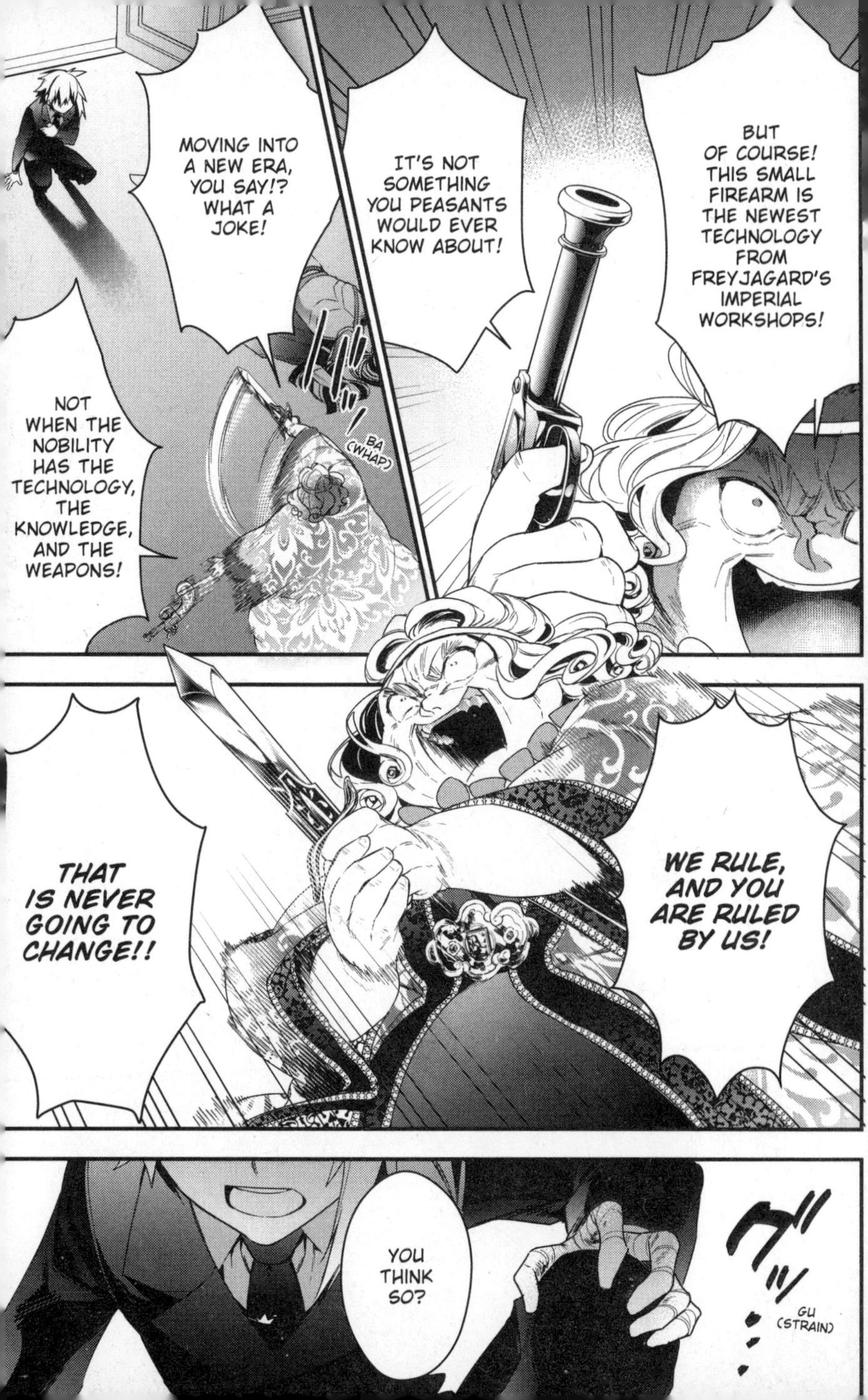
BUT OF COURSE! THIS SMALL FIREARM IS THE NEWEST TECHNOLOGY FROM FREYJAGARD'S IMPERIAL WORKSHOPS!
IT'S NOT SOMETHING YOU PEASANTS WOULD EVER KNOW ABOUT!
MOVING INTO A NEW ERA, YOU SAY!? WHAT A JOKE!
BA (WHAP)
NOT WHEN THE NOBILITY HAS THE TECHNOLOGY, THE KNOWLEDGE, AND THE WEAPONS!
WE RULE, AND YOU ARE RULED BY US!
THAT IS NEVER GOING TO CHANGE!!
GU (STRAIN)
YOU THINK SO?

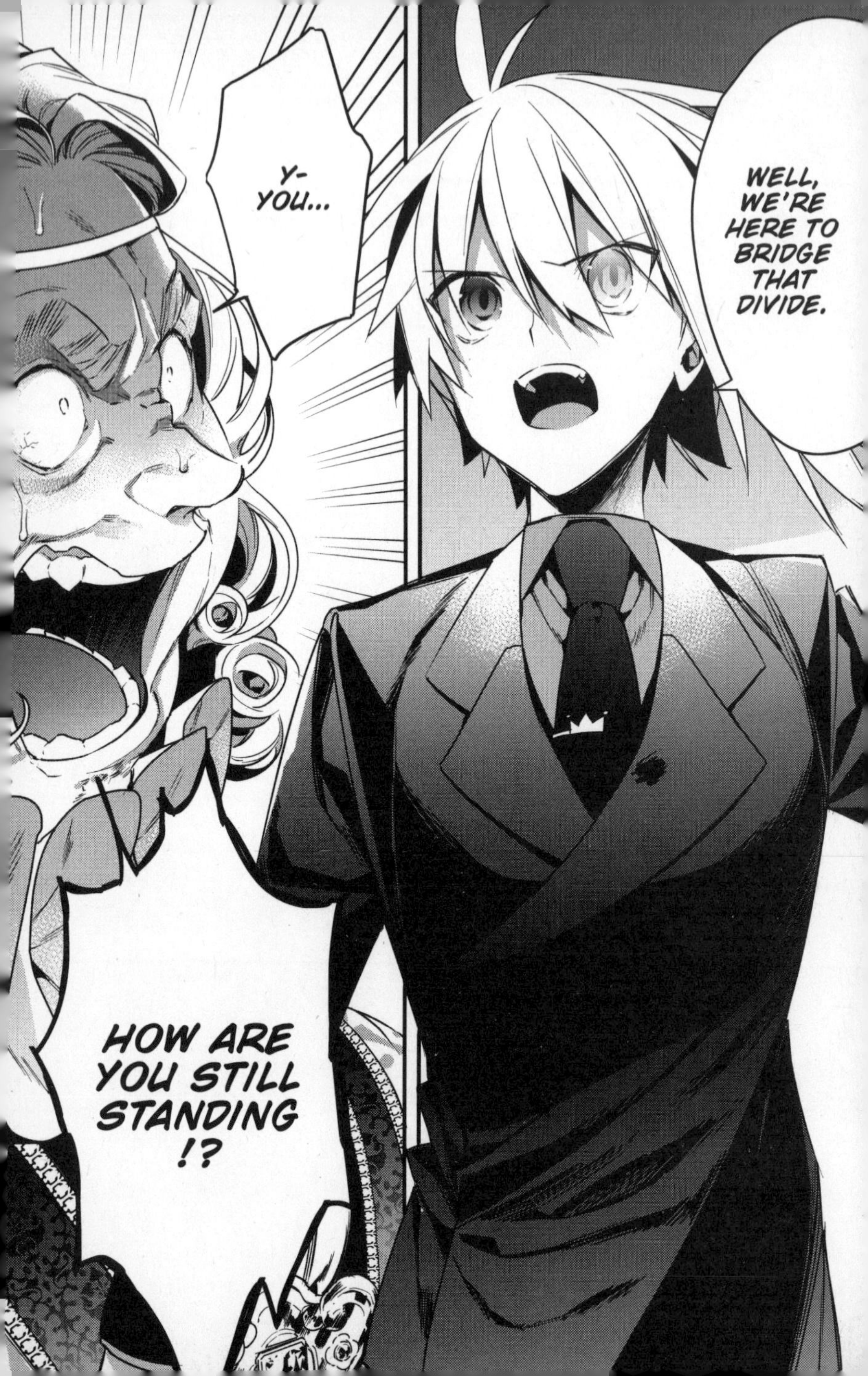
WELL, WE'RE HERE TO BRIDGE THAT DIVIDE.
Y-YOU...
HOW ARE YOU STILL STANDING!?

HIGH SCHOOL
PRODIGIES HAVE
IT EASY EVEN IN
ANOTHER
WORLD!

IT'S A
SECRET!

CHAPTER 17:
REVOLUTION'S START AND SHIFTING SHADOWS

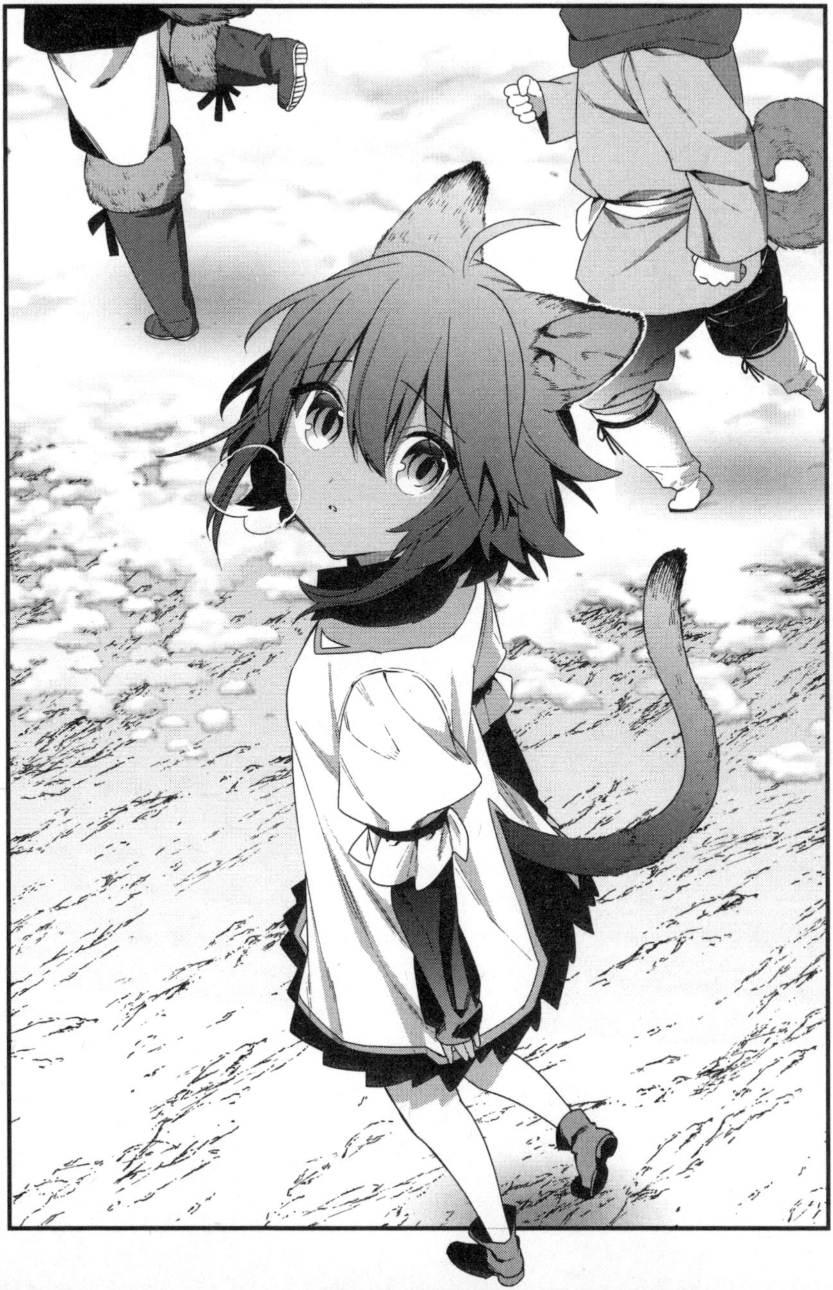

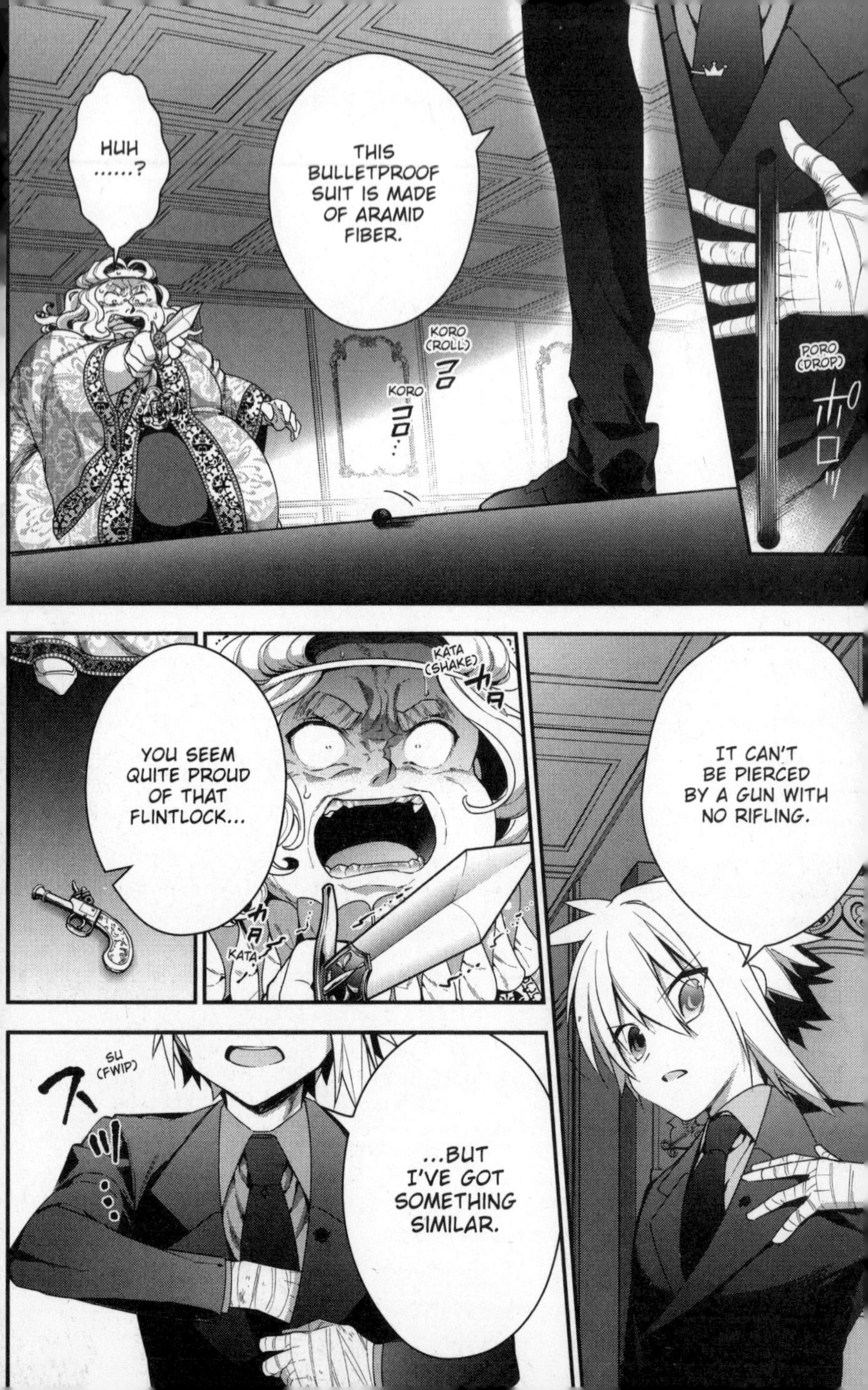
PORO (DROP)
ポロッ
THIS BULLETPROOF SUIT IS MADE OF ARAMID FIBER.
KORO (ROLL)
コロ
KORO
コロ…
HUH ......?
IT CAN'T BE PIERCED BY A GUN WITH NO RIFLING.
KATA (SHAKE)
カタ
KATA
YOU SEEM QUITE PROUD OF THAT FLINTLOCK...
...BUT I'VE GOT SOMETHING SIMILAR.
SU (FWIP)
ス

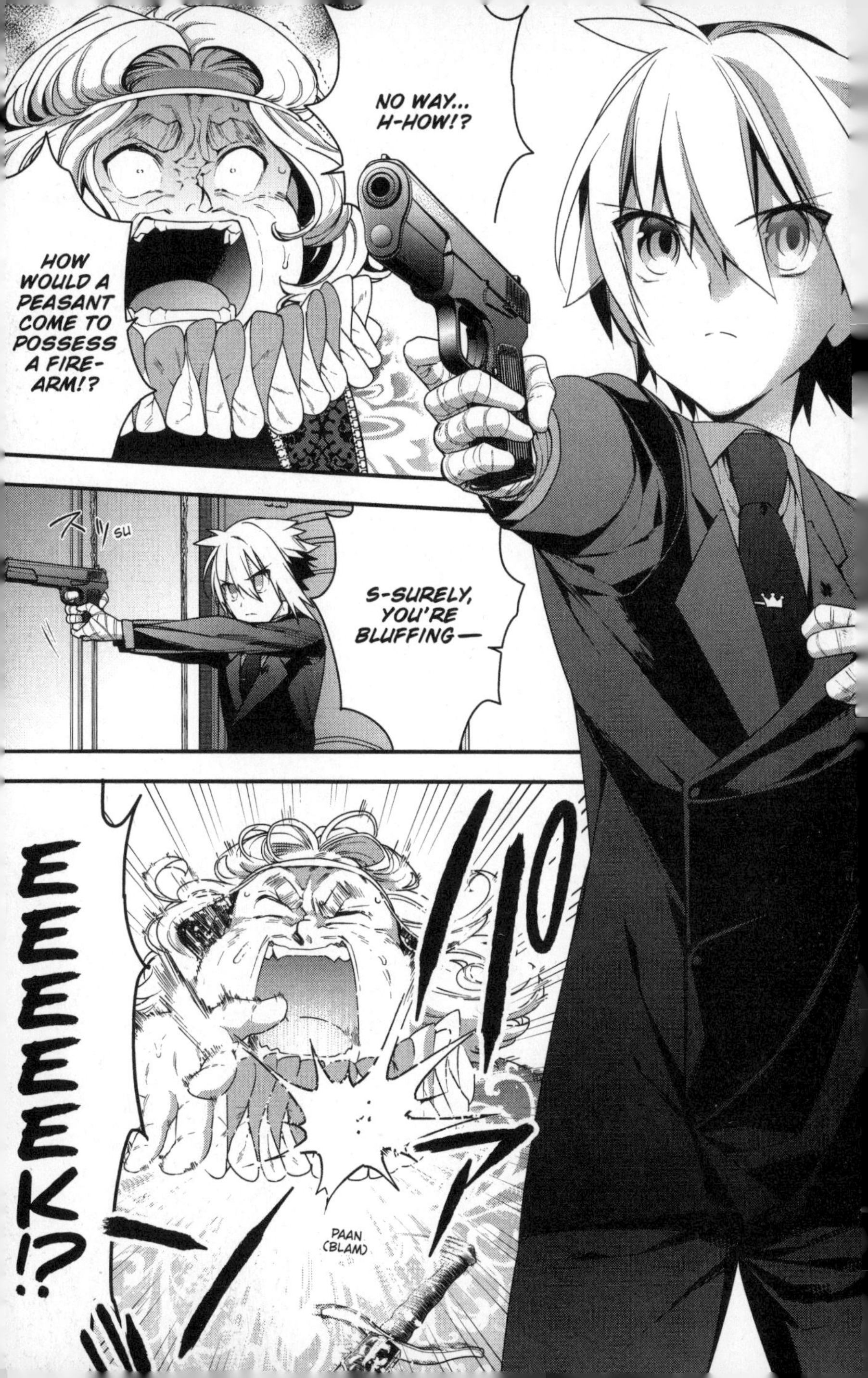
NO WAY... H-HOW!?
HOW WOULD A PEASANT COME TO POSSESS A FIRE-ARM!?
S-SURELY, YOU'RE BLUFFING—
SU
EEEEEK!?
PAAN (BLAM)

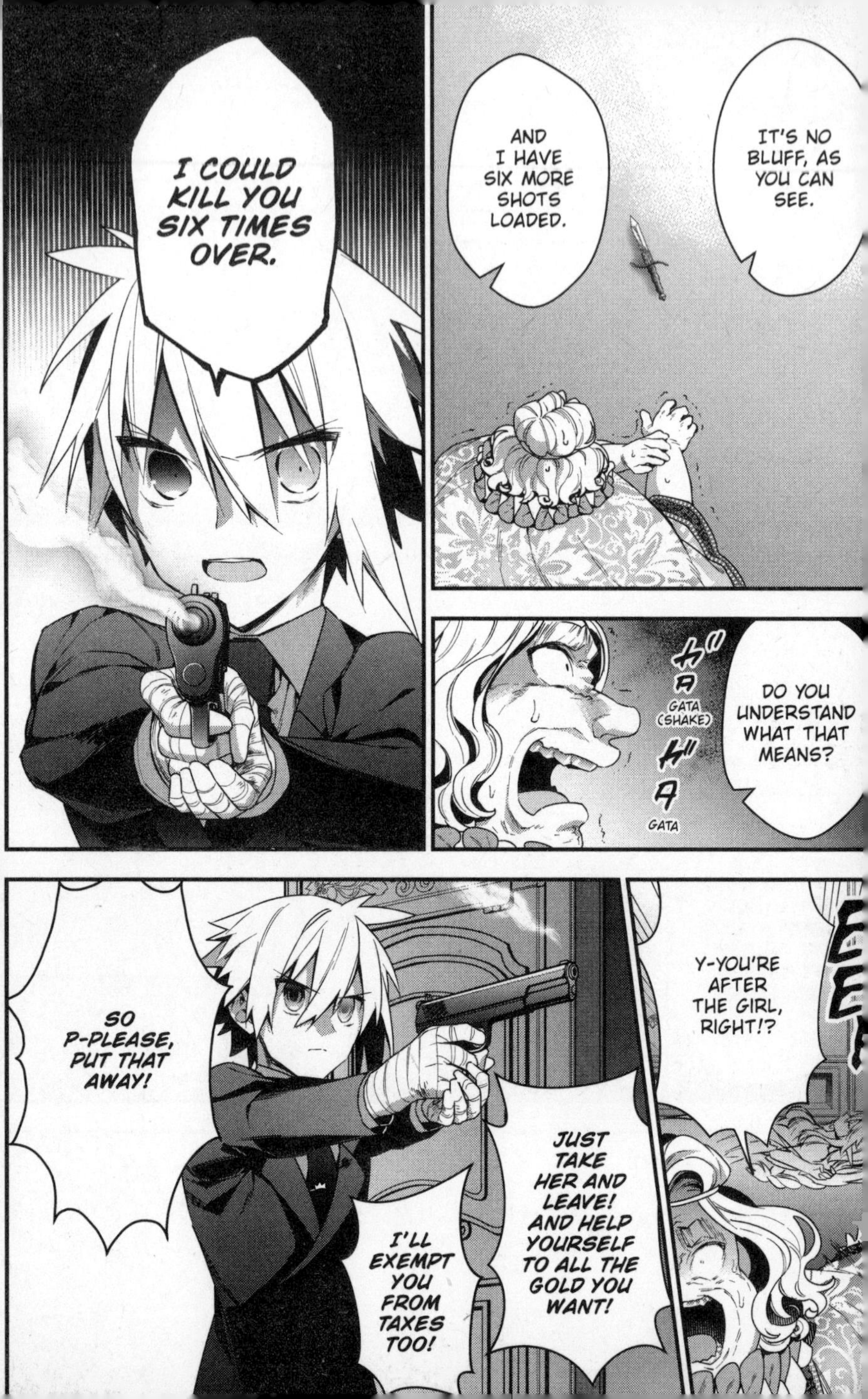
IT'S NO BLUFF, AS YOU CAN SEE.
AND I HAVE SIX MORE SHOTS LOADED.
DO YOU UNDERSTAND WHAT THAT MEANS?
ガタ
GATA (SHAKE)
ガタ
GATA
I COULD KILL YOU SIX TIMES OVER.
Y-YOU'RE AFTER THE GIRL, RIGHT!?
JUST TAKE HER AND LEAVE! AND HELP YOURSELF TO ALL THE GOLD YOU WANT!
I'LL EXEMPT YOU FROM TAXES TOO!
SO P-PLEASE, PUT THAT AWAY!

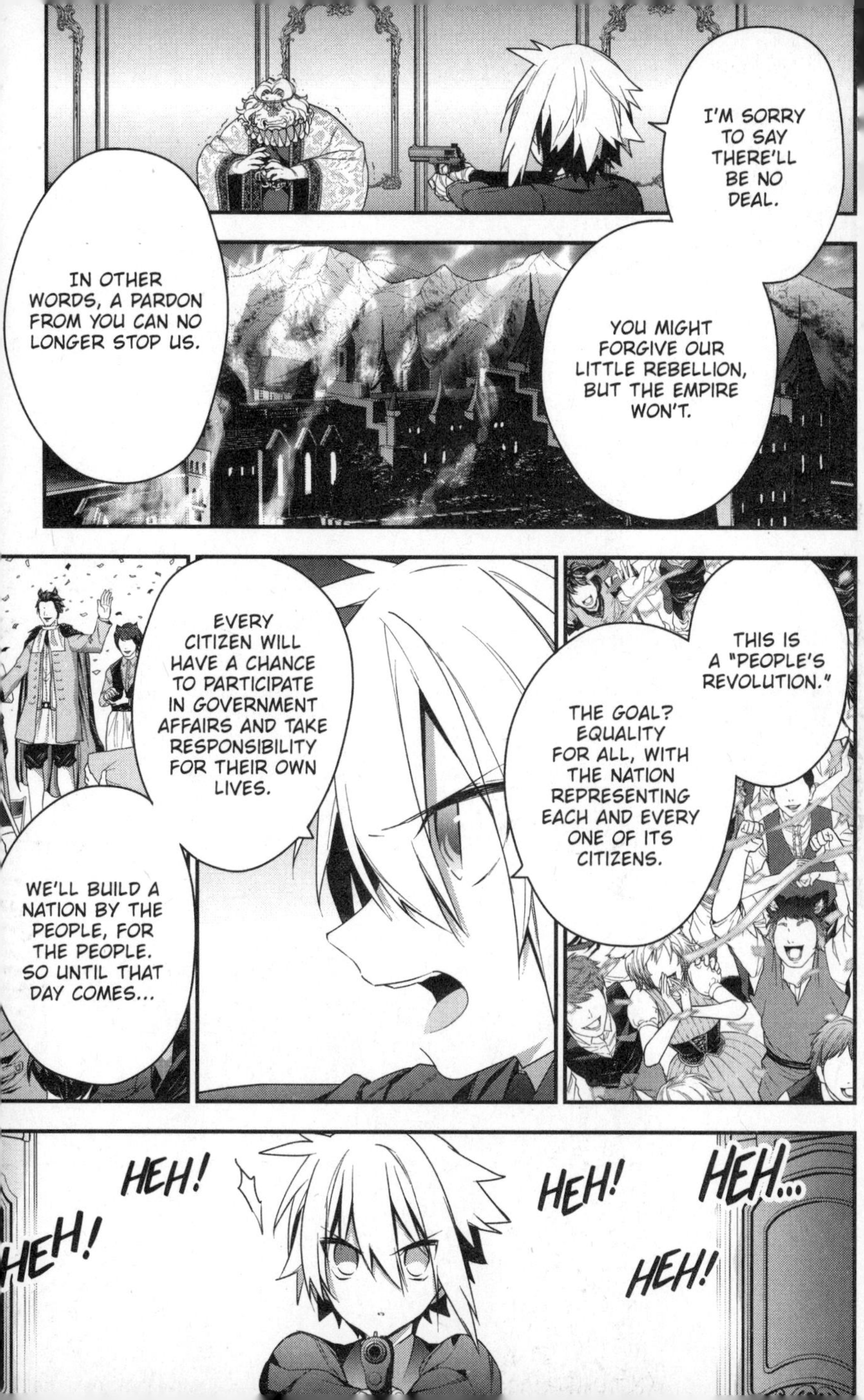
I'M SORRY TO SAY THERE'LL BE NO DEAL.
YOU MIGHT FORGIVE OUR LITTLE REBELLION, BUT THE EMPIRE WON'T.
IN OTHER WORDS, A PARDON FROM YOU CAN NO LONGER STOP US.
THIS IS A "PEOPLE'S REVOLUTION."
THE GOAL? EQUALITY FOR ALL, WITH THE NATION REPRESENTING EACH AND EVERY ONE OF ITS CITIZENS.
EVERY CITIZEN WILL HAVE A CHANCE TO PARTICIPATE IN GOVERNMENT AFFAIRS AND TAKE RESPONSIBILITY FOR THEIR OWN LIVES.
WE'LL BUILD A NATION BY THE PEOPLE, FOR THE PEOPLE. SO UNTIL THAT DAY COMES...
HEH...
HEH!
HEH!
HEH!
HEH!

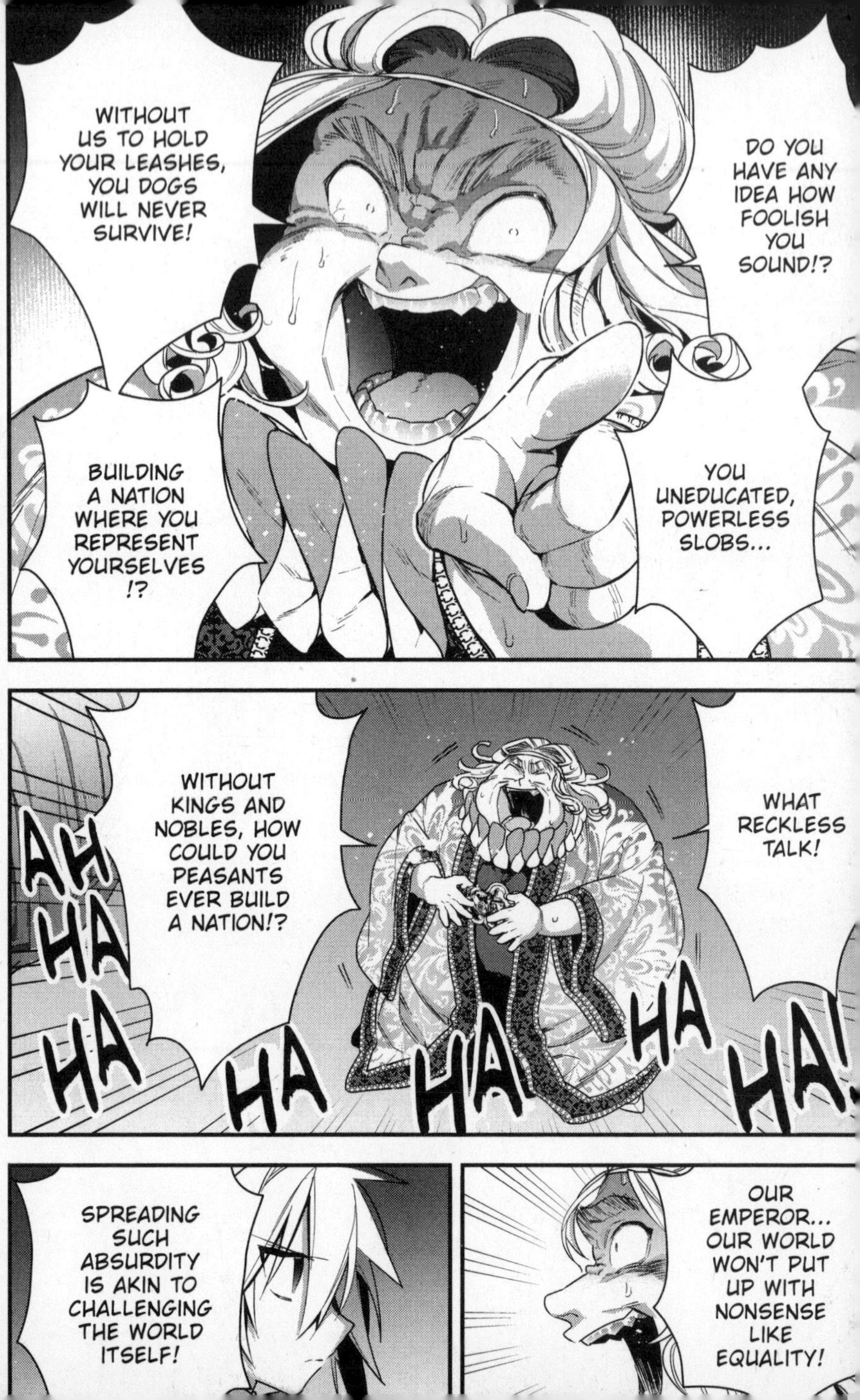
DO YOU HAVE ANY IDEA HOW FOOLISH YOU SOUND!?
WITHOUT US TO HOLD YOUR LEASHES, YOU DOGS WILL NEVER SURVIVE!
YOU UNEDUCATED, POWERLESS SLOBS...
BUILDING A NATION WHERE YOU REPRESENT YOURSELVES!?
WHAT RECKLESS TALK!
WITHOUT KINGS AND NOBLES, HOW COULD YOU PEASANTS EVER BUILD A NATION!?
AH HA HA HA HA HA HA HA!
OUR EMPEROR... OUR WORLD WON'T PUT UP WITH NONSENSE LIKE EQUALITY!
SPREADING SUCH ABSURDITY IS AKIN TO CHALLENGING THE WORLD ITSELF!

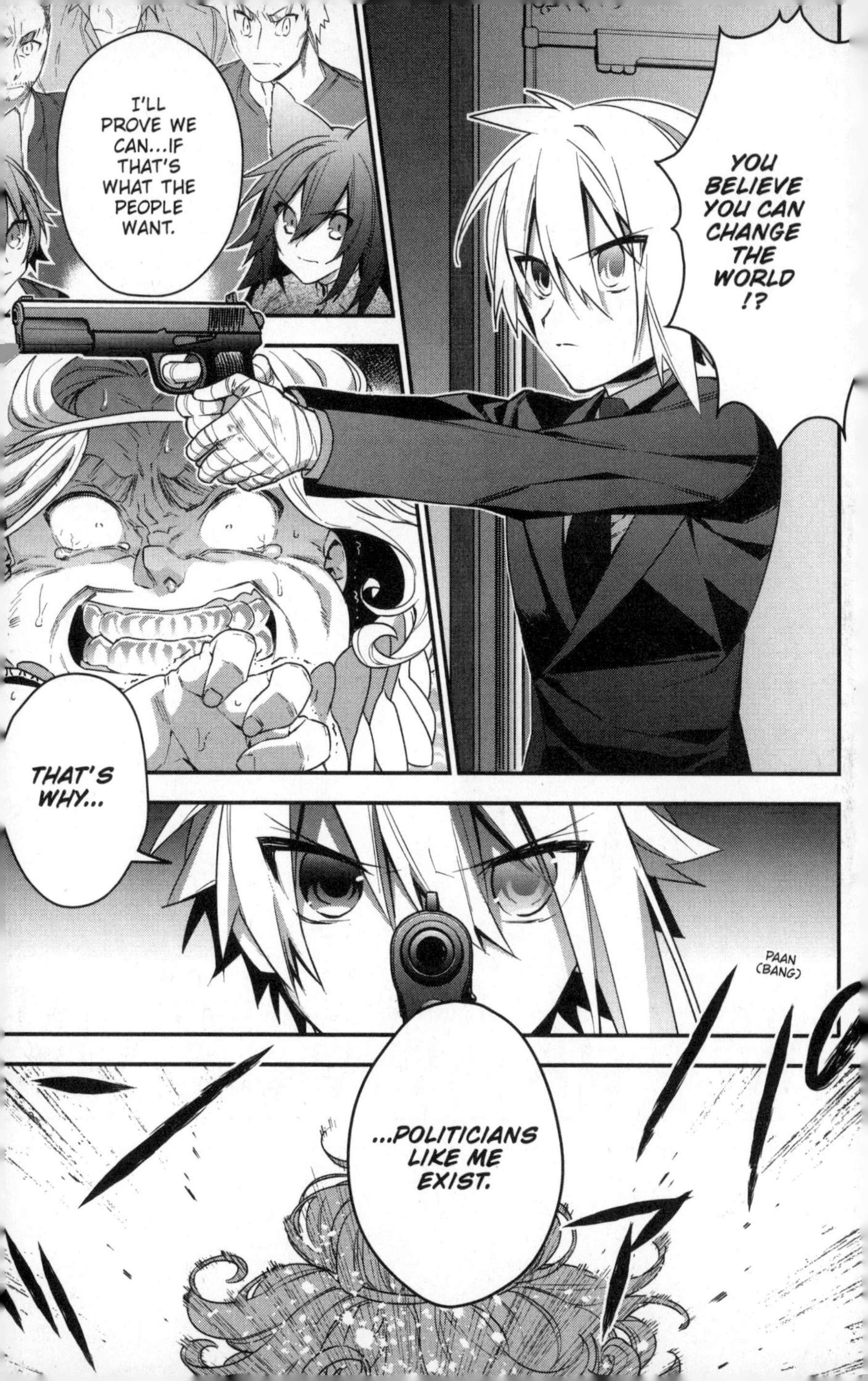

YOU BELIEVE YOU CAN CHANGE THE WORLD!?
I'LL PROVE WE CAN...IF THAT'S WHAT THE PEOPLE WANT.
THAT'S WHY...
PAAN (BANG)
...POLITICIANS LIKE ME EXIST.

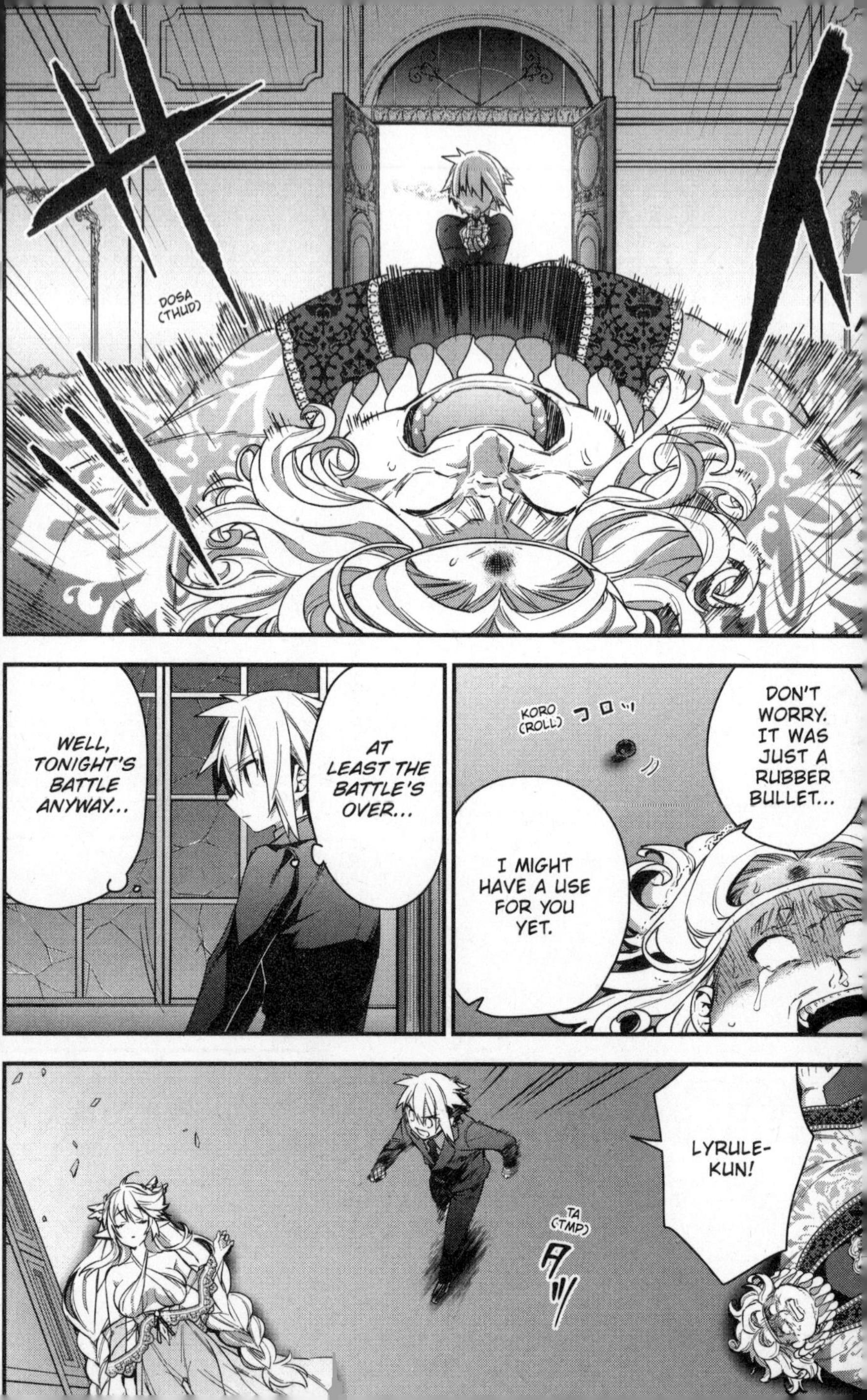
DOSA (THUD)
KORO (ROLL)
コロッ
DON'T WORRY. IT WAS JUST A RUBBER BULLET...
I MIGHT HAVE A USE FOR YOU YET.
AT LEAST THE BATTLE'S OVER...
WELL, TONIGHT'S BATTLE ANYWAY...
LYRULE-KUN!
TA (TMP)
タッ

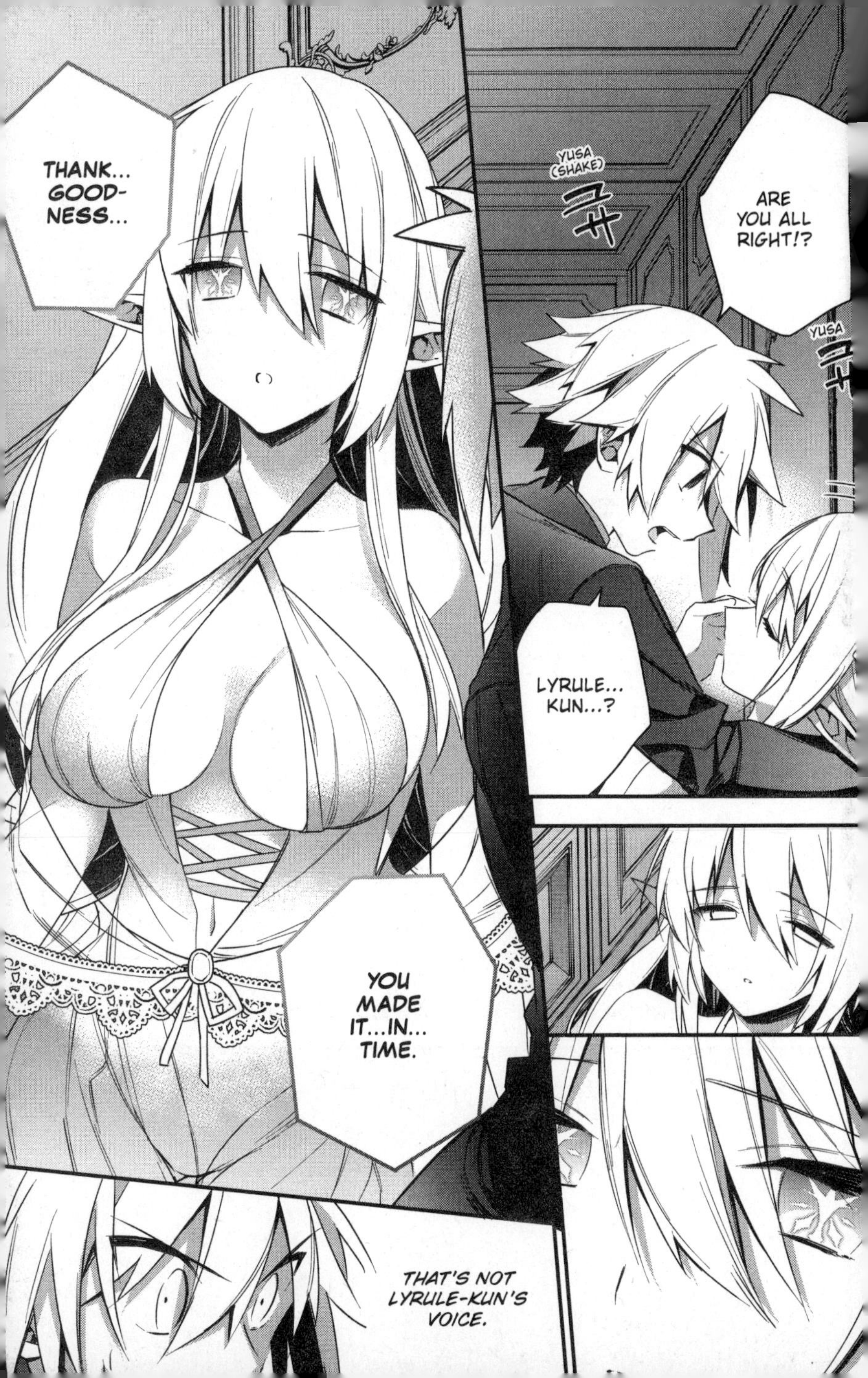
ARE YOU ALL RIGHT!?
YUSA
YUSA (SHAKE)
LYRULE... KUN...?
THANK... GOODNESS...
YOU MADE IT...IN... TIME.
THAT'S NOT LYRULE-KUN'S VOICE.

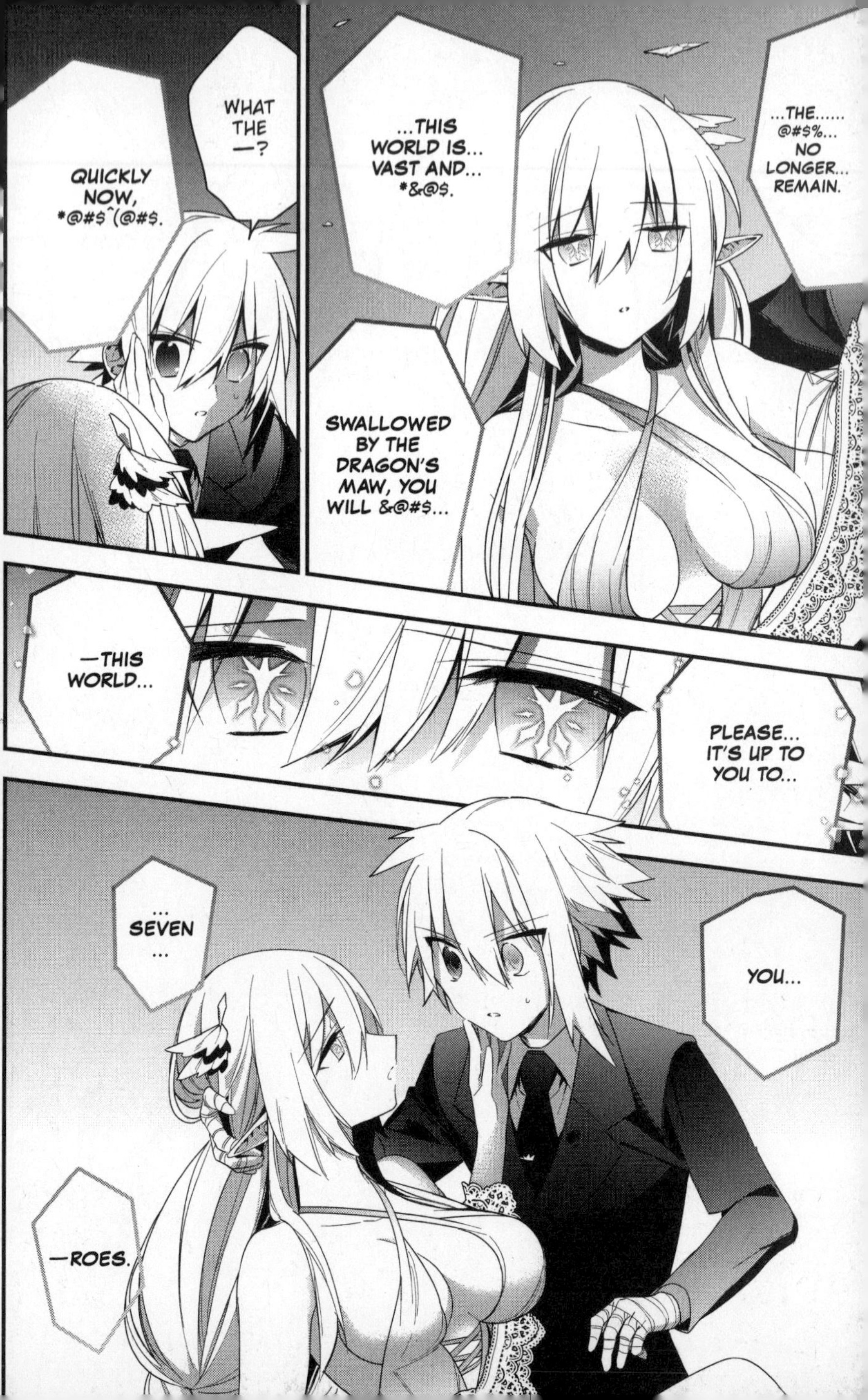
...THE...... @#$%... NO LONGER... REMAIN.
...THIS WORLD IS... VAST AND... *&@$.
SWALLOWED BY THE DRAGON'S MAW, YOU WILL &@#$...
WHAT THE —?
QUICKLY NOW, *@#$^(@#$.
PLEASE... IT'S UP TO YOU TO...
—THIS WORLD...
YOU...
... SEVEN ...
—ROES.

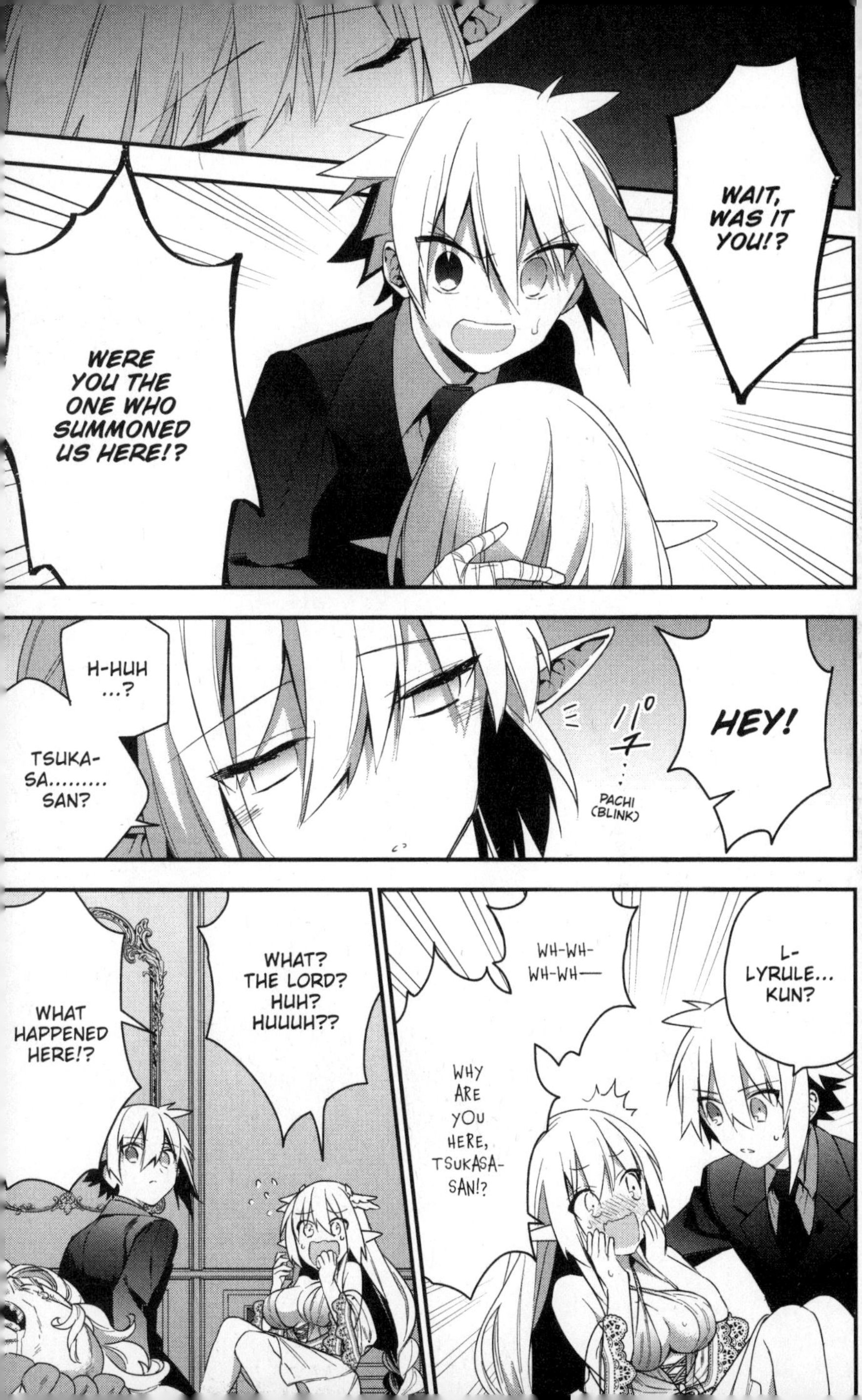
WAIT, WAS IT YOU!?
WERE YOU THE ONE WHO SUMMONED US HERE!?
HEY!
パチ
PACHI (BLINK)
H-HUH ...?
TSUKASA- SA......... SAN?
L- LYRULE... KUN?
WH-WH- WH-WH—
WHY ARE YOU HERE, TSUKASA- SAN!?
WHAT? THE LORD? HUH? HUUUH??
WHAT HAPPENED HERE!?

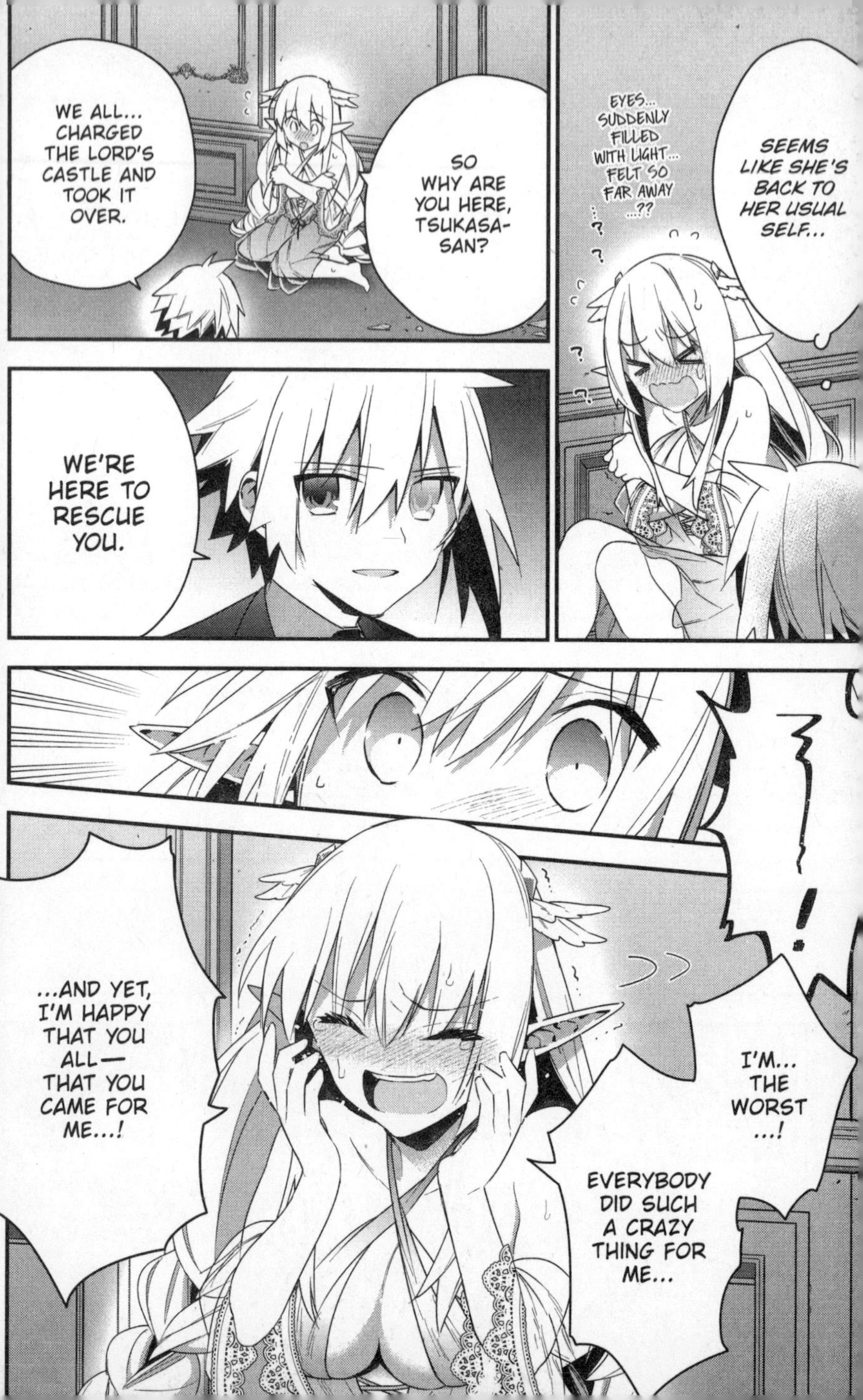
SEEMS LIKE SHE'S BACK TO HER USUAL SELF...
EYES... SUDDENLY FILLED WITH LIGHT... FELT SO FAR AWAY ...??
SO WHY ARE YOU HERE, TSUKASA-SAN?
WE ALL... CHARGED THE LORD'S CASTLE AND TOOK IT OVER.
WE'RE HERE TO RESCUE YOU.
!
I'M... THE WORST ...!
EVERYBODY DID SUCH A CRAZY THING FOR ME...
...AND YET, I'M HAPPY THAT YOU ALL— THAT YOU CAME FOR ME...!

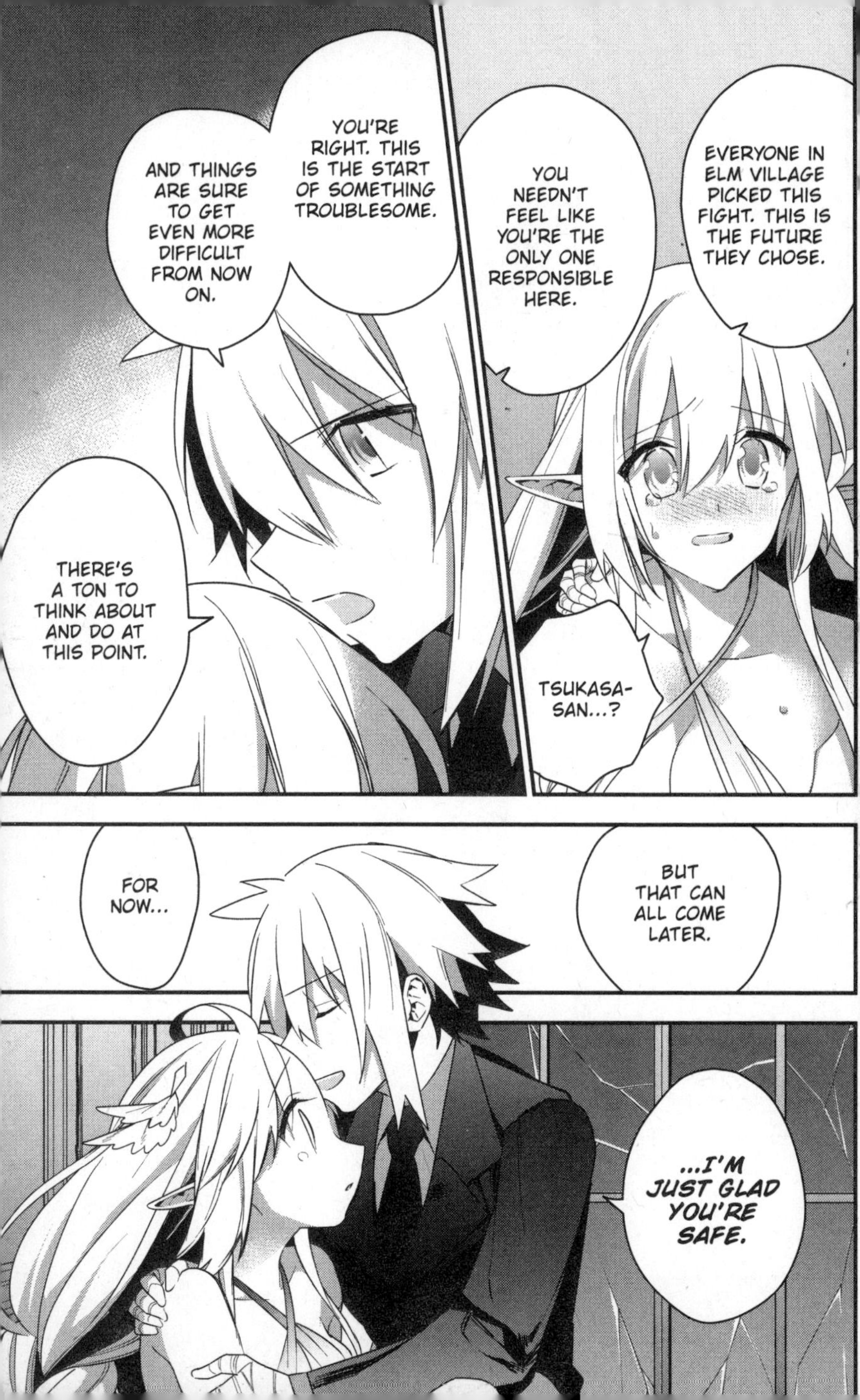
EVERYONE IN ELM VILLAGE PICKED THIS FIGHT. THIS IS THE FUTURE THEY CHOSE.
YOU NEEDN'T FEEL LIKE YOU'RE THE ONLY ONE RESPONSIBLE HERE.
TSUKASA-SAN...?
YOU'RE RIGHT. THIS IS THE START OF SOMETHING TROUBLESOME.
AND THINGS ARE SURE TO GET EVEN MORE DIFFICULT FROM NOW ON.
THERE'S A TON TO THINK ABOUT AND DO AT THIS POINT.
BUT THAT CAN ALL COME LATER.
FOR NOW...
...I'M JUST GLAD YOU'RE SAFE.

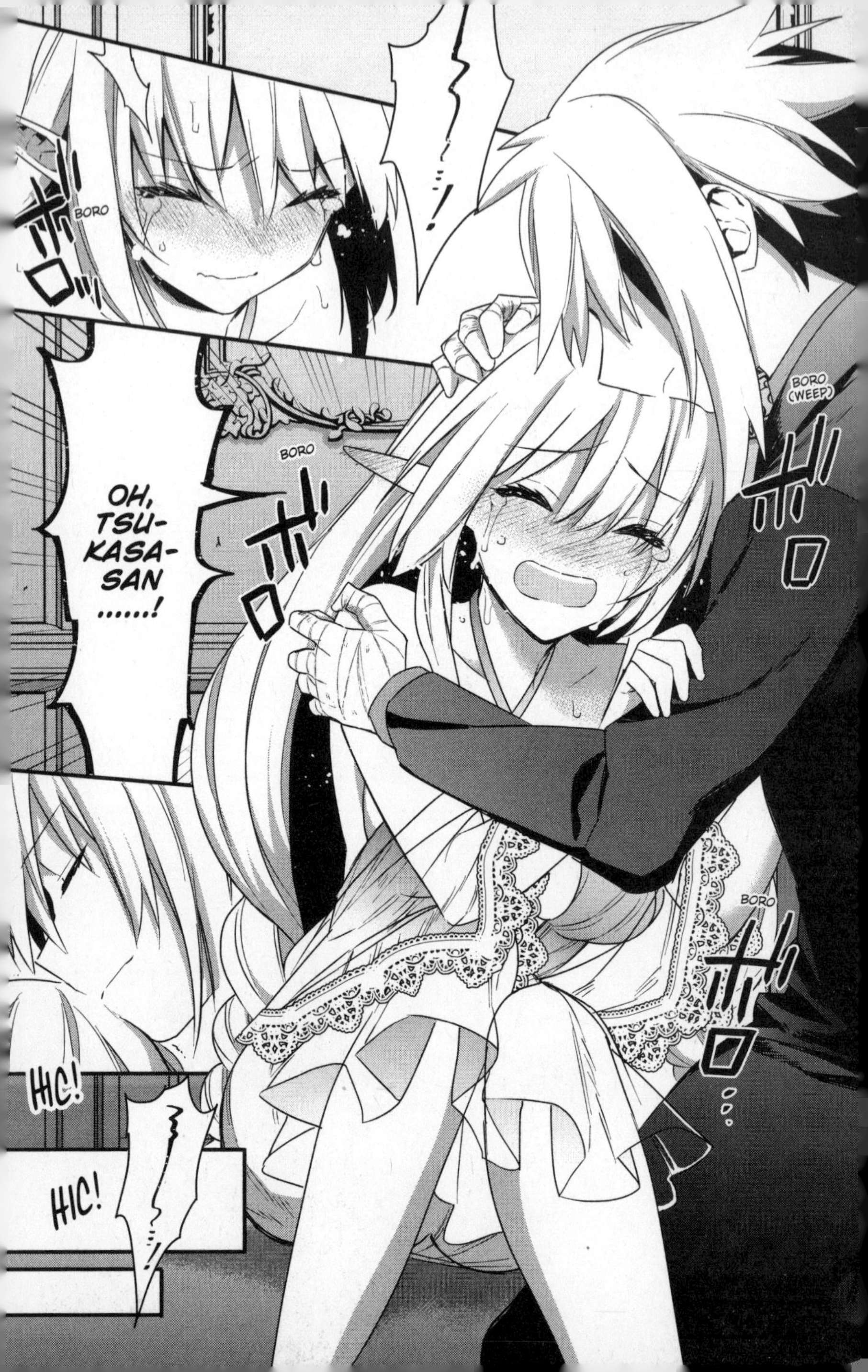
BORO (WEEP)
BORO
BORO
BORO
OH, TSU-KASA-SAN......!
HIC!
HIC!

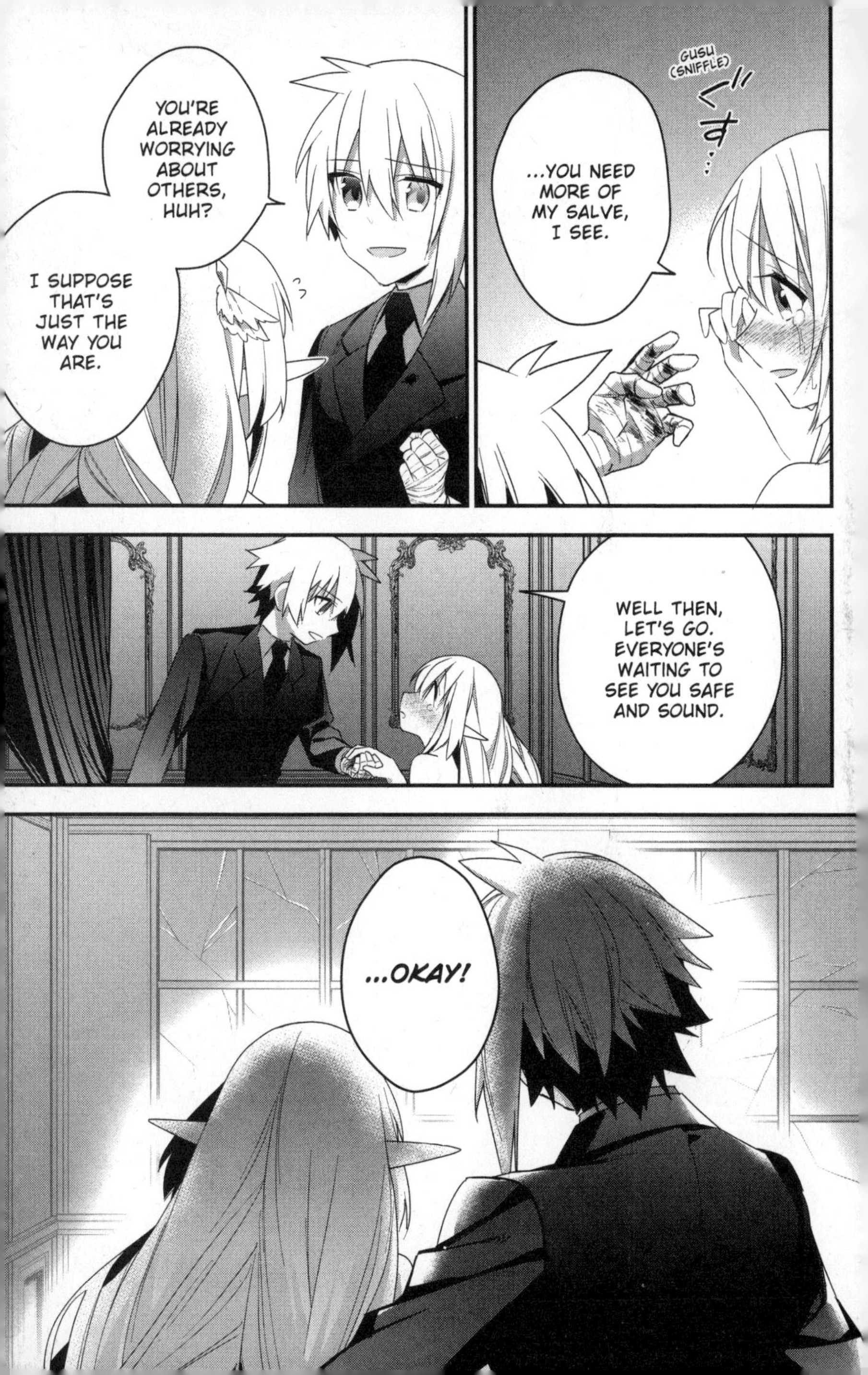
GUSU (SNIFFLE)
ぐす…
...YOU NEED MORE OF MY SALVE, I SEE.
YOU'RE ALREADY WORRYING ABOUT OTHERS, HUH?
I SUPPOSE THAT'S JUST THE WAY YOU ARE.
WELL THEN, LET'S GO. EVERYONE'S WAITING TO SEE YOU SAFE AND SOUND.
...OKAY!

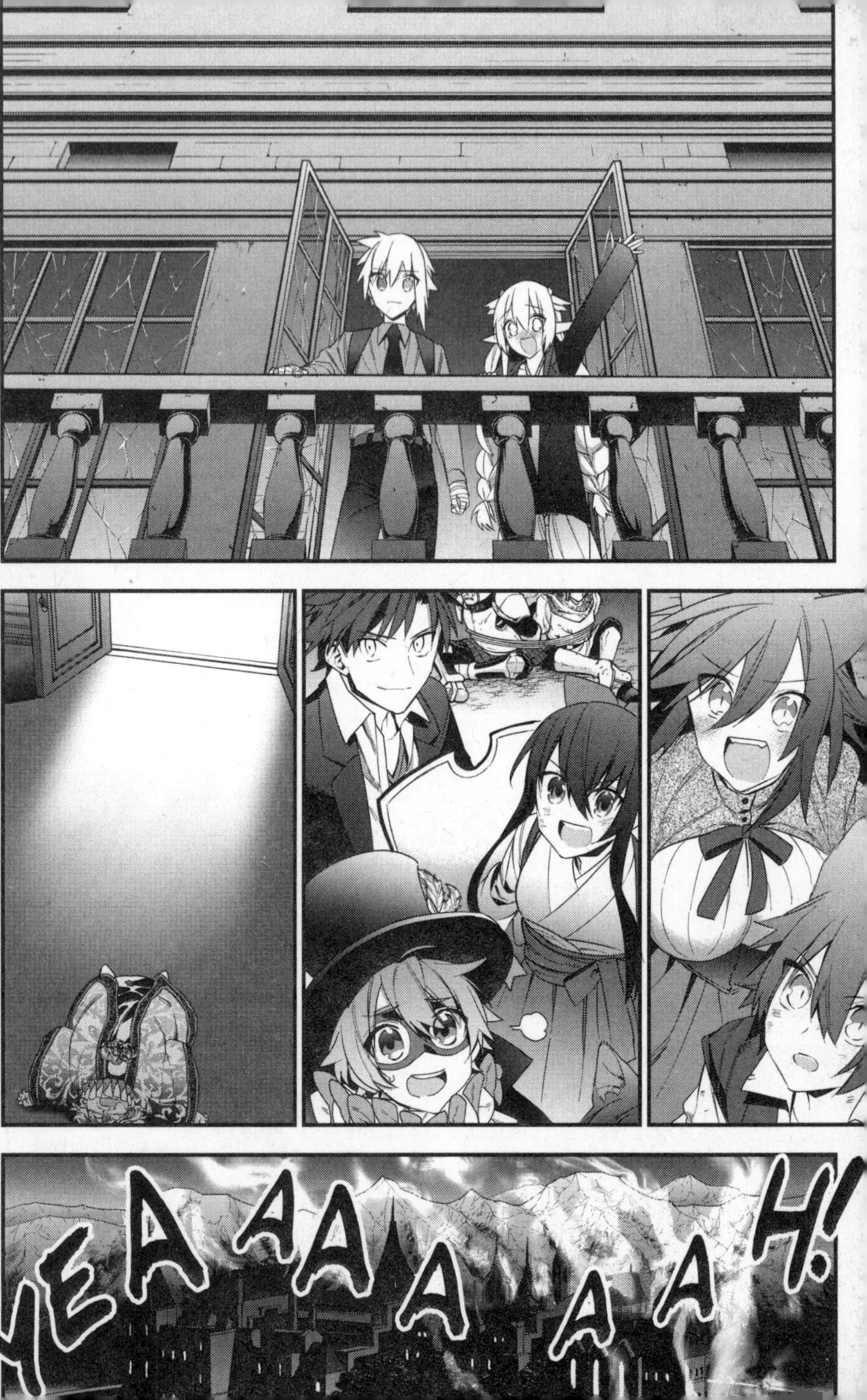
HEAAAAAAAH!

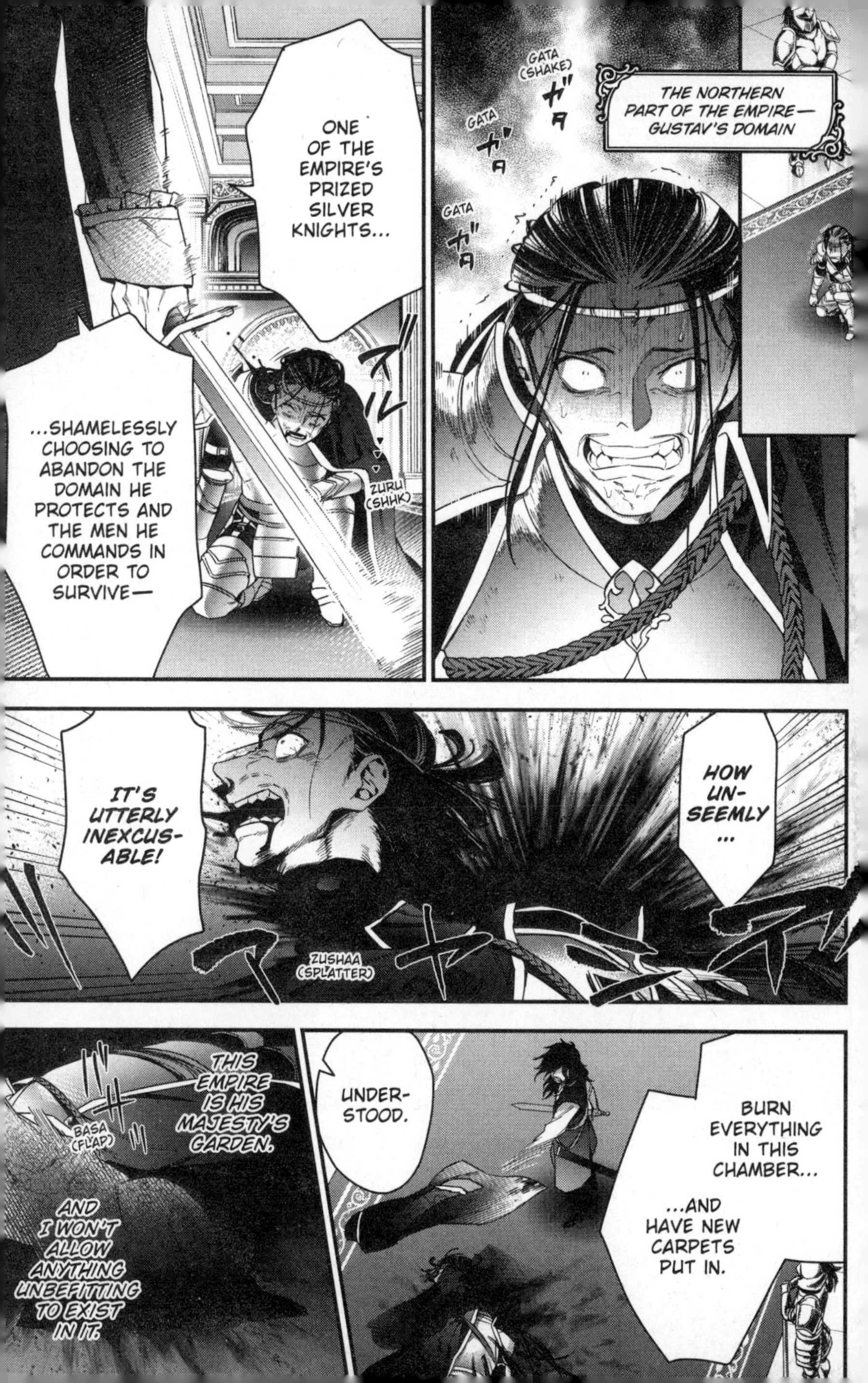
THE NORTHERN PART OF THE EMPIRE—GUSTAV'S DOMAIN
GATA (SHAKE)
GATA
GATA
ONE OF THE EMPIRE'S PRIZED SILVER KNIGHTS...
...SHAMELESSLY CHOOSING TO ABANDON THE DOMAIN HE PROTECTS AND THE MEN HE COMMANDS IN ORDER TO SURVIVE—
ZURU (SHHK)
HOW UN-SEEMLY...
IT'S UTTERLY INEXCUS-ABLE!
ZUSHAA (SPLATTER)
BURN EVERYTHING IN THIS CHAMBER...
...AND HAVE NEW CARPETS PUT IN.
UNDER-STOOD.
THIS EMPIRE IS HIS MAJESTY'S GARDEN.
BASA (FLAP)
AND I WON'T ALLOW ANYTHING UNBEFITTING TO EXIST IN IT.

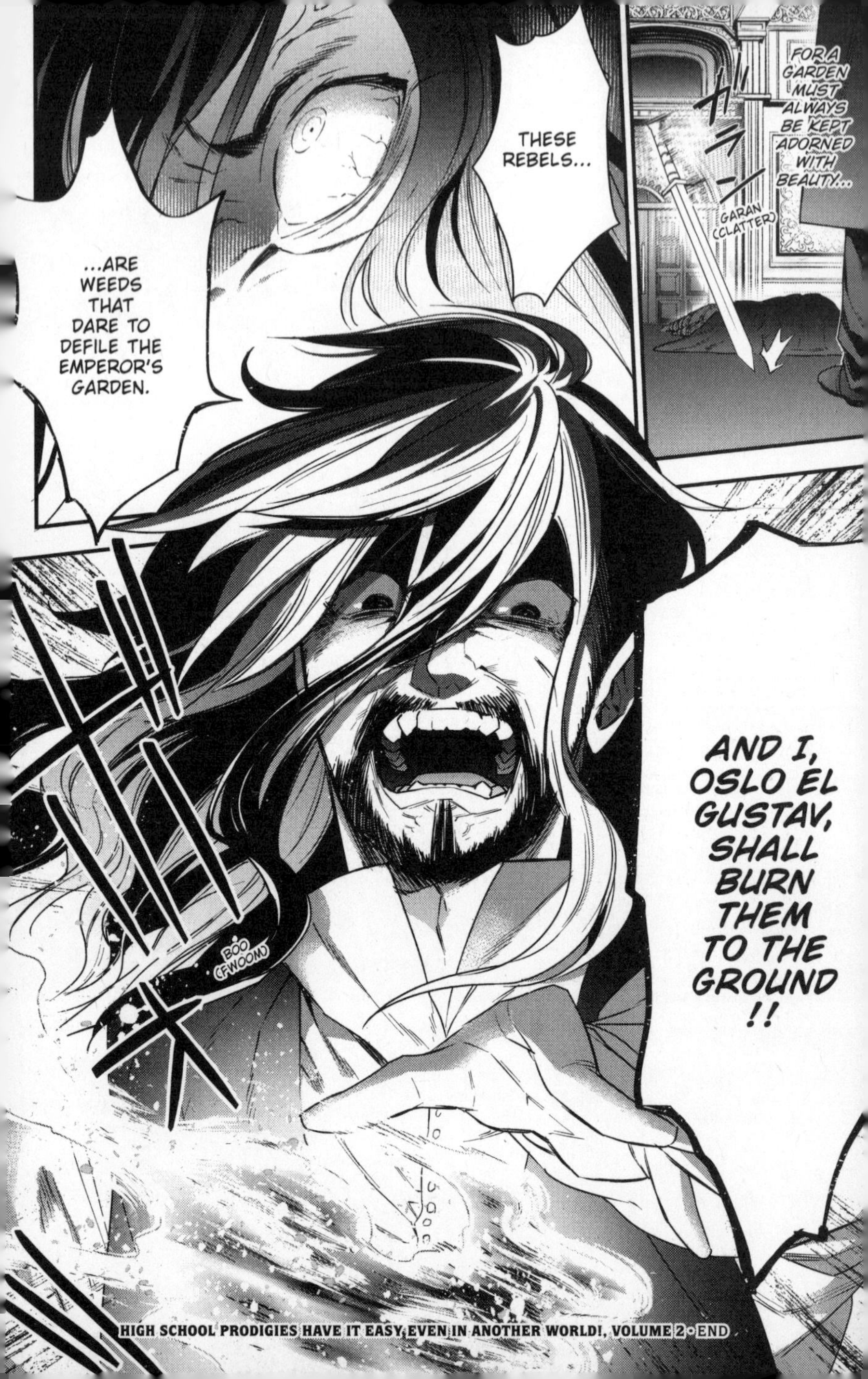
FOR A GARDEN MUST ALWAYS BE KEPT ADORNED WITH BEAUTY...
GARAN (CLATTER)
THESE REBELS...
...ARE WEEDS THAT DARE TO DEFILE THE EMPEROR'S GARDEN.
AND I, OSLO EL GUSTAV, SHALL BURN THEM TO THE GROUND!!
BOO (FWOOM)
HIGH SCHOOL PRODIGIES HAVE IT EASY EVEN IN ANOTHER WORLD!, VOLUME 2 • END

TRANSLATION NOTES

COMMON HONORIFICS

no honorific: Indicates familiarity or closeness; if used without permission or reason, addressing someone in this manner would constitute an insult.

-san: The Japanese equivalent of Mr./Mrs./Miss. If a situation calls for politeness, this is the fail-safe honorific.

-sama: Conveys great respect; may also indicate that the social status of the speaker is lower than that of the addressee.

-kun: Used most often when referring to boys, this indicates affection or familiarity. Occasionally used by older men among their peers, but it may also be used by anyone referring to a person of lower standing.

-chan: An affectionate honorific indicating familiarity used mostly in reference to girls; also used in reference to cute persons or animals. Variants include **-chin**.

-senpai: A suffix used to address upperclassmen or more experienced coworkers.

-sensei: A respectful term for teachers, artists, or high-level professionals.

-dono: A respectful term typically equated with "lord" or "master," this honorific has an archaic spin to it when used in colloquial parlance.

Page 13
As in the Japanese edition, Shinobu's "**G'mooornin-nin'**" combines the greeting "Good morning" with her exclamation of "nin" indicating her ninja heritage in a play on words.

Page 145
Shinobu calls Tsukasa **Micchan** as a nickname, combining the first syllable of his family name Mikogami with the honorific -chan. While indicating that the two are good enough friends for her to address him in this way, it is also a reflection of her personality and casual manner of speech.

Page 155
The term for **lady ninja** is kunoichi, used specifically for female ninja. In the Japanese edition, Shinobu also refers to herself as a shinobi, which is interchangeable with the term ninja.

Page 161
The Japanese phrase for Tsukasa's "**We'll just have to take your emperor's head before he takes ours**" carries a double meaning. While metaphorically, it could mean to fire someone, as a boss does to an employee; at face value, it can also mean to literally take someone's head.

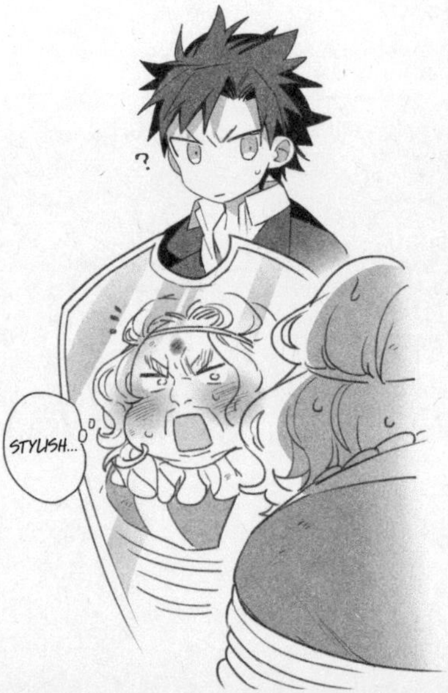
STYLISH...

High School Prodigies Have It Easy Even in Another World!

special thanks

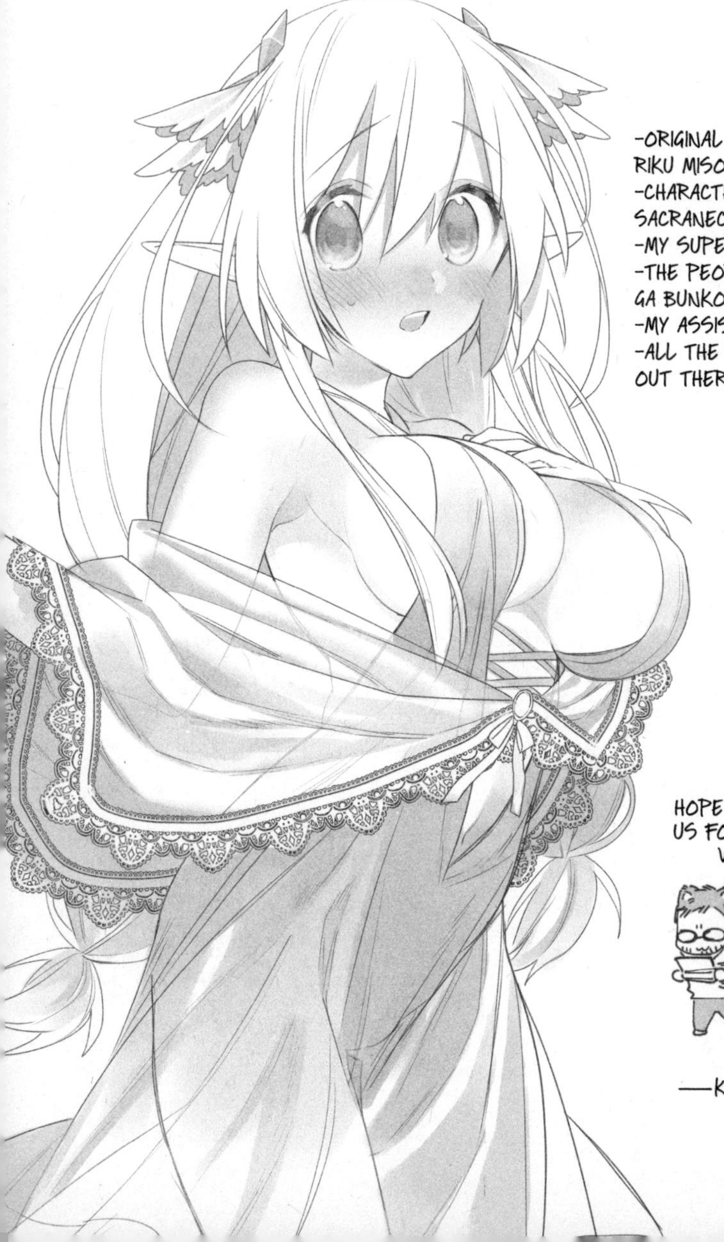

-ORIGINAL STORY:
RIKU MISORA-SENSEI
-CHARACTER DESIGN:
SACRANECO-SENSEI
-MY SUPERVISOR
-THE PEOPLE AT
GA BUNKO
-MY ASSISTANTS
-ALL THE READERS
OUT THERE

HOPE YOU'LL JOIN
US FOR THE NEXT
VOLUME!

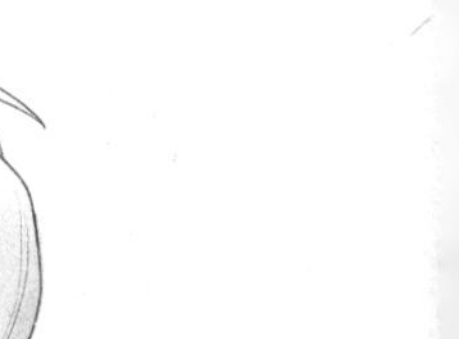

—KOTARO YAMADA

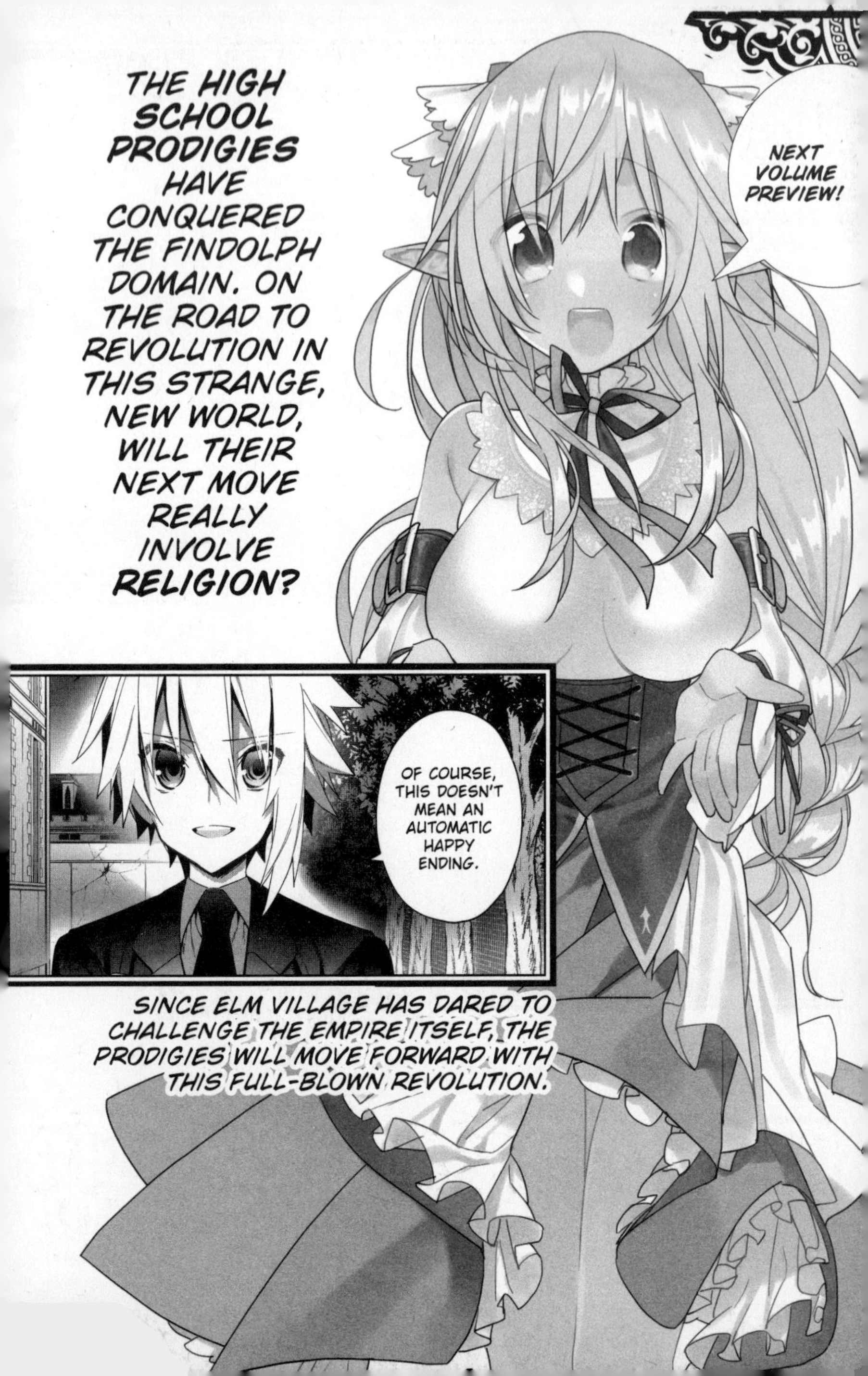
NEXT VOLUME PREVIEW!
THE HIGH SCHOOL PRODIGIES HAVE CONQUERED THE FINDOLPH DOMAIN. ON THE ROAD TO REVOLUTION IN THIS STRANGE, NEW WORLD, WILL THEIR NEXT MOVE REALLY INVOLVE RELIGION?
OF COURSE, THIS DOESN'T MEAN AN AUTOMATIC HAPPY ENDING.
SINCE ELM VILLAGE HAS DARED TO CHALLENGE THE EMPIRE ITSELF, THE PRODIGIES WILL MOVE FORWARD WITH THIS FULL-BLOWN REVOLUTION.

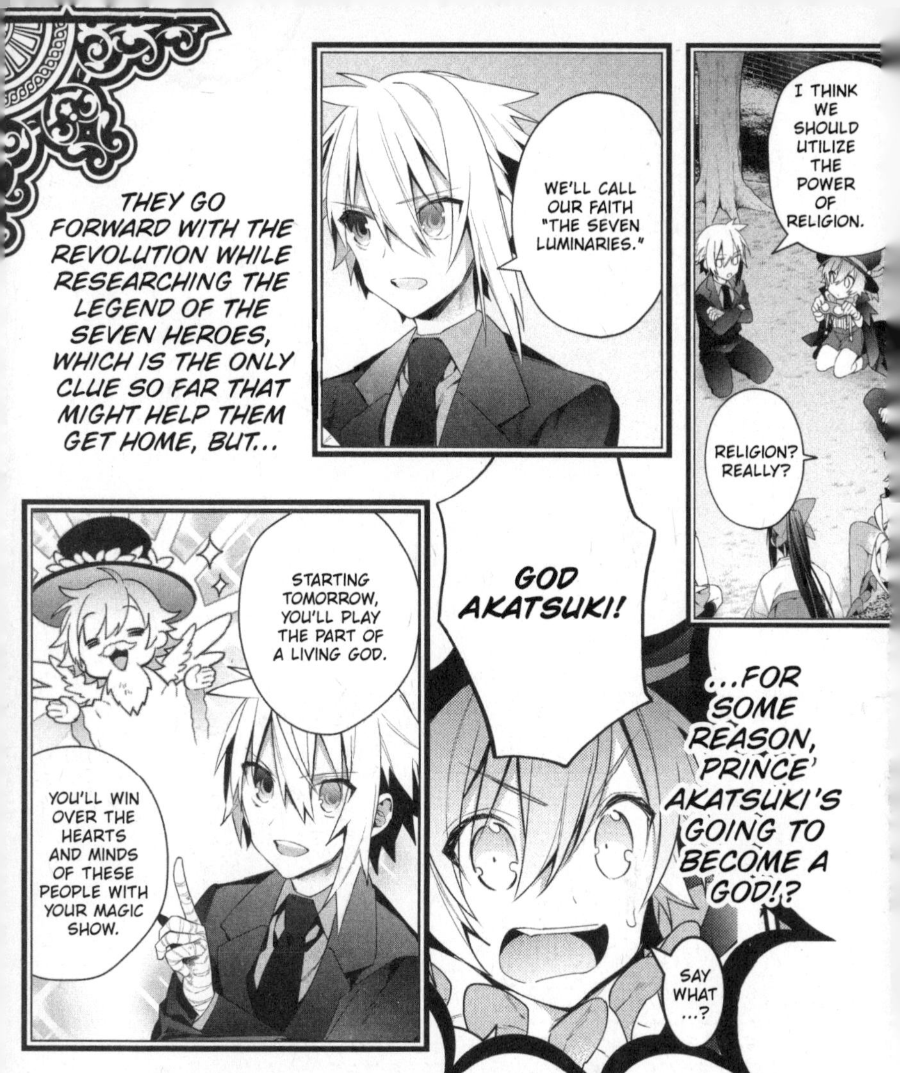
I THINK WE SHOULD UTILIZE THE POWER OF RELIGION.
RELIGION? REALLY?
WE'LL CALL OUR FAITH "THE SEVEN LUMINARIES."
THEY GO FORWARD WITH THE REVOLUTION WHILE RESEARCHING THE LEGEND OF THE SEVEN HEROES, WHICH IS THE ONLY CLUE SO FAR THAT MIGHT HELP THEM GET HOME, BUT...
GOD AKATSUKI!
...FOR SOME REASON, PRINCE AKATSUKI'S GOING TO BECOME A GOD!?
SAY WHAT ...?
STARTING TOMORROW, YOU'LL PLAY THE PART OF A LIVING GOD.
YOU'LL WIN OVER THE HEARTS AND MINDS OF THESE PEOPLE WITH YOUR MAGIC SHOW.

High School Prodigies Have It Easy Even in Another World! 2

STORY BY **Riku Misora**   ART BY **Kotaro Yamada**

CHARACTER DESIGN BY **Sacraneco**

Translation: Caleb D. Cook
Lettering: Brandon Bovia

CHOUJIN KOUKOUSEI TACHI WA ISEKAI DEMO YOYU DE IKINUKU YOUDESU! vol. 2
© Riku Misora / SB Creative Corp. Character Design: Sacraneco
© 2017 Kotaro Yamada / SQUARE ENIX CO., LTD.
First published in Japan in 2017 by SQUARE ENIX CO., LTD.
English translation rights arranged with SQUARE ENIX CO., LTD.
and Yen Press, LLC through Tuttle Mori Agency, Inc.

English translation © 2019 by SQUARE ENIX CO., LTD.

Yen Press
1290 Avenue of the Americas
New York, NY 10104

Visit us at yenpress.com

facebook.com/yenpress
twitter.com/yenpress

yenpress.tumblr.com
instagram.com/yenpress

First Yen Press Edition: January 2019

Yen Press is an imprint of Yen Press, LLC.
The Yen Press name and logo are trademarks of Yen Press, LLC.

The publisher is not responsible for websites (or their content) that are not owned by the publisher.

Library of Congress Control Number: 2018948324

ISBNs: 978-1-9753-0137-8 (paperback)
978-1-9753-0138-5 (ebook)

10 9 8 7 6 5 4 3 2 1

WOR

Printed in the United States of America

conⵜenⵜs

HIGH SCHOOL
PRODIGIES HAVE
IT EASY EVEN IN
ANOTHER WORLD!

High School Prodigies Have It Easy Even in Another World!

2

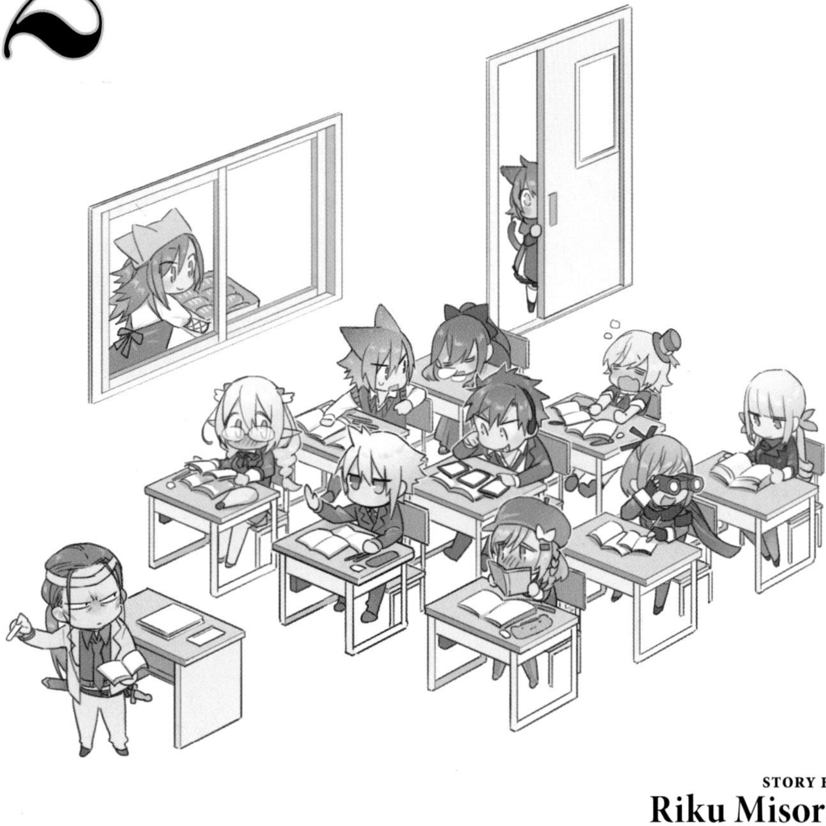

STORY BY
Riku Misora

ART BY
Kotaro Yamada

CHARACTER DESIGN BY
Sacraneco